MORAL MAZES

MORAL MAZES

The World of Corporate Managers

Robert Jackall

New York   Oxford
OXFORD UNIVERSITY PRESS
1988

Oxford University Press

Oxford   New York   Toronto
Delhi   Bombay   Calcutta   Madras   Karachi
Petaling Jaya   Singapore   Hong Kong   Tokyo
Nairobi   Dar es Salaam   Cape Town
Melbourne   Auckland

and associated companies in
Beirut Berlin Ibadan Nicosia

Copyright © 1988 by Oxford University Press, Inc.

Published by Oxford University Press, Inc.
200 Madison Avenue, New York, New York 10016

Oxford is a registered trademark of Oxford University Press

Library of Congress Cataloging-in-Publication Data
Jackall, Robert.
Moral mazes: the world of corporate managers/Robert Jackall.
p.   cm.
Bibliography: p.
Includes index.
ISBN 0-19-503825-8
1. Business ethics—United States.
2. Executives—Professional ethics—United States.
3. Corporations—United States—Corrupt practices.
I. Title.
HF5387.J29 1988   87-31845
174'.4—dc19   CIP

I am grateful to the editors of several publications for permission to use previously
published materials. Several basic themes of this book first appeared in my article
"Moral Mazes: Bureaucracy and Managerial Work," *Harvard Business Review*,
Vol. 61, No. 5 (September–October, 1983), which I use freely here with the permission of the *Harvard Business Review*. The material from *The Apologia of Robert
Keayne: The Self-Portrait of a Puritan Merchant*, edited by Bernard Bailyn
(Gloucester, Mass.: Peter Smith, 1970) that appears in the notes to Chapter 1 is
reprinted with the permission of Peter Smith Publishers. The excerpts from the
newspaper columns of Dr. Peter Gott that appear in the notes to Chapter 6 are
reprinted by permission of Newspaper Enterprise Association, Inc. Finally, the
excerpts from Harry Reichenbach (with David Freedman), *Phantom Fame* (New
York: Simon & Schuster, 1931) in Chapter 7 are reprinted by permission of Simon
& Schuster, Inc.

2 4 6 8 9 7 5 3 1

Printed in the United States of America
on acid-free paper

In Memory of
Joseph Bensman
and for
Arthur J. Vidich and Robert F. Murphy

Acknowledgments

This book studies the world of corporate managers. It examines managers' work, the intricate social contexts of their organizations, their striving for success, the habits of mind they develop, and especially the occupational ethics that they construct to survive and flourish in their world. The book does not treat these issues abstractly. Rather, it reports firsthand fieldwork among corporate managers in a few organizations. Through such a focused appraisal of an institutionally central occupational group, the book tries to explore in some depth situations and experiences that are widespread in our social order.

This book has been a long time in the making and owes a great deal to many people. My first debt is to the organizations that allowed me to do the study (many would not) and especially to the managers, of high, middle, and low rank, who spent many hours patiently educating me in how their world works. The sociologist's first task is to get things right and, if I have done that, I owe it to this sizable group of unacknowledged co-authors. Managers may disagree with some of the broader interpretations of their experiences suggested here. I have tried, however, to capture the complexities, ambiguities, and anxieties of their world.

The research would not have been possible without strong institutional support. I am especially indebted to the National Endowment for the Humanities for a year-long fellowship which, together with an Adsit Fellowship for junior faculty from Williams College, enabled me to do intensive fieldwork in the corporations in 1980–1981. Several small research grants from Williams College helped support the years of more sporadic fieldwork that followed. Also, a grant-in-aid from the Wenner-Gren Foundation for Anthropological Research enabled me to pursue work on organizational dissenters, some of which is reported here. I received valuable assistance in this latter phase of my study from Michael Baker and Albert Feliu, formerly of the Educational Fund for Individual Rights, and especially from Louis Clark of the Government Accountability Project. My very special thanks to the men and women who agreed to be interviewed for this portion of my work.

I want to thank my students at Williams College who have listened patiently and responded creatively to my grapplings with the data over the last several years. Opportunities for more formal presentations of various portions of my work were also important. In this regard, I especially want to thank Lawrence Graver, William Moomaw, and Francis Oakley of Williams College, James Kuhn of Columbia University and Donald Shriver of Union Theological Seminary, Troy Duster of the University of California, Berkeley, and Arthur J. Vidich of the New School for Social Research. The lectures and seminars that they arranged were valuable in bringing this work to fruition.

The library staffs at Columbia University, the National Archives in Washington, D.C., the New York Public Library, and especially at Williams College were very helpful, as were staff at the Textile Workers Union of America in New York. I extend special thanks also to Donna Chenail, Shirley Bushika, and especially Peggy Bryant who helped type, print, and revise various editions of the manuscript. I am very grateful too to Roger Davis who assisted in checking sources and especially to Duffy Graham who wrote several research memoranda summarizing pertinent secondary materials and who helped in many other phases of my work.

My thanks to Susan Rabiner, my first editor at Oxford University Press, who nurtured the project in many ways, and to Bill Sisler and Joan Bossert who brought it to completion. Linda Grossman did a fine copyediting job.

Many colleagues and friends have taken time to read and comment on my work. Lila Abu-Lughod, Michael F. Brown, Gillian Feeley-Harnik, Joseph Ferrie, Clara Park, and Laszlo Versenyi each read a portion of the work in early versions and helped me sharpen my treatment. Gene Bell-Villada read several chapters in different stages, always with a keen eye both for content and style. Joseph Bensman, Arthur Vidich, Robert Murphy, Hans Speier, Janice Hirota, Stanford Lyman, Michael Hughey, Charles Payne, Robert Friedrichs, Marty White, Elizabeth Tice, and Duffy Graham, as well as a person in one of the corporations I studied who wishes to remain anonymous, carefully read the entire manuscript and provided me with a great many thoughtful critiques and suggestions. I am most grateful to these men and women for their help. But I separate them from any untoward consequences of their kindness.

Janice Hirota and Yuriko Hirota Jackall sustained me in every way throughout this work. My deepest gratitude and love to them.

The book has its origins in a conversation with Arthur Vidich more than a decade ago while we reflected on puzzling issues that emerged during my first fieldwork experience, also in a large organization. As I began fieldwork for this book, I got to know the late Joseph Bensman. Our many conversations over the next few years were invaluable in helping me grasp and articulate my data. And even his last ravaging illness did nothing to deter his relentless editing. Finally, during this same period, I came to know Robert Murphy and appreciate his particular and remarkable anthropological sensibilities. In their work, all three have explored the puzzles of humanity and modernity by looking at the world as it is with a skeptical and unflinching eye, with a characteristic passionate dispassion, and with an expansive social imagination that disregards conventional disciplinary boundaries. With deep affection and respect, I am happy to dedicate this work to these fine scholars, fine teachers, and fine men.

New York   R. J.
October 1987

Contents

INTRODUCTION: Business as a Social and Moral Terrain   3

1. Moral Probations, Old and New   7

2. The Social Structure of Managerial Work   17

3. The Main Chance   41

4. Looking Up and Looking Around   75

5. Drawing Lines   101

6. Dexterity with Symbols   134

7. The Magic Lantern   162

8. Invitations to Jeopardy   191

AUTHOR'S NOTE   205

NOTES   207

SUGGESTIONS FOR FURTHER READING   235

INDEX   239

MORAL MAZES

INTRODUCTION

Business as a Social
and Moral Terrain

Corporate leaders often tell their charges that hard work will lead to success. Indeed, this theory of reward being commensurate with effort has been an enduring belief and a moral imperative in our society, one central to our self-image as a people, where the main chance is available to anyone of ability who has the gumption and persistence to seize it. Hard work, it is also frequently asserted, builds character. This notion carries less conviction because business people, and our society as a whole, have little patience with those who, even though they work hard, make a habit of finishing out of the money. In the end, it is success that matters, that legitimates striving, and that makes work worthwhile. What if, however, men and women in the corporation no longer see success as necessarily connected to hard work? What becomes of the social morality of the corporation—the everyday rules-in-use that people play by—when there is thought to be no fixed or, one might say, objective standard of excellence to explain how and why winners are separated from also-rans, how and why some people succeed and others fail? What rules do people fashion to interact with one another when they feel that, instead of ability, talent, and dedicated service to an organization, politics, adroit talk, luck, connections, and self-promotion are the real sorters of people into sheep and goats?

This is one important puzzle that confronted me while doing the extensive fieldwork in several large corporations that is the basis of this book. I went into these organizations to study how bureaucracy—the prevailing organizational form of our society—shapes moral consciousness. I stayed to study managers' rules for survival and success in the corporation because these goals

proved to be uppermost in their minds. I suggest in this book that managers'
rules for survival and success are at the heart of what might be called the
bureaucratic ethic, a moral code that guides managers through all the dilemmas and vicissitudes that confront them in the big organization.

This book analyzes the occupational ethics of corporate managers. By
occupational ethics, I mean the moral rules-in-use that managers construct to
guide their behavior at work, whether these are shaped directly by authority
relationships or by other kinds of experiences typical in big organizations. I
refer here to experiences such as the deep anxiety created by organizational
upheavals that jumble career plans, or the troubling animosity generated by
intense rivalries that pit managers against one another in struggles for prestige
and say-so, or the emotional aridity caused by continually honing one's self
to make hard choices with ambiguous outcomes.

As they are popularly used, of course, the notions of morality and ethics
have a decidedly prescriptive, indeed moralistic, flavor. They are often rooted
in religious doctrines or vague cultural remnants of religious beliefs, like the
admonition to follow the Golden Rule. However, this book treats ethics and
morality sociologically, that is, as empirical, objective realities to be investigated. Therefore, in using the terms morality and ethics, I do not refer to any
specific or given, much less absolute, system of norms and underlying beliefs.
Moreover, I imply no judgment about the actions I describe from some fixed,
absolute ethical or moral stance, as the terms are often used in popular discourse, sometimes even by corporate managers themselves.

I mean to explore rather the actual evaluative rules that managers fashion
and follow in their work world, the rules that govern their stances toward and
interaction with their superiors, subordinates, and peers; their friends, allies,
and rivals; their business customers and competitors; regulators and legislators; the media; and the specific publics they address and the public at large.
I examine, as well, the particular conceptions of right and wrong, of proper
and improper, that underpin those rules. Even more specifically, I analyze
how the work that managers do and, in particular, how the social and bureaucratic context of their work—the warp across which the threads of their
careers are stretched—shape their occupational moralities. In this sense, the
book is also a sociology of the peculiar form of bureaucracy dominant in
American business.

As it happens, the field of business ethics is rapidly becoming big business.
Among other developments, the last fifteen years have seen the proliferation
of a great number of books and articles on ethical problems in business;[1] the
emergence of several centers and institutes at least partly dedicated to the
subject or to related problems like the role of values in scientific, technological, or public policy work;[2] the spread of business ethics courses in both college and business school curricula;[3] and even, in some corporations, the development of seminars in ethics for executives. This groundswell of attention to
ethical issues in business continues a historical tradition that in different
forms dates at least to the turn of this century, when the big corporation
became a paramount institution in our society.[4] The current upsurge in con-

cern over ethics was prompted undoubtedly by the Watergate crisis and its spillover into business. It has been stimulated more recently by a series of corporate and governmental scandals headed by revelations about insider trading on the stock market and by glimpses of high federal officials illegally diverting funds and systematically deceiving Congress and the public during the Iran-contra affair. At the same time, the accelerating pace of scientific and technological change that continually overturns taken for granted notions about our universe has prompted widespread discussions of ethical issues. All of this has been a boon to moral philosophers, normally a precariously positioned occupational group in a social order where the mantle of intellectual supremacy has long since passed from a discipline once called the queen of the sciences. With the titles of "ethicist" or even "ethician,"* moral philosophers have applied their considerable mental acumen to unraveling the conundrums of the fast-paced, hurly-burly worlds of commerce and industry or more sedate scientific milieux. In doing so, they have extended in quite new directions the much longer tradition of moral casuistry, that is, the process of applying general principles to specific situations in order to resolve moral quandaries, an art that may involve the invention of wholly new rules and legitimations for action.⁵ Unfortunately, most of this analysis has been of hypothetical cases, of real-life situations abstracted from their intricate organizational contexts, of public testimony before various commissions and hearings by officials who, as it happens, are well-versed in fencing with their adversaries, or of the journalistic accounts of the many highly publicized corporate scandals in recent years. In fact, certain vocabularies have become so institutionalized in some philosophical circles that whole sets of assumptions and taken for granted analyses, often complete with settled moral judgments, are often invoked simply by cryptic references to, say, the "Pinto Case" or the "Dalkon Shield Affair." Despite the emergence of a new industry that one might call Ethics Inc., however, the philosophers at least have done little detailed investigation of the day-to-day operations, structure, and meaning of work in business and of how the conditions of that work shape moral consciousness.

But only an understanding of how men and women in business actually experience their work enables one to grasp its moral salience for them. Bureaucratic work shapes people's consciousness in decisive ways. Among other things, it regularizes people's experiences of time and indeed routinizes their lives by engaging them on a daily basis in rational, socially approved, purposive action; it brings them into daily proximity with and subordination to authority, creating in the process upward-looking stances that have decisive social and psychological consequences; it places a premium on a functionally rational, pragmatic habit of mind that seeks specific goals; and it creates subtle

---

*Throughout the book, I use quotation marks in the text proper to indicate words, phrases, or quotes actually voiced in the interviews, conversations, and discussions described in Chapter 1 and in the Author's Note that form the basis of my analysis. The only exceptions to this are occasional words or phrases borrowed from other authors where the citations make this usage clear. I do not use quotation marks to emphasize or self-consciously bracket ideas.

measures of prestige and an elaborate status hierarchy that, in addition to fostering an intense competition for status, also makes the rules, procedures, social contexts, and protocol of an organization paramount psychological and behavioral guides. In fact, bureaucratic contexts typically bring together men and women who initially have little in common with each other except the impersonal frameworks of their organizations. Indeed, the enduring genius of the organizational form is that it allows individuals to retain bewilderingly diverse private motives and meanings for action as long as they adhere publicly to agreed-upon rules. Even the personal relationships that men and women in bureaucracies do subsequently fashion together are, for the most part, governed by explicit or implicit organizational rules, procedures, and protocol. As a result, bureaucratic work causes people to bracket, while at work, the moralities that they might hold outside the workplace or that they might adhere to privately and to follow instead the prevailing morality of their particular organizational situation. As a former vice-president of a large firm says: "What is right in the corporation is not what is right in a man's home or in his church. *What is right in the corporation is what the guy above you wants from you.* That's what morality is in the corporation."* Of course, since public legitimacy and respectability depend, in part, on perceptions of one's moral probity, one cannot admit to such a bracketing of one's conventional moralities except, usually indirectly, within one's managerial circles where such verities are widely recognized to be inapplicable except as public relations stances. In fact, though managers usually think of it as separate from decision making, public relations is an extremely important facet of managerial work, one that often requires the employment of practitioners with special expertise.

Managers do not generally discuss ethics, morality, or moral rules-in-use in a direct way with each other, except perhaps in seminars organized by ethicists. Such seminars, however, are unusual and, when they do occur, are often strained, artificial, and often confusing even to managers since they frequently become occasions for the solemn public invocation, particularly by high-ranking managers, of conventional moralities and traditional shibboleths. What matters on a day-to-day basis are the moral rules-in-use fashioned within the personal and structural constraints of one's organization. As it happens, these rules may vary sharply depending on various factors, such as proximity to the market, line or staff responsibilities, or one's position in a hierarchy. Actual organizational moralities are thus contextual, situational, highly specific, and, most often, unarticulated.

This book, then, examines business as a social and moral terrain. I offer no programs for reform, should one think that reform is necessary. Nor, I am afraid, do I offer tips on how to find one's way onto the "fast track" to managerial success. This is, rather, an interpretive sociological account of how managers think the world works.

---

*All italics within quotations from interviews represent the subject's own emphasis, as noted by the author.

1

Moral Probations, Old and New

I

To understand the connections between managerial work, bureaucracy, success, and morality, one must look at the great transformations, both social and cultural, that produced managers as an occupational group. A grasp of the moral significance of work in business today begins, in fact, with an understanding of the original Protestant ethic, Max Weber's term to describe the comprehensive worldview of the rising middle class that spearheaded the emergence of capitalism. The term Protestant ethic refers to the set of beliefs and, more particularly, to the set of binding social rules that counseled "secular asceticism"—the methodical, rational subjection of human impulse and desire to God's will through "restless, continuous, systematic work in a worldly calling."[1]

This is not, of course, to suggest that Protestantism has ever known theological unity. Even among pious Calvinists, whom Weber saw as the chief carriers of secular asceticism, interpretive disputes about theological matters were always rife from the very beginnings of this austere doctrine that posited a vast abyss between an inscrutable God and mankind. Sometimes such disputes were rooted in deep social divisions. In the early seventeenth century, for instance, New England Puritan merchants—worldly, urban men of great raw vitality and drive—clashed repeatedly with the genteel, land-based official guardians of the Puritan Covenant. The merchants drew largely practical and individualistic lessons from the Calvinist tradition; the more churchly Puritans felt that the community must always come first and that individuals had to bend their wills to the community's needs, defined of course by themselves. Activities vital to the common weal like trade, the lifeblood of the merchants, had to be watched and regulated with special vigilance.[2] Such doctrinal disputes, reflecting as they did the splits within the middle class as well as the inevitable conflicts over the meaning of the common good in a society that extolled individualism, could be rancorous and, in at least one well-documented case, emotionally ravaging for individuals.[3] But, as Weber suggests, doctrines or doctrinal quarrels are less important than the everyday conduct of one's life guided by sanctioned norms.[4] The social organization of moral probation—how one proves one's worth to other people—outweighs theological beliefs.

The enduring significance of the Protestant ethic was due to the way it linked the probation of self, work in the world, and eternal salvation. An individual served an unknowable God, not by prayer or by almsgiving but by faithfully, continually, and unremittingly performing his or her worldly work. This rational and methodical pursuit of a worldly vocation, when it was crowned with economic success, proved a person before others. Their approbation helped the individual convince himself that he had proved himself to God and attained salvation.

This powerful intellectual construction, this ethic of ceaseless work combined with ceaseless renunciation of the fruits of one's toil, provided both the economic and the moral foundations for modern capitalism. On one hand, secular asceticism was a ready-made prescription for building economic capital; on the other, it became for the upward-moving middle class—self-made industrialists, merchants, farmers, and enterprising artisans—the social myth, the ideology that justified their attention to this world, their accumulation of wealth, and indeed the social inequities that inevitably followed such accumulation. This pragmatic bourgeois ethic, with its imperatives for self-reliance, hard work, frugality, and rational planning, and its clear definition of success and failure, came to dominate a whole historical epoch in the West, even in time among sectors of the middle class that eschewed classical Protestant theology as such.

But, for the most part, the ethic in its traditional form came under assault from two directions. First, the very accumulation of wealth that the original Protestant ethic made possible gradually stripped away its religious basis, especially among the rising middle class that benefited from it. There have been, of course, periodic reassertions of the old religious context of the ethic, as in the case of John D. Rockefeller and his turn toward Baptism, or in the recent resurgence of Protestant fundamentalism. Indeed, the ethic has been unwittingly revived in nearly pristine form among Korean-Americans, who have melded their traditional Confucian cultural values of self-control and self-abnegation with a newfound version of Protestantism.[5] But on the whole, by the late 1800s the specifically religious meaning of the ethic survived principally among independent farmers and proprietors of small businesses in rural areas and small towns across America. Even there the religious meaning was more ambiguous than before. By 1904, when Max Weber attended a baptism with his backwoods farmer relatives in western North Carolina, the meaning of the event seems to have been indisputably religious to most participants, but colored as well with extremely pragmatic calculations of the material advantages of affiliation with the sect conducting the ceremony.[6]

In the mainstream of an emerging urban America, the ethic had become secularized into the work ethic, rugged individualism, and especially the success ethic. The latter generated, and continues to generate, a vast outpouring of popular cultural myths, stories in the melodramatic, heroic mold, and practical guides for the uninitiated.[7] By the beginning of this century, among most of the economically successful, frugality had become an aberration, conspicuous consumption in varying degrees the norm. And with the shaping of the mass consumer society later in this century, accompanied by the commercialization of leisure, the sanctification of consumption fueled by consumer debt became widespread, indeed crucial to the maintenance of the economic order.

Affluence and the emergence of the consumer society were responsible, however, for the demise of only some aspects of the old ethic—namely, the imperatives for saving and investment. The core of the ethic, even in its later, secularized form—self-reliance, unremitting devotion to work, and a morality that postulated just rewards for work well done—was undermined by the complete transformation of the organizational form of work itself. The hallmarks of the emerging modern production and distribution system were administrative hierarchies, standardized work procedures, regularized timetables, uniform policies, specialized expertise, and, above all, centralized control—in a word, the bureaucratization of the economy.

This bureaucratization was heralded at first by a very small class of salaried managers. In the mid-1800s, mass wholesalers and retailers suddenly had great opportunities to expand their internal markets due, first, to the coming of the railroads and improvements in waterways, and, second, to the communications revolution initiated by the telegraph. Somewhat later, these same innovations in transportation and communications, as well as the technological breakthroughs made possible by new sources of energy, especially coal, spurred the development of the factory system. Mass distribution required greater administrative coordination for its success, and mass production demanded the centralization of operations to achieve efficiency.[8] Both processes stimulated the emergence of internal administrative hierarchies to guide and coordinate such developments. In the last quarter of the nineteenth century, mass distribution and mass production facilities were integrated within the same firms, producing big business as we know it today and requiring the addition of new layers of management. These burgeoning administrative hierarchies were later joined by legions of clerks who, as support staff to management, began to handle the enormously detailed work that underpins mass production. Still later, as needs for increasingly refined expertise grew, technicians and professionals of every stripe joined the process.

In this century, of course, the tide of bureaucratization spilled over from the private to the public sector, and government bureaucracies came to rival those of industry. The chief forces here have been the erection of the massive apparatus of the welfare state during the New Deal, the militarization of American society during World War II and the subsequent importance to key economic sectors of administered military spending, and the proliferation of the multitude of legislative and regulatory bodies at every level of government that make rules designed to meet the many claims that both citizens and businesses make on governments, as well as to protect citizens, businesses, and governments from each other.[9] This unrelenting societal push toward bureaucracy may be briefly gauged by the growth of the white-collar sector of the American work force, that is, the highly stratified category of men and women who perform the myriad of functions—from typing letters to providing technical know-how, from selling products to making crucial decisions about plant location—that make big organizations work.[10] Over the course of this century, the work force has shifted from the farm, through the factory, and into the lower, middle, and upper reaches of administrative hierarchies—into the great shipping offices permeated with the smell of carbon paper; into the sprawling, chaotic floors of stock exchanges and the busy but orderly banking halls; into the cavernous windowless rooms, guarded by mantraps and armed guards, that house hundreds of blinking computer consoles; into honeycombed government bureaus with desks piled nearly on top of one another, separated only by Plexiglas windows; into the "rabbit warrens" of advertising and public relations firms; into the antiseptic, pastel or blanch-white, Muzak-filled corridors of suburban corporate headquarters; or into the designer-decorated private executive suites. No major occupation or profession in our society has escaped the process of bureaucratization. They are all—from assembly-line workers to physicians—specialized, standardized, certified, arranged in a hierarchy, and coordinated by higher authorities. Moreover, bureaucracy is never simply a technical system of organization. It is also always a system of power, privilege, and domination. The bureaucratization of the occupational structure therefore profoundly affects the whole class and status structure, the whole tone and tempo of our society.

The changes in our social landscape brought about by this bureaucratization can hardly be exaggerated. This great transformation produced the decline of the old middle class of entrepreneurs, free professionals, independent farmers, and small independent businessmen—the traditional carriers of the old Protestant ethic—and the ascendance of a new middle class of salaried employees, that is, clerks, managers, executives, officials, technicians, and professionals alike, whose chief common characteristic was and is their dependence on the big organization. In the bargain, bureaucratization has shredded and reknit whole communities by making individual life chances almost wholly dependent on bureaucratic career lines that often require an unusual willingness to be geographically mobile.

Any understanding of what happened to the worldview that we call the old Protestant ethic and to the old morality and social character it seemed to embody—and therefore any understanding of the moral significance and texture of work in business today—is inextricably tied to an analysis of the historical and, especially, the contemporary structural significance of bureaucracy. I mean by the latter neither a treatment of bureaucracy as a practical administrative science nor a piecemeal investigation of how some particular facets of bureaucratic work affect aspects of people's experiences. Such directions have largely dominated the sociological and business studies of bureaucracy, fields usually called complex organizations or organizational behavior. I mean instead a comprehensive look at how the unique form of bureaucracy that has evolved in American business shapes the daily experiences, the social, cognitive, and evaluative frameworks, the self-images and worldviews, and, of course, the occupational morality of corporate managers.

The actual workings of American bureaucracy differ, in important respects, from the classical notion of the phenomenon as articulated by Max Weber.[11] Weber constructed a formal model of bureaucracy based to some extent on his perception of the Prussian state apparatus. In its pure form, bureaucracy is characterized by a kind of legalistic objectivity, by close attention to details and to orders, by an adherence to standardized procedures, by thorough written documentation of daily business in well-maintained files, by impartial and fair treatment under law, by a consequent impersonality, and by a separation of offices from persons. Ideally, the very rationality of such a bureaucracy produces greater efficiency. The model still guides much of the research in organizational theory. And, of course, all modern bureaucracies incorporate to some degree these ideal features. Indeed, certain American bureaucracies, like the civil service and some professional schools dedicated to advanced specialized training, approximate Weber's Prussian model.

But bureaucratic impersonality in its pure form lacks affinity with the American character. Our frontier experience emphasized individualistic solutions to problems, even if they were illegal; in any event, the law was often remote. The millions of immigrants who later flooded into the nation's expanding cities were mostly of peasant origins; with the possible exception of the Irish, they were not attracted to the formalities of the bureaucratic milieu. Moreover, big city bosses based their quasifeudal regimes on personal loyalty and on the delivery of personal services. By the time American corporations began to bureaucratize, they instituted as a matter of course many of the features of personal loyalty, favoritism, informality, and nonlegality that marked crucial aspects of the American historical experience. The kind of bureaucracy that developed in America, especially in the corporations but even in the higher reaches of government, was a hybrid; it incorporated many structural features of the pure form of bureaucracy but it also resembled patrimonial bureaucracy.

Patrimonial bureaucracy was the organizational form of the courts of kings and princes. There, personal loyalty was the norm, not loyalty to an office. In a patrimonial bureaucracy, one survives and flourishes by currying favor with powerful officials up the line who stand close to the ruler. It is a system marked by patronage and by intrigues and conspiracies among various factions to gain the favor of the ruler and the perquisites that accompany his good grace. Of course, in America, kings and princes were unavailable as objects of personal attachment. But the hierarchies of bureaucratic milieux allow the hankerings for attachment generated by the intense personalism of our historical experience to be focused on chief executive officers of corporations, as well as on certain high elected and appointed officials.

This hybrid bureaucracy, then, this peculiar combination of modern organizational features and the re-creation of patrimony in the context of the corporation, is the framework of this inquiry. In short, I want to examine the ethos of this kind of bureaucracy and the ethic it produces in managers.

It is precisely the study of managerial groups within bureaucracies that enables one to grasp the large shifts in moral viewpoints that the bureaucratic transformation has helped fashion in our society as a whole. Although managers only constitute 9.9 percent of the labor force (in 1980), they are nonetheless the quintessential bureaucratic work group in our society. Until and unless they reach the pinnacles of their administrative hierarchies, managers not only fashion bureaucratic rules but they are also bound by them. They not only implement rational procedures and plans, often in an attempt to control irrational forces, but they are also affected by the methodical rationality that they, their peers, and their superiors put into place. Often, too, they are affected by the irrationalities that rational efforts generate. They are not only bosses, but bossed; they are not only the beneficiaries of the privileges and power that authority in bureaucracies bestows, but in most cases they are also subordinates who want to climb higher. If they do struggle to the top of their organizations, they become not just the stuff of legend and the models for the ambitious below them, but also the objects of gossip, rumor, envy, resentment, and fear. Whether they stay at the middle or reach the top, managers typically are not only in the big organization but, because their administrative expertise and knowledge of bureaucratic intricacies constitute their livelihood, they are also of the organization. Unlike public servants, they need not avow allegiance to civil service codes or to any ethic of public service. Their sole allegiances are to the very principle of organization, to the market which itself is bureaucratically organized, to the groups and individuals in their world who can demand and command their loyalties, and to themselves and their own careers.

Managers are thus the paradigm of the white-collar salaried employee.[12] Their conservative public style and conventional demeanor hide their transforming role in our society. In my view, they are the principal carriers of the bureaucratic ethic in our era. Their pivotal institutional position as a group not only gives their decisions great reach, but also links them to other important elites. As a result, their occupational ethics and the way they come to see the world set both the frameworks and the vocabularies for a great many public issues in our society. Moreover, managers' experiences are by no means unique; indeed, they have a deep resonance with those of a great many other white-collar occupational groups, including men and women who work in the academy, in medicine, in science, and in politics. Work—bureaucratic work in particular—poses a series of intractable dilemmas that often demand compromises with traditional moral beliefs. Men and women in positions of authority, like managers, face these dilemmas and compromises in particularly pointed ways. By analyzing the kind of ethic bureaucracy produces in managers, one can begin to understand how bureaucracy shapes actual morality in our society as a whole.

II

The moral dilemmas posed by bureaucratic work are, in fact, pervasive, taken for granted, and, at the same time, regularly denied. Managers do, however, continually assess their decisions, their organizational milieux, and especially each other to ascertain which moral rules-in-use apply in given situations. Such assessments are always complex and most often intuitive. Essentially, managers try to gauge whether they feel "comfortable" with proposed resolutions to specific problems, a task that always involves an assessment of others' organizational morality and a reckoning of the practical organizational and market exigencies at hand. The notion of comfort has many meanings. When applied to other persons, the idea of comfort is an intuitive measure of trustworthiness, reliability, and predictability in a polycentric world that managers often find troubling, ambiguous, and anxiety-laden. Such assessment of others' organizational morality is a crucial aspect of a more general set of probations that are intrinsic to managerial work.

Getting into the corporations presented me with much of what I eventually learned, although I realized this only in retrospect.* When I approached my field study of managers, I had, for example, no firm grasp of the subtle, ambiguous process by which managers assess their colleagues' moral fitness, so to speak, for managerial life. Moreover, I did not know, or at least did not consciously understand, that managers would subject me, an outsider desiring to study their occupational morality, to the same searching assessment that they continuously make of each other.

Thirty-six corporations on both coasts refused permission for the study during a search for access from January to October, 1980. This was an instructive experience in itself. About half of these refusals came after extended and complicated negotiations with various levels of management, indeed all the way to the top of some firms. Most of these refusals were based, of course, on wholly practical rationales, although, as I later recognized, these often contained clues to themes that proved important in my subsequent work. The most common rationales, often given in concert, were: that there were no tangible organizational benefits to be gained from a study of managerial ethics because the project lacked a specific practical focus, or that the timing for the study was inappropriate because of "transitions" in a particular organization. Taken together and translated in light of later understanding, these mean that managers can afford to give approbation only to studies that officially are on a short leash and that can be publicly defended with the vocab-

---

*See Author's Note (preceding the Notes section at the end of the book) for a description of the data on which this study is based.

ularies of justification normally at hand in the corporation. I came to understand that such wariness is warranted because corporate hierarchies are almost always in political turmoil. The endless search for an organizational handle on the market—that is, rational structures to deal with the irrational—coupled with managers' ambitions and what I shall call their mobility panic, fuel a never-ending succession of personnel changes, marked by intense personal rivalries, in virtually all big corporations. Nosy outsiders can only complicate already troublesome, or potentially troublesome, situations.

Some managers seemed sympathetic to the study, although they encouraged me to recast it as a technical issue, such as the "problem of executive succession in multinationals." They objected in particular to those aspects of my brief written proposal that discussed the ethical dilemmas of managerial work. They urged me to avoid any mention of ethics or values altogether and concentrate instead on the "decision-making process" where I could talk about "trade-offs" and focus on the "hard decisions between competing interests" that mark managerial work. Taking these cues, I rewrote and rewrote the proposal couching my problem in the bland, euphemistic language that I was rapidly learning is the *lingua franca* of the corporate world. But such recasting eroded whatever was distinctive about the project and some managers dismissed the study as a reinvention of the wheel. Moreover, following managers' advice led me into ambiguous moral terrain with some of my academic colleagues. For instance, at one point, I approached a prominent academic ethicist, who had expressed a willingness to help me, with the sanitized proposal. He was "uncomfortable" with the revised version, arguing that I was not following the norms of "full disclosure." He preferred instead the earlier proposal with the more explicit references to managerial ethics and, with the agreement that I would use this version, put me in touch with a high-ranking executive in a major corporation. Unfortunately, this executive felt "uncomfortable" with the idea of suggesting to his colleagues that an outsider, untested in the corporate world, examine their ethics. In effect, I could not get access to study managers' moral rules-in-use because I seemed unable to articulate the appropriate stance that would convince key managers that I already understood those rules and was thus a person with whom they could "feel comfortable" enough to trust.

In the end, I gained access to several corporations through fortuitous circumstances and for reasons independent of any intrinsic merit that my proposed study of managerial ethics might have had. The search contained still further clues to what became main themes in my subsequent work; these are all reported in this book. As I crisscrossed managerial circles in different corporations, becoming known in some segments of the corporate world and running into managers that I had met in the course of my search, often in odd places, my personal contacts increased as managers referred me to each other. In the process, I became acutely aware of the importance that managers place on "being known" to one another and on having someone who is known vouch for one's probity. Institutional affiliations performed this role in two cases. Essentially through school ties, I gained limited access to a small chemical company and to a large defense contractor. My access to these companies was, however, restricted to interviews with top management, some observation, and use of a few internal company documents, all data that I have treated as preliminary despite some valuable insights. Eventually more personal referrals were the crucial keys to access. Through a totally chance meeting with a scholar who is also interested in social aspects of the business world, I was introduced to an executive, an expert in public relations, who befriended me. As had another executive earlier in the process with less successful results, this man encouraged me to reconstruct my own self-presentation in order to make managers feel comfortable with the proposed project. The process centered on the written proposal that I had been circulating and consisted essentially of a furthering of my linguistic education in the art of indirect rather than pointed statement and, more particularly, a reformulation of my inquiry that recast the moral issues of managerial work as issues of public relations. When, after several rewritings, the proposal satisfied him, he approached a well-placed executive in a large textile firm that I have given the pseudonym of Weft Corporation and vouched for me. At that point, the proposal itself became meaningless since, to my knowledge, no one except the two executives who arranged access ever saw it. The personal vouching, however, was crucial. This was based on what both men took to be a demonstrated willingness and ability to be "flexible" and especially on their perception that I already grasped the most salient aspect of managerial morality as managers themselves see it—that is, how their values and ethics appear in the public eye.

A somewhat more haphazard chain of events brought me access into Alchemy Inc., a pseudonym for the chemical company of a large conglomerate. An academic colleague's chance meeting on a tennis court with an executive from Covenant Corporation, a pseudonym for the parent corporation, led, after extremely complicated negotiations, to this man's vouching for me to a well-placed executive in Alchemy Inc. The latter admitted me to one of his groups, but only to study the intricacies of pending regulation on chlorofluorocarbons. Once admitted, however, I was able to find my way into managerial networks where one manager after another vouched for me to other managers, enabling me to broaden my inquiry unobtrusively with the active assistance of the executive who officially and publicly had framed my access as a narrow technical study. I ended up doing the bulk of my research in Weft Corporation and especially in Alchemy Inc.

Somewhat later, I had the opportunity to do research in a large public relations firm and this experience rounded out my fieldwork. My unplanned introduction to the world of public relations came during my search for access to large corporations in 1980. A scholarly acquaintance invited me to attend with him regular monthly meetings at a public relations agency that I shall call Images Inc., a large firm (by agency standards) that counsels every kind of corporate, governmental, and public service organization, and provides a full range of public relations services. The meetings, organized as seminars, discussed a variety of difficult cases facing the agency's management. Initially, it was understood that I would not study this firm but would simply use the seminars to become alert to managerial problems. However, since my discussions with managers at Weft Corporation and Alchemy Inc. on subjects like cotton dust and toxic waste disposal were leading me repeatedly to public relations issues, and more importantly, since an internal crisis prompted a top executive of Images Inc. to invite me to study the agency, I began systematic work there in 1982.

Given the problems that I had in gaining access to these corporate worlds, I cannot claim strictly scientific procedures, like random selection, in choosing the organizations that I studied. I do not claim, moreover, that this book describes all of American business; the limits of any inquiry based on studies of a few firms are self-evident. But only detailed fieldwork, which necessarily limits breadth, can yield in-depth knowledge of a subject like occupational ethics. Moreover, the great size of both Weft and Alchemy Inc., their intricate bureaucratic hierarchies in both line and staff, and the complex technological, regulatory, legal, administrative, and public relations problems that their managers face not only made both fit all my initial selective criteria but make them, I think, sites which enable one to understand many of the central issues of managerial work. Further, Images Inc. is at the very center of the public relations world. Finally, within the confines of the circles to which I had access, I made every effort to get structured representative samples of people to interview, that is, groups in all three firms that ranged across official rank, salary, organizational function and responsibility, age, and sex.

My search for access involved me in some of the crucial bureaucratic intricacies that shape managers' experiences. These include organizational upheavals, political rivalries, linguistic ambiguity, the supremacy of chance and tangled personal connections over any notion of intrinsic merit, the central significance of public relations, and, perhaps especially, the ceaseless moral probations for inclusion in a managerial circle. Managers keep their eyes on the organizational premiums that shape behavior, values, ethics, and worldviews in corporate bureaucracies. I focus on those premiums as well and, in particular, on those men and women whose ambition impels them to internalize those premiums in a thorough way, since it is they who create and re-create their organizational milieux.

2

The Social Structure of Managerial Work

I

The hierarchical authority structure that is the linchpin of bureaucracy dominates the way managers think about their world and about themselves. Managers do not see or experience authority in any abstract way; instead, authority is embodied in their personal relationships with their immediate bosses and in their perceptions of similar links between other managers up and down the hierarchy. When managers describe their work to an outsider, they almost always first say: "I work for [Bill James]" or "I report to [Harry Mills]" or "I'm in [Joe Bell's] group,"* and only then proceed to describe their actual work functions. Such a personalized statement of authority relationships seems to contradict classical notions of how bureaucracies function but it exactly reflects the way authority is structured, exercised, and experienced in corporate hierarchies.

American businesses typically both centralize and decentralize authority. Power is concentrated at the top in the person of the chief executive officer (CEO) and is simultaneously decentralized; that is, responsibility for decisions and profits is pushed as far down the organizational line as possible. For example, Alchemy Inc., as already noted, is one of several operating companies of Covenant Corporation. When I began my research, Alchemy employed 11,000 people; Covenant had over 50,000 employees and now has over 100,000. Like the other operating companies, Alchemy has its own president, executive vice-presidents, vice-presidents, other executive officers,

---

*Brackets within quotations represent words or phrases changed or added by the author, either to protect identity or to provide grammatical fluency.

business area managers, staff divisions, and more than eighty manufacturing plants scattered throughout the country and indeed the world producing a wide range of specialty and commodity chemicals. Each operating company is, at least theoretically, an autonomous, self-sufficient organization, though they are all monitored and coordinated by a central corporate staff, and each president reports directly to the corporate CEO. Weft Corporation has its corporate headquarters and manufacturing facilities in the South; its marketing and sales offices, along with some key executive personnel, are in New York City. Weft employs 20,000 people, concentrated in the firm's three textile divisions that have always been and remain its core business. The Apparel Division produces seven million yards a week of raw, unfinished cloth in several greige (colloquially gray) mills, mostly for sale to garment manufacturers; the Consumer Division produces some cloth of its own in several greige mills and also finishes—that is, bleaches, dyes, prints, and sews—twelve million yards of raw cloth a month into purchasable items like sheets, pillowcases, and tablecloths for department stores and chain stores; and the Retail Division operates an import-export business, specializing in the quick turnaround of the fast-moving cloths desired by Seventh Avenue designers. Each division has a president who reports to one of several executive vice-presidents, who in turn report to the corporate CEO. The divisional structure is typically less elaborate in its hierarchical ladder than the framework of independent operating companies; it is also somewhat more dependent on corporate staff for essential services. However, the basic principle of simultaneous centralization and decentralization prevails and both Covenant and Weft consider their companies or divisions, as the case may be, "profit centers."[1] Even Images Inc., while much smaller than the industrial concerns and organized like most service businesses according to shifting groupings of client accounts supervised by senior vice-presidents, uses the notion of profit centers.

The key interlocking mechanism of this structure is its reporting system. Each manager gathers up the profit targets or other objectives of his or her subordinates and, with these, formulates his commitments to his boss; this boss takes these commitments and those of his other subordinates, and in turn makes a commitment to his boss.* At the top of the line, the president of each company or division, or, at Images Inc., the senior vice-president for a group of accounts, makes his commitment to the CEO. This may be done directly, or sometimes, as at Weft Corporation, through a corporate executive vice-president. In any event, the commitments made to top management depend on the pyramid of stated objectives given to superiors up the line. At each level of the structure, there is typically "topside" pressure to achieve higher goals and, of course, the CEO frames and paces the whole process by applying pressure for attainment of his own objectives. Meanwhile, bosses and subordinates down the line engage in a series of intricate negotiations—managers often call these "conspiracies"—to keep their commitments respectable but achievable.

---

*Henceforth, I shall generally use only "he" or "his" to allow for easier reading.

This "management-by-objective" system, as it is usually called, creates a chain of commitments from the CEO down to the lowliest product manager or account executive. In practice, it also shapes a patrimonial authority arrangement that is crucial to defining both the immediate experiences and the long-run career chances of individual managers. In this world, a subordinate owes fealty principally to his immediate boss. This means that a subordinate must not overcommit his boss, lest his boss "get on the hook" for promises that cannot be kept. He must keep his boss from making mistakes, particularly public ones; he must keep his boss informed, lest his boss get "blindsided." If one has a mistake-prone boss, there is, of course, always the temptation to let him make a fool of himself, but the wise subordinate knows that this carries two dangers—he himself may get done in by his boss's errors, and, perhaps more important, other managers will view with the gravest suspicion a subordinate who withholds crucial information from his boss even if they think the boss is a nincompoop. A subordinate must also not circumvent his boss nor ever give the appearance of doing so. He must never contradict his boss's judgment in public. To violate the last admonition is thought to constitute a kind of death wish in business, and one who does so should practice what one executive calls "flexibility drills," an exercise "where you put your head between your legs and kiss your ass goodbye." On a social level, even though an easy, breezy, first-name informality is the prevalent style of American business, a concession perhaps to our democratic heritage and egalitarian rhetoric, the subordinate must extend to the boss a certain ritual deference. For instance, he must follow the boss's lead in conversation, must not speak out of turn at meetings, must laugh at his boss's jokes while not making jokes of his own that upstage his boss, must not rib the boss for his foibles. The shrewd subordinate learns to efface himself, so that his boss's face might shine more clearly.

In short, the subordinate must symbolically reinforce at every turn his own subordination and his willing acceptance of the obligations of fealty. In return, he can hope for those perquisites that are in his boss's gift—the better, more attractive secretaries, or the nudging of a movable panel to enlarge his office, and perhaps a couch to fill the added space, one of the real distinctions in corporate bureaucracies. He can hope to be elevated when and if the boss is elevated, though other important criteria intervene here. He can also expect protection for mistakes made, up to a point. However, that point is never exactly defined and depends on the complicated politics of each situation. The general rule is that bosses are expected to protect those in their bailiwicks. Not to do so, or to be unable to do so, is taken as a sign of untrustworthiness or weakness. If, however, subordinates make mistakes that are thought to be dumb, or especially if they violate fealty obligations—for example, going around their boss—then abandonment of them to the vagaries of organizational forces is quite acceptable.

Overlaying and intertwined with this formal monocratic system of authority, with its patrimonial resonance, are patron-client relationships. Patrons are usually powerful figures in the higher echelons of management. The patron might be a manager's direct boss, or his boss's boss, or someone several levels higher in the chain of command. In either case, the manager is still bound by the immediate, formal authority and fealty patterns of his position but he also acquires new, though more ambiguous, fealty relationships with his highest ranking patron. Patrons play a crucial role in advancement, a point that I shall discuss later.

It is characteristic of this authority system that details are pushed down and credit is pulled up. Superiors do not like to give detailed instructions to subordinates. The official reason for this is to maximize subordinates' autonomy. The underlying reason is, first, to get rid of tedious details. Most hierarchically organized occupations follow this pattern; one of the privileges of authority is the divestment of humdrum intricacies. This also insulates higher bosses from the peculiar pressures that accompany managerial work at the middle levels and below: the lack of economy over one's time because of continual interruption from one's subordinates, telephone calls from customers and clients, and necessary meetings with colleagues; the piecemeal fragmentation of issues both because of the discontinuity of events and because of the way subordinates filter news; and the difficulty of minding the store while sorting out sometimes unpleasant personnel issues. Perhaps more important, pushing details down protects the privilege of authority to declare that a mistake has been made. A high-level executive in Alchemy Inc. explains:

> If I tell someone what to do—like do A, B, or C—the inference and implication is that he will succeed in accomplishing the objective. Now, if he doesn't succeed, that means that I have invested part of myself in his work and I lose any right I have to chew his ass out if he doesn't succeed. If I tell you what to do, I can't bawl you out if things don't work. And this is why a lot of bosses don't give explicit directions. They just give a statement of objectives, and then they can criticize subordinates who fail to make their goals.

Moreover, pushing down details relieves superiors of the burden of too much knowledge, particularly guilty knowledge. A superior will say to a subordinate, for instance: "Give me your best thinking on the problem with [X]." When the subordinate makes his report, he is often told: "I think you can do better than that," until the subordinate has worked out all the details of the boss's predetermined solution, without the boss being specifically aware of "all the eggs that have to be broken." It is also not at all uncommon for very bald and extremely general edicts to emerge from on high. For example, "Sell the plant in [St. Louis]; let me know when you've struck a deal," or "We need to get higher prices for [fabric X]; see what you can work out," or "Tom, I want you to go down there and meet with those guys and make a deal and I don't want you to come back until you've got one." This pushing down of details has important consequences.

First, because they are unfamiliar with—indeed deliberately distance themselves from—entangling details, corporate higher echelons tend to expect successful results without messy complications. This is central to top executives' well-known aversion to bad news and to the resulting tendency to kill the messenger who bears the news.

Second, the pushing down of details creates great pressure on middle managers not only to transmit good news but, precisely because they know the details, to act to protect their corporations, their bosses, and themselves in the process. They become the "point men" of a given strategy and the potential "fall guys" when things go wrong. From an organizational standpoint, overly conscientious managers are particularly useful at the middle levels of the structure. Upwardly mobile men and women, especially those from working-class origins who find themselves in higher status milieux, seem to have the requisite level of anxiety, and perhaps tightly controlled anger and hostility, that fuels an obsession with detail. Of course, such conscientiousness is not necessarily, and is certainly not systematically, rewarded; the real organizational premiums are placed on other, more flexible, behavior.

Credit flows up in this structure and is usually appropriated by the highest ranking officer involved in a successful decision or resolution of a problem. There is, for instance, a tremendous competition for ideas in the corporate world; authority provides a license to steal ideas, even in front of those who originated them. Chairmen routinely appropriate the useful suggestions made by members of their committees or task forces; research directors build their reputations for scientific wizardry on the bricks laid down by junior researchers and directors of departments. Presidents of whole divisions as well are always on the lookout for "fresh ideas" and "creative approaches" that they can claim as their own in order to put themselves "out in front" of their peers. A subordinate whose ideas are appropriated is expected to be a good sport about the matter; not to balk at so being used is one attribute of the good team player. The person who appropriates credit redistributes it as he chooses, bound essentially and only by a sensitivity to public perceptions of his fairness. One gives credit, therefore, not necessarily where it is due, although one always invokes this old saw, but where prudence dictates. Customarily, people who had nothing to do with the success of a project can be allocated credit for their exemplary efforts. At the middle levels, therefore, credit for a particular idea or success is always a type of refracted social honor; one cannot claim credit even if it is earned. Credit has to be given, and acceptance of the gift implicitly involves a reaffirmation and strengthening of fealty. A superior may share some credit with subordinates in order to deepen fealty relationships and induce greater efforts on his behalf. Of course, a different system obtains in the allocation of blame.

Because of the interlocking character of the commitment system, a CEO carries enormous influence in his corporation. If, for a moment, one thinks of the presidents of operating companies or divisions as barons, then the CEO of the corporation is the king. His word is law; even the CEO's wishes and whims are taken as commands by close subordinates on the corporate staff, who turn them into policies and directives. A typical example occurred in Weft Corporation a few years ago when the CEO, new at the time, expressed mild concern about the rising operating costs of the company's fleet of rented cars. The following day, a stringent system for monitoring mileage replaced the previous casual practice. Managers have a myriad of aphorisms that refer to how the power of CEOs, magnified through the zealous efforts of subordinates, affects them. These range from the trite "When he sneezes, we all catch colds" to the more colorful "When he says 'Go to the bathroom,' we all get the shits."

Great efforts are made to please the CEO. For example, when the CEO of Covenant Corporation visits a plant, the most significant order of business for local management is a fresh paint job, even when, as in several cases, the cost of paint alone exceeds $100,000. If a paint job has already been scheduled at a plant, it is deferred along with all other cosmetic maintenance until just before the CEO arrives; keeping up appearances without recognition for one's efforts is pointless. I am told that similar anecdotes from other corporations have been in circulation since 1910, which suggests a certain historical continuity of behavior toward top bosses.

The second order of business for the plant management is to produce a book fully describing the plant and its operations, replete with photographs and illustrations, for presentation to the CEO; such a book costs about $10,000 for the single copy. By any standards of budgetary stringency, such expenditures are irrational. But by the social standards of the corporation, they make perfect sense. It is far more important to please the king today than to worry about the future economic state of one's fief, since, if one does not please the king, there may not be a fief to worry about or indeed vassals to do the worrying.

By the same token, all of this leads to an intense interest in everything the CEO does and says. In all the companies that I studied, the most common topic of conversation among managers up and down the line is speculation about their respective CEO's plans, intentions, strategies, actions, style, public image, and ideological leanings of the moment. Even the metaphorical temper of a CEO's language finds its way down the hierarchy to the lower reaches of an organization. In the early stages of my fieldwork at Covenant Corporation, for example, I was puzzled by the inordinately widespread usage of nautical terminology, especially in a corporation located in a landlocked site. As it happens, the CEO is devoted to sailboats and prefers that his aides call him "Skipper." Moreover, in every corporation that I studied, stories and rumors circulate constantly about the social world of the CEO and his immediate subordinates—who, for instance, seems to have the CEO's ear at the moment; whose style seems to have gained approbation; who, in short, seems to be in the CEO's grace and who seems to have fallen out of favor. In the smaller and more intimate setting of Images Inc., the circulation of favor takes an interesting, if unusual, tack. There, the CEO is known for attaching younger people to himself as confidants. He solicits their advice, tells them secrets, gets their assessments of developments further down in the hierarchy, gleans the rumors and gossip making the rounds about himself. For the younger people selected for such attention, this is a rare, if fleeting, opportunity to have a place in the sun and to share the illusion if not the substance of power. In time, of course, the CEO tires of or becomes disappointed with particular individuals and turns his attention to others. "Being discarded," however, is not an obstacle to regaining favor. In larger organizations, impermeable structural barriers between top circles and junior people prevent this kind of intimate interchange and circulation of authoritative regard. Within a CEO's circle, however, the same currying and granting of favor prevails, always amidst conjectures from below about who has edged close to the throne.

But such speculation about the CEO and his leanings of the moment is more than idle gossip, and the courtlike atmosphere that I am describing more than stylized diversion. Because he stands at the apex of the corporation's bureaucratic and patrimonial structures and locks the intricate system of commitments between bosses and subordinates into place, it is the CEO who ultimately decides whether those commitments have been satisfactorily met. The CEO becomes the actual and the symbolic keystone of the hierarchy that constitutes the defining point of the managerial experience. Moreover, the CEO and his trusted associates determine the fate of whole business areas of a corporation.

Within the general ambiance established by a CEO, presidents of individual operating companies or of divisions carry similar, though correspondingly reduced, influence within their own baronies. Adroit and well-placed subordinates can, for instance, borrow a president's prestige and power to exert great leverage. Even chance encounters or the occasional meeting or lunch with the president can, if advertised casually and subtly, cause notice and the respect among other managers that comes from uncertainty. Knowledge of more clearly established relationships, of course, always sways behavior. A middle manager in one company, widely known to be a very close personal friend of the president, flagged her copious memoranda to other managers with large green paperclips, ensuring prompt attention to her requests. More generally, each major division of the core textile group in Weft Corporation is widely thought to reflect the personality of its leader—one hard-driving, intense, and openly competitive; one cool, precise, urbane, and proper; and one gregarious, talkative, and self-promotional. Actually, market exigencies play a large role in shaping each division's tone and tempo. Still, the popular conception of the dominance of presidential personalities not only points to the crucial issue of style in business, a topic to be explored in depth later, but it underlines the general tendency to personalize authority in corporate bureaucracies.

Managers draw elaborate cognitive maps to guide them through the thickets of their organizations. Because they see and experience authority in such personal terms, the singular feature of these maps is their biographical emphasis. Managers carry around in their heads thumbnail sketches of the occupational history of virtually every other manager of their own rank or higher in their particular organization. These maps begin with a knowledge of others' occupational expertise and specific work experience, but focus especially on

previous and present reporting relationships, patronage relationships, and alliances. Cognitive maps incorporate memories of social slights, of public
embarrassments, of battles won and lost, and of people's behavior under pressure. They include as well general estimates of the abilities and career trajectories of their colleagues. I should mention that these latter estimates are not
necessarily accurate or fair; they are, in fact, often based on the flimsiest of
evidence. For instance, a general manager at Alchemy Inc. describes the
ephemeral nature of such opinions:

> It's a feeling about the guy's perceived ability to run a business—like
> he's not a good people man, or he's not a good numbers man. This is
> not a quantitative thing. It's a gut feeling that a guy can't be put in one
> spot, but he might be put in another spot. These kinds of informal
> opinions about others are the lifeblood of an organization's advance-
> ment system. Oh, for the record, we've got the formal evaluations; but
> the real opinions—the ones that really count in determining people's
> fates—are those which are traded back and forth in meetings, private
> conferences, chance encounters, and so on.

Managers trade estimates of others' chances within their circles and often
color them to suit their own purposes. This is one reason why it is crucial
for the aspiring young manager to project the right image to the right people
who can influence others' sketches of him. Whatever the accuracy of these
vocabularies of description, managers' penchant for biographical detail and
personal histories contrasts sharply with their disinclination for details in general or for other kinds of history. Details, as I have mentioned, get pushed
down the ladder; and a concern with history, even of the short-run, let alone
long-term, structural shifts in one's own organization, constrains the forward
orientation and cheerful optimism highly valued in most corporations. Biographical detail, however, constitutes crucial knowledge because managers
know that, in the rough-and-tumble politics of the corporate world, individual
fates are made and broken not necessarily by one's accomplishments but by
other people.
    One must appreciate the simultaneously monocratic and patrimonial char-
acter of business bureaucracies in order to grasp the personal and organizational significance of political struggles in managerial work. As it happens,
political struggles are a constant and recurring feature in business, shaping
managers' experience and outlooks in fundamental ways. Of course, such
conflicts are usually cloaked by typically elaborate organizational rhetorics of
harmony and teamwork. However, one can observe the multiple dimensions
of these conflicts during periods of organizational upheaval, a regular feature
of American business where mergers, buyouts, divestitures, and especially
"organizational restructuring" have become commonplace occurrences.[2] As
Karl Mannheim, among others, has pointed out, it is precisely when a social
order begins to fall apart that one can discern what has held it together in the
first place. A series of shake-ups that occurred in Covenant Corporation, all

within a period of a few years, present a focused case study of political processes basic to all big corporations.

II

In 1979, a new CEO took power in Covenant Corporation. The first action of most new CEOs is some form of organizational change. On the one hand, this prevents the inheritance of blame for past mistakes; on the other, it projects an image of bare-knuckled aggressiveness much appreciated on Wall Street. Perhaps most important, a shake-up rearranges the fealty structure of the corporation, placing in power those barons whose style and public image mesh closely with that of the new CEO and whose principal loyalties belong to him. Shortly after the new CEO of Covenant was named, he reorganized the whole business, after a major management consulting firm had "exhaustively considered all the options," and personally selected new presidents to head each of the five newly formed companies of the corporation—Alchemy, Energy, Metals, Electronics, and Instruments. He ordered the presidents to carry out a thorough reorganization of their separate companies complete with extensive "census reduction," or firing as many people as possible. The presidents were given, it was said, a free hand in their efforts, although in retrospect it seems that the CEO insisted on certain high-level appointments.

The new president of Alchemy Inc.—let's call him Smith*—had risen from a marketing background in a small but important specialty chemicals division in the former company. Specialty chemicals are produced in relatively small batches and command high prices, showing generous profit margins; they depend on customer loyalty and therefore on the adroit cultivation of buyers through professional marketing. Upon promotion to president, Smith reached back into his former division, indeed back to his own past work in a particular product line, and systematically elevated many of his former colleagues, friends, clients, and allies. Powerful managers in other divisions, particularly in a rival process chemicals division, whose commodity products, produced in huge quantities, were sold only by price and who exemplified an old-time "blood, guts, and courage" management style were: forced to take big demotions in the new power structure; put on "special assignment"—the corporate euphemism for Siberia, sent to a distant corner office where one looks for a new job (the saying is: "No one ever comes back from special assignment"); fired; or given "early retirement," a graceful way of doing the same thing. What happened in Alchemy Inc. was typical of the pattern in the other companies of the conglomerate. Hundreds of people throughout the whole corporation lost their jobs in what became known as "Bloody Thursday," the "October Revolution," or in some circles, the "Octoberfest." I shall refer back to this event as the "big purge."

Up and down the chemical company, former associates of Smith were

---

*All personal names in the field data throughout the book are pseudonyms.

placed in virtually every important position. Managers in the company saw all of this as an inevitable fact of life. In their view, Smith simply picked those managers with whom he was comfortable. The whole reorganization could easily have gone in a completely different direction had another CEO been named, or had the one selected picked someone besides Smith, or had Smith come from a different work group in the old organization. Fealty is the mortar of the corporate hierarchy, but the removal of one well-placed stone loosens the mortar throughout the pyramid. And no one is ever quite sure, until after the fact, just how the pyramid will be put back together.

The year after the "big purge," Alchemy prospered and met its financial commitments to the CEO, the crucial coin of the realm to purchase continued autonomy. Smith consolidated his power and, through the circle of the mostly like-minded and like-mannered men and women with whom he surrounded himself, further weeded out or undercut managers with whom he felt uncomfortable. At the end of the year, the mood in the company was buoyant not only because of high profits but because of the expectation of massive deregulation and boom times for business following President Reagan's first election. On the day after the election, by the way, managers, in an unusual break with normal decorum, actually danced in the corridors.

What follows might be read as a cautionary tale on the perils of triumph in a probationary world where victory must follow victory. Elated by his success in 1980, and eager to make a continued mark with the CEO vis-à-vis the presidents of the other four companies, all of whom were vying for the open presidency of Covenant Corporation, Smith became the victim of his own upbeat marketing optimism. He overcommitted himself and the chemical company financially for the coming year just as the whole economy began to slide into recession. By mid-1981, profit targets had to be readjusted down and considerable anxiety pervaded Smith's circle and the upper-middle levels of management, whose job it became both to extract more profits from below and to maintain a public facade of cheerful equanimity. A top executive at Alchemy Inc. describes this anxiety:

> See, the problem with any change of CEO is that any credibility you have built up with the previous guy all goes by the board and you have to begin from scratch. This CEO thinks that everybody associated with the company before him is a dummy. And so you have to prove yourself over and over again. You can't just win some and lose some. You have to keep your winning record at least at 75 percent if not better. You're expected to take risks. At least the CEO says that, but the reality is that people are afraid to make mistakes.

Toward the end of the year, it became clear that the chemical company would reach only 60 percent of its profit target and that only by remarkable legerdemain with the books. Publicly, of course, managers continued to evince a "cautious optimism" that things would turn around; privately, however, a deepening sense of gloom and incipient panic pervaded the organization. Stories began to circulate about the CEO's unhappiness with the company's shortfall. To take but one example, managers in chemical fertilizers were told by the CEO never again to offer weather conditions or widespread farmer bankruptcy as excuses for lagging sales. Rumors of every sort began to flourish, and a few of these are worth recounting.

Smith was on his way out, it was feared, and would take the whole structure of Alchemy Inc. with him. In fact, one of the CEO's most trusted troubleshooters, a man who "eats people for breakfast," was gunning for Smith and his job. (This man distinguished himself around this time by publicly accusing those who missed a 9:00 A.M. staff meeting, held during one of the worst snowstorms in two decades, of being disloyal to Covenant.)

Smith would survive, it was said, but would be forced to sacrifice all of his top people, alter his organization's structure, and buckle under to the increasingly vigorous demands of the CEO.

The CEO, it was argued, was about to put the whole chemical company on the block; in fact, the real purpose of creating supposedly self-contained companies in the first place might have been to package them for sale. At the least, the CEO would sell large portions of Alchemy Inc., wreaking havoc with its support groups at corporate headquarters.

There were disturbing rumors too about the growth of personal tension and animosity between Smith and the CEO. The CEO was well-known for his propensity for lording it over his subordinates, a behavioral pattern that often emerges in top authority figures after years of continual suppression of impulses. He was now said to have targeted Smith for this kind of attention. Managers up and down the line knew instinctively that, if the personal relationship between Smith and the CEO were eroding, the inevitable period of blame and retribution for the bad financial year might engulf everyone, and not just well-targeted individuals. Managers began to mobilize their subordinates to arrange defenses, tried to cement crucial alliances, and waited. In the meantime, they joked that they were updating their résumés and responding graciously to the regular phone calls of headhunters.

While reorganizations by CEOs have the broadest impact in a corporation, such shake-ups are not made by CEOs alone. Shake-ups are in fact the first line of defense against a CEO's demands by presidents of operating companies or divisions in trouble. At Alchemy Inc., invoking a commissioned study by management consultants, Smith eliminated a layer of top management early in 1982 to give himself and his top aides "greater access to the business areas." In the process, he got rid of Brown, the chemical company's executive vice-president. Brown was an anomaly in the higher circles of the company. Although his formal training had been in marketing, he had ended up performing a financial function in the executive vice-president slot—that is, riding herd on business managers about costs. His principal rise had been through the old specialty chemicals division; however, his original roots in the corporation were in the Energy Division where he had been a friend and close associate of the man who later rose to the presidency of that company in the "big purge." This biographical history made Brown suspect, especially when the tension between the CEO and Smith intensified and some of the presidents of the other companies were thought to be seizing the chance to extend their own influence. Brown's straitlaced personal style was also out of keeping with the back-slapping bonhomie that marked Smith's inner circle. Managers often note that one must stay at least three drinks behind one's boss at social functions; this meant that Brown's subordinates might never drink at all on such occasions. As it happens, however, the CEO, himself a financial man, saved Brown and appointed him an executive vice-president of the Electronics company, in charge of what had become known as the "corporate graveyard," a place with decaying businesses that one buries by selling off.

Many managers were amused at Brown's reassignment. They felt that, as soon as he had succeeded in disposing of the unwanted businesses, he would be out of a job. He was, in effect, being told to dig his own grave in an appropriate location. Some managers, however, were more wary; they saw the move as a complicated gambit, in fact as a cover-up by the CEO himself who had invested heavily in several businesses in the electronics area only to have them expire. In any case, Brown had not been popular at Alchemy and his departure was greeted, as one manager describes it, "by a lot of people standing on the sidelines, hooting, and hollering, and stamping our feet. We never thought we'd see old [Brown] again."

In Brown's place, Smith appointed two executive vice-presidents, one a trusted aide from his favorite product group in the old specialty chemicals division and the other an outsider whose expertise was, it was said, in selling off commodity businesses, that is, what was left of the old process chemicals division. Though badly scarred, Smith managed to deflect blame for the bad year onto the heads of a few general managers, all from the old process division, whom he fired. One ominous note was Smith's loss of administrative control of the corporate headquarters site, a function that had fallen to the chemical company during the "big purge." A fundamental rule of corporate politics is that one never cedes control over assets, even if the assets are administrative headaches. More ominous was the CEO's gift of responsibility for headquarters to the man "who eats people for breakfast," mentioned earlier. On the whole, however, managers felt that not only had Smith reasserted the supremacy of his own alliances but that he had in the bargain bought himself eight months—time enough perhaps for the economy to turn around.

As it happened, however, the economy continued to worsen and the CEO's pressure on Smith increased. In the late spring of 1982, the CEO began sending a series of terse notes to company executives accompanied by photocopied articles written by a well-known management consultant in *The Wall Street Journal* about the necessity of trimming staff to streamline operations. Only companies that aggressively cut staff during the recession, the articles argued, would emerge lean and poised for the economic recovery. The CEO's notes usually said simply: "This article merits your careful attention." Smith's aides privately referred to the CEO as a "tinhorn tyrant" and muttered about his "henchmen" being sent to extract information from them to be used against Smith. One executive describes the chemical company's growing feeling toward corporate staff: "The boys he [the CEO] has over there are not very nice . . . they never miss a chance to stomp on you when you're down." As time passed, this feeling became more acerbic. Another executive describes how he sees "internal auditors," that is, the CEO's people who were overlooking Alchemy's operations:

> Have I ever told you my definition of an auditor? An auditor is some-one who situates himself up on a hill overlooking a battle, far from the noise of the guns and the smoke of the explosions. And he watches the battle from afar, and when it is over and the smoke is cleared, he goes down onto the battlefield and walks among the wounded. And he shoots them.

Finally, in the early summer, the CEO demanded a 30 percent cut in staff in the chemical company, even asking for the names of those to be terminated. Smith had little choice but to go along and he fired 200 people. Most of these, however, were technical support people, Indians rather than chiefs. Smith was thus able to maintain a basic rule of management circles, namely that management takes care of itself, at least of other known managers, in good times and bad.

As the economy continued to flounder throughout the summer, Alchemy's earnings dipped even further, and the CEO's demands on Smith became relentless. By this point, the watchword in the corporation had become "manage for cash" and the CEO wanted some businesses sold, others cut back, still others milked, and costs slashed. Particular attention began to be focused on the chemical company's environmental protection staff, a target of hostility not only from the CEO's people but from line managers within Alchemy itself. In response to an environmental catastrophe in the late 1970s, and to the public outrage about chemical pollution in general, Smith had erected, upon his ascendancy to the presidency, an elaborate and relatively free-roaming environmental staff. Though costly, Smith felt that this apparatus was the best defense against another severely embarrassing and even more expensive environmental debacle. The company had, in fact, won an industrial award and wide public recognition for its program; the CEO himself, of course, had been a principal beneficiary of all this public praise and he basked in that attention. But, as the political atmosphere in the country changed with the conservative legislative, budgetary, and regulatory triumphs after President Reagan's election, line managers in Alchemy began chafing under staff intrusions. They blamed the environmental staff for creating extra work and needless costs during a period of economic crisis. The CEO agreed with these sentiments, and his opinion helped deepen the splits in the chemical company. In the early fall, faced with unremitting pressure because of the company's declining fortunes, internal warring factions, and, worse, the prospect of public capitulation to the CEO on the structure of his supposedly autonomous company, Smith chose to resign to "pursue other interests," pulling the cord on his "golden parachute" (a fail-safe plan ensuring comfortable financial landing) as he left.

His parting letter to the company typifies the peculiar combination of in-house humor, personal jauntiness in the face of adversity, and appeals to some of the classical legitimations of managerial work that one may observe among high-ranking managers. It reads in part:

> Hi!
>
> Someone from the stockroom just called and said there were reams of my stationery left downstairs—what did I want to do with it? Not only have I relocated myself to a distant corner office, but it appears that I've also freed up space on the stockroom shelves as well! Since I will be leaving on October 15, I want to take this opportunity to thank each and every one of you for the never-failing support and understanding you have given me throughout my years with [Alchemy]. I have had the privilege of knowing many of you personally, and the greatest satisfaction in my job here has been, throughout the years, to be able to walk down the hall and have so many of you say "Hi, [Joe]."
>
> I would like to invite you to have a drink with me after work on October 6th. My first inclination was that it would be great to pitch a tent in the front parking lot and have hotdogs, too, but somehow I don't think that one would fly. So the [nearby hotel] it is, and I promise you—no speeches, no presentations, no formalities. Just a chance to personally say thank you for being part of a great team—one that I will never forget.

It is important to note that many managers were deeply moved by Smith's letter and particularly by the social occasion to which he invited them. It became not only a farewell party for a fallen leader, but was seen as a small act of rebellion against the CEO.

Alchemy Inc. went into a state of shock and paralysis at Smith's resignation, and the rumor mills churned out names of possible replacements, each tied to a scenario of the future. Once again, the mortar of fealty loosened throughout the pyramid even as it bound managers to their pasts. Managers know that others' cognitive maps afford little escape from old loyalties, alliances, and associations. At the same time, they realize that they must be poised to make new alliances in a hurry if their areas get targeted for "restructuring."

As things turned out, a great many managers found themselves in exactly that position. To almost everyone's astonishment, and to the trepidation of many, the CEO brought Brown back from the electronics graveyard after a "thorough assessment of all the candidates," which took two days, and made him the new president of Alchemy. No laughter or jeering was heard in the corridors, although some wags suggested nominating Brown as the "Comeback Player of the Year." Whatever Brown's previous affiliations, there was no doubt about where his fealty now lay. He became known throughout the corporation as the "CEO's boy" and everyone recognized that he had a mandate to "wield a meat axe" and to wreak whatever mayhem was necessary to cut expenditures. At every level of the company, managers began furiously to scramble—writing position papers, holding rushed meetings, making deals—to try to secure their domains against the coming assault. Within a short time, Brown had fired 150 people, mostly at the managerial level, focusing particular attention on "streamlining" the environmental staff, slashing it by 75 percent. The survivors from the environmental staff were "moved close to the action," that is, subordinated to the business units, each of which was made more "free-standing," and thus the staff was effectively neutralized. The official rationale was as follows. The company had gone through an extraordinary learning experience on environmental issues and had benefited greatly from the expertise of the environmental staff. It had, however, by this point fully integrated and institutionalized that knowledge into its normal operations. Moreover, since there were no longer any environmental problems facing the company, a modest reduction in this area made good business sense. Privately, of course, the assessments were different. Brown himself said at a managerial meeting that good staff simply create work to justify their own existence. Many line managers echoed this opinion. More to the point, the feeling was that work on environmental issues had lost any urgency in the Reagan era. The Environmental Protection Agency (EPA) was dead. Moreover, the only real threat to corporations on environmental issues was in the courts, which, however, judge past actions, not present practices. By the time the courts get to cases generated by contemporary practices, typically in fifteen years, those executives presently in charge will have moved on, leaving any problems their policies might create to others. Managers noted, some ruefully, some with detached bemusement, the irony of organizational reform. The public outcry against Covenant after the environmental disaster of the late 1970s produced thoroughgoing internal reform designed to ward off such incidents in the future. But the reforms also unintentionally laid down the bases of resentment among managers who did not benefit from the staff increase. During a crisis, these managers grasped the chance to clamor for dismantling the safeguards that might prevent future catastrophes.

Brown's "housecleaning" created extreme anxiety throughout Alchemy. Even managers who agreed with Brown's attack on the staff and his wholesale pruning of other areas expressed astonishment and sometimes outrage that mostly persons of managerial rank had been fired. This seemed an ominous violation of the managerial code. Those that survived were "looking over their shoulders" and "listening for footsteps behind them." Bitter jokes circulated freely, like: "Opening Day at the chemical company; Brown comes in and throws out the first employee." Some managers even passed around among their colleagues a list of thirteen tough questions to throw at Brown at an internal news conference.

Throughout this entire period, the CEO had been pursuing an aggressive policy of acquisitions, picking up small and medium-sized companies and adding them to one or another of the operating companies' holdings. No one could discern the pattern of the acquisitions. High-technology industries with rapid growth potential were the officially stated targets; in fact, however, mostly mature businesses were purchased and unsuccessful bids were made for several others. Suddenly, in the midst of Alchemy's crisis, the CEO announced the acquisition, publicly called a merger, of another major corporation with mostly mature businesses and large, complicated corporate and company staffs. The announcement precipitated both consternation and excitement throughout Covenant Corporation; up and down the ladder of every company both line and staff managers began to mobilize their forces and to gear their troops for the inevitable and dangerous showdown with the personnel of the newly acquired firm. Showdowns following the acquisition of a smaller company are wholly predictable and are virtually no contest. The apprehension of Covenant managers in this case stemmed from their wariness of the bureaucratic battle skills of their opposite numbers in the firm acquired. Everything, of course, would depend on which leaders emerged from the crucible.

In the meantime, Alchemy Inc. staggered into the following year. Six months after the national economy took an upswing, its own fortunes began to improve, a typical pattern for industrial supply companies. Suddenly, in the spring of 1983, the CEO announced another major reorganization in order to integrate the newly acquired corporation, citing yet another thorough appraisal by a management consulting firm. Once again the entire corporation was divided into several "sectors," each section with different companies. This time, the Industrial Supplies Sector incorporated Alchemy, Metals, and Plastics. Brown did not get the call to head the whole Industrial Supplies Sector but remained as the president of Alchemy. The leadership of the whole sector fell instead to a man who had emerged out of the Metals company where he had been president in the old order. He in turn gave the presidencies of Metals and Plastics to metals people, and a new cycle of ascendancy with its own patterns of fealty, patronage, and power cliques began. Managers noted, with some satisfaction, the irony of Brown being passed over by the CEO for the sector presidency after performing the CEO's dirty work. Their satisfaction was short-lived. After a stint at the helm of chemicals, Brown returned to his original home in the corporation as the aide-de-camp of the president of the new Energy Sector—his old mentor. When the latter retired, Brown assumed control of that sector.

III

This sequence of events is remarkable only for its compactness. One need only regularly read *The Wall Street Journal,* the business section of *The New York Times,* any of the leading business magazines, let alone more academic publications, to see that these sorts of upheavals and political struggles are commonplace in American business. In Weft Corporation, one could observe exactly similar patterns, though played out over a much longer period of time. For instance, more than a decade ago, a new CEO was brought into the company to modernize and professionalize what had been up to that point a closely held family business. His first act was to make a rule that no executives over sixty years old could hold posts above a certain high-ranking management grade. In one stroke, he got rid of a whole cohort of executives who had ruled the company for a generation. He then staffed all key posts of each division, as well as his own inner circle, either with people who had served under him in the Army during World War II, or with whom he had worked in another corporation, or with former consultants who had advised him on how to proceed with the reorganization, or with people from the old organization with whom he felt comfortable. All of these managers in turn brought in their own recruits and protégés. They established a corporate order notable for its stability for many years. As the CEO and his subordinates grew older, of course, he eliminated the rule governing age. Eventually, however, retirement time did come. The new CEO was handpicked by the outgoing boss from the high reaches of another corporation where he had been vice-chairman and thus effectively dead-ended. He graciously bided his time until the old CEO had entirely left the scene and then moved decisively to shape the organization to his liking. The most important move in this regard was the rapid elevation of a man who had been a mere vice-president of personnel, normally the wasteland of the corporate world. Within a year of the new CEO's ascendancy, this manager was given control over all other staff functions. He then moved into an executive vice-president post as the closest aide and confidant of the CEO on the Central Management Committee, with decisive say-so over financial issues and thus over operations. Tough, seasoned managers in the operating divisions—men and women of great drive and ambition—began to see their own chances for future ascendancy possibly blocked. Many began to depart the corporation. The posts of those who left were filled by men and women whose loyalties and futures lay with the new regime. Thus, the compressed sequence of events at Covenant Corporation simply allows one to be particularly attentive to ongoing, and usually taken for granted, structural and psychological patterns of corporate life.

Here I want to highlight a few of these basic structures and experiences of managerial work, those that seem to form its essential framework. First of all, at the psychological level, managers have an acute sense of organizational contingency. Because of the interlocking ties between people, they know that a shake-up at or near the top of a hierarchy can trigger a widespread upheaval, bringing in its wake startling reversals of fortune, good and bad, throughout the structure. Managers' cryptic aphorism, "Well, you never know ... ," repeated often and regularly, captures the sense of uncertainty created by the constant potential for social reversal. Managers know too, and take for granted, that the personnel changes brought about by upheavals are to a great extent arbitrary and depend more than anything else on one's social relationships with key individuals and with groups of managers. Periods of organizational quiescence and stability still managers' wariness in this regard, but the foreboding sense of contingency never entirely disappears. Managers' awareness of the complex levels of conflict in their world, built into the very structure of bureaucratic organizations, constantly reminds them that things can very quickly fall apart.

The political struggles at Covenant Corporation, for instance, suggest some immediately observable levels of conflict and tension.

First, occupational groups emerging from the segmented structure of bureaucratic work, each with different expertise and emphasis, constantly vie with one another for ascendancy of their ideas, of their products or services, and of themselves. It is, for instance, an axiom of corporate life that the greatest satisfaction of production people is to see products go out the door; of salesmen, to make a deal regardless of price; of marketers, to control salesmen and squeeze profits out of their deals; and of financial specialists, to make sure that everybody meets budget. Despite the larger interdependence of such work, the necessarily fragmented functions performed day-to-day by managers in one area often put them at cross purposes with managers in another. Nor do competitiveness and conflict result only from the broad segmentation of functions. Sustained work in a product or service area not only shapes crucial social affiliations but also symbolic identifications, say, with particular products or technical services, that mark managers in their corporate arenas. Such symbolic markings make it imperative for managers to push their particular products or services as part of their overall self-promotion. This fuels the constant scramble for authoritative enthusiasm for one product or service rather than another and the subsequent allocation or re-allocation of organizational resources.

Second, line and staff managers, each group with different responsibilities, different pressures, and different bailiwicks to protect, fight over organizational resources and over the rules that govern work. The very definition of staff depends entirely on one's vantage point in the organization. As one manager points out: "From the perspective of the guy who actually pushes the button to make the machine go, everyone else is staff." However, the working definition that managers use is that anyone whose decisions directly affect profit and loss is in the line; all others in an advisory capacity of some sort are staff. As a general rule, line managers' attitudes toward staff vary directly with the independence granted staff by higher management. The more freedom staff have to intervene in the line, as with the environmental staff at Alchemy or Covenant's corporate staff, the more they are feared and resented by line management. For line managers, independent staff represent either the intrusion of an unwelcome "rules and procedures mentality" into situations where line managers feel that they have to be alert to the exigencies of the market or, alternatively, as power threats to vested interests backed by some authority. In the "decentralized" organizations prevalent today in the corporate world, however, most staff are entirely dependent on the line and must market their technical, legal, or organizational skills to line managers exactly as an outside firm must do. The continual necessity for staff to sell their technical expertise helps keep them in check since line managers, pleading budgetary stringency or any number of other acceptable rationales, can thwart or ignore proffered assistance. Staff's dependent position often produces jealous respect for line management tinged with the resentment that talented people relegated to do "pine time" (sit on the bench) feel for those in the center of action. For instance, an environmental manager at Weft Corporation comments on his marginal status and on how he sees it depriving him of the recognition he feels his work deserves:

> I also want recognition. And usually the only way you get that is having a boss near you who sees what you do. It rubs me raw in fact. . . . For instance, you know they run these news releases when some corporate guy gets promoted and all? Well, when I do something, nothing ever gets said. When I publish papers, or get promoted, and so on, you never see any public announcement. Oh, they like me to publish papers and I guess someone reads them, but that's all that's ever said or done. . . . I can get recognition in a variety of arenas, like professional associations, but if they're going to recognize the plant manager, why not me? If we walked off, would the plants operate? They couldn't. We're *essential*.

This kind of ambivalent resentment sometimes becomes vindictiveness when a top boss uses staff as a hammer.

Staff can also become effective pitchmen; line managers' anxious search for rational solutions to largely irrational problems, in fact, encourages staff continually to invent and disseminate new tactics and schemes. Alternatively, social upheavals that produce rapid shifts in public opinion—such as occurred in the personnel or environmental areas in the aftermath of the 1960s—may encourage proliferation of staff. In either circumstance, staff tend to increase in an organization until an ideological cycle of "organizational leanness" comes around and staff, at least those of lower rank, get decimated.

Third, powerful managers in Alchemy Inc., each controlling considerable resources and the organizational fates of many men and women, battle fiercely with one another to position themselves, their products, and their allies favorably in the eyes of their president and of the CEO. At the same time, high-ranking executives "go to the mat" with one another striving for the CEO's approval and a coveted shot at the top. Bureaucratic hierarchies, simply by offering ascertainable rewards for certain behavior, fuel the ambition of those men and women ready to subject themselves to the discipline of external exigencies and of their organization's institutional logic, the socially constructed, shared understanding of how their world works. However, since rewards are always scarce, bureaucracies necessarily pit people against each other and inevitably thwart the ambitions of some. The rules of such combat vary from organization to organization and depend largely on what top management countenances either openly or tacitly.

Nor are formal positions and perquisites the only objects of personal struggle between managers. Even more important on a day-to-day basis is the ongoing competition between talented and aggressive people to see whose will prevails, who can get things done their way. The two areas are, of course, related since one's chances in an organization depend largely on one's "credibility," that is, on the widespread belief that one can act effectively. One must therefore prevail regularly, though not always, in small things to have any hope of positioning oneself for big issues. The hidden agenda of seemingly petty disputes may be a struggle over long-term organizational fates.

At the same time, all of these struggles take place within the peculiar tempo and framework each CEO establishes for an organization. Under an ideology of thorough decentralization—the gift of authority with responsibility—the CEO at Covenant actually centralizes his power enormously because fear of derailing personal ambitions prevents managers below him from acting without his approval. A top official at Alchemy comments:

> What we have now, despite rhetoric to the contrary, is a very centralized system. It's [the CEO] who sets the style, tone, tempo of all the companies. He says: "Manage for cash," and we manage for cash. The original idea . . . was to set up free-standing companies with a minimum of corporate staff. But . . . we're moving toward a system that is really beyond what we used to have, let alone modeled on a small corporate staff and autonomous divisions. What we used to have was separate divisions reporting to a corporate staff. I think we're moving away from that idea too. I think what's coming is a bunch of separate businesses reporting to the corporation. It's a kind of portfolio management. This accords perfectly with [the CEO's] temperament. He's a financial type guy who is oriented to the bottom line numbers. He doesn't want or need intermediaries between him and his businesses.

In effect, the CEO of Covenant, who seems to enjoy constant turmoil, pits himself and his ego against the whole corporation even while he holds it in vassalage. Other CEOs establish different frameworks and different tempos, depending on self-image and temperament. The only firm rule seems to be that articulated by a middle-level Covenant manager: "Every big organization is set up for the benefit of those who control it; the boss gets what he wants."

Except during times of upheaval, the ongoing conflicts that I have described are usually hidden behind the comfortable and benign social ambiance that most American corporations fashion for their white-collar personnel. Plush carpets, potted trees, burnished oak wall paneling, fine reproductions and sometimes originals of great art, mahogany desks, polished glass tables and ornaments, rich leather upholstery, perfectly coiffured, attractive and poised receptionists, and private, subsidized cafeterias are only a few of the pleasant features that grace the corporate headquarters of any major company. In addition, the corporations that I studied provide their employees with an amazing range and variety of services, information, and social contacts. Covenant Corporation, for instance, through its daily newsletter and a variety of other internal media, offers information about domestic and international vacation packages; free travelers' checks; discounted tickets for the ballet, tennis matches, or art exhibits; home remedies for the common cold, traveling clinics for diagnosing high blood pressure, and advice on how to save one's sight; simple tests for gauging automotive driving habits; tips on home vegetable gardening; advice on baby-sitters; descriptions of business courses at a local college; warning articles on open fireplaces and home security; and directions for income tax filing. The newsletter also offers an internal market for the sale, rental, or exchange of a myriad of items ranging from a Jamaican villa, to a set of barbells, to back issues of *Fantasy* magazine. Covenant offers as well intracompany trapshooting contests, round-robin tennis and golf tournaments, running clinics, and executive fitness programs. Weft Corporation's bulletin is even more elaborate, with photographic features on the "Great Faces" of Weft employees; regular reports on the company's 25- and 50-year clubs; personal notes on all retirees from the company; stories about the company's sponsorship of art exhibits; human-interest stories about employees and their families—from a child struggling against liver cancer to the heroics of a Weft employee in foiling a plane hijacker; and, of course, a steady drumbeat of corporate ideology about the necessity for textile import quotas and the desirability of "buying American."

My point here is that corporations are not presented nor are they seen simply as places to work for a living. Rather the men and women in them come to fashion an entire social ambiance that overlays the antagonisms created by company politics; this makes the nuances of corporate conflict difficult to discern. A few managers, in fact, mistake the first-name informality, the social congeniality, and the plush exterior appointments for the entire reality of their collective life and are surprised when hard structural jolts turn their world upside down. Even battle-scarred veterans evince, at times, an ambivalent half-belief in the litany of rhetorics of unity and cohesive legitimating appeals. The latter are sometimes accompanied by gala events to underline the appeal. For instance, not long after the "big purge" at Covenant Corporation when 600 people were fired, the CEO spent $1 million for a "Family Day" to "bring everyone together." The massive party was attended by over 14,000 people and featured clowns, sports idols, and booths complete with bean bag and ring tosses, foot and bus races, computer games, dice rolls, and, perhaps appropriately, mazes. In his letter to his "Fellow Employees" following the event, the CEO said:

> I think Family Day made a very strong statement about the [Covenant] "family" of employees at [Corporate Headquarters]. And that is that we can accomplish whatever we set out to do if we work together; if we share the effort, we will share the rewards. The "New World of [Covenant]" has no boundaries only frontiers, and each and everyone can play a role, for we need what *you* have to contribute.

The very necessity for active involvement in such rituals often prompts semicredulity. But wise and ambitious managers resist the lulling platitudes of unity, though they invoke them with fervor, and look for the inevitable clash of interests beneath the bouncy, cheerful surface of corporate life. They understand implicitly that the suppression of open conflict simply puts a premium on the mastery of the socially accepted modes of waging combat.

The continuous uncertainty and ambiguity of managerial hierarchies, exacerbated over time by masked conflict, causes managers to turn toward each other for cues for behavior. They try to learn from each other and to master the shared assumptions, the complex rules, the normative codes, the underlying institutional logic that governs their world. They thus try to control the construction of their everyday reality. Normally, of course, one learns to master the managerial code in the course of repeated, long-term social interaction with other managers, particularly in the course of shaping the multiple and complex alliances essential to organizational survival and success.

Alliances are ties of quasiprimal loyalty shaped especially by common work, by common experiences with the same problems, the same friends, or the same enemies, and by favors traded over time. Although alliances are rooted in fealty and patronage relationships, they are not limited by such relationships since fealty shifts with changing work assignments or with organizational upheavals.

Making an alliance may mean, for instance, joining or, more exactly, being included in one or several of the many networks of managerial associates that crisscross an organization. Conceptually, networks are usually thought of as open-ended webs of association with a low degree of formal organization and no distinct criteria of membership.[3] One becomes known, for instance, as a trusted friend of a friend; thought of as a person to whom one can safely refer a thorny problem; considered a "sensible" or "reasonable" or, especially, a "flexible" person, not a "renegade" or a "loose cannon rolling around the lawn"; known to be a discreet person attuned to the nuances of corporate etiquette, one who can keep one's mouth shut or who can look away and pretend to notice nothing; or considered a person with sharp ideas that break deadlocks but who does not object to the ideas being appropriated by superiors.

Alliances are also fashioned in social coteries. These are more clublike groups of friends that, in Weft Corporation, forge ties at the cocktail hour over the back fence on Racquet Drive, the road next to the company's tennis courts where all important and socially ambitious executives live; or in Friday night poker sessions that provide a bluff and hearty setting where managers can display their own and unobtrusively observe others' mastery of public faces, a clue to many managerial virtues. In other companies, coteries consist of "tennis pals" who share an easy camaraderie over salad and yogurt lunches following hard squash games or two-mile jogs at noon. They are also made up of posthours cronies who, in midtown watering holes, weld private understandings with ironic bantering, broad satire, or macabre humor, the closest some managers ever get to open discussion of their work with their fellows; or gatherings of the smart social set where business circles intersect with cliques from intellectual and artistic worlds and where glittering, poised, and precisely vacuous social conversation can mark one as a social lion. In one company, a group of "buddies" intertwine their private lives with their organizational fates in the most complete way by, for example, persuading an ambitious younger colleague to provide a woodsy cabin retreat and local girls for a collegial evening's entertainment while on a business trip. At the managerial and professional levels, the road between work and life is usually open because it is difficult to refuse to use one's influence, patronage, or power on behalf of another regular member of one's social coterie. It therefore becomes important to choose one's social colleagues with some care and, of course, know how to drop them should they fall out of organizational favor.

Alliances are also made wholly on the basis of specific self-interests. The paradigmatic case here is that of the power clique of established, well-placed managers who put aside differences and join forces for a "higher cause," namely their own advancement or protection. Normally, though not always, as Brown's case at Covenant shows, one must be "plugged into" important networks and an active participant in key coteries in order to have achieved an organizational position where one's influence is actively counted. But the authority and power of a position matter in and of themselves. Once one has gained power, one can use one's influence in the organization to shape social ties. Such alliances often cut across rival networks and coteries and can, in fact, temporarily unite them. Managers in a power clique map out desired organizational tacks and trade off the resources in their control. They assess the strengths and weaknesses of their opponents; they plan coups and rehearse the appropriate rationales to legitimate them. And, on the other hand, they erect requisite barriers to squelch attempted usurpations of their power. Cliques also introduce managers to new, somewhat more exclusive networks and coteries. Especially at the top of a pyramid, these social ties extend over the boundaries of one's own corporation and mesh one's work and life with those of top managers in other organizations.

I shall refer to all the social contexts that breed alliances, fealty relationships, networks, coteries, or cliques, as circles of affiliation, or simply managerial circles. Now, the notion of "circles," as it has been used in sociological literature[4] as well as colloquially, has some drawbacks for accurately delineating the important features of the web of managerial interaction. Specifically, a circle suggests a quasiclosed social group made up of members of relatively equal status without defined leadership and without formal criteria for membership or inclusion. In a bureaucratic hierarchy, nuances of status are, of course, extremely important. Moreover, since business cannot be conducted without formal authorization by appropriate authorities, one's formal rank always matters even though there is ample scope for more informal charismatic leadership. Finally, the most crucial feature of managerial circles of affiliation is precisely their establishment of informal criteria for admission, criteria that are, it is true, ambiguously defined and subject to constant, often arbitrary, revision. Nonetheless, they are criteria that managers must master. At bottom, all of the social contexts of the managerial world seek to discover if one "can feel comfortable" with another manager, if he is someone who "can be trusted," if he is "our kind of guy," or, in short, if he is "one of the gang." The notion of gang,[5] in fact, insofar as it suggests the importance of leadership, hierarchy, and probationary mechanisms in a bounded but somewhat amorphous group, may more accurately describe relationships in the corporation than the more genteel, and therefore preferable, word "circle."

In any event, just as managers must continually please their boss, their boss's boss, their patrons, their president, and their CEO, so must they prove themselves again and again to each other. Work becomes an endless round of what might be called probationary crucibles. Together with the uncertainty and sense of contingency that mark managerial work, this constant state of probation produces a profound anxiety in managers, perhaps the key experience of managerial work. It also breeds, selects, or elicits certain traits in ambitious managers that are crucial to getting ahead.

3

The Main Chance

I

Within this complicated and ambiguous authority and social structure, always subject to upheaval, success and failure are meted out to those in the middle and upper-middle managerial ranks. Managers rarely speak of objective criteria for achieving success because once certain crucial points in one's career are passed, success and failure seem to have little to do with one's accomplishments.

Corporations do demand, of course, a basic competence, and sometimes specialized training and experience. For the most part, hiring patterns ensure these. Corporations rely on other institutions—principally the schools—to establish what might be called competence hurdles. The demonstrated ability of a student to leap over successively higher hurdles in school is taken as evidence of the ability to weather well the probationary trials of corporate life. This fundamental institutional correspondence gets complicated by corporate executives' perceptions of their organizations' chances in the external prestige market. Covenant Corporation actively recruits younger managers from the leading business schools, that is, Harvard, Stanford, Wharton, Columbia, and others, a policy that reflects its top executives' self-images as leaders of American industry. The higher management circles at Weft Corporation, by contrast, are acutely aware of the backward public image of the textile industry, and the organization is satisfied to recruit from the lesser business schools of the South and Southwest. These choices also reflect judgments about whether a corporation can offer the hard-charging MBAs from the top-ranked schools enough quick variety to retain them long enough to justify their inflated salaries.

Schooling, of course, not only demonstrates requisite hurdling abilities but also provides rudimentary training in specific skills. Internal training programs in most companies complement, extend, and deepen those abilities. When highly developed skills or extensive experience are needed immediately, outsiders from other companies can be hired to provide them. However, a few companies—Covenant Corporation is one of these, as are the Big Eight accounting firms—have such extensive internal training programs that they almost always have needed talent on hand. Other companies, of course, raid Covenant regularly for trained managers, obviating the need to structure similar programs themselves.

A weeding-out process takes place among the lower ranks of managers during the first several years of their experience. The early careers of promising young managers are highly variegated; the more promise managers show, the more probations they must undergo. Take, for example, the case of a young man newly graduated in 1965 from one of the South's leading universities. He joined Weft Corporation and spent the next two years in the company's production management training program. Then he became a first-line supervisor on the third shift at a small mill. Shortly thereafter, he was promoted to the night superintendent's job of that mill and given overall responsibility for the night shift. After six months, he became a department head for weaving operations in another mill. After another six months, he was assigned to head a larger weaving department in yet another plant. After still another six months, he became assistant plant manager at a medium-sized mill and kept that job for four years. Then he moved to a still larger mill in the same capacity for another two years. Then he became plant manager of a medium-sized mill for two years. Finally, he was named one of two group managers with six plant managers reporting to him. At the age of 36, he has reached grade 20, the "breaking point" on a scale of 29, placing him in the top 12.17 percent of management in Weft Corporation with, he hopes, a clear shot at becoming vice-president of manufacturing. Similarly variegated careers are evident for young marketing and sales managers in Weft's northern offices. In Alchemy Inc., whether in sales, marketing, manufacturing, or finance, the "breaking point" in the hierarchy is generally thought to be grade 13 out of 25 or the top 8.5 percent of management. By the time managers reach such a numbered grade in an ordered hierarchy—and the grade is socially defined and varies from company to company—managerial competence as such is taken for granted and assumed not to differ greatly from one manager to the next. One continues, of course, in a state of probation, and one's competence is always subject to review and to redefinition. One must, therefore, always avoid being associated with big mistakes since a reputation carefully wrought over a number of years can be twisted out of shape in a day by a major blunder. As it happens, the nature of managerial work itself is to oversee others' work and therefore to depend on others. The higher one rises in a management hierarchy, however, the more layers accrue between oneself and actual work tasks where crucial mistakes can be made; therefore, the more one's continued assertion of competence becomes hostage to others' efforts as well as to others' interpretations. It goes without saying that one must always make sure that significant others higher in the organization recognize and appreciate one's continuing efforts. Unless he attends to this basic rule, even the best "can-do guy" runs the risk of getting stuck with work without recognition.

Striving for success is, of course, a moral imperative in American society. In the corporate world, this means moving up or getting ahead in the organization. For some managers, the drive for success is a quest for the generous financial rewards that high corporate position brings. For others, success means the freedom to define one's work role with some latitude, to "get out from under the thumb of others." For still others, it means the chance to gain power and to exert one's will, to "call the shots," to "do it my way," or to know the curiously exhilarating pleasure of controlling other people's fates. For still others, the quest for success expresses a deep hunger for the recognition and accolades of one's peers.

Despite this general imperative, however, not everyone has or sustains a burning desire for getting ahead. Some managers, usually men or women in their forties or fifties, reach a certain point in their careers and either accept or resign themselves to immobility. In a very few cases, they feel that they have reached the outer limit of their own potential and that only better managers than they will advance. But such self-assessments are rare. More generally, those who accept immobility are unwilling to sacrifice family life or free-time activities to put in the extraordinarily long hours at the office required in the upper circles of their corporations. Or they have made a realistic assessment of the age structure, career paths, and power relationships above them and conclude that there is no longer real opportunity for them. They may see that there is an irreparable mismatch between their own personal styles and the kinds of social skills being cultivated in well-entrenched higher circles. In many cases, they decide that they do not wish to put up with the great stress of higher management work that they have witnessed. An upper-middle manager at Covenant Corporation elaborates the last point:

> Once I thought I wanted to be president. I thought I *had* to be president to do what I wanted with my life. But now my personal life is more important than my business life. I look at [Smith, the president of Alchemy] and I ask what his motivations are. [The CEO] shits on [Smith] *all the time.* Is this what you struggle for all your life? To be shit on in public? Is that what $326,000 a year buys you? It must be what you have to put up with. You know, I didn't think that this sort of thing happened at that level, but it does. [The CEO] is crude and demanding and loves to exert his will over others. . . . [He] has to exert his own will and I don't need that.

Whatever their reasons or perceptions, some managers find therefore comfortable organizational niches and settle into them. Tacit agreements are reached about them, a kind of silent barter—as long as they continue to perform their functional roles, they can stay. To some extent, they even become protected against reprisals during upheavals because the high stakes players in the corporation generally recognize that every organization needs such a core of people. One manager in Alchemy Inc. explains:

> You always need a core of people who will do the work in an orga-
> nization whether it's creative or not. You just can't have all superstars.
> Potential is important but you need some people who are, well, drones.
> You don't *want* them to move. You need people who will stay in a job
> for year after year and do the necessary work that is essential to an
> organization's survival.

Moreover, and just as important, drones threaten no one and can therefore maintain their anomalous position. They are, however, without influence and subject therefore to the faint contempt that the powerful, and especially the would-be powerful, reserve for the impotent. Such weakness can, of course, invite more direct abuse. To guard against this, even those managers who are happy where they are usually adopt, at least in public, the rhetoric of mobility.

But for managers driven to get ahead—a category that includes inciden-tally virtually all young managers—even standing still for an instant, symbol-ically or actually, can be dangerous. A young manager in the chemical company:

> The whole thing becomes a complicated game of maintaining the pub-
> lic perception—the illusion really—that I'm on the move. In an inflat-
> ing economy, if you just get 10–12 percent a year, you're standing still,
> going nowhere. So the illusion of being a comer is crucial to success
> in the long run. . . . If you let them for one minute give you just the
> 10 percent cost of living increase, you're finished. Or if other people
> in the organization think for one minute that you've begun to slip,
> you're finished and your influence—whatever it is—evaporates.

Only rising stars validate the ethos of the corporation and can claim and win the respect and perhaps the anticipatory fear of others.

Hard work, unremitting effort, it is said, is the key to success. Some top executives often state this connection between hard work and success as a necessary, taken for granted relationship. When asked who gets ahead, an executive vice-president at Weft Corporation says:

> The guys who want it [get ahead]. The guys who work. You can spot
> it in the first six months. They work hard, they come to work earlier,
> they leave later. They have suggestions at meetings. They come into a
> business and the business picks right up. They don't go on coffee
> breaks down here [in the basement]. You see the parade of people
> going back and forth down here? There's no reason for that. I never
> did that. If you need coffee, you can have it at your desk. Some people
> put in time and some people work.

Such statements of the equation between work and success not only implicitly exhort others to greater efforts, but also legitimate one's own rise. These kinds of rationales filter down through an organization changing shape and meaning in the process. They survive in their most pristine form in those managerial occupations where the results of work are clearly measurable. Sales managers, in particular, who can graph with great precision the upward or downward trajectories of their charges' work often remain as addicted to the instant gratification of consummated deals as college boys "carrying a bag" for the first time. Plant managers who can measure their output by gallons of sulfuric acid, tons of soda ash, or yards of cloth also tend to see success directly tied to hard work. For instance, a plant manager at Weft Corporation:

> Who gets ahead? It's the person who performs.... I'm not going to get promoted if I don't make progress.... You could be [a] real smart guy but unless you have the numbers you're not going to make any progress in manufacturing.... I honestly feel that I'm going to be capable of managing plant managers before long.... I want my boss's job. And I think that ultimately I can be Chairman of the Board.

There may, of course, be little connection between such beliefs and one's future. Quantifiable work, however, provides some managers, often for long stretches of their careers, comforting measures of accomplishment and promises of progress that renew old faiths and, a point that I shall elaborate later, a framework that enables one to make sense out of one's work and life.

For most managers, however, future chances in an organization, after the crucial break points in a career are reached, are seen to depend not on competence nor on performance as such. Instead, managers see success depending principally on meeting social criteria established by the authority and political alignments—that is, by the fealty and alliance structure—and by the ethos and style of the corporation. Again, the formal word criteria dignifies what is actually a fairly rudimentary process. A manager at the chemical company explains:

> See, once you are at a certain level of experience, the difference between a vice-president, an executive vice-president, and a general manager is negligible. It has relatively little to do with *ability* as such. People are all good at that level. They wouldn't be there without that ability. So it has little to do with ability or with business experience and so on. All have similar levels of ability, drive, competence, and so on. What happens is that people perceive in others *what they like*—operating styles, lifestyles, personalities, ability to get along. Now these are all very subjective judgments. And what happens is that if a person in authority sees someone else's guy as less competent than his own guy, well, he'll always perceive him that way. And he'll always pick—as a result—his own guy when the chance to do so comes up.

The criteria that individuals in authority may apply are, of course, bounded by the particular style and ethos of their corporation.

II

One can, however, discern several criteria that are universally important in managerial circles. Bureaucracies not only rationalize work; they rationalize people's public faces as well. A person's external appearances, modes of self-presentation, interactional behavior, and projection of general attitude together constitute his public face. Large corporations create highly standardized rules to regulate the public faces of lower-level white-collar workers, for instance at the clerical level. In a large bank that I studied some years ago, these include a formalized dress code, regularly updated, that prescribes details of clothing down to skirt length for women; manuals with a whole variety of sample conversations to guide interaction with customers; and detailed evaluation procedures that place a great premium on displaying cheerful cooperativeness toward coworkers and supervisors. Aware of the importance of the bank's public image toward customers and of the need for smooth, harmonious work relationships in pressure-packed, highly routinized contexts, bank managers try to establish and control the principal aspects of workers' public faces. For their part, workers chafe under the public faces the bank prescribes and experience as little control over the social presentation of themselves as they do over the sea of paperwork that engulfs them.[1] But managers both at the bank and in all the corporations I studied more recently see the matter of public faces differently. For them, the issue is not a reluctant donning of organizationally prescribed masks but rather a mastery of the social rules that prescribe which mask to wear on which occasion.

Such social mastery and the probations that test it begin early in managers' careers. Every spring at elite colleges and universities throughout the land, a small but instructive transformation takes place when corporate recruiters from a wide variety of large companies descend on campuses to screen graduating seniors for entry-level managerial jobs. The jeans, ragged shirts, beards, mustaches, and casual unkemptness of youth that typify college life, particularly in rural areas, give way to what is called the corporate uniform—three-piece, wool pin-striped suits or suited skirts; button-down collars or unfrilled blouses; sedate four-in-hand foulards for men and floppy printed bow ties for women; wing-tipped shoes or plain low-heeled pumps; somber, straighforward hues; and finally, bright, well-scrubbed, clean-shaven or well-coiffured appearances. It is, in short, a uniform that bespeaks the sobriety and seriousness appropriate to the men and women who would minister to the weighty affairs of industry, finance, and commerce. Perhaps the only noteworthy aspect of this unremarkable rite is that underclassmen and seniors evaluate it quite differently. Underclassmen, surprised and bemused by the symbolic intrusion of the real world into their youth ghettoes, see seniors' capitulation to the norms of the managerial milieu as a callow moral compromise, as a first but ominous step toward de-individualizing conformity. Seniors, however, approach the crisis more pragmatically, though not without ironic self-deprecation and biting sarcasm. They know that managers have to look the part and that all corporations are filled with well-groomed and conventionally well-dressed men and women. They consciously decide to alter their external appearance to fit these well-known and widely disseminated criteria.

Such small probations are the stuff of everyday managerial life. Businesses always try to epitomize social normality, and managers, who must both create and enforce social rules for lower-level workers and simultaneously embody their corporation's image in the public arena, are expected to be alert to prevailing norms. Managers in different corporations joke with bemused detachment about the rules that govern their appearances—the rule against sports jackets (too casual); the rule against leaving one's floor without one's suit jacket (improper attire in a public arena); the unspoken rule against penny loafers (comfortable looking shoes suggest a lackadaisical attitude); the suspicion of hair that is too long or too short (there is no place for hippies or skinheads); the mild taboo against brown suits (brown is dull, a loser's color; winners choose blue); the scorn for polyester suits (strictly lower class, wool is better); the preference for red ties or red on blue (red symbolizes power and authority); the indulgent tolerance of the person who slightly overdresses if this is done tastefully (classy); and the quiet but forceful admonition of the person who does not dress properly or who is in some way unkempt. Anyone who is so dull-witted or stubborn that he does not respond to social suggestions and become more presentable is quickly marked as unsuitable for any consideration for advancement. If a person cannot read the most obvious social norms, he will certainly be unable to discern more ambiguous cues. At the same time, managers also suspect that clothes and grooming might indeed make the man. The widespread popularity of recent self-promotional literature on this point—I mean the *Dress for Success* books and the like,[2] even though its principal role is probably to disseminate techniques of image management to less fortunate social classes—underlines knowledge taken for granted among managers. Proper management of one's external appearances simply signals to one's peers and to one's superiors that one is prepared to undertake other kinds of self-adaptation.

Managers also stress the need to exercise iron self-control and to have the ability to mask all emotion and intention behind bland, smiling, and agreeable public faces. One must avoid both excessive gravity and unwarranted levity. One must blunt one's aggressiveness with blandness. One must be buoyant and enthusiastic but never pollyannish. One must not reveal one's leanings until one's ducks are in a row. One must be able to listen to others' grievances and even attacks upon oneself while maintaining an appropriately concerned, but simultaneously dispassionate countenance. In such situations, some managers don masks of Easter-Island-statuelike immobility; others a deadpan fisheye; and the most adroit, a disarming ingenuousness. One must remember, for instance, that in our litigious age the best rule in dealing with angry subordinates is to say nothing or as little as possible since whatever one says may be used against oneself and one's organization. Sometimes this may mean suppressing the natural desire to defend oneself. Moreover, one must always guard against betraying valuable secret knowledge (for instance, knowledge of pending organizational upheaval, knowledge of firings, promotions, or demotions, or knowledge of private deals between one's colleagues) or intentions through some relaxation of self-control (for example, an indiscreet comment or a lack of adroitness in turning aside a query). Such lapses can not only jeopardize a manager's immediate position but can undermine others' trust in him. Furthermore, one must not enter any sexual involvements that might jeopardize other important social relationships or one's public image. One does not, therefore, sleep with one's boss's secretary ("You should never get your meat where you get your bread and butter"), and one should never, of course, allow oneself to become infatuated with another person so that one loses control.

These last admonitions on sexual behavior bear some reflection. The corporation stimulates the natural impulses of the erotic sphere through its gathering together of an abundance of attractive and energetic men and women and through its continual symbolic celebration of vitality, power, and success. At the same time, the managerial ethic of self-control imposes solemn rules for self-abnegation, at least in public. Managers' interpretations of an unusually public situation that was a continual subject of conversation in one corporation that I studied show the profound importance that they attach to self-control. The president of a division was widely known to have a long-term sexual relationship with a woman who was a middle manager in his organization. The president's wife knew of the liaison and had, it was rumored, threatened to use her own considerable holdings in the company's stock to undercut him if he did not break off the illicit relationship. The husband of the woman involved with the president had, it was rumored, already been paid a substantial sum of money not to sue the president. No one in the organization seemed certain about the source for such "hush money" but many managers, in recounting the story, pointedly noted the rapid rise to a director's position of a man who, in their view, was truly remarkable for his dull-witted incompetence. Only extraordinary services of some sort—like a willingness to dip into suddenly inflated training budgets—could, they felt, justify such an appointment.

The matter was even more complicated. The president was also known to be "sharing" his mistress with his executive vice-president, his "asshole buddy," in managers' terms, and his closest organizational ally. Neither man made any attempt to hide or disguise the affair. The president drove his conference scheduling manager to distraction by regularly undoing weeks and sometimes months of work by insisting at the last minute that travel arrangements, conference days, and housing arrangements be altered to accommodate his mistress. The executive vice-president once held a posthours cocktail party for his whole staff in his office. To everyone's puzzlement, he was not present when the party began. However, shortly afterward, a young staff person happened to glance out the window and the entire crowd was regaled with the amorous front seat embraces of the executive vice-president and the middle manager in the company parking lot. There were also several reports of the trio "carrying on," "horsing around," and "giggling like kids" in the back of the company jet or limousine en route to business meetings.

Managers who recounted the story, with one exception, had no moral qualms about their bosses' sexual behavior as such. They felt that both men were constantly under great stress, especially the president, and "if he wants a little honey on the side, who is going to say that he shouldn't have it?" Nor did managers have any qualms about the mysterious monies supposedly used to pay off the woman's husband, although some felt that the imposition of such a hopelessly dumb director was a high price to ask others to pay to obtain a "bag man." However, without exception, managers condemned both the president and his aide for being "out of control," for "losing their cool," for "acting irrationally." Their precipitous flouting of norms, although this is clearly recognized as one of the prerogatives of authority, was seen as a reckless endangerment not only of themselves and their positions but of the whole fealty and alliance structure that they had built. Despite their high positions, both men were after all still subordinates and subject to the judgments of higher-ups. The price of bureaucratic power is a relentlessly methodical subjection of one's impulses, at least in public. To yield to one's desires in a public setting in a way that others can use against one, whether by giving in to the wish for open sexual conquest or proprietary claim or by submitting to the temptation to show one's anger, is seen as irrational, unbefitting men or women whose principal claim to social legitimacy is dispassionate rational calculation.

It is also crucial to be perceived as a team player. This multifaceted notion has its metaphorical basis in team sports, principally football, a game that parallels managerial work in its specialization, segmentation, strategy, hierarchy, and the possibility of sudden bursts of spectacular individual effort made possible by the group. Of all major sports, football resonates most deeply with managers' preferred image of what they do and lends a myriad of phrases to managerial argot. For instance:

Football Phrases	Metaphorical Meaning for Managers
Players	Anyone who has a stake in and is therefore involved in a decision
Carrying the ball	Responsible for an assignment
Taking the ball and running with it	Showing initiative and drive
Fumbling the ball	Messing up in an assignment
Passing the ball	Getting rid of a responsibility
Punt	Employ a defensive strategy while waiting for things to sort out

Football Phrases	*Metaphorical Meaning for Managers*
Sidelined	Getting taken out of the game; benched
Run the clock down	Wear out an opponent by stalling
Huddle	A quick meeting
Reverse or Reversing fields	Changing one's story or public rationale for an action; changing strategies
Going over the top	Achieving one's commitments
Running interference or Blocking	A patron using personal influence to knock down opposition to a client's ideas or plans
Broken field run	A virtuoso individual performance
Getting blindsided	Being unexpectedly undercut by another in public
Quarterback	The boss

Cooperative teamwork can, of course, produce enormous accomplishments and every corporation that I have studied has stories of great victories achieved through team play, all cast into dramatic form. Alchemy managers recall both staff and line personnel working side by side to contain the damage done by an accidental explosion at a plant; managers in the Consumer Division of Weft Corporation remember how they frantically turned their whole cloth finishing operation around to get the jump on competitors in producing a printed fabric suddenly desirable to New York designers; and managers and workers alike in a now defunct book publishing firm recall fondly how the entire company was mobilized for the herculean task of producing one million copies of the Warren Commission report in three days.[3] Managers often point, too, to the coordination and cooperation achieved through team play in the space program, sentiments voiced before the string of Challenger disasters. These images of the possibilities of cooperative effort, of coordinating people and resources to meet a crisis or great challenge, seem to legitimate for managers their actual day-to-day experiences with the ethos of team play.

The main dimensions of team play are as follows.

1. One must appear to be interchangeable with other managers near one's level. Corporations discourage narrow specialization more strongly as one goes higher. They also discourage the expression of moral or political qualms. One might object, for example, to working with chemicals used in nuclear power, or working on weapons systems, and most corporations today would honor such objections. Publicly stating them, however, would end any realistic aspirations for higher posts because one's usefulness to the organization depends on versatility. As one manager in Alchemy Inc. comments: "Well, we'd go along with his request but we'd always wonder about the guy. And in the back of our minds, we'd be thinking that he'll soon object to working in the soda ash division because he doesn't like glass." Strong convictions of any sort are suspect. One manager says:

If you meet a guy who hates red-haired persons, well, you're going to wonder about whether that person has other weird perceptions as well. You've got to have a degree of interchangeability in business. To me, a person can have any beliefs they want, as long as they leave them at home.

Similarly, one's spouse's public viewpoints or activities could reduce others' perceptions of a manager's versatility or indeed ability. In reference to another manager whose wife was known to be active in environmental action groups, lobbying in fact for legislation on chemical waste disposal, one Alchemy manager says: "If a guy can't even manage his own wife, how can he be expected to manage other people?" Interchangeability means then not just generalized skills but a flexibility of perspective that will permit rapid adjustment to internal and external exigencies.

2. Another important meaning of team play is putting in long hours at the office. The norms here are set, of course, by higher-ups and vary from corporation to corporation. The story is told in Covenant Corporation about how the CEO was distressed, upon first taking power, to find no one at work when he reached corporate headquarters at his accustomed hour of 6:30 A.M. He remedied the loneliness of the situation by leaving notes on the desks of all his top executives saying, "Call me when you get in." Since he usually stays in the office well into the evening, he had effectively lengthened the work day for everyone by several hours. Higher level managers in all the corporations I studied commonly spend twelve to fourteen hours a day at the office. This requires a great deal of sheer physical energy and stamina, even though much of this time is spent not in actual work as such, but in social rituals—like reading and discussing articles in *The New York Times, The Wall Street Journal, Harvard Business Review*, and *Forbes*; having informal conversations; casually polling the opinions of participants in upcoming meetings; or popping in and out of other managers' offices with jokes, cartoons, or amusing or enraging journalistic articles. These kinds of readily observable rituals forge the social bonds—what might be called the professional intimacy—that make real managerial work, that is, group work of various sorts, possible. One must participate in the rituals to be considered effective in the work. Managers who do not put in the time at the office or who do not engage in the endless round of face-to-face encounters that make up daily managerial life and that provide the opportunity to prove one's trustworthiness will find themselves "sidelined" or off the team altogether. For this reason, executives do not like to take extended business trips and many break up their vacations into one-week segments rather than risk being away from the office for too long. The public reason for such attentiveness to one's duties is, of course, one's devotion to the organization. The real reason is a fear that prolonged absence from one's everyday interactional milieux will cause or tempt others to forget that one exists.

3. Team playing means being seen as an effective group member, sticking to one's assigned position. The good team player is not a prima donna. This

holds true even when one is considered a rising star. For example, a top executive of Weft Corporation says:

> Who gets ahead? They are people who are good team players. Most are not prima donnas. Prima donnas are very disruptive in this company. Even if a person is a prima donna, he usually tries hard not to look like one. The success of the operating divisions depends on the close cooperation of a number of people—in sales and merchandising and in the South. So that the person who is to really succeed here has to be a team player first and foremost.

Striking, distinctive characteristics of any sort, in fact, are dangerous in the corporate world. One of the most damaging things, for instance, that can be said about a manager is that he is brilliant. This almost invariably signals a judgment that the person has publicly asserted his intelligence and is perceived as a threat to others. What good is a wizard who makes his colleagues and his customers uncomfortable? Equally damaging is the judgment that a person cannot get along with others—he is "too pushy," that is, he exhibits too much "persistence in getting to the right answers," is "always asking why," and does not know "when to back off." Or he is "too abrasive," or "too opinionated," unable "to bend with the group." Or he is a "wildman" or a "maverick," that is, someone who is "outspoken." Or he may be too aloof, too distant, "too professional." A manager who has "ice water in his veins" or is thought to be a "cold fish" might impress others with his tough pragmatism, but he will win few alliances and in time his social standing and effectiveness will be eroded. Women, in particular, face a troublesome dilemma here. If a female executive's public face presents a warm, engaging femininity that distinguishes her from the minions of female clerical workers adopting the "corporate clone" look and practicing the new techniques of self-assertiveness, she runs the risk of being seen by her male colleagues as a "cookie" or a "fluff-head" and dismissed as inconsequential. If she, on the other hand, assumes a public severity in her demeanor, especially if she seems ambitious, she may be labeled a "calculating bitch," a difficult label to shake. Moreover, an effective group member looks to others in making decisions, recognizes that one must always think defensively to protect one's boss and one's associates, and knows that he must "keep his nose clean" and stay out of trouble because "people who have made big mistakes are very damaging to the team approach."

4. Team play also means, as one manager in the chemical company puts it, "aligning oneself with the dominant ideology of the moment" or, as another says, "bowing to whichever god currently holds sway." Such ideologies or gods may be thought of as official definitions of reality. As I suggested earlier, bureaucracies allow their employees a diverse range of private motives for action in return for assent to common rules and official versions of reality, that is, explanations or accounts that serve or at least do not injure the orga-

nization itself. Organizations always try, of course, to mobilize employees' belief in manufactured realities; such efforts always meet with some success particularly at the middle levels among individuals who still labor under the notion that success depends on sincerity. However, the belief of insiders in abstract goals is not a prerequisite for personal success; belief in and subordination to individuals who articulate organizational goals is. One must, however, to be successful in a bureaucratic work situation, be able to act, at a moment's notice, as if official reality is the only reality. The contexts for understanding this meaning of team play are the complicated levels of conflict within corporations and the probationary state of mind endemic to managerial work. The knowledgeable practitioners of corporate politics, whether patrons or leaders of cliques and networks, value nothing more highly than at least the appearance of unanimity of opinion among their clients and allies, especially during times of turmoil. They invoke the vocabulary of team play to bring their own people into line as well as to cast suspicion on others who pose some threat to them. If one examines the way team play is defined, invoked, and experienced at different levels of a hierarchy, one can see its use as an ideology. For instance, a top official at Alchemy Inc. states:

> Now I would define a team player as someone who sinks his personal ambition to the good of the company; someone who agrees to the consensus on a decision even though he might see things differently.

Another highly ranking executive in Covenant Corporation says:

> Team play means the sacrifice of one's individual feelings for the sake of the unified effort. It doesn't mean that you don't express your own views but your objective is not your own advancement. Rather you're working for the correct solution to some problem.

Some managers at the upper-middle and middle levels echo and reinforce these official sentiments. An upper-middle level manager in the chemical company says:

> Well, I strongly believe in [team play]. I've seen enough to know that you have to work together; there has to be a common understanding. Sometimes you don't like the assignment you might get but you've got to look at it like a football . . . team. The management has to assign the roles. . . . Management . . . wants a team that works well together. This means an understanding of what has to be done and having the access to the resources to do it the right way, the best way. And not having people who are going to say—I don't want to do that.

Many other managers, however, see the pronouncements of their superiors and some of their peers with a skeptical eye. An upper-middle level executive in the chemical company demonstrates the accepted rhetoric of team play:

Team play—it's each individual on a team doing his job to the best of his ability and the combination of each person with each other leading to an objective. It means fulfilling your assignment on a project to the best of your ability to the end that the objective is met in a timely and efficient manner. That's team play.

He goes on to discuss what he considers the real meaning of the ideology, shifting back and forth between the perspective of subordinate and boss:

Now what it really means is going with the flow and not making waves. If you disagree with something, bowing to the majority without voicing your disagreement. You can indict a person by saying that he's not a team player. That doesn't mean he won't follow directions. It's because he voices an objection, because he argues with you before doing something, especially if he's right. That's when we really get mad—when the other guy is right. If he's wrong, we can be condescending and adopt the "you poor stupid bastard" tone. . . .

The skillful boss uses ideologies such as team play adroitly, counting on subordinates to get the message and do what he wants. The same executive continues:

Another meaning of team play is its use as a club. You use it to push people into corners without seeming to. If I say to you, do this and you say that you don't really want to, but I insist, well, you've put the guy in an uncomfortable position and yourself too. But if you do it skillfully, the guy is not going to go away boxed. So, on one hand, you can't force them to do something, but you also can't manipulate them to do it; people resent this. What you do is to appeal to something like teamwork and they choose to do it because they know how important and valued it is in the organization. The boss has the extra vote but he has to cast it with some skill.

A team player is a manager who does not "force his boss to go to the whip," but, rather, amiably chooses the direction his boss points out. Managers who choose otherwise or who evince stubbornness are said to "have made a decision," a phrase almost always used to describe a choice that will shorten a career.

A middle-level manager in Alchemy Inc. puts a sharp edge on the same sentiment:

Someone who is talking about team play is out to squash dissent. It's the most effective way to tell people who have different perspectives to shut up. You say that you want a team effort. . . . You can and you have to learn to keep your mouth shut. My boss is like that. Everyone likes him because he is like that. It's hurt me because I have spoken out. It might be that someone has formed the opinion that I have interesting things to say, but more likely, it gives you a troublemaker label and that's one that is truly hard to get rid of. The troublemaker is often a creative person but truly creative people don't get ahead; to get ahead you have to be dependable and a team player. You have to be steady. . . . When I hear the word, I immediately think it's an effort to crush dissent. . . . [Bosses] say they don't want a yes man, but, in fact, most bosses don't want to hear the truth. And this is particularly true if it disagrees with what they want to do.

Younger managers learn quickly that, whatever the public protestations to the contrary, bosses generally want pliable and agreeable subordinates, especially during periods of crisis. Clique leaders want dependable, loyal allies. Those who regularly raise objections to what a boss or a clique leader really desires run the risk of being considered problems themselves and of being labeled "outspoken," or "nonconstructive," or "doomsayers," "naysayers," or "crepehangers."

Organizations vary in this respect and some tolerate, and indeed encourage, high degrees of dissent and controversy within particular work groups or within given strata of managers, that is, between peers or managers of different rank who consider themselves colleagues. Moreover, generally speaking, dissent on points of demonstrable fact is acceptable provided that one corrects others, even superiors, tactfully and does not make others look foolish in public. However, when interpretive judgments or plain desires are involved, or when an issue spills out of smaller groups into the larger political structures of an organization, or when higher authorities get involved, a new dynamic takes over. What are "frank perspectives" in a strictly collegial context can get interpreted in the political or hierarchical arenas as "downbeat negativism" or even "disloyalty." Wise and ambitious managers know that public faces of cheerful cooperativeness, which of course they generally require from their own subordinates, put superiors and important allies at ease. And, of course, the ability to put others at ease is an important skill in a world where one must be continually on guard against the eruption of usually suppressed conflict.

5. Team players display a happy, upbeat, can-do approach to their work and to the organization. A vice-president in the Metals Division of Covenant Corporation states:

Your degree of happiness is important. If someone is always pissing and moaning then that affects your evaluation of them. . . . If you're not happy in what you do, you can generate a synergism of apathy. If everybody talks about failure, you're going to fail. Happy people are nicer to be around. It's important to be an up person. And to keep an up perspective. I mean, how do you like it when you ask a guy how things are and he says: "Well, I have a corn on my toe and I don't feel well and so on and on"? He's telling you more than you want to know.

And that attitude will poison everyone around him. I always start looking for a positive result. . . . You have to feel that way. People don't
want to parade in unison into a vale of doom.

A world geared toward pragmatic accomplishments places a great premium
on the appearance of buoyant optimism. Looking on the bright side of things,
always "try[ing] to see the glass as half full rather than half empty," is felt to
be a prerequisite for any action at all, let alone managerial work that involves
imparting energy, enthusiasm, and direction to others, indeed a sense of social
cohesiveness.

In a word, a team player is alert to the social cues that he receives from
his bosses, his peers, and the intricate pattern of social networks, coteries,
and cliques that crisscross the organization. Depending on the vocabulary of
his company, a team player "fits in," "gets along with others," is "a good old
country boy," "knows how to schmooze." He is a "role player" who plays
his part without complaint. He does not threaten others by appearing brilliant,
or with his personality, his ability, or his personal values. He masks his ambition and his aggressiveness with blandness. He recognizes trouble and stays
clear of it. He protects his boss and his associates from blunders. When he
disagrees with others, he does so tactfully, preferably in private, and then in
ways that never call others' judgments into question. Even in dark times, he
keeps a sunny disposition and learns always to find the bright side of bleak
news. In short, he makes other managers feel *comfortable*, the crucial virtue
in an uncertain world, and establishes with others the easy predictable familiarity that comes from sharing taken for granted frameworks about how the
world works.

Top corporate executives are rarely described as "team players" and middle managers are rarely described as "leaders." Such terms, however, depend
less on personal attributes than on social position in the organization. All but
the topmost person in a hierarchical organization is a subordinate to others
and must, to some extent, cultivate the virtues of team play. Otherwise he will
never reach a position where subordinates come to think of him as a leader.

Moreover, to keep rising, managers must have the proper style to differ-
entiate themselves from other managers and to push themselves into the organizational limelight. One of the top executives in the chemical company says:

Now I'll admit that the majority of the work is done at G-13 or around
that level, say G-12, G-13, and G-14. That's where the real *work* work
is done. Beyond that level is more management, more planning, more
promotion, more accountability oriented. There's less day-to-day
work involved. Now at the G-13 or G-14 levels, the same kind of
skills are needed as later on, but higher up a different set of skills
become *predominant*. It's *style*. You have to remember that a firm gets
very narrow after a certain point and, when you get right down to it,
if you have an ability and others have the same ability, what is going

to make the difference? Not intellectual ability. It's going to be *style* ... that differentiates one person from the next.

He goes on to discuss the principal constituents of style.

[It's] being able to talk with and interrelate with people, all kinds of people. Being able to make a good case for something. Being able to sell something. Being able to put things well; being articulate. [It's] presentation ability in particular.

Other managers emphasize the crucial importance of presentational ability. A middle-level product manager at Weft Corporation explains:

Persons who can present themselves well, who can sell themselves the best are the kind of people who get ahead. It's an image type thing. Not just doing the job right but being able to capitalize on it in certain ways. Some people are gifted at doing that. They handle themselves very well. They may not be take-charge people but they give you the impression that they are. They dress properly and dress is very important. And how they handle themselves at a meeting is extremely important. This is especially true at pressure-cooker-type meetings which is what divisional meetings are. People get up and review their numbers. It's a stagelike atmosphere. People have to justify their numbers. And everybody knows why things fall apart sometimes, but some people are able to explain things better and highlight the good points in ways that impress other people. It's having a certain grace, charm, adroitness, and humor. . . . I think what's important is to portray yourself as very decisive, as being able to think on your feet. There are some people who will go after you and the important thing is not to get flustered. Most people work at this self-presentation. They rehearse their slides before they have to give a talk. . . . Or they'll rehearse their speech again and again and stay up going over the numbers.

A general manager at Alchemy emphasizes the importance of seeming to be in command:

[Style] is being able to talk easily and make presentations. To become credible easily and quickly. You can advance quickly even without technical experience if you have style. You get a lot of points for style. You've got to be able to articulate problems, plans, and strategies without seeming to have to refer to all sorts of memos and so on. The key in public performances and presentations is in knowing how to talk forcefully without referring to notes and memoranda. To be able to map out plans quickly and surely.

An upper-middle executive in the chemical company points out how certain occupational specialties in management offer more opportunities than others to make presentations. The ability to seize these chances, using the requisite skills, can propel a manager's career in a hurry:

> Sales people and business people [are] constantly being exposed to management, making presentations to the Operating Committee. If they are articulate, well-dressed, articulate their program well, they make an indelible impression. I've seen many guys who on the basis of *one presentation* have been promoted beyond their abilities. And if they're telling the top guys good news in the bargain, well, that just helps them. I'm always astonished by this emphasis on appearances. I mean ... *if they like the way you look,* you have a good chance to impress them.... When the top guys see a guy and say: "Hey, he's great," the myth about the guy is perpetuated. If they say to a plant manager that some guy is great, the plant manager is not going to say that he can't find his ass in a rainstorm. And suddenly the guy is on the fast track.

Having the right style also means mirroring the kind of image that top bosses have of themselves, "mak[ing] the people most responsible for [one's] fate *comfortable.*" Without such a clear meshing of styles, and this is a central meaning of the notion of comfort, managers have little chance of being taken into the higher circles of an organization. A top Alchemy executive states:

> When you get to the very top—and this is an observable thing—your style cannot be in conflict with the style of the guys on top. If there is a conflict, you're not going to last very long.

The style that most large corporations want their up-and-coming managers to project both within the organization and in other public arenas is that of "the young, professional, conservative person" who "knows what is going on in the world" and who is "broad as a person" with interests that transcend the work milieu. When top corporate circles mesh with high intellectual, artistic, political, and civic social circles of metropolitan areas—this is particularly true of Weft Corporation and Images Inc.—breadth, here measured by social poise and conversational ability, becomes crucial. A top official of Weft explains:

> We want someone with breadth, with some interests outside the business, someone who is broad as a person. And this can be in anything—the arts, sports, or both, in local politics, in Toastmasters, in Little League, in the eleemosynary organizations. Why? Because they're bigger people and they can do the job better in the long run if they have bigger interests, broader interests. We'd like to think that they represent [Weft Corporation] well when they're in public—that when

someone asks them what they do and they say that they work for [Weft Corporation] the person has a good impression of the company through them. And you can sense what kind of people will create that kind of impression.

In short, managers with the right style possess a subtle, almost indefinable sophistication and polish, essentially a *savoir faire*, marked especially by an urbane, witty, graceful, engaging, and friendly demeanor. They are men and women of discriminating taste, of ostensibly balanced judgment, marked with an open-minded tolerance towards others' foibles and idiosyncrasies, at least in public, and with an ability to direct social interaction and conversation into well-grooved and accepted channels. They are able to frame issues with a graceful flair, subtly but forcefully dramatizing themselves in the process. Finally, men and women with the right style know how to assess and adjust themselves with poised ease and an air of quiet decisiveness to the nuances, exigencies, and shifting moralities of social situations.[4]

Some observers have interpreted such conformity, team playing, continual affability, and emphasis on social finesse as evidence of the decline of the individualism of the old Protestant ethic.[5] To the extent that commentators take the public faces that managers wear at face value, and I include here the predictable trappings of upper-middle-class affluence that mark managers' lifestyles, these writers miss the main point. Managers up and down the corporate ladder adopt their public faces quite consciously; they are, in fact, the masks behind which the real struggles and moral issues of the corporation can be found.

Karl Mannheim's conception of self-rationalization[6] or self-streamlining, that is, the systematic application of functional rationality to the self to attain certain individual ends, is useful in understanding one of the central social psychological processes of organizational life. In a world where appearances—in the broadest sense—mean everything, the wise and ambitious manager learns to cultivate assiduously the proper, prescribed modes of appearing. He dispassionately takes stock of himself, treating himself as an object, as a commodity. He analyzes his strengths and weaknesses and decides what he needs to change in order to survive and flourish in his organization. And then he systematically undertakes a program to reconstruct his image, his publicly avowed attitudes or ideas, or whatever else in his self-presentation that might need adjustment. As I have suggested, this means sharply curbing one's impulses, indeed spontaneity of any sort, and carefully calculating instead both the appropriate modes of packaging oneself and the social consequences of one's every action. Such self-regulation requires simultaneously great discipline and "flexibility," since one must continually adjust oneself to meet the ever-changing demands of different career stages and, of more immediate consequence, the expectations of crucial social circles in ever-changing organizational milieux. An enterprising young manager, touching on all the crucial aspects of public faces treated here, describes how he tailors his style to criteria valued by key circles in Alchemy Inc. after the "big purge" of October

1979. His view is more fully articulated than that of most managers but his
high degree of self-consciousness about his self-streamlining helps illuminate
the self-adjustment that other managers take for granted.

There are two aspects which are important—tangible and intangible.
First, looks are crucial. The image that they want—if you go to the
management committee, they all look the same. They're not robots in
a Wall Street firm; but they're clean-cut young executives—short hair,
no mustaches, button-down collars, Hickey Freeman suits. . . . Then
there are the mannerisms. They like you to be well-organized, well-
spoken. They like presentations, briefings. The greatest thing for your
career is to go before the Operating Committee and talk. It's your day
in the sun, or rather your five minutes in the sun. What they like are
the slick presentations with slides, with overheads. Short, succinct.
Tell them what they want to hear. I've been sent to two courses in
public speaking for executives. For guys on the really fast track,
they've even got this charm school for executives—a finishing school
. . . I think it's up at Harvard. They learn about "management theory"
and so on. People who are *comers*—the fair-haired boys—all exhibit
the same traits. They are all fast on their feet, well-spoken. They all
send *visibility* memos. You know, get your name out, let people know
you're managing. Cultivate pseudo-leadership. Develop a habit of calling somebody back in a hurry. Wearing your [Covenant] tie.

. . . My long suit is my personality. I have the gift of gab and the way
to move up is to know as many people as you can. . . . You get ahead
by being noticed by others. . . . I think going to a school like [Amherst,
Dartmouth, or William and Mary] matters in this regard. You develop
your social perception; you learn to size people up. And things like
this are the biggest asset in the corporation.

The key in all of this is to find the right time and place to say something. You gain a lot of respect both for saying something and for
knowing when to say it. You keep it humorous. The higher up you
go, the more people you deal with, and everybody wants something
from you. Everybody has a sense of humor but the top guys can't joke
around in their jobs, they can't joke around with those above and
below them. They can't let their guard down. So if [I] keep things
light, humorous, offhand, they tend to be open with me. I build on the
[*Covenant*] connection—you know, the "we're all in this together"
thing—and he begins to think, well, if I have any problems in [his area
of expertise], I'll call him. You try to develop *trust* with them. The
other day, I walked into the Credit Union downstairs and there was
[a vice-president] ahead of me in line with a check in his hand. And as
he was giving it to the girl, I said, "Don't drop that check; it'll bounce
to the ceiling." And the girl cringed but [the vice-president] turned
around and laughed and then we got into a ten-minute conversation

about things. And I asked him about his kids and he asked about mine and I told him that the baby is still waking up at night. . . . You don't clam up. You keep it light; make it humorous. And you keep things rolling; draw him out of his shell.

I don't háve the responsibility for a salesman's job in this company, but I sell everybody every day. What I sell is *me*—myself.

Later reorganizations in the chemical company brought new circles of managers to power and with them an emphasis on different criteria. Increasingly, the notion of "lean, hungry, and aggressive management" became the company watchword and the bonhomie of the old regime became dangerous. Wise and ambitious managers assessed the situation and altered their public faces to fit the new circumstances, the occasion, the circle, the need.

Such adroit self-rationalization demands continual self-scrutiny, a constant private monitoring of one's adaptation to socially defined criteria. One not only displays correct appearances, social finesse, and the proper attitudes but one always reflexively examines one's performance, as if glancing in a mirror. Even seasoned managers whose external performances are so smooth as to seem instinctive suggest in their interviews a high degree of self-consciousness. This is one of the principal roots of the narcissism that Joseph Bensman has noted among managers and related professionals in our society.[7] Such self-scrutiny places managers in yet another probationary crucible, one from which there is no ready escape. But such attention to self makes perfect sense since one's personality becomes one's most valuable asset. As one manager says: "Personality spells success or failure, not what you do on the field." In such a world, not only new skills, but wholly new moralities that allow one to use those skills readily, become imperative. The very nature of their work numbers managers among the great actors of our time; they rarely, however, receive credit for their thespian abilities because their best performances take place not on front stage but in the corridors and back rooms of their bureaucratic warrens.

To advance, a manager must, as suggested earlier, have a patron, also called a mentor, a sponsor, a rabbi, or a godfather. A patron provides his client with opportunities to get "visibility," to "showcase" his abilities, to step out of the crowd at the middle levels, to make connections with others of high status. A patron cues his client to crucial political developments in the corporation, helps arrange lateral moves if the client's upward progress is thwarted by a particular job or a particular boss, applauds his presentations or suggestions at meetings, introduces his client to the right people at the right times, and promotes his client during an organizational shake-up, usually to posts where the patron needs someone of unswerving loyalty. The signs of favor from a patron and, of course, a client's reciprocal obligations, vary widely. One powerful manager, for example, adopts a succession of bright young protégés with whom he shares work, troubles, and secrets in return for steadfast loyalty and for the enlivening enthusiasm of the young. If he becomes disappointed with his charges, they fall back into the obscurity from which he plucked them. But under his tutelage, many have gone on to high positions, extending the patron's influence in subtle but important ways. More generally, to the extent that a patron "invests" in a client, to that extent will he make sure that the client does not fail since a client's failure can damage a patron's reputation for picking winners. The client, in turn, cheers his patron's strategies in public and arranges support for them in private. Most important, he makes sure that the patron always has access to vital information—technical and political—lest the patron make a public mistake and lose "credibility." The more powerful a patron, the more other managers fear his clients, since to oppose the clients is to call the patron's judgment into question. One must, of course, be lucky in one's patron. If the patron gets caught in a political cross fire, the arrows are likely to find his clients as well.

A manager must, of course, also develop the intricate alliances with other managers that will provide him with a secure political base to weather storms and that will make him attractive to patrons. To the extent that a manager can master whatever social criteria are posed for admission to the matrices of crisscrossing networks, coteries, and cliques, to that extent will a patron's actions on a client's behalf be seen to serve the interests and reflect the judgments of many.

Surely, one might argue, there must be more to success in the corporation than appearances, personality, team play, style, chameleonic adaptability, and fortunate connections. What about the bottom line—profits, performance? After all, whole forests have been demolished to print the endless number of tracts designed to assure and extol "results-oriented management."

Unquestionably, "hitting your numbers"—that is, meeting the profit commitments already discussed—or achieving expected levels of performance in other areas is important, but only within the social context I have described. For instance, a general manager in the chemical company explains:

> You can lose money and still be an insider; you can make money and still be an outsider. If you're not part of the team being developed, well, your chances are slim. . . . It's crucial to be both making money *and* be included in the developing team.

More generally, there are several rules that apply here. First, no one in a line position—that is, with responsibility for profit and loss—who regularly "misses his numbers" will survive, let alone rise. Second, a person who always hits his numbers but who lacks some or all of the required social skills will not rise. Third, a person who sometimes misses his numbers but who has all the desirable social traits will rise.

Performance is thus always subject to a myriad of interpretations. Profits and other kinds of results matter, but managers see no *necessary* connections between performance and reward. Although meritocratic ideologies are constantly invoked in the corporate world to explain or justify promotions, demotions, or other organizational changes, such rationales are always viewed by managers with a measure of skepticism. First, the contingency of corporate life, most evident, as discussed earlier, during shake-ups, erodes traditional notions of loyalty or of "trust in the system" and creates a deep and unsettling uncertainty about how, in fact, one is to "get on." A young manager, discussing one of the shake-ups at Alchemy Inc., says:

> You know, these things are always very arbitrary and capricious. And what that means is that there is no concept of loyalty anymore. You've got to position yourself continually so that you can get a good job when you're bounced. . . . People feel that they could be rewarded for doing a good job, but they also realize that despite doing good work, their careers could be terminated in a minute.

Such troubling uncertainties, marked especially by the felt lack of any objective standards to measure and reward excellence, get compounded by managers' perceptions of basic inequities in evaluation and reward processes. Merit pay systems, for instance, are widely considered to be used simply as sophisticated, highly rational legitimations for what is in practice a complicated political patronage system. In Covenant Corporation, criticism of merit pay focuses on the CEO's insistence on a rigid bell curve distribution of performance ratings that determines salary increases. The official rationale is that such a distribution forces supervisors to make the hard judgments necessary to maintain performance standards. In actuality, the judgments that are made are seen to reflect other interests. For instance, a middle-level manager in a large staff division of Alchemy explains:

> There is a companywide bell curve for our [performance] ratings. It goes from 1 to 5; one means that you walk on water, five means that you hit the streets. And they have to balance these out. It means that *somebody's gain is somebody else's loss*. If they give me a 2.5, they have to give somebody else a 3 to even out the curve. It also means that I'm competing for limited spots with people who have high grades. If I do well, are they going to knock down somebody who is a director to give me what I deserve? Not very likely. [Our] whole . . . group is competing with each other for the same grades; the irony is that although people at the top of the group are evaluated by [our vice-president], they in turn will evaluate us even though we're competing with them for limited grades.

The system has the curious effect of simultaneously underlining the already existing fierce competition between managers but also of bunching the crowd at the middle levels ever more closely. For example, according to a high-ranking manager in Covenant Corporation:

> You have a bell curve system and it's got to be a normal curve and nobody breaks that curve. . . . So [people] don't see what they do, or

don't do, as related to their situation in the corporation. Because they are all rated by their bosses as *typical*. And they know that they don't all perform *typically*. So the underachievers get satisfaction because they are rated the same as hard workers, even though they are coasting. And the overachievers get bent out of shape because they see that their work is not recognized.[8]

Work comes to be seen as separated from reward. One might surmise that bonus systems, tied to specific accomplishments, could mend such a breach at least for those included in such plans. Some executives at Weft Corporation claim that this is the case. There, a handful of key "mistake makers" receive a somewhat reduced salary and have to make up the difference, and an increment, by "shooting crap"—that is, by meeting goals negotiated through the commitment system. However, managers not in the bonus system, who are also experienced in the art of arranging "reasonable" commitments, resent their exclusion from what they see as a sure thing. In their view, the bonus system is an inequitably administered bonanza that implicitly devalues their own work. In Covenant Corporation, the resentment of those managers excluded from the bonus system is complemented by a certain guilty knowledge of those who are part of it (all grade 15s and up, plus a few selected grade 14s); even during the corporation's rocky red-ink years described earlier, generous bonuses were regularly passed out to the chosen few.

Finally, except at the lower levels of management that directly oversee actual production of goods, managers see the intrinsic ambiguity of their work as impossible to evaluate with any objectivity. The very categories of management evaluation in the companies I have studied—judgment and decision-making ability, creativeness, leadership, communication, working with others, and so on—lend themselves to multiple, subjective, and extremely divergent interpretations. Of course, to the extent that measures of performance are vague, to that extent are standards of accountability vague.

The real task for the ambitious manager then becomes how to shape and keep shaping others' perceptions of oneself—that is, how to influence favorably or alter if necessary the cognitive maps of others in the central political networks of the organization—so that one becomes seen as "promotable." The promotable person is the manager who possesses a desirable combination of the important managerial skills already described. Of course, not all cognitive maps are equally important. A high-ranking Alchemy executive describes how authoritative perceptions shape the maps of others:

This whole informal body of knowledge is a crucial set of maps to the organization. It helps you gauge how you relate to others—what you can and can't do. And this knowledge and the relationships themselves ebb and flow. Sometimes a guy is nonpromotable today and tomorrow he is the very best man. Everything depends on who is on top and how he perceives you and other people.

Managers know that patrons and powerful allies protect those already selected as rising stars from the negative judgments of others; and only the foolhardy point out even egregious errors of those in power or those destined for it.

III

Failure is also socially defined. The most damaging failure is, as one middle manager in Alchemy Inc. puts it, "When your boss or someone who has the power to determine your fate says: 'You failed.'" Such a godlike pronouncement means, of course, out-and-out personal ruin; one must, at any cost, arrange matters to prevent such an occurrence.

Except in cases of major public blunders covered by the media—managers say that those who have suffered such misfortune might as well have the word "asshole" branded on their foreheads—things rarely come to such a dramatic pass even in the midst of an organizational crisis. Rather, "failure is perception," that is, a set of coinciding judgments that one "cannot cut the mustard" or, especially, that one is "nonpromotable." Managers can be thought to be nonpromotable for many reasons—a manager "doesn't fit in," he "doesn't communicate well," he is "too consumed with detail," he is "not flexible enough," or he is "not a self-starter" (meaning one has to pressure him to get anything done). An Alchemy executive explains the ambiguous nature of such attribution and how reputations about a manager develop in people's cognitive maps:

> You can put the damper on anyone who works for you very easily and that's why there's too much chemistry in the corporation. There's not enough objective information about people. When you really want to do somebody in, you just say, well, he can't get along with people. That's a big one. And we do that constantly. What that means, by the way, is that he pissed me off; he gave evidence of his frustration with some situation. Another big one is that he can't manage—he doesn't delegate or he doesn't make his subordinates keep his commitments. So in this sort of way, a consensus does build up about a person and a guy can be dead and not even know it.

Sometimes assessments about an individual vary sharply. What matters then, as always in a hierarchical situation, are the impressions top management has of a person. A high-ranking member of Weft Corporation, who sits on its Central Management Committee (CMC), talks about such conflicts:

> An executive will make a presentation and say, "Well, Sam Sausage is wonderful and I think we should promote him." But others know him and we'll say, "I just don't agree with you. Our assessment is that he is in his niche. We've seen him in various situations and we don't have

the sense that he can be successful in a new environment." This gets particularly tough with a senior executive. Like we have one guy—whom the division president is particularly high on moving up. But in the perception of all of us on the CMC, we don't see him moving into another job. There's simply no job higher up for that guy. We'd be happy to have him stay here—I mean where he is—forever, if he wants that. But if he wants to get ahead, he can't do it here.

Those publicly labeled as failures normally have no choice but to leave the organization; those adjudged nonpromotable can remain, provided they are willing to stop moving ahead, or, as their influence inevitably wanes with their decreased mobility, accept being shelved, sidelined, sidetracked, or, more colorfully, "mushroomed"—that is, kept in a dark place, fed manure, and left with nothing to do but grow fat. This too, of course, is a kind of failure, indeed a serious one, and I shall discuss its consequences shortly.

Normally, despite official policies and good intentions to the contrary, those considered to be nonpromotable are not told of negative judgments about them. An Alchemy executive explains:

Well, usually you don't tell people the truth. I once knew a guy whom I knew was about to be fired and I asked if he had been told and he had never been told. I think you should tell people explicitly. Things like that shouldn't have to be decoded. But you can understand how it happens. Suppose you have a guy and the consensus is that he isn't promotable. You wouldn't *ever*—or very seldom—tell him.

He goes on to justify his silence:

There are people who go through life thinking they can do a lot more than they really can do. And the reason is that losing or changing jobs is a very high stress situation and most people prefer to hang on to what they've got—to their routine. They're not happy but they go through life like prisoners of war not recognizing their true situation.

A top-ranking executive in Weft offers the same account:

You get the situation where a lot of people don't really want to know. . . . Like one guy we have, he will retire on his job. He's in my division. He knows it. I know it. And he doesn't want me to tell him about that. Now don't ask me how I know that but, believe me, I do.

Illusions of every sort are, of course, the stuff of life, but dreams of mobility become particularly important in hierarchical situations dominated by the moral imperative to get ahead. Managers simply recognize here the links between personal illusions and institutional needs and choose not to upset an ambiguous but useful coincidence. Perhaps even more to the point, however, managers avoid telling their immediate subordinates about harsh organizational realities not only because they have to deal with these people face-to-face on a daily basis but also because such a confrontation might jeopardize images that they have nurtured in others and indeed in themselves. Another high-ranking executive in Weft Corporation explains:

> Why does it happen? Because people are afraid of confrontations. People want to be thought of as kind, sensitive, and compassionate. Being compassionate has a good significance in our society. The easy way out is not to do anything, don't tell the guy. That happens a lot.

The ambiguity of not knowing where one stands thus not only reflects the ambiguity of the judgments that determine one's organizational fate, but also the tangled motivations, self-perceptions, and projection of images of those who make the judgments.

As a result, subordinates are generally expected to get the message after they have been repeatedly overlooked for promotions. In fact, middle managers interpret staying in the same job for more than two or three years as evidence of a negative judgment. This leads to a mobility panic at the middle levels, complete with elaborate knowledge in one's cognitive map of the retirement schedule of personnel in desired organizational slots and mental timetables to have reached such and such a grade and salary point by a certain age. All of this, in turn, has crucial consequences for pinpointing responsibility in the organization.

It is worth reflecting a bit more deeply on the significance and social consequences of failure in a world where there is such a strong moral imperative for success. Every corporation has cautionary tales of egregious failures, of managers who fell from great heights, and also tales and usually living examples of once promising managers now shivering in Siberia or sidelined and thought of as has-beens. Certain common themes run through all of these stories, and a case from the chemical company illustrates these. Patterson was an executive vice-president in the old process chemicals division, the backbone of Covenant Corporation before the new CEO took power in 1979. He was closely allied with two powerful patrons—the president of his division and the president of the whole corporation—both of whom were fired with the ascendancy of the new CEO. Like many managers during that period, Patterson became "naked to his enemies." Moreover, Patterson's caustic, sometimes downright unpleasant style contrasted sharply with the smooth marketing image cultivated by Smith and his ascendant specialty chemicals clique. Patterson found himself faced either with dismissal or a double demotion in grade and rank all the way down to general manager status. He chose the latter and was put in charge of a "dog," that is, a declining business area.

Although Patterson's personal catastrophe was considered "a fall from grace of the highest order," the really remarkable aspect of it to managers who accept such contingency as commonplace was Patterson's decision to take the demotion and the public humiliation that accompanied it. Managers who formerly ranked well below Patterson in status and authority were now his bosses. Younger managers in particular felt that Patterson had "lost his guts," exhibited "a lack of self-esteem," and had "laid down and died." They felt only contempt for his choice and saw his acceptance of demotion as a resignation to a kind of civil death. Older managers, around Patterson's age of 48 years, saw the matter differently. At the time of his demotion, Patterson had only a few years to go before he reached the magic number of 80, a combination of years of age and of organizational service which qualifies one for the company's pension plan. His age peers understood his need to maintain income during a difficult economic period with the financial responsibilities of middle-class life, mortgage payments, college tuition bills for children, and so on. Still, they said that they had little respect for Patterson's choice. Managers know that to be weak in a world that extols strength and power is to invite abuse. This is exactly what happened to Patterson. After a time, Smith took away the only lucrative part of Patterson's business and gave it to a rising star who needed fail-safe line experience. Patterson was then ordered to sell almost all the rest of his business, except for one plant to produce enough of an essential ingredient to service the chemical company's internal needs.

For the most part, other managers avoided Patterson "as one would a leper," a common pattern of behavior toward failures in a competitive environment. Managers stayed away from him at company social occasions, and one manager, in the community where both he and Patterson lived, thwarted all efforts on Patterson's part to get together socially. Such social distancing has two purposes: it undermines in advance or lays the groundwork for refusal of any claims that a person considered a failure might make on another, and it forestalls the possibility of being linked with that person in others' cognitive maps. This becomes particularly important when there has been a known past association between oneself and one thought to have failed in some way. One executive describes this distancing:

> Our motives are purely selfish. We're not concerned about old Joe failing, but we're worried about how his failure will reflect on us. When you pick somebody, say, you invest part of yourself in him. So his failure and what it means to his kids and so on mean nothing. What you're worried about is your own ass with your superiors for having picked him in the first place. . . . What we do essentially when somebody fails is to put him in a little boat, tow him out to sea, and cut the rope. And we never think about him again.

In fact, when it is even suspected that a person might be headed for trouble, anticipatory avoidance is the rule. Since one never knows what standards or criteria might be invoked to determine fates, it certainly makes little sense to be associated with those whose career threads seem already to be measured for cutting.

As a result, the managerial world is not notable for its compassion. In this, it affirms Max Weber's note about the irreconcilable opposition between the ethical requirements of *caritas* and the exigencies of the market and of public life in general.[9] A high-ranking staff official at Covenant explains:

> Anxiety is endemic to anyone who works in a corporation. By the time you get to be middle management, it's difficult to make friends because the normal requirement for friendship—that is, *loyalty*—doesn't fit in this context. You have to look out for number one more than anything else.

Moreover, the prevailing view is that managers are big boys and girls, well-paid, and should be able to take care of themselves. Besides, one person's failure represents another person's opportunity.

By hanging on after his political downfall, instead of accepting a quick "golden handshake" (a departure encouraged by financial reward), Patterson presented his colleagues with the difficult problem of how they could avoid, both socially and psychologically—that is, not become associated with or emotionally entangled with—a fellow manager with whom they had to work every day. Perhaps because Patterson's continuing presence constantly reminded others that they too could quickly fall from grace, managers searched Patterson's character for faults that might make what happened to him more intelligible. Typically, and characteristically, they focus not on his work performance as such but on his social manner of carrying out that performance. For instance, a peer of Patterson's says:

> You know, there are people who derive their strength by being cooperative, friendly. Still others by being decisive and cooperating not at all. When a fall comes, it's the guy in the second category that falls the furthest. See, the important thing in managing is not to show your authority too much. You've got to get people to think an idea is theirs; you've got to get them to accept "hints" so that they perform the way you want them to. [Patterson] doesn't really seem to be able to do this; he's decisive but without allowing other opinions, and so he comes across as abrasive and rough with others.

Managers see the old corporate saw as salient here: you should treat others well on your way up so that they will treat you well on your way down. If one cannot avoid the contingencies of organizational life, one can at least try to master the social niceties that might buffer one's fate. Managers know that there is no safety outside managerial circles.

One may also note in passing that, with the exception of his occasional importuning of others, Patterson collaborated with other managers in arranging their avoidance of him, something that won their quiet admiration. He was aided in doing so by his own complete acceptance of the institutional logic of corporate power struggles. Had he triumphed in the game, he argues, he would have done exactly to others what was done to him. Specifically, he would have selected a team of managers that he trusted and with whom he felt comfortable, and then he would have gotten rid of any potentially opposing groups. However, since things turned out differently, Patterson adopted a public face of stoic professional acceptance, never referring publicly to the events that precipitated his downfall or to his own difficult personal situation, not even indulging in the macabre humor that became commonplace in some circles. With only a few lapses, he maintained this public face of cool detachment for more than three years despite what he acknowledges to be constant feelings of suppressed rage. Finally, his reaching the magic number of 80 coincided with one of Smith's purges and he was fired. Although other managers were not sorry to see him go, they knew that his departure marked the closing of a virtuoso performance.

Finally, managers feel that there is a tremendous amount of plain luck involved in advancement. It is striking how often managers who pride themselves on being hardheaded rationalists explain their own career patterns and those of others in terms of luck. The continual probations of managerial life and especially its ambiguous uncertainties shape this perception.

One uncertainty, of course, is managers' pervasive sense of organizational contingency that I have already discussed. Another is the uncertainty of the markets that undercuts the perceived connection between one's work and economic results. A product manager in the chemical company talks about the lack of connection between work and results:

> I guess the most anxiety provoking thing about working in business is that you are judged on *results* whether those results are your fault or not. So you can get a guy who has tried really hard but disaster strikes; and you can get a guy who does nothing and his business makes a big success. And so you just never know which way things are going to go and you're never sure about the relationship of your work to the outcome.

One of the top executives in Weft Corporation echoes this sentiment:

> I always say that there is no such thing as a marketing genius; there are only great markets.

Assuming a basic level of corporate resources and managerial know-how, real economic outcome is seen to depend on factors largely beyond organizational or personal control. Managerial planning becomes elaborate guesswork, though it remains a central organizational ritual—a kind of ceremony of rationality—closely linked to the commitment system that underpins fealty relationships. It is interesting to note in this context that a line manager's long-run credibility suffers just as much from missing his numbers on the up side (that is, achieving profits higher than predicted) as from missing them on the down side although, as one might expect, the immediate consequences of such different miscalculations vary. Both outcomes, however, undercut the ideology of managerial planning and control. Moreover, planning serves as one of the few psychological bulwarks managers have against market irrationality. Planning is the basis for the legitimacy of resource allocation. A top staff official at Covenant Corporation explains:

> By putting the money in this business, you're taking the money away from others. In human terms, that's what you're doing. It's money that you could provide jobs with to others. So when you get a guy in the business who comes in under or over the plan, well, both are equally suspect. Because you're making major decisions based on your plan. . . . Like when we shut down [business A] and put the money into [business B], the whole legitimacy of the operation depends on the [business A] guys accepting the rationale that more money can be made in another operation.

Another bulwark against market irrationality, of course, is "working hard," that is, putting in long hours at the office. For many managers, this is a psychological necessity to relieve the anxiety of being responsible for what one cannot control. One manager explains:

> This [lack of control] doesn't mean you don't work hard; at least in my case, that's my answer. I have to believe I can influence events. That way, I feel good about myself even if my boss doesn't.

Many managers also note with irony that they work hardest, that is, put in the most hours, when economic times are bad, when even they see few practical results for their efforts. They do not do so because they actually expect their hours of work to produce an economic boom; rather, they know that, unless they are seen toiling with other managers, they might not be around when the good times start to roll.

Public opinion and government regulations also create great uncertainties for managers. These are treated extensively later in this book, but two examples are appropriate here. The public concern in recent years about chemical pollution, called "chemophobia" by managers, a "hysteria" that ignores the incalculable societal benefits of chemical research and engineering, has triggered a widespread retreat from chemical production in several corporations. Executives at Weft Corporation refer to possible regulation on the formaldehyde resin used in producing permanent-press materials as the "piano hanging over our heads." Such unsureness reaches far into the corporate structure and affects even those managers in staff positions who are quite removed from the turmoil of the market. Occupational safety specialists, for instance, know that the bad publicity from one serious accident can jeopardize years of work and devalue scores of safety awards. Such inevitable uncertainties of managerial work create further probationary crucibles; past accomplishments crumble under today's pressures. A managerial commonplace says: "In the corporate world, 1,000 'Attaboys' are wiped away with one 'Oh, shit!'"

Because of such uncertainties, managers continually speak of the great importance of being in the right place at the right time. An upper-middle level manager says:

> If I were just out of school and somebody told me that it doesn't matter what you do and how well you do it but that what matters is being in the right place at the right time, I'd have said that hard work is still the key. You know, the old virtues. But now as I have gotten older, I think it's pure happenstance—luck. Things *happen* to people and being in the right time and place and knowing the right people is the key.

A top-ranking executive suggests that the axiom of being in the right place at the right time has literal as well as broader figurative meaning:

> It's being the right man at the right time. . . . It's recognizing that among people with equal abilities, sometimes just luck, plain luck, makes the difference. If there were a job open here at [company headquarters] and two people were being considered for it and one of them was right here and one of them on assignment in some other state, who do you think would get the job?

Corporations do try to establish mechanisms to maximize their employees' perceptions of rationality and equity and to minimize perceptions of chance and favoritism. Computerized skill banks, for instance, where managers regularly update reports of their abilities for review by an organizational development committee, are a widespread practice. Some junior managers see great value in such systems. They try to guess what skills will be valued in the future and assiduously enroll in whatever development courses are offered by their companies, taking care to make sure that even their smallest achievements are noted in their files. The longer one stays in the corporate world, however, the less rational such highly rational systems seem. A middle-aged, upper-middle level manager at Alchemy Inc. says:

> You know, there is this huge computerized inventory of skills which people update each year; it's called a skills inventory. . . . But all the computerized lists in the world don't amount to much in the corporation. What matters is a bunch of guys sitting informally in a room and deciding who should get jobs and who shouldn't. The real job decisions are made on that basis. And circumstances determine your fate.

In such a chance-filled world, the great catastrophe is to end up at the wrong place at the wrong time. There are any number of ways that this can happen. A top executive in the chemical company talks about one typical pattern:

> You can also end up at the wrong place at the wrong time. I've seen some very capable guys destroyed. They get caught in some situation, things go on for awhile and then somebody in power decides to *do* something about it. And they get sacrificed to the virgin gods. Or the market can suddenly go sour. But the typical case is that something has been going on for thirty to forty years and someone decides to *do* something about it.

Circumstances, personal and social, are seen to shape destiny. My interview materials are filled with stories of people who were transferred immediately before a big shake-up and, as a result, found themselves riding the crest of a wave to power; of people in a promising business area who were terminated because top management suddenly decided that the area no longer fit the corporate image desired; of two ambitious young managers who joined Weft Corporation at the same time, and were adopted by and assigned to "track," that is, follow the footsteps of, the same powerful and knowledgeable patron when suddenly the whole cohort of top managers retired and all three were propelled to the upper echelons of the company; of another executive in the same company who began his career in the manufacturing side of textiles when the southern mills dominated the industry and the company, only to see the ground shift under his feet and ascendancy pass to marketing managers based in the North; of still another Weft executive, a cinch in his own mind for a newly vacant divisional presidency, suddenly stricken with a mysterious viral infection that kept him out of work for six weeks, long enough for his arch rival to get the nod and become his new boss; of a product manager whose plant accidentally produced an odd color batch of chemicals, who sold them as a premium version of the old product, and who is now thought to be a marketing genius; of a young manager who, while at a company conference, went out for his weight-controlling 5:30 A.M. jog only to meet a vice-president similarly engaged, a powerful executive who now cheers the younger man's work and presentations and introduces him to other influential senior managers; of a plant manager who, when his machinery had ground to a halt and his technicians were baffled and everyone turned to him to make a decision, told his crew, without the faintest idea of the right thing to do and with the great fear that all he had worked for was about to crumble before him, to dump ten pounds of phosphate into the machine. The machine sprang to life and he became a hero.

The point is that managers have a sharply defined sense not only of the contingency but of the capriciousness of organizational life. Luck seems to be as good an explanation as any of why, after a certain point, some people succeed and others fail. The upshot is that many managers decide that they can do little to influence external events in their favor. This does not mean that they stop working or worrying; indeed, as noted earlier, the uncertainty and anxiety at the core of managerial life often make the social requirements for long hours at the office personal compulsions as well. One must not, however, let tasks distract one from the main chance. Even in an irrational world, one can at least exert rational control over oneself. Above all, one must learn to streamline oneself shamelessly, learn to wear all the right masks, learn all the proper vocabularies of discourse, get to know all the right people, and cultivate the subtleties of the art of self-promotion. One can then sit tight and wait for things to happen.

4

Looking Up and Looking Around

I

Authority and advancement patterns come together in the decision-making process. The core of the managerial mystique is decision-making prowess, and a multitude of scientific theories as well as mythologies about decision making abound in every corporation. Two widely held ideals, for instance, are that of the "consensus manager" who brings his team together through adroit persuasion to achieve a communally defined goal and of the "take-charge guy" whose vision and dynamic leadership galvanizes others into concerted action. Although one can observe aspects of these and of many other managerial styles in any hierarchy, such images, popular among managers themselves, are fictions of a sort that conceal the essential political and personal problems that managers face in making decisions.

Of course, large areas of managerial decision making are thoroughly routinized. Though routine decisions are not my principal concern, it is worth noting the highly rationalized context within which all managerial decisions are made. Historically, managers have been the architects and the directors of the rationalization of the modern workplace. As a group, at least at the lower and middle levels of organizational hierarchies, managers have been subject to the same discipline, systems of control and evaluation, and fragmentation of discretionary judgment that they have imposed on others. Many lower echelon managers see themselves as little more than highly paid clerks. Such routinization characteristically is devoid of substantive critical evaluation. I refer here to what Max Weber and later Karl Mannheim respectively called formal or functional rationality, that is, activity consciously planned and calculated to attain some goal, any goal.[1] Weber and Mannheim distinguished functional

75

rationality from substantive rationality. The latter refers to a critical reasoned reflectiveness with which one assesses and evaluates particular goals themselves and which guides one's decisions. In bureaucratic settings, which are institutionalized paradigms of functional rationality, technique and procedure tend to become ascendant over substantive reflection about organizational goals, at least among lower and middle-level managers, where, of course, one is expected to implement policy rather than fashion it or much less criticize it. Even at higher levels of management, one sees ample evidence of an overriding emphasis on technique rather than on critical reasoning. In Alchemy Inc., to take but one example, high-level managers were recently given a handbook called "Procedures for Creativity in Management." Moreover, scientific theories of decision making, often highly specified step-by-step procedures, are the staple of administrative science, business school curricula, and management consultant programs. These theories provide managers with a whole range of conceptual tools—cost/benefit analysis, risk/benefit analysis, several measures to calculate capital utilization as well as profit, and so on—that purport to "take the black magic out of management" and routinize administration. It is worth noting that even managers who are skeptical about the efficacy of such measures are among the principal consumers of such techniques and of analytical devices of every sort. In trying to come to grips with what seem at times to be incalculable, irrational forces, one must be willing to use whatever tools are at hand. Moreover, in an increasingly professionalized managerial environment, to eschew a vocabulary of rationality or the opportunity to routinize decisions when possible, can only make one vulnerable to the charge of "managing by the seat of the pants."

All of this, of course, is complicated by the difficulties of assessing to what extent functionally rational devices actually are used in making decisions, particularly by higher-ups. Vocabularies of rationality are always invoked to cloak decisions, particularly those that might seem impulsive when judged by other standards. The CEO of Covenant Corporation, for instance, sold the sporting goods business from one of his operating companies to the president of that company and some associates in a leveraged buyout. The sale surprised many people since at the time the business was the only profitable operation in that particular operating company and there were strong expectations for its long-term growth. Most likely, according to some managers, the corporation was just not big enough to hold two egos as large and bruising as those of the president and the CEO. However, the official reason was that sporting goods, being a consumer business, did not fit the "strategic profile" of the corporation as a whole. Similarly, Covenant's CEO sold large tracts of land with valuable minerals at dumbfoundingly low prices. The CEO and his aides said that Covenant simply did not have the experience to mine these minerals efficiently, a self-evident fact from the low profit rate of the business. In all likelihood, according to a manager close to the situation, the CEO, a man with a financial bent and a ready eye for the quick paper deal, felt so uncomfortable with the exigencies of mining these minerals that he ignored the fact that the prices the corporation was getting for the minerals had been negotiated forty years earlier. Such impulsiveness and indeed, one might say from a certain perspective, irrationality, is, of course, always justified in rational and reasonable terms. It is so commonplace in the corporate world that many managers expect whatever ordered processes they do erect to be subverted or overturned by executive fiat, masquerading, of course, as an established bureaucratic procedure or considered judgment.

Despite such capriciousness and the ambiguity it creates, many managerial decisions are routine ones based on well-established and generally agreed upon procedures. For the most part, these kinds of decisions do not pose problems for managers. But, whenever nonroutine matters, or problems for which there are no specified procedures, or questions that involve evaluative judgments are at issue, managers' behavior and perspective change markedly. In such cases, managers' essential problem is how to make things turn out the way they are supposed to, that is, as defined or expected by their bosses.

A middle-level designer in Weft Corporation's fashion business provides a rudimentary but instructive example of this dynamic at work. She says:

You know that old saying: "Success has many parents; failure is an orphan"? Well, that describes decision making. A lot of people don't want to make a commitment, at least publicly. This is a widespread problem. They can't make judgments. They stand around and wait for everybody else's reaction. Let me tell you a story which perfectly illustrates this. There was a [museum] collection coming, the [Arctic] collection, and there was a great deal of interest among designers in [Arctic] things. My own feeling was that it wouldn't sell but I also recognized that everybody wanted to do it. But in this case, [our] design department was spared the trouble. There was an independent designer who had access to our president and he showed him a collection of [Arctic] designs. There were two things wrong: (1) it was too early because the collection hadn't hit town yet; (2) more important, the designs themselves were *horrible*. Anyway, [the collection] was shown in a room with everything spread out on a large table. I was called down to this room which was crowded with about nine people from the company who had seen the designs. I looked at this display and instantly hated them. I was asked what I thought but before I could open my mouth, people were jumping up and down clapping the designer on the back and so on. They had already decided to do it because the president had loved it. Of course, the whole affair was a total failure. The point is that in making decisions, people look *up* and look *around*. They rely on others, not because of inexperience, but because of fear of failure. They look up and look to others before they take any plunges.

Looking up and looking around becomes particularly crucial when managers face what they call "gut decisions," that is, decisions that involve big money, public exposure, or significant effects on one's organization. The term probably derives from the gut-wrenching anxiety that such troublesome decisions cause. At all but the highest levels of both Covenant Corporation and Weft Corporation, and frequently there as well, the actual rules for making gut decisions are quite different from managerial theories or rhetoric about decision making. An upper-middle level manager explains:

> There's a tremendous emphasis put on decision making here and in business in general. But decision making is not an individual process. We have training programs to teach people how to manage, we have courses, and all the guys know the rhetoric and they know they have to repeat it. But all these things have no relationship to the way they actually manage or make decisions. The basic principles of decision making in this organization and probably any organization are: (1) avoid making any decision if at all possible; (2) if a decision has to be made, involve as many people as you can so that, if things go south, you're able to point in as many directions as possible.

Decision-making paralysis is, predictably enough, most common at the middle levels. A lawyer talks about the difficulty he has in extracting decisions from the managers he advises:

> It's tough for people to make decisions. Like today, I needed a decision from a business guy involving $200,000 and he just didn't want to make the decision. It involved a claim from another company. They claimed that a certain clause in the contract that we have with them is unfair to a partner of theirs and that it is costing them money and that to be equitable we owed them 200 grand. I reviewed the contract and checked with a couple of other lawyers and decided that we didn't owe them a dime. It was a pretty straightforward case in our view. But it's not our decision to make so we went to the proper business guy and he didn't want to decide. So we said we need a decision and we would have to go to the next highest guy, his boss, and get it. He said: "No, no, don't do that, because he'll send it back to me." And he wanted us to send it to some other guy, a counterpart of his in a business area that isn't even related. He felt uncomfortable about making the decision because of the amount of money involved. Also, he was afraid of making a mistake. And he was afraid of impacting others in areas he couldn't even see. Now, clearly, he should have just taken the decision up to his boss. But people don't want to do that. People have a very hard time making decisions and there's no question that this guy had the *authority* to make this decision. You see this sort of thing all the time. If you just walk around and look at people's desks, you'll see them piled with paper and that's an indication of their paralysis.

Senior managers are generally better at making decisions precisely because their positions allow them to establish the evaluative frameworks against which their choices will be measured. But even they evince the same kind of paralysis if they sense trouble or if their purported autonomy is really a mirage. For example, a financial planning manager, in discussing one of the cycles of financial commitment making in Alchemy Inc. when Smith was still in power, describes how even very high-ranking managers look up and look around:

> People are fearful to make decisions on their own, and that goes all the way up to [the president, Smith]. [The CEO] says that he wants [a] 10 percent reduction in administrative costs and there's no question that [Smith] will do that. But all the way up to [Smith], everybody hedges and waits to see what he wants. And then [Smith] in turn waits to see what [the CEO] wants.

> People try to cover themselves. They avoid putting things clearly in writing. They try to make group decisions so that responsibility is not always clearly defined. This is obvious to me in the planning process; and all the plans end up on my desk. [Smith] looks for decisions from the vice-president and general manager levels and the decisions are never forthcoming. I've been in any number of meetings where [Smith] hears out what business management was presenting and then relies on their recommendations up to the point where he had to go to [the CEO]. But [the CEO] says that that is not good enough and then [Smith] had to go back and make some decisions about what to do. The business people would present something and wait for a decision from [Smith], but no decision would be forthcoming. Then [Smith] would go to [the CEO] and get his own signals and then he would come back to the business people. There's no question that [the CEO] centralizes authority and that he makes the decisions. He has [Smith] over in the main building all the time to review matters.

Two aspects of looking up and looking around deserve particular, though brief, mention. First, the social psychology of the phenomenon is rooted in the pervasive social uncertainty of the organization. Managers' sense of organizational contingency, of authoritative capriciousness, and of the lack of firm connections between work and reward lead many to doubt whatever abilities they may actually have. Many managers live in constant fear, in one manager's words, of "being found out," of not measuring up to the expectations in their social world. An upper-middle manager explains:

> There's a lot of it [fear and anxiety]. To a large degree it's because people are more honest with themselves than you might believe. People know their own shortcomings. They know when they're over their heads. A lot of people are sitting in jobs that they know are bigger than they should be in. But they can't admit that in public and, at still another level, to themselves. The organizational push for advancement produces many people who get in over their heads and don't know

what they are doing. And they are very fearful of making a mistake and this leads to all sorts of personal disloyalty. But people know their capabilities and know that they are on thin ice. And they know that if they make mistakes, it will cost them dearly. So there's no honesty in our daily interaction and there's doubt about our abilities. The two go together.

Of course, one must never betray such uncertainty to others. Here the premium on self-control comes into play and many a manager's life becomes a struggle to keep one's nerve and appear calm and cool in the bargain. Making a decision, or standing by a decision once made, exposes carefully nurtured images of competence and know-how to the judgments of others, particularly of one's superiors. As a result, many managers become extremely adept at sidestepping decisions altogether and shrugging off responsibility, all the while projecting an air of command, authority, and decisiveness, leaving those who actually do decide to carry the ball alone in the open field.

Second, aspects of the structure of bureaucratic work itself prompt managers to look up and look around. I shall mention here only a nonobvious and somewhat paradoxical influence. Bureaucracy breaks work into pieces and, in the process, the knowledge required and conferred by each piece of work. Generally speaking, only managers with a "need to know" something in order to complete their own work are privy to certain crucial details of decisions in other business areas. Of course, rumors, gossip, and the actual trading of secrets within alliances mean that such admonitions are often more honored in the breach than in the keeping; moreover, an adroit manager who "keeps his ear to the ground" can pick up enough details from various sources to piece together a coherent picture of events when such fragments are coupled with cognitive maps. However, even when such knowledge is possessed, and known to be possessed, organizational protocol usually demands that it be concealed behind public faces of discreet unconcern. Such a demand for secrecy or at least its appearance separates managers emotionally, except for shared confidences between trusted friends or allies, but it actually provides an important stimulus to link them socially. When a manager gets into a difficult situation that demands a hard decision, even when he knows that others are fully aware of his decision, he must actively involve them in his problems if he is to hope for their support later. Committees thus reduce the plausibility of "deniability" although, of course, when things go wrong, instant amnesia always seems to become a widespread malady.

Decisions involving huge outlays of capital are almost always classic gut decisions; they involve risky, inherently ambiguous judgments between unclear alternatives. In mature industries, like textiles and chemicals, managers are regularly faced with troubling reinvestment decisions. An upper-middle level manager in Weft Corporation discusses the complexities of such choices:

A particular problem for our industry is that the textile machinery is simply not developed fast enough, so that the technology in process hasn't developed fast enough to make old equipment economically obsolete. Technically yes, but economically no. We are such a mature industry. Even though you can up the speed of the looms, you don't necessarily change the cost enough to make it economical. You also have to guess about the long-term economic value of the machines themselves. So you're faced with a dilemma. There's no question that the new equipment helps in other ways. It's quieter; it makes it easier to recruit people to work the machines; it's helped the industry improve its image problem; it doesn't make seconds; the machine is probably worth more to you in the future; and, of course, it's hard to compete with other companies if they had had these machines and we didn't. Now in [one] plant, we're replacing the older looms with the newer air-jet looms. In the sewing plant, we now have a sheet folder. Now there's an interesting contrast for you to see the problem between choosing different types of machinery. Now there's no question that we should have bought the sheet hemmers. And we did. You get the price and it's clear you ought to buy those machines. Because that's a *technology that's still in its infancy.* And you have to buy the machines to keep pace with your competitors. But then you get to the question of replacing your basic machinery—your looms, your spinning equipment and so on—and the issue is not the machinery. New machinery is not the issue. The issue is how much labor cost per unit of production will there be on the new machinery versus the old. That's the key issue because that's the meaning of productivity. It's not economically justifiable as yet for us to replace things like looms. There's another issue here. There is a point when old looms will simply up and die on you. How do you determine when to put money back into old looms, or to buy new looms, or to put the money into another business altogether?

Numerical measures and other seemingly sophisticated analytical tools can only be "guideposts" in making such choices. Satisfactory rates of return are socially determined; they vary from industry to industry, indeed, from firm to firm, and involve complicated assessments of competitors' strategies, actual, possible, or pending regulation, possible alternative investments, and, most important, key managers' determinations of what levels of return are desirable, acceptable, and defensible. Since, as described earlier, credit flows up and details get pushed down in corporate hierarchies, managers at the middle and upper-middle levels are often left to sort out extremely complicated questions about technology, investment, and their bosses' desires and intentions.

Consider, for instance, the case of a large coking plant of the chemical company. Coke making requires a gigantic battery to cook the coke slowly and evenly for long periods; the battery is the most important piece of capital equipment in a coking plant. In 1975, the plant's battery showed signs of weakening and certain managers at corporate headquarters had to decide whether to invest $6 million to restore the battery to top form. Clearly, because of the amount of money involved, this was a gut decision.

No decision was made. The CEO had sent the word out to defer all unnecessary capital expenditures to give the corporation cash reserves for other investments. So the managers allocated small amounts of money to patch the battery up until 1979, when it collapsed entirely. This brought the company into a breach of contract with a steel producer and into violation of various Environmental Protection Agency (EPA) pollution regulations. The total bill, including lawsuits and now federally mandated repairs to the battery, exceeded $100 million. I have heard figures as high as $150 million, but because of "creative accounting," no one is sure of the exact amount.

This simple but very typical example gets to the heart of how decision making is intertwined with a company's authority structure and advancement patterns. As Alchemy managers see it, the decisions facing them in 1975 and 1979 were crucially different. Had they acted decisively in 1975—in hindsight, the only substantively rational course—they would have salvaged the battery and saved their corporation millions of dollars in the long run.

In the short run, however, since even seemingly rational decisions are subject to widely varying interpretations, particularly decisions that run counter to a CEO's stated objectives, they would have been taking serious personal risks in restoring the battery. What is more, their political networks might have unraveled, leaving them vulnerable to attack. They chose short-term safety over long-term gain.

American managers seem regularly to look to the short term rather than the long run. There are several reasons for this. First, in the last few decades, there has been an ascendancy of professional managers in the corporate world whose habit of mind, honed by MBA programs, scores of managerial seminars, and a voluminous and ever-growing literature, stresses the quick turnaround of ailing businesses, deal-making both to unload businesses slow to respond to such ministrations and to acquire "winners," and, of course, the concomitant rapid prospering of one's own career. The training of professional managers increasingly focuses in the main on the techniques of financial wizardry—for example, leveraged buyouts, arbitrage, stock protection and stock kiting—and on quantitative measures of organizational progress. The latter are conceptual tools, the most important purpose of which is to put one on the defensible, high ground of rationality in explaining economic choices in public forums. Many of these tools reflect and illustrate the short-term mentality that characterizes most managerial training. Consider, for example, one basic analytical technique, "discounted cash flow rate of return." This measure determines the cost of capital and the rate of return over and above the cost of capital; it stresses working in the short term, even when one is planning for the long term. Money anticipated for later years is discounted because, due to expected inflation, it simply will not be worth as much as money in the present. Similarly, accounting systems that place a premium on bare-bones inventory reflect the same pressure for short-run profit maximization. For instance, at Covenant Corporation the story is told about a plant that produced a useful by-product at no extra cost. One simply had to store it until it was needed for other internal operations. Covenant, however, works with an accounting system that considers by-products as inventory; moreover, inventory counts against one at the end of a fiscal year. In order to cut costs, managers decided to throw out the by-product at the end of a financial cycle. But a sudden shortage of the material trebled its cost two months later. To service their own operations, managers had to go hat in hand to their competitors to buy the material at the premium prices.

Further, management training today gives little or no time to production management, a lament heard constantly at the lower reaches of management, particularly from "the guys in the trenches" at the plants. As it happens, production is precisely the nexus of the whole economic process where managers try to harness technology and labor to produce value. The growing dominance of new professional managers has helped emphasize the already existing corporate premium on quick returns. In the process, it has placed a new premium on fast deals and on money made in paper transactions rather than on the arduous and necessarily long-term task of taking material out of the ground and creating wealth. Within such a framework, plants and the whole production process become, as one manager notes, "a bother," and managers who work in production get thought of as "necessary but boring."

The troubled and troubling state of the American economy in the last several years has accelerated this development. When, in particular, high rates of inflation and high interest rates coincide, a common enough recent phenomenon, money in hand for quick investment or for short-term parking in financial instruments simply becomes worth more than money down the road. Moreover, the capital markets are increasingly dominated by big institutional investors—among them, large corporations, the insurance companies, the investment funds, and the brokerage houses—whose "quick in, quick out" philosophy wreaks havoc with corporate stocks. This sets the stage for financial sharpshooters who, in takeover strategies, buy large chunks of a company's stock at devalued prices only to be "greenmailed" (persuaded with financial inducements) by the target company's management into surrendering these blocks of holdings at premium prices. In such unsettled times, where virtually any large corporation could become a takeover target, managers feel that they have to keep their companies' stock properly valued. As it happens, the markets honor only short-term gains.

A second reason for managers' short-term perspective is the structure and pace of managerial work itself. Managers' days are punctuated by quick huddles and endless meetings; the reading and dictation of terse one-page memoranda, devoid of nuance; the scanning of fluctuating market reports; "brainstorming" sessions to surface bright ideas; listening to the presentations of line subordinates about output, productivity, or marketing, or those of staff about suggested guidelines for corporate policies; talking to lawyers about the impact of existing or projected regulation; evaluating the work of subordinates; buttonholing or being buttonholed by other managers for a word of advice or warning or simply to pass the time of day; and finally, constant phone calls. Each call, the higher up one goes, usually represents some problem that needs to be addressed. Within such a context of events that seem to be rapidly moving, issues do not "come at" managers in any integrated, coherent way, but rather in piecemeal fashion. Bits and fragments of an issue surface through the reports of subordinates who, of course, are always under pressure to put things in a good light; actions are often taken on an ad hoc basis to address a suddenly pressing aspect of a larger problem but only rarely, usually when matters come to a boiling point, are issues focused on in a complete, integrated way. The very consciousness of managers gets fragmented at work. Fragmentation of consciousness makes the history and structural roots of problems unimportant and therefore long-term solutions unlikely. One plans for the future, of course, but the planning itself is highly standardized and ritualized and subject to precipitous changes should exigencies force one to cast aside old assumptions. Instead, one focuses attention on important problems of the moment that must be solved. Since these are always plentiful, they justify postponing less pressing concerns. Of course, managers know at one level of their consciousness that today's minor issues can quickly become tomorrow's major crises, but the pressure for annual, quarterly, monthly, daily, and even hourly "results," that is, measurable progress plausibly attributed to one's own efforts, crowds out reflection about the future. An upper-middle manager at Alchemy Inc. recalls, for instance, his days as a plant manager when his boss at company headquarters phoned him every three hours to see how many tons of soda ash had been produced in the interval.

This goes to the heart of the problem. Managers think in the short run because they are evaluated by both their superiors and peers on their short-term results. Those who are not seen to be producing requisite short-run gains come to be thought of as embarrassing liabilities. Of course, past work gets downgraded in such a process. The old saw, still heard frequently today, "I know what you did for me yesterday, but what have you done for me lately?" is more than a tired garment district salesman's joke. It accurately reflects the widespread amnesia among managers about others' past accomplishments, however notable, and points to the probationary crucibles at the core of managerial life. Managers feel that if they do not survive the short run, the long run hardly matters, and one can only buy time for the future by attending to short-term goals. As one manager says: "Our horizon is today's lunch."

Within such a context, managers know that even farsighted, correct decisions can shorten promising careers. A manager at Weft Corporation reflects:

> People are always calculating how others will see the decisions that they make. They are always asking: "What are the consequences of this decision?" They know that they have to gauge not just the external . . . market consequences of a decision, but the internal political consequences. And sometimes you can make the right market decision, but it can be the wrong political decision.

This explains why the chemical company managers kept putting off a decision about major reinvestment. After the battery collapsed in 1979, however, the decision facing them was simple and posed little risk. The corporation had to meet its legal obligations; also, it had either to repair the battery the way the EPA demanded or shut down the plant and lose several hundred million dollars. Since there were no real choices, everyone could agree on a course of action because everyone could appeal to inevitability. This is the nub of managerial decision making. As one manager says:

> Decisions are made only when they are inevitable. To make a decision ahead of the time it *has* to be made risks political catastrophe. People can always interpret the decision as an unwise one even if it seems to be correct on other grounds.

When a decision is inevitable, managers say, "The decision made itself." Diffusion of responsibility, in the case of the coke battery by procrastinating until total crisis voided real choices, is intrinsic to organizational life because the real issue in most gut decisions is: Who is going to get blamed if things go wrong?

II

There is no more feared hour in the corporate world than "blame-time." Somewhere, there is a cartoon of President Richard Nixon saying: "I accept all of the responsibility, but none of the blame." Blame is quite different from responsibility. To blame someone is to injure him verbally in public; in large organizations where one's image is crucial to one's "credibility" and therefore one's influence, this poses the most serious sort of threat. For managers, blame—like failure—has little to do with the actual merits of a case; it is a matter of social definition, that is, of public perception of having failed or, more usually, of being associated with a failure, a perception backed or at least tacitly countenanced by authority. Authorities can, of course, also deflect, mitigate, or preempt altogether blame otherwise attributable to favored subordinates by assuming "complete responsibility" even when they did not have a direct hand in what went wrong. As a general rule, when blame is allocated, it is those who are or become politically vulnerable or expendable, who become "patsies," who get "set up" or "hung out to dry" and become blamable.

There are different kinds of blame. Being a "fall guy," that is, "taking the rap" or "taking the heat" for others' decisions or mistakes is probably the most common kind of blame in big organizations. The meaning of being a fall guy depends entirely, of course, on whether acceptance of blame is voluntary or involuntary. Managers recognize that sometimes subordinates might be called upon to "take a fall" without complaint in order to protect one's boss and senior associates. A high-ranking official in Covenant Corporation says:

> Well, we joke about this all the time.... I've often thought that we should appoint a position entitled Chief Fall Guy. Joking, of course. But it would be a good idea. He would be well-paid; plenty of benefits. And if things go wrong, he would go to jail or whatever, and his family would be provided for.

Given the proper assurances and assumptions, acceptance of blame can be an exercise in loyalty, although it is never without risk.

But the more frequent case is when those with the power to do so foist or allow blame to fall on unwary or inexperienced underlings. They do so either to cover up their own mistakes, or to extricate themselves from potentially embarrassing or politically untenable situations. Consider, for instance, the story of Green, a new marketing manager in Alchemy Inc.'s photochemical line. After prolonged discussions at all relevant levels of management, company managers decided to raise photochemical prices substantially. Green was given the task of explaining to the company's largest customer of photochemicals, a major producer of film and developing equipment, the sad necessity of the increase. However, executives at the film company, utilizing personal contacts made over a number of years, went over Green's head all the way to Alchemy's president, suggesting to him that unless the price increase were rescinded, it might be necessary to end many happy years of association. The president, of course, had approved the decision to raise prices but he sent down an edict to drop the increase. None of Green's bosses intervened to protect him. In fact, when the customer was told that an unfortunate mistake had been made, Green's overeagerness and inexperience were cited as the reasons. Certainly, no one at the film company believed such a story, but this is not the point. Instead, Green's supposed naiveté became an acceptable formula, part of a vocabulary of excuses, to smooth a ruffled business relationship and maintain the public image of senior officials.

The most feared situation is to end up inadvertently in the wrong place at the wrong time and get blamed. Yet this is exactly what happens in a structure that systematically diffuses responsibility. It is because managers fear blame-time that they diffuse responsibility; however, such diffusion inevitably means that someone, somewhere is going to become a scapegoat when things go wrong. For instance, as in most large corporations, it is customary for Alchemy executives to take periodic tours of production facilities accompanied by a retinue of staff. Such "flying circuses," as they are called, are not intended to do serious inspections of facilities, despite ostentatious displays of white-glove scrutiny, but rather to give ritualistic endorsements of work performed by local management, some of which, in fact, is often stimulated precisely by such occasions. After Alchemy executives had visited one plant and duly certified it, local workers, distressed by what they thought to be a sham, wrote to the Occupational Safety and Health Administration (OSHA) complaining of numerous health and safety violations that created, they claimed, unsafe conditions. After an inspection, OSHA did in fact cite the company for violations. The story hit the local papers and caused unfavorable publicity. A high-ranking executive, who himself had been part of the flying circus, tells what happened:

So they [top management] wrote the plant manager a check for a half million dollars to clean the place up. And the irony is that it later became a model. But the plant manager was fucking doomed. People would never forget that—especially since the same executives who had walked through the plant and blessed the place had control over his fate. So they scapegoated the plant manager.... The guy never recovered from that incident.

Nothing is supposed to go wrong to mar the illusion that authority is exercised properly.

Big corporations implicitly encourage scapegoating by their complete lack of any tracking system to trace responsibility. Whoever is currently and directly in charge of an area is responsible—that is, potentially blamable—for whatever goes wrong there, even if he has inherited others' mistakes. To take a minor example, one firm that I studied installed a new telephone system at great expense. The bugs in the system—lost calls, mistransfers, dead lines, and so on—were multiple and constant and continued to plague the company well after the installation. A year after the initial installation, a new executive vice-president was brought into the firm to handle internal management affairs; part of his responsibility became the coordination of office technology. One day not long after, in the course of a meeting of all the top executives, the CEO lost an important phone call; with phone still in hand, he turned to the executive vice-president and said: "Well, [Harry], *your* phone system has done it again."

A more serious example from the chemical company illustrates the process further. When the CEO of Covenant Corporation took office, he wanted to rid his capital accounts of all problematic financial drags. The corporation had been operating a storage depot for natural gas which it bought, stored, and then resold. Some years before the energy crisis, the company had entered into a long-term contract to supply gas to a buyer—call him Jones. At the time, this was a sound deal because it provided a steady market for a stably priced commodity.

When gas prices soared, the corporation was still bound to deliver gas to Jones at 20 cents per unit instead of the going market price of $2. The CEO ordered one of his subordinates to get rid of this albatross as expeditiously as possible. This was done by selling the operation to another party—call him Grey—with the agreement that Grey would continue to meet the contractual obligations to Jones. In return for Grey's assumption of these costly contracts, the corporation agreed to buy gas from Grey at grossly inflated prices to meet some of its own energy needs.

In effect, the CEO transferred the drag on his capital accounts to the company's operating expenses. This enabled him to project an aggressive, asset-reducing image to Wall Street. Several levels down the ladder, however, a new vice-president for a particular business in the chemical company found himself saddled with exorbitant operating costs when, during a reorganization, those plants purchasing gas from Grey at inflated prices came under his purview. The high costs helped to undercut the vice-president's division's earnings and thus to erode his position in the hierarchy. The origin of the situation did not matter. All that counted was that the vice-president's division was steadily losing big money. In the end, he resigned to "pursue new opportunities."

One might ask why top management does not institute codes or systems for tracking responsibility. Several plausible reasons come to mind. Changing assumptions and ever shifting personnel would unquestionably make tracking complex and difficult. Moreover, some companies, simply to free up storage space, do not retain any written records, except tax records, for more than ten years. For example, according to an environmental manager searching for requisite information to conform to the Superfund legislation on toxic waste disposal, the whole archives of Covenant Corporation in 1981 consisted of five or six cardboard boxes of materials. His search for chemical waste sites formerly used or operated by Alchemy Inc. revealed the names of 150 such locations, but no further information. For one 29-year period, there was only one document giving any details about the history of the company. On its face, this is somewhat curious since one of the hallmarks of classical bureaucracy is the written record. And, in fact, most big organizations do produce seas of paper, some of which—say, documents detailing the adherence to fair practices in personnel cases or documents verifying the use of stress-resistant steel in building nuclear plants—are crucially important in an increasingly litigious age. But, even where one can follow a paper trail, most written documents in the corporate world constitute simply official versions of reality that often bear little resemblance to the tangled, ambiguous, and verbally negotiated transactions that they purportedly represent. As a result, whatever meaningful tracking does take place occurs within managers' cognitive maps of their world, which, of course, are constantly changing and subject to retrospective interpretation and reinterpretation.

However, the example of the vice-president provides the clue to the more salient reason why top management does not institute tracking systems. An explicit system of tracking accountability would presumably have to apply, at least in the public forum, to top executives as well and would restrict their freedom. Bureaucracy expands the freedom of those on top precisely by giving them the power to restrict the freedom of those beneath.

Managers see what happened to the vice-president as completely capricious but completely understandable. They take for granted the absence of any tracking of responsibility. If anything, they blame the vice-president for not recognizing soon enough the dangers of the situation into which he was being drawn and for not preparing a defense—even perhaps finding a substitute scapegoat. At the same time, they realize that this sort of thing could easily happen to them.

When blame-time comes, managers' immediate reaction is, as they put it, to "CYA" or "cover your ass." A high-ranking executive says:

> The one statement that will paralyze a room is when some guy in authority says: "Now I'm not interested in a witch hunt but . . . ."
> When those words are uttered, the first instinct of people is to immediately hunker down and protect their own flanks.

At the middle levels of the corporation, CYA memos proliferate during a crisis, as managers who sense jeopardy try to "get their views on the record" or stake out defensible ground against opposition or construct plausible alibis. In fact, it is said that one can gauge the seriousness of an issue or the importance of a decision and its potential dangers by the amount of paper it generates.

Documentation can be useful in a CYA operation but only when authorities that count recognize the relevance of a document. In fact, higher authorities themselves frequently institutionalize CYA documentation to shield themselves in the public forum from any untoward or unwanted knowledge. For instance, Covenant Corporation's CEO circulates fully prepared, highly uniform and stylized draft letters, requiring only minor modifications, to all senior line and staff executives in all the operating companies of the conglomerate. These letters "assure" each executive in turn up the line that his subordinates have taken all appropriate steps to guarantee the corporation's conformance to environmental regulations. Assurance here, a staff member close to the operation points out, does not include alerting higher management in writing to potential or actual problems. Such devices seem particularly useful in deflecting and allocating blame but only when one has requisite authority and power. However, when real disaster strikes, the idea that paper protects anyone, at the middle levels in particular, is a vain and naive hope. As one executive says: "When things really go peanut butter, all the goddamn memos in the world are not going to help you."

What does matter when things go wrong is agility and political connections. One manager explains the kind of agility that is necessary:

> The good manager is always aware and always wary. He knows that he has to be able to point the finger at somebody when things go wrong. And he knows that someone can point the finger *at him* at any time. There's no accountability in the corporation. People don't want to hear about that shit. What you hope is that no one is after *your* ass. . . . You have to have the political wherewithal to know you're being set up. You have to be able to turn anything around and be able to point the finger at somebody else when they come after you.

He goes on to link this personal skill with the invaluable inclusion in a network of powerful allies:

> . . . [And] you need a Godfather. They have to know you. . . . You have to remember that you only get to explain things away *once*. When things get screwed up, you get *one* chance. That's why it's important for everybody to be in bed with everybody else. And if they don't like you from the start, you don't have a chance. Because when things go wrong, what people do is sit down and say—without saying it in so many words—look, our jobs are on the line. Let's make sure that it's not us who gets nailed.

Of course, a less agile individual or less powerful group might get nailed as a consequence, but managers do not concern themselves with this. The fundamental rule of corporate life is to protect oneself and, if possible, one's own.

III

Although managers see few defenses against being caught in the wrong place at the wrong time except constant wariness and perhaps being shrewd enough to declare the ineptitude of one's predecessor on first taking a job, they do see safeguards against suffering the consequences of their own errors. Most important, they can "outrun their mistakes" so that when blame-time arrives, the burden will fall on someone else. At the institutional level, the absence of any system for tracking responsibility here becomes crucial. A lawyer explains how this works in the sprawling bureaucracy of Covenant Corporation:

> I look at it this way. See, in a big bureaucracy like this, very few individual people can really change anything. It's like a big ant colony. I really believe that if most people didn't come to work, it wouldn't matter. You could come in one day a week and accomplish the absolutely necessary work. But the whole colony has significance; it's just the individual that doesn't count. Somewhere though some actions have to have significance. Now you see this at work with mistakes. You can make mistakes in the work you do and not suffer any consequences. For instance, I could negotiate a contract that might have a phrase that would trigger considerable harm to the company in the event of the occurrence of some set of circumstances. The chances are that no one would ever know. But if something did happen and the company got into trouble, and I had moved on from that job to another, it would never be traced to me. The problem would be that of the guy who presently has responsibility. And it would be his headache. There's no tracking system in the corporation.

Some managers argue that outrunning mistakes is the real meaning of "being on the fast track," the real key to managerial success. The same lawyer continues:

> In fact, one way of looking at success patterns in the corporation is that the people who are in high positions have never been in one place long enough for their problems to catch up with them. They outrun their mistakes. That's why to be successful in a business organization, you have to move quickly.

It is said that some managers move so quickly that "their feet never touch the ground." These women and mostly men usually have a great deal of energy and "dynamism" that draw others to themselves; with their articulateness and personal magnetism, they can "motivate" others and provide a galvanizing "vision" of the future. They are said to be like "skyrockets" or "shooting stars" or "sparklers" that light up the night sky. All big organizations feed off this kind of renewing energy. Sometimes such men and women seem "annointed," as managers say, predestined for great things.

Of course, many of these stars eventually fizzle and return to the dark obscurity of the middle level crowd out of which they burst. Some, in fact, "disappear in the night" because top managers come to see them, or something about them, as too much of a threat to their own established prerogatives. Another common way of clouding a star's luminosity is to assign him, with no fail-safe guarantees, to a trouble-prone area where big problems and perhaps big mistakes are hard to avoid. Those stars who are successful grasp more surely than others the nature of the complicated mirror game of corporate mobility—to move quickly but always to project an unthreatening and socially accommodating public face upward and, the point I want to stress here, to hit desired numbers without becoming involved in or associated with trouble.

One way to hit desired numbers is by squeezing the resources under one's control, and American corporations generally provide structural inducements to encourage and facilitate this. One can, of course, squeeze both people and equipment but I shall focus only on the latter here. Both Covenant Corporation and Weft Corporation, for instance, place a great premium on a division's or a subsidiary's return on assets (ROA); managers who can successfully squeeze assets are first in line, for instance, for the handsome rewards allotted through bonus programs. One good way for business managers to increase their ROA is to reduce assets while maintaining sales. Usually, managers will do everything they can to hold down expenditures in order to decrease the asset base at the end of a quarter or especially at the end of the fiscal year. The most common way of doing this is by deferring capital expenditures, everything from maintenance to innovative investments, as long as possible. Done over a short period, this is called "starving a plant"; done over a longer period, it is called "milking a plant." An upper-middle level manager in the chemical company discusses how the ethos of rapid mobility and the concomitant mobility panic among managers, short-term pressures, and the lack of tracking come together to produce strategies of milking:

We're judged on the short-term because everybody changes their jobs so frequently. As long as we have a system where I'm told that I am not going to be in a job for the long term, you're going to have this pressure. And you're not tracked from one job to the next, so you can milk your present situation and never have it pinned on you in the future. If we started doing poorly in [this business], I would do everything I could to make my group look good. Now you've got to understand what I'm saying. A plant that is not well maintained will fail in the short term, so you have to spend money there; a plant that has poorly trained people will fail today, so you have to spend money there. But you can still milk it. If a piece of fairly large capital equipment needs to be replaced—well, almost anything can be fixed and you can just keep patching things up, just putting absolutely no money at all into the business. Or you can just make an edict that will cut supplies by 25 percent, [things like] pumps, motors, tools, and so on. You run a risk because the plant could shut down. But there are always things you can do. My favorite things are not to replace my stores inventory and that shows up as direct profit on your balance sheet; not replace people who retire, and stretch everybody else out; cut down on overtime; cut working inventories to the bone. [You can also] lower the quality standards; you can get away with this in the short term because people will accept that for awhile, though in the long term people will stop buying from you. Another thing is to give less money in the paycheck, which is a stupid thing to do. What I mean is give less raise to the salaried people—instead of 10 percent, give 8 percent. That's small and foolish, but it will be done. You can really save a lot of money. In the chemical business, another way to do it is to let waste accumulate. Essentially, when I think of milking a business, I think of shutting off any capital expenditure and anything that is an expense. And you know what happens when you do that? The guy who comes into that mess is the one who gets blamed, not the guy who milked it.

It is important to note that such a philosophy of milking, where it occurs, can be idiosyncratic, but it is often part of an institutionalized and sanctioned management style. Milking was, for instance, standard practice in the old specialty chemicals division of Alchemy and, when that division triumphed in the "big purge" of 1979, milking became the norm throughout the company. Except for some well-maintained operations, usually run by survivors of the old process chemicals division who remained as managers of the same plants for many years, even brand new facilities began to show signs of weathering quickly. An environmental manager who travels around the country inspecting plants comments in 1982:

Just the other day I had to go out to [Utah] where we do [product Y]. This is supposed to be the flagship of our operations now. And you see signs of the same thing—girders rusting, pipes taken out of service and not replaced, poor housekeeping. And the place was only opened in 1979. I was shocked. But it's all part of the same old philosophy. See, when there's a high turnover of plant management, there's a natural selfishness. People want to make the system work *for themselves*. And when they get to the top, they can't criticize the system that got them there because they believe in the system and because they know that others know how they themselves got where they are. And if you let a plant go for five or six years, you can't afford to replace it, especially now with the cost of money. Each year, it gets harder and harder to repair a plant that has been let go.

Of course, the closer one is in the hierarchy to a business being milked, the greater the potential danger of being caught in a catastrophe and the more sure one has to be that one gets out in time. For this reason, managers feel that most milking, though not all, is done by those at the top of the hierarchy who are well removed and insulated from a local situation. An upper-middle level manager sketches a scenario:

> I don't think there are very many plants that are milked by people who are actually running them, I mean at the plant sites. Plants are milked by guys like [Smith, president of Alchemy Inc.]. He does that by controlling the purse strings and by putting money into where his future lies, that is, in the most profitable businesses. So the guy at the plant level may not even know he's being milked.
>
> Let's say that [Smith] wanted to milk my business [product X]. He would go to [his executive vice-president] and say: "Here's the situation. I want you to maximize cash flow. Be frugal. Be tight in all your business areas except [a favorite product]. Keep a special eye on [product X]; you need to watch that one. Cut the capital expenses there." As a matter of fact, he wouldn't even have to say "cut capital." He would just put pressure on him by saying: "Well, sales are down 50 percent; why aren't your expenses down 50 percent?" My boss will come to me, by the time it reaches him, and say: "Cut costs." It's as simple as that. There's no question that most milking comes from the top. Now it can also come from the bottom. It can be milked both ways in other words. But the key thing is that, if you do it from the bottom, you have to be sure to get out in time; otherwise the whole thing will come down around your ears.

A famous story is told in the chemical company about a young plant manager who was dismayed to find a very poorly maintained plant when he assumed his job. He put in a budget request to his bosses at company headquarters for a substantial amount of maintenance work. The request was politely declined. When he insisted on resubmitting his request, he suddenly became as obsolete as the plant that he wished to salvage would soon become.

It is worth noting in passing that sometimes the only way lower-level managers have to break out of such a squeeze is to rely on some external agency to make expenditures inevitable and therefore acceptable. A high-ranking staff person at Alchemy explains:

> Another scenario. The plant manager says that he needs $10 million in his capital budget this year. And he says here is what we will spend it on. And suppose that every plant is saying this and it comes up top-

side. You add it all up and it comes to $200 million. Someone topside says: "Well, you can only have $100 million." So it goes back down and you say to the plant manager: "You can't have $10 million; you can only have $5 million." Well, where is he going to cut? So the plant manager says: "Well, I have to do safety things, I have to fix this, and I have to do this. That means that I'll let this and this go because I don't have the money." In other words, he does what is immediately necessary to keep his operation together and lets the rest go. But suppose that the plant manager says that: "I need $10 million and I need it to fix the floor under the [major capital equipment] otherwise the floor might collapse." And his request is denied and cut down by half again and he's going to do what he needs to do to get by. But then OSHA comes in and says: "Fix that goddamn floor." Well, then he *has* to do it. It's out of his hands and nobody in the corporation can try to fuck around with him when he requests the money to fix the floor.

Even though OSHA or another agency might help managers cut the Gordian knots of corporate politics, it is, of course, imperative that any regulatory interference with the prerogatives of management be severely and loudly criticized. I shall return to these issues later.

Some managers become very adept at milking businesses and showing a consistent record of high returns. They move from one job to another in a company, always upward, rarely staying more than two years in any post. They may leave behind them deteriorating plants and unsafe working conditions or, say, in marketing areas where fixed assets are not at issue, depleted lines of credit and neglected lists of customers, but they know that if they move quickly enough, the blame will fall on others. The ideal situation, of course, is to end up in a position where one can fire one's successors for one's own previous mistakes. A top ranking official explains:

There is a real problem with the [return on assets] measure. If you are going to reward Mr. X on his yearly performance and part of it is his ROA, if you don't have a built-in reward for a longer term performance—say five years—well, you're asking for that guy to maximize his own gain at the expense of the operation over the long run. Most people have a tendency to short-term management. One thing that has always griped me is that Mr. X might take the short-term view and milk a business, or a bunch of them, and move from job to job to job. And meantime, Mr. Y comes in and inherits Mr. X's problems. And the guy who botched up earlier jobs ends up sitting on top overlooking guys who have inherited his own mistakes. There should be some comeuppance for that kind of thing, some penalty.

In fact, however, the manager who "takes the money and runs" is usually not penalized but rewarded and indeed given a license to move onto bigger mistakes. At the highest levels of a corporation, one can make even egregious mistakes with virtual impunity provided that they are not too numerous and that one does so with aplomb. When Smith headed the chemical company, he was persuaded by a bright, enthusiastic ally to make a deal to provide two other major rival chemical manufacturers with an intermediate substance used in making pesticides. Alchemy Inc. already had some capacity to make the substance and Smith got rival A to put up $7 million and rival B several million more—I have no exact figure—to expand plant space. The whole deal was contingent on performance, and, with rival A, subject to a time deadline. Smith assigned a trusted vice-president of engineering to oversee the building of the new plant and ordered him to keep costs low—between $15 and $18 million—so that the chemical company would put up as little money as possible. As a result, the plant was erected without a variety of features—valves, surge tanks, and drains—that would normally be included. As it happened, the plant would not function without these features. The cost of retrofitting the plant mounted quickly to $50 million. In the meantime, because of long delays, rival A withdrew its $7 million and turned elsewhere to satisfy its intermediate needs. When the plant finally did come on line, there was no real steady market for the product and the newly built capacity went into mothballs. Smith promoted the vice-president of engineering, a move that most managers saw as a "golden egg" (even when one makes horrible mistakes, one can prosper). For his own part, Smith acted as if the whole affair had never happened, let alone that he had played any role in it. At the very top of organizations, one does not so much continue to outrun mistakes as tough them out with sheer brazenness. In such ways, bureaucracies may be thought of, in C. Wright Mills's phrase, as vast systems of organized irresponsibility.

This ethos, this institutional logic that I have described, permeates the corporate world not just among managers but among workers as well. For instance, in Weft Corporation, one can see the same pattern of grasping the short-run gain among weavers that is often evident among managers. Weavers work on piece rate, getting paid for each yard of cloth their looms produce. Depending on the age, maintenance, and speed of her looms (75 percent of weavers are women), and on her own skill and experience, a single weaver might tend as many as fifty looms or as few as twenty-five. Weavers work in eight-hour shifts, and the looms, which are fully automated and monitored electronically, are in continuous use. The weaver's job is essentially to move back and forth between her looms trying to prevent loom "stops" and starting the looms up again when they do stop. Loom stops are the crucial index of quality control in a textile mill; any problems in the cotton, in the polyester, in the blending of the two fibers, in the production of yarn, in the "sizing" (the polyvinyl alcohol put on yarn to give it greater tensile strength) all show up at the point of cloth production in the weave room. In an eight-hour shift, the average loom will stop ten times even when it is running well. The new air-jet looms stop like any other loom; it is simply the nature of spun yarn to foul even the best machinery. There are about ten different categories of loom stops that weavers are trained to recognize, and each kind of stop takes a certain number of seconds to repair. When a weaver is unable to repair a stop, she shuts down the loom and flags a "fixer," the most skilled and highest ranking worker on the shop floor, who does the repair or basic maintenance necessary to get the loom working again. However, since weavers are paid by the piece and can make no gain from a loom out of service for repair or maintenance during their own shifts, weavers will tend to remedy stops in any way they can in order to keep their cloth production high, leaving the maintenance and repair of the machinery and the economic cost involved to another weaver on another shift. Supervisors and managers who are evaluated by a plant's overall weaving efficiency are thus forced to monitor the number of loom stops constantly in order to make sure that looms badly in need of repair or maintenance get proper attention. Whenever structural inducements place premiums on immediate personal gains, especially when mistakes are not penalized, there seems to be a sharp decline in the likelihood of men and women sacrificing their own interests for others, for their organizations, or least of all for the common weal.[2]

IV

Sometimes managers become hostages of sorts to this "take the money and run" ethos of short-term gains, outrunning mistakes, and leaving problems for others; the ethos subverts even the best attempts at exercising substantive rationality and can draw managers into disastrous situations. Consider, for instance, the case of Young who, after the "big purge" at Covenant Corporation in 1979, emerged as the general manager of a mature business area producing what I shall call chemical X, an extremely useful agent that has a variety of industrial as well as consumer applications. Covenant held the number two position in an oligopolistic domestic market for this product. All of the company's production facilities for chemical X were concentrated in one plant on a major waterway in [Ohio]; Young himself, of course, was based at corporate headquarters near a major metropolitan area in the East. The plant was old, dating back to the turn of the century, but it had been rebuilt twice since then, most recently in the early 1950s right before Covenant acquired the business.

Young's plant manager was Noll, a man who had fallen from a higher position in a previous purge but, it turned out, liked production work and had developed a reputation for aggressive hard-driving management in a series of assignments. It was said that Noll had milked and milked thoroughly every plant he ever supervised. One day, a story goes, he was accused of this in a public meeting by a vice-president who was then his superior. Noll is said to have responded with great boldness: "[Joe], how can you sit there and say that to me? How in the hell do you think you got to where you are and how do you think you stay there?" The matter was dropped because everyone present, including the vice-president, knew that Noll was right, that is, he was simply pointing out the institutional logic that they all live by. The vice-president had, in fact, broken a cardinal rule of managerial circles. An upper-middle level manager explains:

> The code is this: you milk the plants; rape the businesses; use other people and discard them; fuck any woman that is available, in sight, and under your control; and exercise authoritative prerogatives at will with subordinates and other lesser mortals who are completely out of your league in money and status. *But you also don't play holier than thou.* This last point is as important as all the others.

Managers feel that sermons have a somewhat hollow ring in back rooms.

Young too had benefited from Noll's willingness to do what was necessary to make chemical X a generous "cash cow" for Covenant. The business area regularly provided and was expected to continue to give about $8 million a year back to Covenant, and Young knew that as long as he could produce that kind of regular short-term return (about 18 percent on his assets), his star would burn bright at Covenant.

Young felt, however, that there were serious threats to the business which, if unaddressed, could undermine Covenant's number two market position even in the short run. Briefly, these were: the increasing difficulty and expense of disposing of a highly toxic, allegedly carcinogenic, solid waste because of complicated and unintegrated state regulations; pending OSHA regulations that might lower substantially the current standard of exposure to carcinogens in the workplace, significantly driving up production costs; and the rising cost of mineral Y, essential to the particular older production process of chemical X utilized by Covenant. Recent research had, in fact, begun to tie this older process utilizing mineral Y to the problem of carcinogenicity both in the workplace and in solid waste.

The other two major domestic producers and most major European competitors had already moved to the new "[mineral Y]-free" process, though they had done so only when building new plants, a tribute perhaps to the unforgiving nature of the technology necessary to produce chemical X. Young and his bosses decided that Covenant also had to adopt the new process to remain competitive, but building an entirely new plant was out of the question. For an investment calculated at about $4 million to buy some new equipment and to retrofit the rest of the plant for the mineral Y-free process, they felt that they could dramatically reduce their operating costs by eliminating the expense of mineral Y, by saving energy, and by reducing their solid wastes by about 40 percent and cleaning those that remained of suspected carcinogens as well, probably even saving the wastes for recycled use. Just as important, they could circumvent entirely any future problem with OSHA by eliminating the production process suspected of generating carcinogens. It was, Young said, "Chevrolet, mother, and apple pie all rolled into one package." After a successful laboratory experiment with the new process and a limited field experiment in one portion of the plant, the decision was made to move ahead. A crucial part of that decision was the choice, backed by research, engineering, and management, to deviate from the industrywide practice and to use what we may call here a static rather than a dynamic or continuous subprocess necessary to both drain and cool chemical X at a certain stage of its production. The continuous subprocess, used by everyone else making chemical X, would have brought the total bill for the plant conversion to about $8 million, and it was felt that an appropriations request for that amount would not be approved. In preparation for the switch to the mineral Y-free process, Noll was asked to run the plant harder than usual to build up inventory of chemical X so that Covenant would not lose its regular customers during the necessary shutdown.

The plant did shut down, and the necessary retrofitting and the installation of the mineral Y-free process were completed in early 1982. When, however, Young and his bosses pushed the button to begin production, one disaster after another began to occur. The static subprocess, though it had worked on a small experimental scale, simply did not function at the plant level. It caused, first of all, a severe backup of liquids at one end of the operation. The plant shifted rapidly from being a net water consumer to being in constant danger of spilling contaminated water into the local tributary. The whole plant had to be sandbagged to keep tainted water in. Moreover, the subprocess did not provide quick enough cooling of extremely hot materials so that a precipitate of yet another chemical was formed that encrusted loading cars. Young had to send in men with jackhammers to knock away the encrustation.

The plant was never able to reach a regularized steady-state condition—that is, some sort of equilibrium between the raw materials in the pipeline, the main processing of those materials, and the static subprocessing. Moreover, when the plant was briefly brought into a period of equilibrium, it became evident that the productive capacity was only half of that anticipated and simply could not pay for itself. In the meantime, Covenant had to buy chemical X from its competitors in order to resell it at a loss to its own customers. In the end, after extensive consultations, Young argued that the mineral Y-free process—by now widely known as the "[chemical X]-free process"—would not work in the [Ohio] plant and had to be abandoned. Covenant returned to its old process using mineral Y after losing about $27 million, although if one calculates profit losses over a few years as well, the real loss was closer to $50 million.

Of course, nobody wishes to be associated with such a catastrophe and, predictably enough, a circle of blame developed. The research and development people who had made the static subprocess work on an experimental scale said that there was no good reason why the process should not function and that the fault lay with the practical implementation of their ideas. The engineering people in turn castigated R & D for obviously ill-conceived research. Other managers blamed Young for not supervising more closely the extension of the experimental static subprocess to the rest of the plant. For his part, Young did not know what other safeguards he could have taken; he too blamed the R & D people for failing to appreciate how unforgiving some technology can be. But he also knew where the real blame would fall, although he tried to deflect it from himself by firing Noll. He says:

Well, I'm realistic about the consequences of this whole thing. . . . The fact is that it's affected my credibility. As a general manager, you can't escape the old "buck stops here" axiom. Nobody likes to lose. And I feel that I've lost and the business area has lost too. I feel that I'm tainted by it. . . . The damage has gone beyond the issue of my management of this business area. I think it's had an adverse impact on my career at [Covenant].·

One can surmise the deep anxiety, indeed, the psychological havoc that Young experienced during this whole period by contrasting his external behavior during the two interviews that I conducted with him. In August 1981, on the eve of the installation of the new equipment, Young was quietly ebullient, composed, and looked the interviewer straight in the eye. In November 1982, after almost a year of catastrophes, Young was visibly distressed and agitated, walking around his office picking up imaginary objects from the floor, staring at blank walls with his back to the interviewer, or gazing out the window with his hands shoved deeply in his pockets. His office seems to have become a cell and his behavior like that of a man awaiting sentence.

Only a few managers seemed able to go beyond the personal issue of blame and see what happened to Young in more structural terms. These managers attribute the catastrophe to Young's ignoring of the fundamental rules of the "take the money and run" ethos. An upper-middle manager close to the situation explains:

My own theory is that it was the plant itself that was let to run downhill and that no matter what they had put in there, it wouldn't have worked. Basically, [Noll] milked the plant and the plant would have run poorly in any event. He skimped on maintenance and concentrated on short-term profit. And he made money but he didn't keep the plant in shape to do *anything* with it. . . . Some guys, like [Noll], go into plants and because they cut costs, tighten things up, they become heroes. But the plant is being milked. The question is, does he know he's doing it? I'll bet you he thinks he is a plant man who is frugal. . . . It's easy to make money in the short term; you just don't spend money. And this is what happened . . . if the plant had been a well-oiled machine, a new program like this would have had a greater chance of success.

The same manager goes on to stress that he has no objection to milking under certain conditions:

[Milking] works well if [a guy] gets out in time. If a guy keeps moving, he can say, "Look, I ran this plant better than my predecessors." And people have to concede that. A lot of people do that. Then you get the guy who takes his place and tries to run things right and he has to spend a lot of money. And people look at the guy who was there before and they say: "Well, old [Noll] ran the plant well and he didn't have to spend any money like you're claiming you do."

I don't think there is anything wrong with milking a plant. As long as you know you're milking it. As long as you know you're going to run it for three or four years and then sell it to some unsuspecting fool. And you show him the papers on the plant and you don't tell him what money you haven't put back into the operation. But, one thing you don't do. You don't spend millions of dollars on new equipment if you're milking a plant. That's what happened in [Ohio].

Young tried to position his business for the future while continuing to meet short-run profit pressures. This is a difficult task since the institutional logic that the pressure for short-run results sets in motion, while lucrative for a time, undercuts the possibilities of lasting achievement, however reasonably planned. Within the institutional logic of the corporation, Young's fatal error was pausing on the track, in the middle of the race, and thinking about the future. Instead of outrunning his mistakes, they overran him.

5

Drawing Lines

The moral ethos of managerial circles emerges directly out of the social context that I have described. It is an ethos most notable for its lack of fixedness. In the welter of practical affairs in the corporate world, morality does not emerge from some set of internally held convictions or principles, but rather from ongoing albeit changing relationships with some person, some coterie, some social network, some clique that matters to a person. Since these relationships are always multiple, contingent, and in flux, managerial moralities are always situational, always relative. Business bureaucracies thus place a great premium on the virtue of "flexibility," as it is called, and in this chapter and the next, I shall explore the key features of this central characteristic. I shall begin by examining the personal moral dilemmas of two managers.

Consider, for example, the case of White, a health professional in 1981 with some supervisory responsibilities in the corporate headquarters of Weft Corporation. White, who had extensive graduate training in audiology, had principal responsibility for the company's hearing conservation program. As it happens, noise is inescapable in the textile industry because its basic technology, in particular the loom and spinning equipment, cannot operate without making a certain amount of noise. Old shuttle looms, many of which have been in continuous operation since World War I, are extremely noisy, usually creating a decibel level of 95–105 dB(A), that is, decibels measured on the "A" scale of a sound level meter rather than on the older "C" scale,[1] in a weave room of fifty looms. It is important to note that the intensity of sound doubles with every three dB increase. Even with new air-jet shuttleless looms to which the textile industry is slowly moving because of their greater efficiency and lower rate of second-grade cloth, decibel readings in weave rooms still reach between 93–94 dB(A). Spinning rooms with old equipment register 96 dB(A); with the newer equipment that was developed to produce better, more durable yarn, the readings are still at 89 dB(A). In 1981, the Occupational Safety and Health Administration (OSHA) promulgated an amendment to its occupational noise standard specifying that workers whose noise exposure exceeded an eight-hour time-weighted average of 85 dB must be included in a hearing conservation program. Along with other industries, the textile manufacturers opposed the amendment; the industry was, in fact, unhappy with the existing standard which set the maximum eight-hour time-weighted average at 90 dB.

White disagreed with his industry and strongly supported the OSHA hearing amendment that would lower the critical threshold 5 dB. White's opinion, strongly endorsed professionally, was that the danger to workers rested in the way hearing loss occurs with continual exposure to noise at 90 dB and above; in his view, prolonged exposure even at 85 dB was risky. In order to function socially, people need to be able to hear in the frequency range of 300 to 3,400 "hertz" (Hz). Without that frequency range, conversational ability becomes severely impaired. However, prolonged exposure to high levels of noise, such as one experiences in industrial work in textiles, erodes people's hearing at higher frequency levels first—at between 3,500 to 6,000 Hz. A person first begins to lose his ability to perceive higher frequency speech sounds beginning with the fricative consonants; further prolonged exposure spreads the damage to lower frequency ranges. People come to have problems interpreting sounds and in gauging the intensity and loudness of sounds. The crucial issue is that noise-induced hearing loss occurs gradually and is not felt until damage is irreversible and becomes evident late in life. Hearing aids can only amplify sounds, not clarify indistinct sounds. With heavy impairment, older people sink into isolation and incommunicability in their retirement.

Within this general context, White's work conducting and analyzing the audiograms required by OSHA's existing standard on noise presented him with what he saw as a serious dilemma. In analyzing incidence data from a representative plant, and by extrapolating to the rest of the firm's mills, White discovered that 12 percent of all greige mill workers had already suffered hearing loss severe enough to be immediately compensable under state law for as much as $3.5 to $5.7 million. This, however, was only the thunder before a summer storm. Another 63 percent of greige mill workers had already suffered substantial, though not yet compensable, damage that could only worsen the longer they stayed in the industry. In brief, three-quarters of all the greige mill workers in Weft Corporation (more than 10,000 employees) had already suffered significant hearing loss. As it happens, the hearing compensation law in the state at the time allowed workers to make claims for hearing loss only up to two years after leaving employment. The textile industry in the state was, in fact, fighting to have this law reinterpreted to allow claims only while workers were still employed. (As I have already mentioned, severe hearing loss that might impair social functioning becomes evident principally in workers' later years.)

White was disturbed by the extent of the damage indicated by his data. He saw only one solution to the problem, namely to make the hearing conservation program already mandated by OSHA a vital force in the greige mills. This meant strictly enforcing workers' use of hearing protection—that is, earplugs—while motivating both supervisors and workers alike with extensive and regular educational programs on the dangers of hearing loss. Engineering controls are almost impossible to implement on this issue. The use of physical space in what is essentially a machine tending industry, where each worker, for instance, in weaving or spinning tends a large number of machines, obviates any practical and reasonably affordable engineering remedies. Even if the large spaces presently used could be broken up into smaller units, a step that would completely alter the social organization of work, this would baffle noise only in the far field of sound, not in the near field where workers tend individual machines. Moreover, in the weave rooms where the noise problem is greatest, the extensive and difficult training of weavers (in Weft Corporation, this lasts thirteen weeks with only a 32 percent success rate) makes job rotation impractical. White wrote a report detailing his analysis of the data collected and proposing the extensive and regular educational programs he felt were necessary. For White, both because of his professional training and because of his personal religious background (he had been in a seminary for some years), this was a clear moral issue and he felt that he had to act as the conscience of the company.

White's report and his suggestions did not fare well. First of all, White stood at the margin of the intricate fealty and patronage structure of his organization. He was unlucky in his boss, the medical director of the company. The latter was an older man who had completed a long career in the military and then had begun a second life with the textile company, a relatively common pattern for company doctors in southern textile firms. The director saw himself as a guardian of the textile industry's interests against increasingly vociferous and hostile critics. For him, the hearing issue, like the cotton dust problem, was simple. If workers did not smoke cigarettes, he argued, they would not have pulmonary disorders such as the alleged disease byssinosis; if they wore earplugs, they would not go deaf. In fact, the director joked about the imminent formation of a "Brown Ear Association." The director took White's report and rewrote it extensively to emphasize the financial liability of the company, while only mentioning the desirability of more educational programs. White was caught in a fealty relationship with all of its obligations—especially those of protocol—but with little likelihood of support for his work or of future rewards. Nor had White been adopted by a powerful godfather higher in the organization who could fight for him in forums to which White himself had no access. In White's case, the logical patron would have been his boss's boss, the senior vice-president for human resources, who was known to be favored by the new CEO and, as things have turned out, destined for much higher things. However, it was almost certainly the senior vice-president who buried even the recast report on the hearing issue and with it any opportunity that White might have had for a patron-client relationship with him.

White never heard about the report from his superiors again. It took him a while to understand that he was opposed by powerful interests rooted in the occupational group structure of the company. The group of top executives, first of all, had two concerns. First, the company faced potentially enormous liability costs if those workers who were already severely damaged were fully alerted to their hearing problems; there was also the even greater liability threat of the large reservoir of workers whose hearing was steadily worsening to the compensable level each day should they also fully grasp the threat to their health. Second, workers' health benefits could not, on this issue, be linked with any productivity gains, always the goal in the implementation of safety and health programs, an issue I shall discuss later. Even the latest technology could not solve the hearing problem; moreover, implementing vigorous educational programs, in addition to raising the liability specter, could only reduce production time. The plant managers who would have to implement any educational programs echoed the latter concern, and most of these that White contacted wanted nothing to do with anything but the most perfunctory required annual notification to workers. Group meetings do not produce cloth, the principal criterion by which plant managers rise or fall. Finally, staff in related health fields, sensing top management's reluctance to act in the absence of forceful external compulsion from OSHA, also refused to help; they had their own bailiwicks to protect.

In addition, White had never gained access to the numerous intersecting managerial circles that crisscross the formal occupational structure of his organization. This is not to say that other managers were unfriendly to him; the textile company prides itself on its smiling courtly geniality extended to everyone. But White's weak fealty links with his boss and the refusal of his boss's boss, the senior vice-president, to extend patronage to him even though this executive had a sizable barony, made White suspect; marginal managers cannot further a network's interests. Moreover, though the company publicly pointed with pride to its employment of someone with training in audiology, the fact is that White's moral squint on the hearing issue, manifested by his obvious emotional commitment to the problem and his insistence on the company's obligation to workers, made other managers uncomfortable. The only publicly acceptable way to discuss such an issue, of course, is in rational/technical, emotionally neutral terms like "liability consequences," the "trade-off between noise reduction and efficiency," or the "linkage of compliance with regulation to productivity improvement"; such desiccated language permits a freer exercise of functional rationality and the necessary calculation of the real costs of resolving the problem. All of this put White in a double bind. He was unwanted in the circles where his opinion would count, in some measure because he defined the hearing issue as a moral concern instead of approaching it practically. If, however, he were to frame the issue as a rational/technical problem, powerful interests rooted in the occupational group structure of the hierarchy would oppose him on every score.

White's frustration, isolation, and moral unease finally led him to apply for completely different work in the organization, an office manager's job. He was, however, passed over for this post and he left the company. The OSHA Hearing Conservation Amendment did become a final rule.[2] The only significant change in Weft Corporation's practice is that now the company has to give workers, instead of requiring them to buy, replacement earplugs.

One might say that White suffered from a peculiar kind of disability for his particular occupation, that is, an unwillingness, perhaps an actual inability, to see the hearing issue in more pragmatic terms. But, one might ask, why should his moral stance make other managers uncomfortable? Managers are, after all, men and women with exactly the same kind of moral sensibilities that White possesses although they may express them in different arenas of their lives. Here the political vagaries typical of corporations provide the clue to the riddle. Without clear authoritative sanctions, moral viewpoints threaten others within an organization by making claims on them that might impede their ability to read the drift of social situations. As a result, independent morally evaluative judgments get subordinated to the social intricacies of the bureaucratic workplace. Notions of morality that one might hold and indeed practice outside the workplace—say, some variant of Judeo-Christian ethics—become irrelevant, as do less specifically religious points of principle, unless they mesh with organizational ideologies. Under certain conditions, such notions may even become dangerous. For the most part, then, they remain unarticulated lest one risk damaging crucial relationships with significant individuals or groups. Managers know that in the organization right and wrong get decided by those with enough clout to make their views stick.

Consequently, a principal managerial virtue and, in fact, managers' most striking actual characteristic is an essential, pervasive, and thoroughgoing pragmatism. The social rather than the purely personal origins of this characteristic come into sharp focus in analyzing the following case of a man who tried to "blow the whistle" on practices in his organization, contrasted with other managers' appraisals of what he did.

II

Brady was educated in England as a chartered public accountant, a profession that he values highly and one that carries considerably more status, respect, and public trust in Britain than the American equivalent, that is, certified public accountant. After a stint with a major auditing firm in England and then Canada, Brady got a job in the United States as vice-president of finance for the international company of a large, multidivisional food-processing corporation (I am fictionalizing the industry here). The CEO of the whole corporation was himself a financial man and had initiated a dual reporting system for all of his corporation's divisions. Each major financial officer, like Brady, had to report not only directly up the line to the president of his own company, who in turn reported to the president of his particular division, but also laterally to the corporate vice-president for finance who in turn reported to the CEO himself. The fundamental rule of the reporting system required that any discrepancy in financial figures—budgets exceeded, irregularities in payments, unplanned raises (even, Brady says, an unanticipated salary boost of $11 a week to a secretary in Brazil)—be documented through a Treasurer's Report (called a TR). In due course, this would end up on the CEO's desk. The system was stringent and quite extraordinary in the detail that it required to be sent up the ladder. Year after year, Brady and other financial officers tried to eliminate this dual reporting system but always without success. The CEO relished financial detail and, it is said, reviewed every TR carefully. Brady describes the CEO's style in some detail:

> He was a penny-pincher of the most extreme sort. So it was a matter of discipline with him. Anyone who persistently broke the rules that he set up, well, that was a sign to him that that person was not his man. What this kind of system did was help keep [him] aware of and in charge of a very far-flung company. And when he asked questions of his business people, he would have such a grasp of detail that it would shake their back teeth. He knew more about the numbers than the guys running the business. And he made people pay for working for him, especially when he demonstrated that he knew more than they did. He made people grovel before him. . . . And he treated people very badly. At meetings, he would give a little snap of the whip in front of others and that was humiliating. So people would want to go up there with every little question answered because they knew that he would have the answers too. . . . People didn't like to be in a position where [the CEO] could crack the whip over them.

Brady is a very conscientious man, one deeply imbued with the ethos of his profession. He was disturbed to discover, upon first taking office, that there were a number of financial irregularities occurring in his company, including sizable bribery payments to officials of developing countries. Brady immediately had himself and his staff examined by his company's internal auditors, sent them to Mexico and Venezuela to do detailed field investigations of the bribes, and had the auditors send copies of the report to the CEO. In effect, he "blew the whistle on himself" and was later glad he did since the U.S. Attorney's office subsequently came in to investigate the matter; with the aid of the federal investigation, Brady was able to eliminate the irregular payments.

Closer to home, however, another matter surfaced that proved to be more intractable. A peer of Brady's on his company's managerial ladder, the vice-president for marketing, had overshot his budget and had doctored $75,000 worth of invoices to cover the difference. Brady had pointed out to the vice-president the discrepancy in his numbers earlier and was dismayed later to see information falsified to get rid of the problem. Brady felt that he himself was now in jeopardy from the CEO's scrutiny because he had no verifiable numbers to put in the book to cover the amount. He submitted a TR reporting the matter with the approval of his immediate boss, the international company's president. However, he discovered that his boss's boss, the divisional president, refused to sign off on the report, the requisite procedure before the TR could go on to the corporate vice-president for finance on its way to the CEO. The matter languished for some time despite Brady's repeated efforts to have it go forward. The divisional president sent three emissaries to Brady, only one of them a friend of Brady's, to get him to drop the whole affair. The divisional president had risen to power on the whirlwind success of a particular product suddenly discovered to have many other uses than that originally intended. He was relatively new in his post and unsure of his relationship to the CEO. The bribery matter in the international company had been embarrassing enough; he did not wish more dirty linen from companies under his purview to be washed in public. In short, he wanted the discrepancy in finances hidden somewhere. Eventually, Brady had to acquiesce to a highly sanitized report, although by that point the real issue had become, as Brady saw it, the "question of [the divisional president] having the power of crunching me, of flattening me." Brady felt that his relationship with the divisional president was dead from that point on.

Around this time, the president of the international company, Brady's immediate boss, retired and was replaced by a close associate of the divisional president. Brady suddenly found himself frozen out of key decisions, his authority cut back, and crucial information even about his chief area of responsibility denied. Coincidentally, he had to have a minor surgical operation and entered the hospital for a short period. He returned to find himself broken in grade and salary and transferred to the corporate division where now, as an assistant treasurer, he reported directly to the corporate vice-president for finance. The move, he feels, was intended basically to keep him under control. As it happened, however, he soon came across much more serious and potentially damaging information. Key people in the corporation—at this stage, Brady was not sure just who was involved—were using about $18 million from the employee pension fund as a profit slush fund. Essentially, there was too much money in the pension fund. Explicit rules govern such a contingency but these were being ignored. The money was not declared as an asset but concealed and moved in and out of the corporation's earning statements each year so that the corporation always came in exactly on target. In fact, each October key officials could predict earnings per share for the year to the penny even though one-third of all earnings were in foreign currency. This uncanny accuracy assured top executives, of course, of completely reliable bonus payments. These were tied to hitting profit targets and gave top managers in the company up to 100 percent of their annual salary in deferred income in stock on top of whatever benefits they had accrued in the pension plan. Whatever money was not needed to make the incentive program work to its maximum immediate benefit was set aside for a rainy day.

This knowledge deeply upset Brady. He feels that there are rules in accounting that one can break and rules that one cannot break. The key thing is to explain what one is doing at all times. In his view, the point of being an accountant is precisely to account, that is, to find out the facts—Brady uses the word "truth"—and report them accurately. When one deals with other people's money, one has to be especially careful and forthright. Brady saw the pension fund manipulation as a direct violation of fiduciary trust, as depriving stockholders not only of their rightful knowledge but also of material benefits and as a misuse of other people's money for personal gain. It was, he felt, a practice that could in hard times jeopardize the employees' pension fund. He now had no way of reporting the matter through normal channels. His boss, the corporate vice-president for finance, had been hostile to him ever since Brady came under his control, distrusting Brady, it seems, because of his attempted reporting of the doctored invoices; the vice-president was friends with Brady's old boss's boss, the divisional president. Brady felt, however, that if the CEO were informed about the manipulation of funds, he would act decisively to end the violation. The CEO was "the captain of the boat; the man who wanted a report on everything; [the man] who wanted perfection."

Brady discussed the matter with a close friend, a man who had no defined position but considerable influence in the company and access to the highest circles of the organization. He was Mr. Fixit—a lobbyist, a front man, an all-around factotum, a man who knew how to get things done. Most big corporations have such men, often stashed in their public relations division. He was rewarded for his adroitness with a company Cadillac, a regular table at the 21 Club, and a very sizable expense account. Brady's information alarmed this man, and, with a detailed memorandum written anonymously by Brady, he approached a key director of the corporation who chaired the directors' audit committee. The director took the memorandum into a meeting with the CEO and his top aides, including the corporate vice-president for finance. Immediately after the meeting, Brady's friend was fired and escorted from the building by armed guards.

Only at this point did Brady realize that it was the CEO himself who was fiddling with the numbers. The entire dual reporting system that the CEO had personally initiated was in part an elaborate spy network to guard against discovery of the slush fund manipulation, and perhaps other finagling, rather than a system to ensure financial honesty. The top people still did not know that Brady had written the memo, but he was under suspicion. In time, the pressure on him mounted, with adverse health effects, and Brady had had enough. While his boss, the corporate vice-president, was in Europe, Brady went to the chief lawyer in the whole corporation and laid out the case for him. The lawyer "did not want to touch the issue with a barge pole." He sent a friend of Brady's, yet another corporate vice-president, to Brady to cool things down. According to Brady, the vice-president argued: "Look, why don't you just forget the whole thing. Everyone does it. That's just part of the game in business today." When Brady persisted, the vice-president asked if Brady could not just go along with things even if he did not agree. Brady said that he could not. Brady mentioned the managerial bonus program and acknowledged that that too could be adversely affected by his action. The vice-president blanched and became quite upset. Right after Brady's boss returned from Europe, Brady was summarily fired and he and his belongings were literally thrown out of the company building.

It is important to note the sharp contrast between Brady's reasons for acting as he did and other corporate managers' analyses of his actions. For Brady, the kinds of issues he confronted at work were distinctly moral issues, seen through the prism of his professional code. He says:

> So what I'm saying is that at bottom, I was in jeopardy of violating my professional code. And I feel that you have to stick up for that. If your profession has standing, it has that standing because *someone stood up for it*. If the SEC [the Securities and Exchange Commission] had come in and did an analysis and then went into the details of the case and put me up on the stand and asked me—What is your profession? Was this action right or wrong? Why did you do it then? I would really be in trouble . . . with myself most of all. I am frightened of losing respect, my self-respect in particular. And since that was tied with my respect for my profession, the two things were joined together. I had such a fear of losing that precisely because of my high respect for it.

He goes on to comment further about his relation to professional standards and how those standards contrast with the prevailing ethos of corporate life.

> I have fears in a situation like that. . . . It's not exactly a fear of what could happen to me, although that certainly crossed my mind. What it is is a fear of being found out not to stand up to standards that I have claimed as my own. It is a fear of falling down in a place where you have stuck a flag in the ground and said: "This is where I stand." I mean, why is it in life today that we have to deny any morality at all? But this is exactly the situation here. I was just too honest for that company. What is right in the corporation is not what is right in a man's home or in his church. *What is right in the corporation is what the guy above you wants from you.* That's what morality is in the corporation.

The corporate managers to whom I presented this case see Brady's dilemma as devoid of moral or ethical content. In their view, the issues that Brady raises are, first of all, simply practical matters. His basic failing was, first, that he violated the fundamental rules of bureaucratic life. These are usually stated briefly as a series of admonitions. (1) You never go around your boss. (2) You tell your boss what he wants to hear, even when your boss claims that he wants dissenting views. (3) If your boss wants something dropped, you drop it. (4) You are sensitive to your boss's wishes so that you anticipate what he wants; you don't force him, in other words, to act as boss. (5) Your job is not to report something that your boss does not want reported, but rather to cover it up. You do what your job requires, and you keep your mouth shut.

Second, the managers that I interviewed feel that Brady had plenty of available legitimations to excuse or justify his not acting. Clearly, they feel, a great many other executives knew about the pension fund scam and did nothing; everybody, especially the top bosses, was playing the game. The problem fell into other people's areas, was their responsibility, and therefore their problem. Why, then, worry about it? Besides, Brady had a number of ways out of the situation if he found it intolerable, including resigning. Moreover, whatever action he took would be insignificant anyway so why bother to act at all and jeopardize himself? Even a fool should have known that the CEO was not likely to take whatever blame resulted from the whole affair.

Third, these managers see the violations that disturbed Brady—irregular payments, doctored invoices, shuffling numbers in accounts—as small potatoes indeed, commonplaces of corporate life. One cannot, for example, expect to do business abroad, particularly in the Third World, without recognizing that "one man's bribe is another man's commission." As long as one does not try to extort an unfair market advantage but rather simply facilitates or speeds along already assigned duties, bribes are really the grease that makes the world work. Moreover, as managers see it, playing sleight of hand with the monetary value of inventories, post- or predating memoranda or invoices, tucking or squirreling large sums of money away to pull them out of one's hat at an opportune moment are all part and parcel of managing in a large corporation where interpretations of performance, not necessarily performance itself, decide one's fate. Furthermore, the whole point of the corporation is precisely to put other people's money, rather than one's own resources, at risk.

Finally, the managers I interviewed feel that Brady's biggest error was in insisting on acting according to a moral code, his professional ethos, that had simply no relevance to his organizational situation. "When the rubber hits the road," they say, abstract ethical and moral principles are not of much use. Moreover, by insisting on his own personal moral purity, his feeling that if he did not expose things he himself would be drawn into a web of corruption, he was, they feel, being disingenuous; no one reaches his level of a hierarchy without being tainted. Even more to the point, Brady called others' organizational morality, their acceptance of the moral ethos of bureaucracy, into question, made them uncomfortable, and eroded the fundamental trust and understanding that make cooperative managerial work possible. One executive elaborates a general sentiment:

> What it comes down to is that his moral code made other people uncomfortable. He threatened their position. He made them uncomfortable with their moral standards and their ethics. If he pursued it,

the exposé would threaten their livelihood and their way of life. So they fired him. I personally believe that people in high places in big companies at some stage lose sight of the objectives òf their companies and begin to focus on their positions. That's the only way you can really rationalize the pension fund issue.

But any time you begin to threaten a person's position . . . make him *uncomfortable*, well, in that situation, confrontation is inevitable.

The guy's an evangelist. Under the guise of honesty, he's going to get at the truth no matter what. And those guys are going to lose. Eventually, if the thing hits the newspapers, the big guys will lose. But, in the meantime, within the organization that guy is going to lose. And he will go through life feeling that he was honest and wasn't as crooked as the guys above him.

Brady refused to recognize, in the view of the managers that I interviewed, that "truth" is socially defined, not absolute, and that therefore compromise, about anything and everything, is not moral defeat, as Brady seems to feel, but simply an inevitable fact of organizational life. They see this as the key reason why Brady's bosses did him in. And they too would do him in without any qualms. Managers, they say, do not want evangelists working for them.

The finale to the story is worth recounting. After Brady was fired, the CEO retired and elevated to his position a man known throughout the company as "Loyal Sam." The latter had "tracked" the CEO throughout his career. The CEO went back to his old corner office on a middle floor, his home before he ascended to power, and took an emeritus position with the firm—chief of the internal audit department. He now travels around the world, writing scrutinizing reports about the same companies on which he worked his legerdemain when he was CEO. When the managers to whom I present the case hear the outcome, they laugh softly, nod their heads, and give even an outsider like myself one of the sharp, knowing looks that one imagines they usually reserve for trusted others in their world.

Karl Mannheim points out that bureaucracy turns all political issues into matters of administration.[3] One can see a parallel alchemy in managers' responses to Brady's dilemma. Bureaucracy transforms all moral issues into immediately practical concerns. A moral judgment based on a professional ethic makes little sense in a world where the etiquette of authority relationships and the necessity for protecting and covering for one's boss, one's network, and oneself supercede all other considerations and where nonaccountability for action is the norm. As a matter of survival, not to mention advancement, corporate managers have to keep their eye fixed not on abstract principles but on the social framework of their world and its requirements. Thus, they simply do not see most issues that confront them as moral concerns even when problems might be posed in moral terms by others. Managers' essential pragmatism stems thus not only from the pervasive matter of factness engendered by the expertise so typical of bureaucracies, but from the priority that managers assign to the rules and social contexts of their bureaucratic world.

III

It could scarcely be otherwise. Managers know that whatever efficacy they may have in their occupational world they have through their bureaucratic milieux. The exigencies that they confront both in the market and in their organizations have to be met, if they are to be met at all, through organizational resources and in accordance with the institutional logic of their situations. The notion of institutional logic, a phrase that I have already used several times, does not refer, as I am using it, to any notion of blind functional necessity somehow inherent in organizations or systems rather than in individuals. Instead, I mean the complicated, experientially constructed, and therefore contingent, set of rules, premiums, and sanctions that men and women in a particular context create and re-create in such a way that their behavior and accompanying perspectives are to some extent regularized and predictable. Put succinctly, institutional logic is the way a particular social world works; of course, although individuals are participants in shaping the logic of institutions, they often experience that logic as an objective set of norms. And, of course, managers' own fates depend on how well they accomplish defined goals in accordance with the institutional logic of their situation.

Corporate bureaucracies thus place a great premium on what might be called an alertness to expediency, that is, the accurate assessment of the intersection between exigencies, institutional logic, and, of course, personal advantage. One can gauge the importance of this kind of sensitivity by looking at another case, that of a manager who insisted on adhering to principles rooted outside his immediate occupational milieu and ended up taking a stand against his bosses. Again, I shall contrast his experience with corporate managers' assessment of his predicament.

Joe Wilson (a pseudonym at his request) was trained in marine engineering in the merchant marines, where, among other work experiences, he had key responsibilities on a nuclear vessel. After leaving the marines, Wilson worked in a variety of engineering fields, including the space program, eventually returning to the nuclear field. After work with nuclear submarines, he became the senior systems engineer for a large nuclear plant and later plant superintendent at another nuclear station.[4]

In June 1980, Wilson began working for General Public Utilities, Nuclear (GPUN) at Three Mile Island, Unit-2 (TMI-2). He quickly rose through three levels of management and eventually became Site Operations director, supervising between 260 to 340 employees and, at various points, between 47 to 100 contractors.

The structure of authority on Three Mile Island was multilayered and complex. In March 1979, TMI-2 had, of course, suffered a serious accident that had worldwide negative repercussions for the nuclear power industry. Since TMI-1 was also inoperative due to its own problems, almost all the effort on the Island was directed toward the cleanup of TMI-2, a task seen as urgent in light of the vast national and international media coverage and FBI and Congressional investigations that followed the 1979 accident. There were essentially three organizations operating on the Island: GPUN; Bechtel Corporation, the principal contractor to GPUN for the cleanup; and the Nuclear Regulatory Commission (NRC), which had to approve each step of the cleanup. In the background was General Public Utilities (GPU), the parent corporation of GPUN. GPUN had a chief executive officer who was also a board member of GPU, a president, and an executive vice-president. The latter was director for both TMI-1 and TMI-2. Reporting to this executive vice-president were two deputy directors for TMI-2, one from the GPUN organization and the other from Bechtel Corporation. Wilson, as Site Operations director, reported to both of these men and, in turn, had a number of people reporting to him, including directors and managers of key operations. Parallel to Wilson were other directors also reporting to the two deputy directors. Some of these directors were Bechtel people, others were GPUN employees. Overseeing the whole operation was the NRC, which had a program officer on site. The basic ambiguity of the authority structure, one should note, stemmed from the incorporation of Bechtel employees into GPUN's regular line of authority. There had been a reorganization on the Island in September 1982, which saw leadership in the cleanup pass from GPUN to Bechtel.

The ambiguity of authority relationships after September 1982 was to become one of Wilson's principal concerns. But even from the earliest days of his employment at TMI, Wilson was worried about other management practices. In fact, he says that his first instinct on coming to TMI in 1980 and seeing all of GPUN's organizational and operational problems was to get out. He did not leave, however, not least because he had spent the better part of his working life in the nuclear power field and was deeply committed to the development of nuclear energy. He felt that cleaning up TMI properly was crucial to the industry's future. During his time on the Island, he worked an average of sixty to seventy hours a week and instituted a number of important managerial control systems. These included, to take but two examples: a follow-up system to reduce backlogged work requests from Site Operations (in a year-and-a-half, backlogged requests were reduced from 3,700 to 350), and a unit work instruction (UWI) system that involved sign-offs up and down the line to fix responsibility for work done. This program was part of a commitment to the NRC to address serious safety concerns in the aftermath of a radiation contamination incident caused by crucial drains out of a containment building being merely taped rather than plugged shut.

From Wilson's standpoint, his inclination to thoroughness became harder to implement after Bechtel's integration into the management hierarchy and its ascendancy to leadership in the cleanup. Wilson became increasingly concerned about a number of issues. First, Bechtel's management both above

Wilson and parallel to him in other sectors of the organization began pushing very hard to meet schedules to satisfy Department of Energy (DOE) demands that the cleanup be accomplished promptly. There had indeed been long delays in the cleanup and both the DOE and the NRC were nervous about the possible effect of these delays on other nuclear programs. During one period, in fact, the DOE allocated monies to GPUN only on a task by task basis as each project was completed. Wilson felt that one of the key reasons for the delays was the lack of any integrated schedule for all departments working on particular projects; he made this point many times both verbally and in writing. One of his superiors, the GPUN deputy director, responded to one such protest with a note asking what Wilson was trying to prove and saying that Wilson was making a bad example. Integrated schedules never were developed. Instead, as Wilson sees it, Bechtel addressed the scheduling delays by instituting a series of shortcuts around established procedures. These shortcuts were so multiple and obvious that Wilson feels that the NRC must have either approved or tacitly acquiesced in them.[5] To take but one example, Bechtel substituted its own "work package system" for Wilson's UWI system. Bechtel's work packages required either no signatures at all for work done or only Bechtel personnel signatures. This system did speed up work but it also clouded responsibility for the accomplishment of important procedures.

Second, Wilson had broader concerns regarding responsibility and the exact delineation of authority after Bechtel's ascendancy in 1982. Wilson felt that he and others legally responsible for decisions were overruled or bypassed by other managers and departments. Bechtel's ascendancy to prominence in the cleanup had prompted, it seems, a typical loosening of the authority and fealty relationships throughout GPUN's structure. On issue after issue, from a dilution in the authority of the designated emergency director (in the event of a catastrophe) to increased confusion about the lines of responsibility for significant repairs, Wilson felt that his authority was diminished but that his responsibility—and as he defines it in retrospect, his "blamability"—remained unchanged. He pushed hard to clarify lines of authority and was partially successful in doing so only toward the end of his tenure at TMI.

Third, Wilson saw the kinds of issues he was raising come to a head in a dispute, later widely publicized, about the safety of a piece of equipment called a polar crane, which is wholly contained and operated inside the nuclear reactor building. The polar crane is normally used during refueling to lift off the 163-ton nuclear reactor vessel head and then to remove the rods that make up the fuel for the nuclear reaction. In cleaning up TMI-2, the crane would have to be used repeatedly: first, to remove the four missile shields, ranging in weight from thirty-two to forty tons, that protect the reactor's steel top; then to remove the steel top itself; and finally to clean the rubble and debris from the reactor core, partially destroyed as a result of the 1979 accident. The crane had not been used since the 1979 accident and Bechtel was placed in charge of refurbishing it and load testing it for safety. Even after Bechtel had

refurbished the crane at a cost of several million dollars, key engineers reporting to Wilson, one of whom was a Bechtel employee, felt that the crane might
have suffered structural damage due to radiation and to rust caused by water
on the floor of the containment building. These engineers felt that Bechtel's
proposed tests for the crane's safety and reliability were technically inade-
quate and posed a possible hazard to public health and safety. In basic terms,
the issue was this: Bechtel wanted to perform the test required by the NRC
code on the crane while doing, in stages, the actual lifts necessary to get on
with the cleanup. The tests would begin with lifts of the four missile shields.
After preliminary lifts, the shields would then be set to one side in order to
construct, along with materials in the building, enough weight to load test the
crane fully before proceeding to lift the 163-ton reactor head. Although the
crane was originally designed to do 500-ton lifts, it would be tested for only
about 200 tons. Site Operations counterargued that, if management were
wrong and the crane failed and dropped one of the missile shields, there could
be a repetition of the 1979 accident. Site Operations wanted a lift made of
other materials either already in the containment building or brought in by
workers to make sure that, to begin with, the crane could sustain a thirty-two
to forty-ton weight. If so, it could then proceed with removing the missile
shields and building the test weight for the reactor head. Wilson and his Site
Operations staff were particularly concerned because when the polar crane
was finally used, it would be Site Operations who used it. They knew that, if
they were in charge when the button was pushed, they could be blamed for
whatever might go wrong. If the polar crane failed, it would be seen as the
fault of Site Operations. Site Operations felt that Bechtel's deputy director at
TMI in particular had exerted pressure to prepare procedures without adequate data and without giving Site Operations enough time to review the program fully. Wilson asked repeatedly for the documentation of crane modifications and for an analysis that Bechtel's plan was safe.[6] He never received
such an analysis, and he felt that his requests were brushed aside.

The NRC complicated the dispute in some ways. It seems to have become
customary for top GPUN and Bechtel officials to submit preliminary materials to NRC officials on site to see if there were any problems. NRC officials
often gave informal approval to work requests before internal reviews within
GPUN were completed. When Site Operations disputed technical issues
with top management, it was told that the NRC had no problem with particular technical specifications and that it was curious that Site Operations
should object. On the polar crane issue, the top official of the NRC later characterized Wilson's and his engineers' concerns as stemming from a philosophy that emphasized procedural matters rather than a focus on final goals.
This characterization was echoed by GPUN management who stressed that
what was at issue in the polar crane dispute was not procedures but results;
at a certain point, they said, decisions had to be made to resolve technical
disputes and work had to proceed toward what everyone acknowledged to be
a worthwhile goal, that is, the cleanup of TMI-2.

As these kinds of disputes intensified, Wilson documented his own and his staff's objections on a variety of issues with ever greater thoroughness, regularly sending memoranda on disputed issues to his two immediate superiors. Wilson knew that his bosses were unhappy with such written objections, but he felt that he had little choice except to register his concerns in this way. He had come to see his protests and his insistence on proper procedures as a moral issue. In his view, not only did public health and safety actually depend on upholding procedural safeguards, but just as important, the appearance of upholding them was crucial to the long-term success of the nuclear industry. Once, when he wrote a memo to the GPUN deputy director about radioactively contaminated sewage being trucked out of the plant and disposed of illegally, his boss replied that he did not need such a memo from Wilson. It was, his boss said, not constructive and wasted his own and Wilson's time. Finally, on February 7, 1983, Wilson requested a meeting with his bosses' boss, the GPUN executive vice-president, to discuss among other things his safety concerns; this meeting was scheduled for February 25, 1983. On February 17, 1983, Wilson and one of his engineers expressed their fundamental disagreement with Bechtel's handling of the polar crane. Then, on February 24, Wilson was suddenly suspended from his post, on the grounds of conflict of interest. Wilson happened to be the part owner of a consulting firm that had one client, a nuclear plant in another state; during his employment at GPUN, Wilson had received no income from his consulting work. Wilson's secretary was told to report to the site's stress control center and she was later fired. One of the engineers under Wilson, who had been particularly vociferous on the polar crane, was also asked to report to stress control for a neuropsychological examination; he was later transferred to a non-nuclear GPUN plant. Another engineer, the Bechtel employee, was later suspended and then transferred across country.

During his month-long suspension, Wilson continued to raise his safety concerns. He met with the GPUN executive vice-president, with special investigators who report to the GPU board of directors, with a member of the Safety Advisory Board for TMI, and with NRC officials on site. There was no investigation during this period into Wilson's involvement with his consulting firm. After the month-long suspension, Wilson was fired. Both Wilson and his engineers went public with their concerns, with one of the engineers singled out for the greatest media attention. Top GPUN officials maintained to both the press and to a Congressional committee that Wilson was fired because of a conflict of interest; one official told the Congressional committee that, had Wilson not been associated with the consulting firm, he would still be working at TMI. However, *The New York Times* cited unnamed corporate officials' characterization of Wilson as someone who "was not a team player."[7]

Eventually, the NRC's Office of Investigations launched a special inquiry into the whole TMI-2 management situation after Wilson and his engineers went public. The office released a report on September 1, 1983 that found that not only were the dissenters' allegations substantiated, but they were "illustrative rather than exhaustive."[8] In particular, the report criticizes

Bechtel's shortcuts around proper procedures and GPUN management's failure to "responsibly monitor Bechtel's work and hold Bechtel accountable."[9] Some weeks later, the chairman of the NRC, in a letter to the chairman of GPU, put the matter in sharp focus:

> In the past, the Commission [NRC] has clearly stated its position advocating a safe and expeditious cleanup. Your organization has stated its commitment to the same goals. However, it appears that in the interest of expediency, proper management controls may have been compromised.[10]

The immediate meaning of expediency here is the swift, expeditious accomplishment of what "has to be done," that is, achieving goals, meeting exigencies defined as necessary and desirable. Top management always exerts pressure on subordinates, and subordinates on themselves, to do what they believe has to be done. There are, in fact, few more effective legitimating rationales in the corporate world than the invocation of one's authoritatively approved "goals," "objectives," or "mission." Indeed, organizations themselves are presumably put together precisely to grapple with some exigency. The managers in other corporations that I interviewed about Wilson's situation all stress this meaning of expediency. They too see the cleanup of TMI-2 as the overriding concern in the whole affair. In their view, GPUN's and Bechtel's general management practices, as well as their specific plan to load test the polar crane, were wholly "reasonable," the word most widely used in managerial circles for "practical." In their view, Wilson's insistence on meticulously following proper procedures, whether mandated by regulation or not, could only "lay logs in the path" of getting the job done at all. Besides, they point out, the local program officer of the NRC went along with the shortcuts, and the regulators, not management, are supposed to be the procedural watchdogs in such cases.

The NRC did eventually approve a modified version of Bechtel's plan for the polar crane,[11] which, these managers feel, clearly indicates that the NRC opposed Wilson all along. The investigation and public reprimand of GPUN were all for public show. Wilson's emphasis on proper procedure is clear evidence, they say, of a "military mind," of "nitpicking," of "straining at a gnat," and of "being out in left field." To make an omelet, one must scramble eggs; to erect a building, one must break some glass; results are what count. A dainty insistence on procedure betrays the zero-risk mentality that has hobbled the nation's economic capabilities.

Moreover, these managers feel, the whole institutional logic at TMI should have been clear to Wilson. He should have been able to read the situation and grasp the appropriate rules for behavior, perceiving that both his own and others' advantage was at stake. In particular, these managers stress the following issues. First, organization-sustaining monies from the Department of Energy, and therefore the fates of many employees and executives, were tied to making progress on the cleanup. Moreover, this task, vital from everyone's perspective, was under the sharp glare of international scrutiny. Therefore, rapid progress toward this goal had to be made. Second, one must not, particularly in such circumstances, make one's view of a technical issue or of procedure into a matter of principle. Authority has the prerogative to resolve technical disputes. Whether Wilson liked it or not, Bechtel had won the power struggle and they had the right, that is the power, to call the shots on the cleanup. One has to bend with prevailing winds. One can be beaten even when one is "right"; therefore, these managers stress that whether Wilson was right or not was irrelevant. What mattered was that key authorities decided that Wilson and his engineers were "wrong." As these managers see it, Wilson should have accepted his defeat gracefully, told the engineers who reported to him to drop the matter, and declared his willingness to do whatever he could to help expedite things. In doing so, he could always defer to the "expert judgments" of others or indeed simply claim that matters had been taken out of his hands. Moreover, these managers point out that the corporation is not a democratic assembly; it is an autocracy and one forgets that at his peril. Corporations allow room for dissent but only up to a point; this is particularly true at Wilson's level. The fact is that most bosses simply do not want to hear bad news. Bad news either requires action, always open to multiple and perhaps pejorative interpretations, or it upsets pre-established plans of action, scattering ducks already set in a row. Besides, one can only criticize something when one has the resources to solve it in a clear and decisive way. Otherwise, one should keep one's skepticism to oneself and get "on board." Third, instead, Wilson violated key rules of managerial circles, and the managers that I interviewed reserve their sharpest criticism of him for this. They recognize that the situation was fraught with potential disaster and subsequent blame that could engulf Wilson and his Site Operations people. They too would be wary. But the solution to this was not to make others vulnerable. One manager compared Wilson to a man on a crowded rowboat on choppy stormy waters who declares that he will guard the provisions and the life preservers. He tried to fix responsibility for action, a tactic certain to shatter the trust required to maintain a kind of cooperative nonaccountability. He put things into writing in a world that, apart from ritual nods to the importance of documentation, actually fosters ambiguity by its reliance on talk as the basic mode of negotiation and command. Talk, of course, lends itself more readily than documents to backtracking, filling in, evasion, subterfuge, and secrecy, all important virtues if one is to do what has to be done while establishing and maintaining the kinds of relationships that alone can protect oneself. These managers are not at all surprised that Wilson's superiors reached for whatever pretext they could find to fire him. Sunday school ethics—the public espousal of lofty principles—do not help managers cut the sometimes unpleasant deals necessary to make the world work.[12]

As a result, principles and those who raise them do not generally fare well in back rooms. Managers are paid, and paid well, to bring rationality into irrational markets, to bring sometimes obdurate technology and always difficult people together to make money, to make difficult choices among unclear alternatives. Such uncompromising tasks demand continual compromises with conventional verities. Only those who make themselves alert to expediency can find their way through the ambiguities and dilemmas such compromises entail.

In effect, one makes oneself alert to expediency by projecting outward the objectifying habit of mind learned in the course of self-rationalization. That is, the manager alert to expediency learns to appraise all situations and all other people as he comes to see himself—as an object, a commodity, something to be scrutinized, rearranged, tinkered with, packaged, advertised, promoted, and sold. The mastery of public faces described earlier is only the outward reflection of an internal mastery, a relentless subjection of the self to objective criteria to achieve success. Such self-abnegation, such stripping away of natural impulses, involves a self-objectification that in fact frames and paces the objectification of the world. To the extent that self-objectification is incomplete—and, of course, even the most thorough secular ascetic has uncharted areas of the self—to that extent do managers experience moral dilemmas in their grapplings with the world. In my view, this is the nub of the moral ethos of bureaucracy. Managers see this issue as a "trade-off" between principle and expediency. They usually pose the trade-off as a question: Where do you draw the line?

IV

Managers sometimes find lines already drawn for them depending on the prevailing norms of their particular corporation or even of their particular division. Typically, such norms apply to known troublesome areas in an industry; their effectiveness depends entirely on sanctions from key management figures. In its northern marketing offices, for instance, Weft Corporation has a strong, authoritatively sanctioned set of norms against bribery in any form. Top managers see such strong admonitions as crucial in an industry where graft, payoffs, trips to Bermuda, new cars that magically appear in driveways, and less obvious deal sweeteners are a way of life. It is said, in fact, that one Weft manager who was on the take for years from customers was fired within a half hour of the discovery of his "inexplicably stupid" acceptance and deposit of a check from his benefactors instead of his normal cash rake-offs. With such authoritative encouragement, managers internalize these norms into their own personal codes of honor; they speak privately of the importance of not being known as men or women "who can be had." Similarly, environmental staff managers at Alchemy Inc. developed, as noted earlier, a strong ethic of environmental vigilance backed by the company's president that prevailed for some years after an environmental debacle. This provided environmental managers with sharply defined rules for adjudicating ambiguous cases and with a private sense of public service. Such codes, particularly when they are set down as formal, written "codes of ethics"[13] may sometimes be used as the basis for effective sermons in certain public arenas. But within management circles themselves, even the most high-minded and carefully elaborated codes get transformed into typically pragmatic vocabularies. Bribery is not countenanced because it "provides an unfair market advantage"; environmental spoilage is "bad for business" or "will ultimately affect us since we're consumers too."

In most situations, however, managers have to draw lines for themselves; for some, this can be a troublesome and anxiety-laden process, one that reaches into every sphere of their work lives. I can focus here on only a few areas that illustrate the kinds of ambiguities some managers confront. Consider for a moment simply the issues that emerge in relationships with customers. As a general rule, managers feel that it is dishonorable to lie or to break one's promises. But some marketplaces, as in finished consumer products in textiles, are like "meeting [a guy] with a knife in an alleyway." Pressures come from every direction. Top management wants more goods sold at higher margins; big customers, especially the huge department stores that are crucial to one's business, want favors, special considerations, and instant service. Where does one draw the line then in violating promises? A merchandising manager at Weft describes a typical situation:

> For instance, you're trying to sell Firm A, say, one half or a million dollars worth of stuff and they may want a small amount of cloth that you don't even have any more because you already sold it to Firm B. They say to you if you want the big sale, get us that other cloth. So you go rob Peter to pay Paul. It depends on how bad you want the business. Now it might be a completely good business decision; maybe the big order of cloth that A wants to take is a loser on the shelf and you've had a real problem moving it. But the small amount of cloth is a real winner. But even if it's a good business decision, it's morally wrong, because you're selling the same goods twice. Usually it's the smaller business which gets screwed. It's a good business judgment, though; get rid of the slow moving cloth, even though it's hurting a smaller customer. Now some people can't live with that switch. They say, well, the goods are already sold to Firm B; but then their boss will come to them and tell them to do it. And it's this kind of pressure that drives managers crazy. The boss will usually say something like, "Come on, you can find a way to do this, can't you?" And you know he wants it done.

Or can one sell to both Peter and Paul and avoid any moral choice? One could after all "soul search . . . scrounge . . . examine every order on your books to see if the orders are good . . . see if you can switch looms . . . see if your workers can work a few Sundays to produce the cloth." What about passing off a competitor's goods as one's own during a period of shutdown at a plant in order not to lose business in the long run? Since there are no intrinsic standards of quality that bind one, may one try to sell off-quality goods as first-class merchandise? What about, in the textile industry, putting out a print to "see how it books" and then withdrawing it "because of a quality problem" if pre-orders are not good, leaving customers who purchased the cloth and made plans around it out of luck? Where does one draw the line in cutting off a small customer entirely because he issues trading stamps, something that one's larger customers find undignified? Or in explaining such actions with the "institutionalized falsehoods"—"the loom broke, the delivery didn't come in, anything but the truth, the standard business reasons for not doing what you said you'd do"—typically employed to extricate oneself from a compromised situation? After all, as one executive says, "We lie all the time, but if everyone knows that we're lying, is a lie really a lie?" Again, generally speaking, no manager would knowingly sell to an American buyer toxic chemicals banned for domestic use by the government. But if there are buyers in other countries, may one ignore the scientific data that prompted the domestic ban and sell whatever lots one can, especially if the U.S. government provides indirect subsidies for doing so?

Again, as a general rule, it is not proper to probe into the ethics of one's customers; one must assume that they are honorable. But many customers in the textile world, for instance, "will lie, cheat, and steal from you without blinking twice." How far does one stretch one's own credulity or actually assist customers in fabricating acceptable vocabularies of excuses for illicitly returning purchased goods? If a retailer returns with goods and says, "Look, I can't sell $50,000 of this stuff. You have to take it back or it's going to break me," may one say, "What's that? I didn't hear you," hoping for the sake of future business that the retailer will say, "Oh, look, you were late delivering and I can't use it now." How far does one go in placating one's customers? Is it all right to subsidize an apparel manufacturer's sale to a big retail chain, crucial to his business, by providing him with free items to pass along for promotion that other customers do not get? Or may one give a good customer "just thirty extra days" on his account? How does one decide which customers get "exclusives" and which do not? Is the size of a customer's account the real measure of one's honor in dealing with him? When "the customer always has the upper hand," is moral choice itself an unwarranted luxury? In the chemical industry, how does one assess, say, the storage and organizational capabilities of a customer to handle extremely toxic materials with safety? Does one "climb the fence in the middle of the night to inspect his facilities" or require an on-site inspection before shipping? Does one review all the customer's records and interview key personnel as well to ascertain commitment to safety? "Do you," one manager asks, "have to make sure a guy is not a hatchet murderer before selling him a hatchet?" Or does one simply have to make a "reasonable" judgment in such cases and hope that nothing goes wrong?

What does one do when, in the course of normal business dealings with a customer, one becomes privy to information about the customer's ethics that suggests his actions might produce harmful consequences for others? Take, for instance, the puzzle that confronted Kelly, an upper-middle executive in Alchemy Inc. Kelly was in overall charge of a food-grade chemical used, among other things, by pharmaceutical firms as an ingredient in consumer drugs. One day, Kelly received a phone call from Blue, an executive at a pharmaceutical company, one of Kelly's largest customers. Blue was not only the purchasing agent for his company but, as Kelly discovered during their phone conversation, he was also responsible for the quality control of the substances purchased. Blue asked Kelly if Alchemy used any glass in storing, shipping, or otherwise handling this substance; Kelly replied that for some years Alchemy had been using only plastic containers. When he asked Blue why the inquiry was being made, Blue told him that sampling analysis of the final product had indicated traces of ground glass in the market-ready drug. Kelly again pointed out that Alchemy at least was in the clear because it did not use glass in any phase of production or shipping. But something in Blue's tone and manner suggested to Kelly that this phone call was the end of the matter and that the drug would be shipped to market. Kelly felt faced with an unwanted dilemma. Should he simply keep quiet or should he pass on his suspicion of trouble to the CEO of the drug company? After all, the sample might be faulty. Any action risked permanently alienating Blue and his lucrative business and possibly the CEO of the drug firm as well, perhaps especially if his suspicions proved correct. No one likes to hear about problems that demand unpleasant decisive action. On the other hand, even though Alchemy was not culpable, people hurt with ground glass would file liability suits against all suppliers to get redress and who could tell what the courts might decide? Besides, what if consumers actually did ingest ground glass? Kelly felt that he could not face that possibility. In the end, he sent a telegram to the CEO at the pharmaceutical firm telling him that it had come to his attention that a certain lot of material had been contaminated with glass. He simply described the problem without evaluation and felt his responsibility ended there. The outcome is typical of other cases. Kelly never heard anything back. He also never had any problems with the account. He has no knowledge of what became of the product. And Blue is still in his post at the drug firm. When one does draw lines in the corporate world, one never knows if, when, or how the lines will be honored or even acknowledged.

Encountering such sudden silences, voids of information, and indeed outright subterfuge are, of course, commonplace experiences in any bureaucratic situation. On one hand, the potentially catastrophic consequences of publicly admitting mistakes prohibits open critical discussion and promotes, in fact, backtracking and evasion. On the other hand, as I have suggested earlier, segmented roles, compartmentalized scarce knowledge where knowledge is power, and the public requirement for judiciously restrained public faces make secrecy a pervasive corporate phenomenon.

Drawing lines when information is scarce becomes doubly ambiguous, a problem that often emerges in shaping relationships with one's colleagues. For instance, Black, a lawyer at Covenant Corporation, received a call from a chemical plant manager who had just been served with an order from the local fire department to build retaining dikes around several storage tanks for toxic chemicals so that firemen would not be in danger of being drenched with the substance should the tanks burst if there were a fire at the plant. The plant manager indicated that meeting the order would cause him to miss his numbers badly that year and he wondered aloud if the fire chief might, for a consideration, be persuaded to forget the whole thing. Black pointed out that he could not countenance even a discussion of bribery; the plant manager laughed and said that he was only joking and would think things over and get back to Black in a few weeks. Black never heard from the plant manager about this issue again; when they met on different occasions after that, the conversation was always framed around other subjects. Black did inquire discreetly and found out that no dikes had been built; the plant manager had apparently gone shopping for a more flexible legal opinion. Should he, Black wondered, pursue the matter or in the absence of any firm evidence just let things drop, particularly since others, for their own purposes, could misconstrue the fact that he had not acted on his earlier marginal knowledge? Feeling that one is in the dark can be somewhat unnerving.

More unnerving, however, is the feeling that one is being kept in the dark. Reed, another lawyer at Covenant, was working on the legal issues of a chemical dumpsite that Alchemy Inc. had sold. He suddenly received a call from a former employee who had been having trouble with the company on his pension payments; this man told Reed that unless things were straightened out in a hurry, he planned to talk to federal officials about all the pesticides buried in the site. This was alarming news. Reed had no documentation about pesticides in the site; if Alchemy had buried pesticides there, a whole new set of regulations might apply to the situation and to Covenant as the former owner. Reed went to the chemical company's director of personnel to get the former employee's file but was unable to obtain it. Reed's boss agreed to help, but still the director of personnel refused to release the file. After repeated calls, Reed was told that the file had been lost. Reed went back to his boss and inquired whether it might be prudent for Covenant to repurchase the site to keep it under control. This was deemed a good idea. However, the asking price for the site was now three times what Covenant had sold it for. Everyone, of course, got hesitant; another lawyer became involved and began working closely with Reed's boss on the issue. Gradually, Reed found himself excluded from discussions about the problem and unable to obtain information that he felt was important to his work. His anxiety was heightened because he felt he was involved in a matter of some legal gravity. But, like much else in the corporation, this problem disappeared in the night. Eventually, Reed was assigned to other cases and he knew that the doors to the issue were closed, locked, and bolted. Such secrecy, of course, both permits and invites expedient action. It also makes the assertion of principles an ambiguous exercise in drawing lines in the dark.

As it happens, there is little escape from such anxieties for those who experience them. The normal press of managerial work and uncontrollable events as well always bring new problems to be confronted. More particularly, less questioning managers intensify the anxieties of those who are uneasy. A manager who responds more fully to the bureaucratic premium on alertness to expediency does not spend much time examining the intrinsic merits of issues with all of their tangled complexities. Instead, when one encounters a troublesome problem that must be addressed, one strips away its emotional and stated moral aspects and asks what outcome would be most congruent with institutional logic and of advantage to oneself and to one's social network. One focuses then on the tactical means necessary to reach that outcome without excessive regard for other considerations, although one may, of course, have to proffer a public face of deep concern.

Bureaucracies encourage the rigorous self-rationalization necessary for alertness to expediency in a number of ways. First, bureaucracy facilitates an abstract rather than a concrete view of problems, an essential component of the nonaccountability discussed earlier. Typically, the abstractness of one's viewpoint increases as one ascends the hierarchy of an organization. The pushing down of details and the growing social distance from the human consequences of one's actions enable the development of an austere, uncluttered perspective. The viewpoints that managers at different levels have on workers and, in particular, on the social dislocation caused to workers by labor reallocation decisions illustrates this point.

Typically, plant managers and staff at Weft Corporation, for instance, who interact daily with workers see these men and women and their problems in complex, detailed ways. On one hand, of course, these managers take pains to separate themselves socially from workers. They mock what they see as workers' preferences for "stock car racing, drinking beer, and watching girls' rear ends." They speak disdainfully of the crude, arm-waving "Assembly of God" Protestantism that many workers favor in contrast to their own high Baptist or, better, Presbyterian leanings. Especially if they are themselves from the working class, they see workers' poor education and stumbling inarticulateness around authority figures as shameful, indeed disgusting. But, at the same time, they understand how social class can wreak psychological havoc on individuals, most often lashing out in antagonisms against self and against other workers—in drug and alcohol abuse; or in fights between blacks and whites, between women "over men or over things said out back in the waterhouse," between men over women or over some real or imagined insult. They see too the entanglements and the rhythms of workers' lives—the high school graduations and the shotgun marriages; the trailer park mobile homes and the early births; and the deaths. They sometimes even become the boss of workers who are living legends, like the wizened old spinner who was born under frame #21 in the [Gilroy] plant. His mother worked that frame for twenty-five years. She had abandoned him in a basket on the street shortly after birth, and he was raised by a "half-caste," half black, half Indian woman whom, when he reached puberty, he married and then returned to the [Gilroy] plant, to frame #21, where he worked for forty years. Managers with such dense and intimate knowledge of workers' lives often find the unpleasant aspects of their managerial duties difficult to discharge. A plant manager at a large manufacturing operation recalls an incident that occurred during the 1974 recession when he made his monthly graveyard shift swing through his plant:

We had to lay off a lot of people with less seniority and I came into the plant at one A.M. to make my rounds—well, I'll never forget it— one young lady came up to me and said, "Mr. [Brook], what am I going to do?" I've never had a question haunt me so much. I'll never forget that girl's look. . . . I wasn't able to get back to sleep that night.

He goes on to talk about the dislocations that are occurring on his shop floor because of the implementation of a new labor-saving piece of machinery:

We're in the midst of large changes in the sewing operation right now. Over the years, we used to have women hem a sheet by hand and drop it into a bin; but last year, we finally found a machine which will sew flat sheets acceptably and that means that we will replace a lot of people with machines. Now they will have the option to learn those machines, but as we get more machines, we will need fewer operators. . . . It will take two-and-a-half years for the transition. And the employees were distressed a little but they accepted it; we let them ask questions and explained it to them and used a scale drawing. We told them all what was happening. . . . Several were worrying about what was going to happen to [themselves], but we have told them that we couldn't tell about . . . individual[s]. We'll give those with seniority their choice of machines and shifts. Once we start the process of letting them select, people will only have the option to remain where they are for a while before they have to go to a new job. We let them have adjustment rights so that if they are qualified to do a new job, then they can bump another person to get it. Within two-and-a-half years, we'll have fewer people on the payroll. I can't guess how many but it will be a substantial reduction. Normal attrition is probably not enough. I hope that they can be absorbed in another plant.

The vice-president for manufacturing of the division, the boss of this same plant manager's boss, has his office in the same building. He is physically insulated from workers by intervening floors, but more importantly, by a considerable gulf of authority, prestige, and money. When he and other high-ranking managers at Weft speak about workers, they do so almost reverentially, calling them the "salt of the earth" and noting the "great feeling" born of *noblesse oblige* that the firm's founder had for his workers and that they try to continue. They find the sometimes coarse characterizations of workers made by plant managers to be "insensitive." The vice-president, however, talks about the same labor reallocation issue on the same day:

Well, when there is an IE [industrial engineering] study and we see that there is an opportunity to reduce the numbers of workers, and it involves a sizable number in a critical area, then I get involved to make sure we're not jeopardizing our operations from a larger standpoint and that the workers are given due consideration as employees. . . . Now [recently] we had a modification which involved twenty-two people. I presented the changes to the supervisors and told them that we were eliminating some jobs because we had discovered that by rearranging some equipment, we could eliminate several jobs by combining [them] and that this meant cutting twenty-two jobs. All the workers were absorbed into other operations.

Social insulation permits and encourages a lofty viewpoint that, on its face, "respects the dignity of workers," but seems devoid of the feel of the texture of workers' lives and of the gut-level empathy that such knowledge can bring.

Of course, at the highest levels of Weft, as in most big corporations, workers become wholly abstract categories. A divisional president in the same company, from the vantage point of his northern office 800 miles away, talks about closing some plants to maximize the productive utilization of capital under the spur of regulations:

> Now, if you're not going to put money into these [plants], it creates a very critical analysis of those assets and what you're going to do with them. I mean, we're probably going to divest some plants.

When I asked if one of the considerations was what would happen to the workers, he says:

> Well, actually, I don't worry about the workers. From my perspective, I don't intend to divest our total overall productive capacity because that would lead to other problems. I presume that those workers who lose their jobs because you close a particular plant will be able to find a job somewhere.

Such a distanced viewpoint can be undercut by sudden encounters. One of the top northern officials of Weft, just returned from a tour of the firm's southern plants, when asked what aspects of his work he finds troublesome, comments:

> I think the thing that bothers me the most—well, have you ever been to a textile mill? It's not an attractive place to work. And then I think of an eighteen-year-old girl going into the mill, and we jam earplugs into her head, and put her into a room with 200 looms with 90–95 decibels of noise for eight hours a day. That's a rather disappointing career start for a young lady. So it's the work environment in our older plants that troubles me the most. . . . I can only imagine what that girl thinks. I've never taken one of them out for a cup of coffee or sat down and talked to one of them. But I can guess what she thinks from our turnover rate.

As a rule, however, the various insulations provided by both office and social status prevent such unpleasant episodes from occurring too often.

The sheer impersonality of the vast markets that corporations service also helps managers to achieve the distance and abstractness appropriate to and necessary for their roles. A high-ranking official of Covenant Corporation muses about this problem, referring to the possible, though controverted, harm that one of Alchemy Inc.'s chemicals might produce:

> It gets hard. Now, suppose that the ozone depletion theory were correct and you knew that these specific fifty people were going to get skin cancer because you produced chlorofluorocarbons [CFCs]. Well, there would be no question. You would just stop production. But suppose that you didn't know the fifty people and it wasn't at all clear that CFCs were at fault, or entirely at fault. What do you do then?

An upper-middle official at the chemical company echoes the same sentiment talking about a different, though similar, problem:

> Certainly no one wants to significantly damage the environment or the health of individuals. But it's a different thing to sit and say that it's OK for twenty people out of one million to die because of chlorinated water in the drinking water supply when the cost of warding off those deaths is $25 million to remove the halogenated hydrocarbon from the water. Is it worth it to spend that much money? I don't know how to answer that question as long as I'm not one of those twenty people. As long as those people can't be *identified,* as long as they are not *specific* people, it's OK. Isn't that strange? So you put a filter on your own house and try to protect yourself.

Impersonality provides the psychological distance necessary to make what managers call "hard choices." The high-ranking Covenant official cited a moment ago extends his reflections on this issue by posing a hypothetical case:

> Suppose that you had a candy bar factory and you were touring the plant and you saw with your own eyes a worker slip a razor blade into a bar. And before you could stop the machine, there were a thousand bars more made and the one with the razor blade was mixed up. Well, there's no question that you would get rid of the thousand candy bars. But what if it were a million bars? Well, I don't know what I'd do.

The big organization provides, of course, conceptual tools that help managers cut through such ambiguous quandaries. Dichotomous modes of thinking like "cost-benefit analysis" are to some extent conceptual paradigms of functional rationality. They help managers apply a thoroughly secular, pragmatic, utilitarian calculus even to areas of experience that, in their private lives, they might still consider sacred.

Finally, as I have already noted, bureaucracies create many mechanisms that separate men and women from the consequences of their actions. Here, some of the social dimensions of such nonaccountability deserve explicit attention. Specifically, the kind of personal trust and comfort that link managers into effective circles has at its core a tacit agreement about taciturnity. As a result, managers who are alert to expediency know that they can usually count on other managers within their own organizational circles both to keep secret sensitive information and, to some extent, to cover up for one's fellows. It goes without saying that only those who can keep secrets are worthy of the faith that confidentiality demands. A manager who cannot keep secrets becomes quickly known as "an old hen," or "Mr. Loose Lips," or "blabbermouth," labels that consign one to marginality if one survives at all. No one tells such a person anything of consequence unless, of course, the point of telling him is precisely to make something known. Further, one has an obligation of sorts to cover up the real or presumed mistakes of one's immediate associates, at least by keeping quiet. Other managers and managerial cliques are always on the lookout for others' mistakes or for actions that can be construed as mistakes and will pounce on anyone foolish enough to admit them. Even if others restrain an immediate attack, the knowledge of someone's mistakes is ammunition for the future. Many managers "lay in the weeds, with rocks, and wait." One who exposes a colleague's errors in such a context and makes him vulnerable to others evinces, of course, only a fundamental untrustworthiness, unless one's colleague has first betrayed oneself or others in some way—say, in one case, by burying important data and thus setting others up to be "sandbagged" or, in another, by revealing secret information to an opponent through what seems to be a compulsive self-destructiveness parading as total openness and honesty. Moreover, even though the mistakes of other managerial groups are fair game, one must be judicious in pointing them out since no matter how elaborate one's cognitive map of an organization might be, the connections between different circles of managers might not be clear. Above all, one must not press for a resolution of an organizational problem involving the mistakes of others if the proper authority for that resolution rests above one's own station. Only those with a reputation for discretion are judged trustworthy. Alertness to expediency is thus linked to a close attention to organizational etiquette. As it happens, the etiquette of most situations is always intricate and often obscure, which in itself is a compelling reason for prudent silence.

I can best illustrate the complicated process of how one comes to be trusted by key associates and how such social acceptance breeds the particular habit of mind vital to an alertness to expediency by recounting two stories that one manager told me about himself.

Tucker, a textile engineer by training, was two years out of school and working as a lower-middle level manager when he was hired by the commercial development section of his company's fibers division. The research and development wing of fibers had developed a new blend of polyester and nylon, reported to combine the many excellent qualities of both materials, among them nylon's elasticity and colorfastness and polyester's tensile strength and versatility. The commercial development group that hired

Tucker was developing all sorts of commercial uses for this new blend. The most promising areas were in automobile tires, industrial carpets, and apparel. All nylon tires have a tendency to develop flat spots; the new blend would, it was thought, eliminate this and improve durability to boot. Further, the blend produced a luxuriously deep carpet pile that seemed to promise years of attractive wear. Moreover, any number of applications for apparel fabrics seemed possible, ranging from intimate garments to heavy durable outerwear. Tucker was hired, in fact, precisely to work in this last area of commercial development and, at that, very late in the game. Extensive plans for launching the blend in both the tire and carpet areas were already in place; a major press conference had been scheduled only one month away to announce these plans. Tucker was assigned to conduct a series of routine tests on the prototypes for the blend's apparel applications in order to speed along this area of the product's development.

Tucker was puzzled by the results of his tests. Dyed apparel fabrics are expected to have a colorfastness of about forty to sixty hours of exposure to strong light, but since both nylon and polyester dye well, an even superior fastness was expected of the blend. However, when Tucker took the material out of the test machines, it was badly faded after only one to two hours. He was, of course, using excellent apparel dye, but, to be sure, he obtained some much stronger carpet dye able to withstand up to 120 hours of direct sunlight. However, when he applied this dye to the apparel fabrics, the results were just as poor. Tucker then surreptitiously got small clips of already dyed carpets made from the blend and tested them. They too faded after about one hour. Impelled both by his own curiosity and a growing sense of foreboding, Tucker then quietly gathered up larger samples of all the carpets that had been done and, with a close friend, went back to the laboratory that weekend to conduct a more extensive series of tests in private.

The results clearly indicated that the fibers division was heading into a liability disaster. The lack of colorfastness was only the beginning. When Tucker conducted abrasion tests, he found that even normal wear quickly eroded the carpet piling. Heavily trafficked areas would wear out rapidly and destroy the optical effect that makes carpets aesthetically pleasing. The apparel fabrics also wore out quickly under Tucker's tests. And Tucker did not even wish to contemplate what normal road abrasion would do to the polyester/nylon blend in automobile tires. He analyzed the fiber with great care and concluded that the polyester was breaking apart from the nylon in unexpected ways. Instead of each material reinforcing the other, the result was a substance that was not as strong as either polyester or nylon. The substance simply burst apart under any duress at all.

Tucker is an ambitious man, one who has cast in his own lot wholeheartedly with business and who is deeply committed to the managerial ethos. Tucker believes firmly in the organizational maxim that bosses do not want to hear bad news, and normally he makes every effort to keep knowledge compartmentalized. But in this situation he knew that he had to act. However, since he had no knowledge of how this project, so many years in the making, could have reached the edge of catastrophe, he also knew that he had to proceed with extreme caution. He informed his boss of his discovery to tie him to the problem and his boss immediately told his own boss. The latter asked Tucker to prepare a written report simply presenting the results of his tests and to follow the organizational protocol for top-secret documents. That protocol required that thirty people be informed. Tucker made up the requisite number of booklets and sent them by special post to those executives authorized to receive secret documents. He kept an extra copy for himself, locked in his office desk drawer.

What follows is a cautionary tale about the virtues of steadfast silence amidst the perils of corporate life. One may gauge the reactions of top executives to Tucker's report from subsequent events. All thirty copies of the report were confiscated. Tucker was asked to surrender all of his working notes. Tucker's desk was entered and his own copy of his report taken. The carpet was never introduced; the tires were never introduced; the press conference was never held. One executive, three levels above Tucker, was quietly fired; two research and development scientists, who apparently had been "fudging data" under pressure from the line, were also sanctioned, one fired, the other demoted. And Tucker never heard about the matter again. He says:

> Now clearly the report got to someone because they stopped the introduction of the product. This was not a light decision because four years of work and a lot of hope had gone into it. There was real panic in the division about it. But our evidence was irrefutable. Yet no one ever told me thank you; no one ever said that I was a good employee.

The last remarks are not made in a complaining way. Rather, Tucker understands that this lack of acknowledgment, this silence on the part of authorities, was, first, an implicit warning.

> Now the key thing is that if I had pursued this issue I would have been fired, no doubt about it. Since I didn't pursue it, I didn't get any credit but I also didn't get fired. I was the messenger that came to the king and told him that his son had been tortured to death and his ears cut off. One of the norms here is to keep quiet once you have done your job in reporting what you see. . . . If you pursue something like this, no one will like you. It's that simple.

Tucker has risen steadily since that episode. He understands now that the silence of his superiors also established the criterion for an implicit probation:

> I think that I've got to where I am today because of this. [His boss's boss] knows that I saved the company a lot of money and a lot of asses to boot. And he and others know that I am someone who can be *trusted*. I can keep my mouth shut. . . . And that's the biggest thing that I have going for me—that people feel that I can be trusted. I can't overemphasize that enough.

One retains the trust and confidence of others only by continually displaying the kind of reputation for discretion that leads to social acceptance in the first place. Despite its inevitable tensions, such ongoing probation has its comforts. It provides a clear set of goals, that is, maintaining social relationships, that greatly facilitates the drawing of lines. One comes to gauge that hard-won access to managerial circles takes precedence over fussing with abstract principles. An episode from Tucker's later career illustrates this.

Tucker moved over to another division of his company for a special project and was invited to remain there. After some years, he had risen to an upper-middle level managerial post heading up a particular product area. One day, Tucker was in conference with two of his peers on the managerial ladder but in a different product area when a newly hired technical aide, who reported to one of these other managers, dropped by with an inquiry. The aide had been doing some extra reading to familiarize himself with the materials and processes of his new company, when he made an accidental discovery. He noticed that there was very strong recent evidence to suggest that a particular substance was a potent carcinogen, though only when inhaled in dust form. The aide did not know how the substance was processed at the company, and he asked casually if any dust were emitted in production. As it happens, Tucker's managerial colleagues had been polishing the substance in question in open drums preparatory to other use; the polishing gave off dust that workers inhaled. Moreover, they had employed this process for years, after inheriting it from their predecessors, never suspecting that anything was wrong. Tucker and the other three men were immediately aware of their guilty knowledge and they sent the workers home. In the next few days, they had the drums encased so that the polishing of the substance emitted no dust. They also decided not to tell the workers the facts of the case. They simply said that a decision had been reached to alter production.

Tucker's main concern in this situation was to maintain solidarity with his managerial colleagues. His construction of accounts and rationales for not informing the workers illustrates the combination of resourceful casuistry and reliance on organizational safeguards that marks a well-developed alertness to expediency. Tucker argues that:

1. The workers had already been exposed to the substance. No known medication would remedy whatever damage the exposure had caused, and it would do the workers no good to know about the dangers they might face. In Tucker's view, the analogue here is the case of the heavy cigarette smoker who quit the habit upon hearing the Surgeon General's first report on the health hazards of smoking. Nothing the smoker did subsequently could alter the damage done while smoking.

2. If, however, some of the workers involved did develop cancer and, say a decade later, filed a compensation suit, Tucker admits that he would have to wrestle with himself to know what to do. He points out, however, that he was basically a bystander in this affair and not really responsible for, that is, he was not immediately in charge of, what happened. He sees himself as more of a witness to events than anything else. He might, he says, call one of the

other managers involved and ask if he were willing to come forward. He thinks it unlikely that any would. After all, they had unwittingly inherited the problem; why should they risk getting blamed for the unintended consequences of someone else's decision? He too would be unwilling to risk his career in business, the inevitable result of coming forward, he feels, just "to give a widow compensation." Moreover, there is a difference, he argues, between a case where people know something is wrong and keep on doing it anyway and the case in point where people stopped their actions as soon as they realized something was amiss.

3. It is unlikely, however, that any workers affected could ever piece things together. First, there is nothing in writing. Second, Tucker feels sure that everyone involved would, if it became necessary, simply deny knowledge and claim that the process was altered solely for production reasons.

4. Finally, he says:

> The basic rule is that you hope that these kinds of things never occur. Nobody wants to hurt people. Nobody would ever consciously plan to do something that would endanger people. But when things happen, well, you cover for yourself and your company.

He also says in a related context:

> The thing that makes . . . the corporation work at all is the support we give to each other no matter what happens. . . . We have to support each other and we have to support the hierarchy. Otherwise you have no management system.

Tucker's and his colleagues' actions were, of course, totally at variance with formal policies later adopted by his company, including a commitment to inform workers of hazards they might confront. The company has, in fact, done so in several cases. These policies resemble a highly formal code of ethics. However, the crucial variables in such situations seem to be: how public the knowledge about a hazard is; whether the people affected by such a hazard, here workers, have independent access to that knowledge; and what a company's recent public history on such issues has been and how that history has shaped internal corporate structure and politics. Of particular importance is the relationship between professional staff working explicitly in these areas and the business areas of a company properly speaking. Business areas, of course, almost always establish the tone, tempo, and ethos of a corporation, monitored or checked by professional staff. As it happens, Tucker's case preceded his company's adoption of elaborate formal policies on environmental, safety, and health issues. But, as Alchemy's case described earlier suggests, there has been in many corporations an assault on professional staff in recent years under the pressures of economic hard times, conservative regulatory triumphs, and organizational backlashes by line managers. Tucker's ethic, rooted in the intricate social structure and demands of daily managerial work, might prove more enduring than formal policies and codes, the implementation of which ebbs and flows with external pressures.

But one has to grasp this situation from Tucker's viewpoint to understand the choices he made. Tucker is not afraid of conflict; in fact, he sees himself as something of a maverick. For instance, he was once a plant manager in the Deep South and appointed a black man to supervise white women, an unpopular decision two decades ago. When the other foremen protested his choice, he threw them out of his office. Moreover, he tries to treat his subordinates forthrightly, firmly believing that one's word is an important measure of a person. In a world, however, where actions are separated from consequences, where knowledge is fragmented and secreted, where private agreements are the only real way to fashion trust in the midst of ongoing competition and conflict, where relationships with trusted colleagues constitute one's only real means both of defense and opportunity, and where, one knows, even coincidental association with a disaster can haunt one's career years later, keeping silent and covering for oneself and for one's fellows become not only possible but prudent, indeed virtuous, courses of action.

The manager alert to expediency sees his bureaucratic world through a lens that might seem blurred to those outside the corporation and even to some inside who are unable to rid themselves of encumbering perspectives from other areas of their lives. It is a lens, however, that enables him to bring into exact focus the rules and relationships of his immediate world. The alert manager pays whatever obeisance is required to the ideological idols of the moment, but he keeps his eye fixed on what has to be done to meet external and organizational exigencies. He wears the masks of bland genteel bonhomie with grace and humor but he comes to appreciate more fully than most people the wisdom of the old proverb "Tis an ill wind that blows nobody good," and he learns that one man's misfortune is another man's opportunity. More generally, he comes to measure all relationships with others by a strict utilitarian calculus and, insofar as he dares, breaks friendships and alliances accordingly. He comes to see the secrecy at the core of managerial circles not as a suppression of dissent but an integral component of a compartmentalized world where one establishes faith with others precisely by proving that one can tolerate the ambiguities that expedient action and stone-faced silence impose. He comes to see also that the nonaccountability of the corporation is really a license to exert one's own will and to improve one's own fortunes by making the system work for oneself, as long as one does not overreach one's power or station, and as long as one maintains crucial alliances and does not get caught.

The logical result of alertness to expediency is the elimination of any ethical lines at all. Sometimes the demands to do what has to be done, the pressures of exigencies that must be faced, make erasure of lines a tempting prospect. But as a practical matter, unless managers can act in complete secrecy, they know that they must be at least prepared to legitimate their actions both in their own organizational milieux and, depending on their positions, in the larger public arena. The truly ambitious manager must work therefore at attaining a certain dexterity with symbols.

6

Dexterity with Symbols

I

The density of the social structure of the corporation is matched by an intricate ideological complexity. At any given moment in most major corporations, one can find a vast array of vocabularies of motive and accounts to explain, or excuse and justify, expedient action; ideas and schemes of every sort peddled to managers by various outside consultants that purport to solve organizational problems or simply provide further rationales for what has to be done; and the ideological constructions of managers grappling with the whirlwinds of discontent and controversy endemic to our society that, it seems, inevitably envelop the corporation. Managers have to be able to manipulate with some finesse these sophisticated, often contradictory, symbolic forms that mask, reflect, and sometimes merely sweep through their world.

The indirect and ambiguous linguistic frameworks that managers employ in public situations typify the symbolic complexity of the corporation. Generally speaking, managers' public language is best characterized as a kind of provisional discourse, a tentative way of communicating that reflects the peculiarly chancy and fluid character of their world.

Managers' public language is, more than anything else, euphemistic. For instance, managers do not generally criticize or disagree with one another or with company policy openly and in public except at blame-time and sometimes not even then, since innuendo is often more effective than direct statements. The sanction against such criticism is so strong that it constitutes, in the view of many managers, a suppression of professional debate. This seems to be rooted in a number of the social conditions of managerial work already discussed. Most importantly, although some top managers consider abusive-

134

ness toward subordinates a prerogative of corporate success, managers' acute sense of organizational contingency makes them speak gingerly to one another since the person one criticizes or argues with today could be one's boss tomorrow. Even if such dramatic reversals of fortune were not at issue, managers know that the remembrance of offenses received, whether real or imagined, occupies a special nook in people's cognitive maps and can undercut effective work, let alone potential alliances. Moreover, the crucial premium in the corporation on style includes an expectation of a certain finesse in handling people, a "sensitivity to others," as it is called. As one manager says: "You just can't push people around anymore." Discreet suggestions, hints, and coded messages take the place of command; this, of course, places a premium on subordinates' abilities to read correctly their bosses' vaguely articulated or completely unstated wishes. One cannot even criticize one's subordinates to one's own superior without risking a negative evaluation of one's own managerial judgment. Still further, the sheer difficulty of penetrating managerial circles other than one's own and finding out what actually happened on a given issue, let alone being able to assess its organizational significance, makes the use of oblique language imperative, at least until one gets the lay of the land.

This leads to the use of an elaborate linguistic code marked by emotional neutrality, especially in group settings. The code communicates the meaning one might wish to convey to other managers, but since it is devoid of any significant emotional sentiment—one might also say here strong conviction or forceful judgment—it can be reinterpreted should social relationships or attitudes change. Here, for example, are some typical phrases describing performance appraisals, always treacherous terrain, followed by their probable intended meaning.[1]

Stock Phrase	Probable Intended Meaning
*Exceptionally well qualified	Has committed no major blunders to date
Tactful in dealing with superiors	Knows when to keep his mouth shut
Quick thinking	Offers plausible excuses
Meticulous attention to detail	A nitpicker
Slightly below average	Stupid
*Unusually loyal	Wanted by no one else
*Indifferent to instruction	Knows more than one's superior
*Strong adherence to principles	Stubborn
*Requires work-value attitudinal readjustment	Lazy and hardheaded

Or, to take an example of a different kind of euphemism, one "talks in circles," that is, one masters the art of juxtaposing several sentences that contain implicit contradictions but that one makes seem related by one's forcefulness or style of presentation. One can thus stake out a position on every side of an issue. Or one buries what one wants done in a string of vaguely related descriptive sentences that demand textual exegesis.

For the most part, euphemistic language is not used with the intent to deceive. Managers past a certain point, as suggested earlier, are assumed to be "maze-bright" and able to "read between the lines" of a conversation or a memorandum and to distinguish accurately suggestions from directives, inquiries from investigations, and bluffs from threats. Managers who are "maze-dense," like the manager at Weft Corporation who, though told somewhat indirectly that he was fired, did not realize his fate until the following day, might consider the oblique, elliptical quality of managerial language to skirt deceit. However, most often when managers use euphemistic language with each other (and it is important to remember that in private among trusted others their language can be very direct, colorful, and indeed earthy), its principal purpose is to communicate certain meanings within specific contexts with the implicit understanding that should the context change, a new, more appropriate meaning can be attached to the language already used. In this sense, the corporation is a place where people are not held to what they say because it is generally understood that their word is always provisional.

Euphemistic language also plays other important roles. Within the corporation, subordinates often have to protect their bosses' "deniability" by concealing the specific dimensions of a problem in abstract, empty terms, thus maximizing the number of possible subsequent interpretations. The rule of thumb here seems to be that the more troublesome a problem, the more desiccated and vague the public language describing it should be. Of course, when a troublesome problem bursts into public controversy, euphemism becomes a crucial tool of those managers who have to face the public in some forum. The task here is to defuse public criticism and sometimes outrage with abstract unemotional characterizations of issues. Thus, to take only a few examples, in the textile industry, cotton dust becomes an "air-borne particulate" and byssinosis or brown lung a "symptom complex." In the chemical industry, spewing highly toxic hydrogen fluoride into a neighboring community's air is characterized as a "release beyond the fence line." The nuclear power industry, precisely because of its publicly perceived danger, is, of course, a wonderland of euphemisms. For example, the "incident" at Three Mile Island in March 1979 was variously called an "abnormal evolution" or, perhaps better, a "plant transient."[2] A firm that speculates in radioactive and chemical waste disposal renamed itself U.S. Ecology Inc., hoping that the new appellation "would make people feel comfortable."[3] The same kinds of rules apply for industrial managers' opposite numbers in the regulatory agencies. For instance, at the request of the food industry, the Department of Agriculture renamed the "powdered bone" increasingly used in processed meats as "calcium";[4] for a time, the Environmental Protection Agency called acid rain "poorly buffered precipitation";[5] and the National Transportation Safety Board in the Federal Aviation Agency Accident Investigation Records names an airplane crash as a "controlled flight into terrain."[6] Such abstractions help obfuscate issues and thus reduce the likelihood of unwanted interference in one's work from some public but it also allows managers themselves to grapple dispassionately with problems that can generate high emotions.

II

The higher one goes in the corporate world, the more essential is the mastery of provisional language. In fact, advancement beyond the upper-middle levels depends greatly on one's ability to manipulate a whole variety of symbols without becoming tied to or identified with any of them. Managers' use of certain kinds of expertise, namely that generated by management consultants of various sorts, themselves virtuosos in symbolic manipulation, aptly illustrates their peculiar symbolic skills.

In order to explore this issue properly, I want to discuss the ethos of management consulting itself in some detail. Except for the most narrowly defined technical areas, management consultants are perfect examples of what might be called ambiguous expertise—that is, their clients possess at least experientially the basic knowledge that management consultants claim. Moreover, because their expertise is therefore subject to continual negotiation, management consultants get drawn into the world of their clients and become subject to the political context and rules of that world.

Historically, management consulting grew and flourished with the ascendancy of the status group of corporate managers. The thrust of the consulting profession from its inception has been to help managers get control of the workplace, first in industrial settings, and then later in the burgeoning white-collar sector. The ethos of the contemporary consulting profession is rooted in three main historical developments that continue to shape it today.

The first of these, of course, was the scientific management movement founded by Frederick Taylor, which emphasized the application of engineering principles to measuring and accelerating efficiency at work.[7] Scientific management developed the assembly line, time-and-motion studies, the speedup, and, more generally, the systematic segmentation and routinization of complex work tasks, all to a fine degree. In manufacturing industries today, in particular, this kind of industrial engineering is pervasive and taken for granted. Weft Corporation, for example, electronically monitors each block of looms of every weaver. A supervisor roaming the shop floor can gauge with a glance at a television screen how many times in an hour each loom in a block is stopping and how many yards of cloth each is producing. The monitor also provides an overall index of weaving efficiency either for an individual loom or for a weaver's entire block as a whole. Such information is crucial for plant management in adjudicating the inevitable competition between workers on a piece system, itself a product of scientific management. It was precisely through such rationalization, on the supposedly neutral ground of scientific and technical rationality, that the scientific management movement aimed to bring capital and labor together. Scientific observation and experimentation could and, it was argued, should be applied to the work process in order to achieve greater efficiency, productivity, and consequently a bigger economic pie. The functionally rational perspective of the movement, of course, meshed completely with the thoroughgoing pragmatism of managers. Almost all management consulting programs today at least purport to help managers systematically calculate the best means to reach prescribed goals, usually under the aegis of an appeal to scientifically derived knowledge.

The theory and practice of scientific management came under assault not only from workers but even from some managers. The logic of Taylor's system extends, of course, to management, and of course, managerial work, especially at the lower levels, is as thoroughly rationalized as that of workers. Elton Mayo and his associates at Harvard[8] began a series of studies aimed at the same general problem that concerned the Taylorites—how to create industrial peace. Specifically, they wanted to establish cooperation between management and labor, the principal warring factions of the chaotic industrial workplace. At the base of Mayo's vision was a notion of "Garden America," a romantic image of an idyllic past that could, he thought, be reestablished with careful study of the informal as well as the formal dimensions of the modern workplace and by institutionalizing ways of making people happy at work. This amelioristic concern in particular became and remains today the hallmark of the human relations approach in industry and is the second important root of the ethos of management consulting. Few major firms today are without sports teams that compete in industrial leagues, in-house newsletters and magazines to keep employees abreast of official versions of reality, counseling programs designed to help employees accept their organizational fates, and, at the white-collar level, various committees to arrange the picnics, dances, danish and coffees, the aesthetic decor of the office, and, of course, the cocktail parties, all thought essential to improve the *esprit de corps* of employees. High morale is variously thought to improve productivity[9] or, at the least, to "make for a family spirit." Only a few managers are willing to voice what a top official of Weft Corporation thinks is actually a widespread managerial sentiment about workers' happiness: "Let them be happy on their own time."

Management consulting is also rooted in the application of social science to help managers establish control of the workplace. This process has included, to name only a few examples, the extensive and haphazard use of psychological tests to ascertain worker characteristics in both blue- and white-collar workplaces,[10] procedures continued today despite their extremely dubious efficacy, the transformation of the sociology of bureaucracy into a branch of administrative science, and the extensive use of pre-tested survey instruments to gauge employee sentiment on a whole range of issues. The strictly pragmatic character of such applications may be gauged from an incident at Images Inc., which prides itself on the surveys it performs for its clients. Alarmed at the markedly low morale among their own employees in the aftermath of some economic reversals and subsequent organizational shake-ups, the firm's top management decided, amidst great fanfare, to conduct an extensive employee survey to locate and address the sources of discontent. When the responses came back, according to insiders, top management itself received severe criticism for, among other things, what employees saw as favoritism, nepotism, mismanagement, and stinginess. The results were buried and no one ever heard about them again. Similarly, the results of a survey on the "corporate cultures" of each of the several operating companies at Covenant Corporation became the closely guarded property of one small segment of the corporate staff, that is, a weapon of sorts in the ongoing battles in that corporation. Important social science knowledge can emerge serendipitously from such pragmatic research, sometimes even years later. But, more typically, the knowledge gained is narrowly focused and yields only crude empirical generalizations.

Whatever contributions to the accumulation of knowledge such pragmatic research may make, there is little doubt that both specific techniques and broader theoretical perspectives of social science are the basic stock in trade of management consultants. Regarding the latter, in fact, management consultants probably play a signal role in the systematic condensation, simplification, and popularization of important thought in all the social sciences. At one private conference of management consultants that I recently attended, one speaker gave a virtuoso performance of such syncretic ability. Among those theorists whose ideas were clearly recognizable, though unacknowledged, were not only Marx, Weber, and Freud, but also Ferdinand Tönnies, Emile Durkheim, Robert Merton, Daniel Bell, and C. Wright Mills. The performance concluded with dire prophecies of corporate disaster unless the consultant's warnings were heeded.

The professionalization of the managerial class itself spurred the real growth of managerial consulting. As corporate managers developed the requisite apparatus and distinctions of professionalism, they turned increasingly toward specialized counseling to service special needs. Reliable estimates on the rate or extent of the growth of consulting firms are difficult to obtain. A publication of the leading newsletter for management consultants says that there were ten consulting firms established before 1900 in the United States.[11] One researcher tracked down 305 management consulting firms in the classified telephone directories of eight major cities in 1938, but this figure includes equipment vendors, trade associations, advertising agencies, and auditing firms, none of which are, properly speaking, considered management consulting today.[12] A more recent estimate (1981) suggests that there are currently more than 2,500 firms plying a $2–$3 billion a year market with as many as 50,000 consultants working full or part-time advising management in a host of areas.[13] By 1983, management consultants had become such a permanent and important part of the corporate scene that they were attacked in *Forbes* magazine as one of the causes of the nation's economic malaise. One of the symbols of social arrival in our society is, of course, to be blamed publicly for social ills.[14]

One must keep in mind both the roots of the ethos of the management consulting profession and the ambiguous expertise consultants offer in order to grasp the meaning of consultants' ideas and programs to managers.[15] The further the consultant moves away from strictly technical issues—that is, from being an expert in the ideal sense, a virtuoso of some institutionalized and valued skills—the more anomalous his status becomes. He becomes an expert who trades in others' troubles. In managerial hierarchies, of course, troubles, like everything else, are socially defined. Consultants have to depend on some authority's definition of what is troublesome in an organization and, in most cases, have to work on the problem as defined. As it happens, it is extremely rare that an executive declares himself or his own circle to be a problem; rather, other groups in the corporation are targeted to be "worked on."

The relationship between the consultant and the group to be worked on may be described as a polite, arms-length embrace. The target group knows that whatever is revealed to the consultant will be passed back to a higher authority; the target group knows too that this information may be used in ways that the consultant never intended and further that the consultant is powerless to prevent such use. At the same time, one cannot refuse to coop-erate with consultants when they are mandated by higher authority without running the risk of validating the original definition of being troublesome. The task, then, for the target group is to persuade the consultant that what-ever problem might exist exists elsewhere in the organization or, failing that, to negotiate with the consultant in an oblique way some amelioristic program that will disrupt a given bailiwick as little as possible.

From the consultant's perspective, maintaining the stance of rational expert in such a situation becomes very difficult and the more contact the consultant has with the target group, the truer this becomes. No one likes to deal with people in trouble, at least on a regular sustained basis, but at the same time, consultants have to make a living too and this involves putting on programs to solve problems defined by others. The temptation to accept the target group's redefinition of the trouble at issue is, therefore, always great if that redefinition is plausible and salable to the authority who hired the con-sultant. Of course, the "real trouble" in any organization may lie completely apart from the authority's definition of the situation or the target group's redefinition. I shall comment further on this shortly.

Sometimes the issues that consultants are retained to address are so benign on their face that no group is likely to be threatened by their presence. How-ever, even benign programs—like special training sessions for executives or promising young managers—may be seen to have hidden organizational func-tions, usually in the area of prestige allocation. In any event, whatever the nature of the consultant's work, it cannot become institutionalized without a continuing commitment from top management. When top management ceases to pay attention to a program, no matter how much time, effort, and money has been poured into it, the program withers and dies. There is scarcely much mystery to this. The whole bureaucratic structure of big corporations fosters and demands attentiveness to top management's whims. Both managers and their consultants must keep up with changing whims. One might ask, of course, why top managers are unable or unwilling to sustain long-term interest in programs that they themselves initiate. Once again, the clue lies in the social structure of corporations.

There is a premium in the higher circles of management on seeming fresh, dynamic, innovative, and up-to-date. In their social minglings and shoptalk with one another, particularly with their opposite numbers in other large companies, say, at the Business Roundtable, at high-level conferences at prestigious business schools, at summer galas in the Hamptons, or at the Super Bowl, the biggest business extravaganza of all, executives need to seem abreast of the latest trends in managerial know-how. No one wants to appear stodgy before one's peers nor to have one's firm defined in managerial networks, and perhaps thence to Wall Street, as "slow on the uptake." Executives trade ideas and schemes and judge the efficacy of consultant programs not by any detached critical standards but by what is socially acceptable, desirable, and, perhaps most important, current in their circles.

There is a dialectical process at work here. The need of executives for fresh approaches fuels the large and growing industry of consultants and other managerial sages who write books and articles and develop new programs to "aid management," that is, get the business of well-placed managers. This burgeoning industry in turn fuels executive anxiety with a never-ending barrage of newly packaged schemes, all highly rational, most ameulioristic, and the great majority making operational some social science insight. Despite their fresh appearances, certain themes recur constantly in the programs offered by consultants. Perhaps the most common are how to sharpen decision making, how to restructure organizations for greater efficiency, how to improve productivity, how to recognize trouble spots in an organization, how to communicate effectively, how to humanize the workplace, and how to raise morale.

The language that consultants use to describe their programs has its own interest, marked as it is by the peculiar combination of appeals to a solid scientific basis, promises of organizational betterment, vague, abstract lingo, and upbeat exhortation. For instance, a leading management consultant firm offers a "unique series of workshops designed for leaders in organizations experiencing significant challenge and change." The basis for these is "extensive research into the management styles and management structures required to increase organizational competitiveness." In addition to helping participating managers "develop a *dynamic* concept of management or leadership," the workshop will "identify the difference between being a problem solver and managing or leading others in opportunity-seeking and problem-solving." It will as well "utilize personal, useful feedback on their style" to "develop action plans that allow them to have a greater positive impact on others and their organization."

A higher level version of the same workshop for an "executive management team" promises a "research-based orientation" to "getting competitive." This orientation "can be tailored to the organization's unique situation" through a series of pre-interviews with participants that form "the basis for a 'real time' case which the executive team works on." Pre-interviews are, of course, a crucial strategy in helping the consultant ascertain just what the defined troubles of an organization are and who does the defining. The contentless quality of the language used here is, of course, related to this strategy; the lack of specificity precludes hasty judgments by prospective clients about the range or limits of a consultant's expertise and implicitly promises nearly infinite adaptability.

Recently, other consultants have promoted the importance of "corporate cultures," that is, the idea that specific values, beliefs, rites, and rituals at the core of particular organizations determine social behavior in them. Through a mastery of stagecraft and an understanding of the "hidden hierarchy"—the real "cultural network" of "spies, storytellers, priests, whisperers, [and] cabals"—gained through a kind of instant ethnography, "symbolic managers" can dominate their situation and provide effective leadership.[16] Another recent approach recycles ideologies and slogans from segments of the 1960s New Left, all tailored for the executive suite. The concerns here are with "empowerment," "energizing the grass roots," learning "power skills," and becoming "corporate entrepreneurs."[17]

In reading such materials, one can discern some basic rules that seem to undergird most of the genre of business consultant writing and program presentation. These rules also tell us something about the managerial audience for such writing. The rules seem to be: (1) suppress all irony, ambiguity, and complexity and assert only the most obvious and literal meanings of any phenomenon; (2) ignore all theoretical issues unless they can be encapsulated into a neat schematic form easily remembered, "operationalized," and preferably diagrammed; (3) always stress the bright side of things, inflating, say, all efforts for change, whether major or minor, into "revolutionary" action; downplay the gloomy, troublesome, crass, or seamy aspects of big organizational life or, better, show managers how to exploit them to their own advantage; (4) provide a step-by-step program tied, of course, to one's own pathbreaking research, that promises to unlock the secrets of organizations; and (5) end with a vision of the future that makes one's book, program, or consulting services indispensable.

The result of the untiring efforts of consultants and the reciprocal anxiety of executives is the circulation at or near the top of organizations of ever changing rhetorics of innovation and exhortation. These rhetorics get disseminated throughout a corporation and become rallying cries for a time, and sometimes are instituted, until new rhetorics overtake them. For some time in Weft Corporation, the magic words were "modernization" and "retraining," as managers developed sets of rationales to quell workers' anxieties about new labor-displacing machinery. For a while, the watchword at Covenant Corporation was "productivity," and, since this was a pet project of the CEO himself, it was said that no one ever went into his presence without wearing a blue *Productivity!* button and talking about "quality circles" and "feedback sessions," organizational devices that had in fact been instituted right down to the plant level. But then managers at the upper-middle levels noticed that there had not been a single mention of productivity at executive meetings, and the program fell into disuse just as managers in charge further down the line felt that the quality circles at least were beginning to bear fruit. Managers kept their ears to the ground to anticipate the newest rumblings from the executive suites. This turned out to be an emphasis on creating "entrepreneurial cultures" in all the operating companies of the conglomerate. The president of one company pushes a series of managerial seminars that endlessly repeat the basic functions of management—planning, organizing, motivating, and controlling. So set are the scripts for these sessions that managers who have already completed the seminars are able to cue friends about to take them to key words to be used in key places. Of course, younger managers come already armed for such situations with the well-honed responsiveness to social expectations that marks their profession. As one comments about these seminars, "Whenever I find myself in a situation like this, I always ask: 'What is it they want from me here? What am I expected to do?'" So they attend the sessions and with a seemingly dutiful eagerness learn literally to repeat the requisite formulas under the watchful eyes of senior managers. Of course, senior managers do not themselves necessarily believe in such programs. In one seminar that I attended, the senior manager in charge startled a room of juniors by saying:

> Fellows, why aren't any of you asking about the total lack of correspondence between what we're preaching here and the way we run our company?

But, such outspokenness is rare. Managers privately characterize such programs as the "CEO's incantations over the assembled multitude," as "elaborate rituals with no practical effect," or as "waving a magic wand to make things wonderful again." They refer to consultants as "whores in pin-stripe suits." They admit, however, that the marvelously high fees that consultants command (currently as high as $2,000 a day in New York City) enhance their legitimacy and encourage managers to lend credence to their schemes. Publicly, of course, managers on the way up adopt with great enthusiasm those programs that have caught their bosses' fancy, participate in or run them very effectively, and then quietly drop them when the time is right.[18]

The short-term ethos is crucial in determining managers' stances toward consultants and their programs. A choice between securing one's own success by jumping on and off the bandwagon of the moment, or sacrificing oneself for the long-run good of a corporation by diverting resources and really seeing a program through is, for most managers, no choice at all. Ambitious managers see self-sacrificing loyalty to a company as foolhardy. Moreover, middle and upper-middle level managers upon whom requests for self-sacrifice for the good of the organization are most likely to fall do not see top executives sacrificing themselves for the common good. For example, just after the CEO of Covenant Corporation announced one of his many purges, legitimated by a "comprehensive assessment of the hard choices facing us" by a major consulting firm, he purchased a new Sabre jet for executives and a new 31-foot company limousine for his own use at $1,000 a foot. He then flew the entire board of directors to Europe on the Concorde for a regular meeting to review, it was said, his most recent cost-cutting strategies. As other managers see it, bureaucratic hierarchy gives top bosses the license to act in their own interests and to pursue with impunity the arts of contradiction.

A few other dimensions of the relationships between consultants and managers are worth mentioning. The consultant encounters particular difficulties when he becomes aware that the "real issues" facing him are the political and social structures of a corporation rather than the problem defined for him. Of course, in such cases one may assume that executives are fully aware of the real issues. Most likely, executives are using the consultant to: legitimate already desired unpleasant changes, such as reorganizations; throw rival networks of executives off the track of one's real strategy by diverting resources to marginal programs; undercut consultants employed by other executive groups by establishing what might be called counterplausibility; or advance, as already suggested, a personal or organizational image of being up-to-date, with-it, and avant-garde. The consultant who perceives such discrepancies has to devise his own strategies for handling them. Some of these include: rejecting the assignment altogether; accepting the problem as defined and confining oneself to it for the sake of future contracts even though one knows that any action will be inefficacious; or accepting the assignment but trying to persuade the client to address the underlying social and political issues, that is, redefining the problem. The consultant's own strategy is limited by the constraint that he present his findings according to a certain etiquette, one that has deep roots in the history of the profession—that is, as a rational, objective, scientific judgment that will improve the organization. The consultant's claim to expertise and legitimacy rests on this. As it happens, even if the consultant sees that the real issues are political and social ones and is willing to address them, this emphasis on a pragmatic rational objectivity often produces a somewhat stultifying reification of abstract concepts rather than a detailed explanation of the intricacies of political networks that might lay bare the actual troubles of an organization. But then, managers need and desire the mask of objectivity to cover the capriciousness and arbitrariness of corporate life; consultants want to maintain their occupational self-image as experts. Each group fuels the other's needs and self-images in an occupational drama where the needs of organizations get subordinated to the maintenance of professional identities.

III

The kind of "flexibility" that is required to maintain such stances can be confusing even to those in inner management circles. For instance, a highly placed staff member whose work requires him to interact daily with the top figures of his company, says:

> I get faked out all the time, and I'm part of the system. I come from a very different culture. Where I come from, if you give someone your word, no one ever questions it. It's the old hard-work-will-lead-to-success ideology. Small community, Protestant, agrarian, small business, merchant-type values. I'm disadvantaged in a system like this.

He goes on to characterize the system more fully and what it takes to succeed within it:

> It's the ability to play this system that determines whether you will rise.... And part of the adeptness [required] is determined by how much it bothers people. One thing you have to be able to do is to play the game, but you can't be disturbed by the game. What's the game? It's bringing troops home from Vietnam and declaring peace with honor. It's saying one thing and meaning another.
>
> It's characterizing the reality of a situation with *any* description that is necessary to make that situation more palatable to some group that matters. It means that you have to come up with a culturally accepted verbalization to explain why you are *not* doing what you are doing.... [Or] you say that we had to do what we did because it was inevitable; or because the guys at the [regulatory] agencies were dumb; [you] say we won when we really lost; [you] say we saved money when we squandered it; [you] say something's safe when it's potentially or actually dangerous.... Everyone knows that it's bullshit, but it's *accepted*. This is the game.

He points out how a game can suddenly change:

> Now what upsets the whole game is when some executive on high says: "Well, we just can't accept such and such a loss," or whatever. That throws the whole game into chaos at the middle levels because it disrupts and changes all the rules of the game. But if the guys on high do call a halt to some game, it's not because they're bothered by the game itself but only by the direction a particular game is taking which threatens some interest of their own.

In this view, top executives go home with the ball when they think they are going to lose. In addition, then, to the characteristics described earlier, it seems that a prerequisite for big success in the corporation is a certain adeptness at inconsistency.

I want to make a few general remarks about consistency and inconsistency in public life. Inconstancies and outright contradictions between actions themselves, between actions and appearances, between actions and their explanations, between different explanations, or between explanations and other beliefs are, of course, commonplace human experiences. However, men and women whose occupational roles thrust them into the public forum are often expected to achieve or at least display a degree of consistency in their overall self-presentations, even as they are also expected to do what has to be done. They must seem to be rational even, perhaps especially, when faced with irrationalities; consistent self-presentation is an important measure of such symbolic rationality. Generally speaking, the greater the public scrutiny of one's role performance, the more likely is one to experience pressure for at least the appearance of consistency. Consistent appearances, after all, often provide the only assurance available to, say, potential clients or the public at large that a person has the expertise, organizational skill, and the proper orientation to perform an important job. When, in fact, one points out inconstancies in a person's or a group's public behavior, or discrepancies between professed values and actual practices, the reaction is predictably defensive and, depending on the social power of the group and the vulnerability of the accuser, can be vengeful. Professionals who in some way blow the whistle on their colleagues, for instance, revealing to the public the underside of their occupations, "the roaches and noodles under the rug" in one manager's words, are particularly distrusted and feared.[19] Professionals of any sort are reluctant to have their masks of consistency stripped away, particularly by one in a position to know intimately the inconsistencies necessarily generated by the tensions between monopolized privilege and ideologies of public service.

In the corporate world, one may observe many different kinds of inconsistency among managers. The segmented, fragmented, and hierarchical structure of bureaucratic work lends itself more than other kinds of work situations to the manufacture of multiple ideologies and mythologies. These include not only the attempts of individuals to make sense of their world and lobby for their own positions with others, but also the semi-official viewpoints disseminated through the impressive communications apparatus common to all bureaucracies—I refer here to plant newsletters, monthly employee newspapers, newsbrief circulars, daily news sheet summaries for executives, magazines for managers, and so on—as well as official authoritative pronouncements that, of course, color all other views. Some managers get caught up in this tangle of ideologies, perspectives, and viewpoints and become inconsistent in at least their explanations of reality even over a very short period of time. For example, an upper-middle level manager in Covenant Corporation points out what he observes among his peers:

What's interesting and confusing at the same time is the way guys around here will switch explanations of things from day to day and not even notice. It is astonishing to hear the things people say. Like they explain the current stagnation of our stock one day by referring to the Falkland Islands war; the next day, it's the bearish stock market; the next, it's the Fed's interest policy; the next, it's unsettled political conditions. And so on and on. And they don't remember the explanations they gave a month ago. They end up going around believing in fairy tales that might have no relationship to reality at all.

Various vocabularies of explanation for issues, trends, or events important to an institution get circulated in different organizational circles. Depending on the range of one's social contacts, one adopts different vocabularies to explain the same event. Of course, explanations carrying high-ranking official imprimaturs, however provisional, are circulated rapidly and carry special weight. Except for the necessity to be alert to the vagaries of official views of reality, corporate bureaucracies do not, however, put any premium on such garden variety inconsistency. There is also no check on it as long as one carefully maintains the requisite appearances and does not get stuck with the label of being "flaky." The organizational premium on adeptness at inconsistency becomes particularly evident in the many areas of public controversies that face managers, especially those of high rank. Here the ability to "throw people off the track" with a certain finesse becomes particularly valuable within an organization. Two things come together to produce this situation—managers' sense of beleaguerment and the necessity for them to address a multiplicity of audiences.

Managers feel beleaguered from a wide array of adversaries who, it is thought, want to disrupt or impede management's attempts to further the economic interest of their companies. In every company that I studied, managers see themselves and their traditional prerogatives as being under siege, and they generally respond with a set of sardonic caricatures of their principal adversaries that often, in fact, ridicule these adversaries' perceived inconsistencies. For example, most government regulators are brash, young, unkempt hippies in blue jeans who know nothing about the businesses for which they make rules; OSHA inspectors, in particular, are so ignorant that they want to turn off the electricity before testing power tools. Consumer activists, the far too many Ralph Naders of this world, want to save the universe but not give up their own creature comforts. Workmen's compensation lawyers are out-and-out crooks who prey on corporations to appropriate exorbitant fees for unwary clients whom they fleece next. Labor activists are radical troublemakers who want to disrupt harmonious industrial communities; union leaders might be reasonable men in back rooms but, in public, act as if they have lost their minds. Academics who criticize business may be able to conjugate difficult Greek verbs; unfortunately, many of them cannot tie their own shoelaces. Most environmental activists—the bird and bunny people—are softheaded idealists who want everybody to live in tents, burn candles, ride horses, and eat berries. The leaders of environmental organizations are people who accuse industry of profiteering on pollution while driving to their meetings in "fat-assed Cadillacs"; they are also upper-middle-class people who can summon up heartfelt anguish for snail darters, but never give a thought to how inflation, caused by the choices they impose on industry through the EPA, "ravages working stiffs on the swing shift." And members of the news media, who link together all of these groups clamoring for air time because of the media's own vested interest in catastrophe, are cynical rabble-rousers propagating sensational antibusiness stories to sell papers or advertising time on shows like "60 Minutes," which lay in wait to edit for their own purposes clips of the "poor schnooks" stupid enough to submit to their inquisitions. Caricatures of the media are honed to a fine point among managers who specialize in public relations.

Managers' sense of beleaguerment, reflected in such portraits, ebbs and flows to a great extent with the national political fortunes of business. These are, as it happens, closely tied to those of the Republican party. The barbed defensive hostility of businessmen during the years of the Carter administration gave way, as I suggested earlier, to a sense of belligerent triumph at President Reagan's first election, concealed after a time by a public face of mellow statesmanship, a stance befitting the return to power of a group long accustomed to receiving deference. Still, American managers' sense of beleaguerment has probably been greater over the last two decades than ever before. There are several reasons for this.

First, businessmen's historical claims to legitimacy, along with those of other public figures, were seriously called into question by the social, cultural, and political upheavals of the 1960s and early 1970s. These movements, that were, as it happens, spearheaded by the sons and daughters of segments of the bureaucratized new middle class, resurrected and sharpened critiques of business civilization that have recurred periodically since the triumph of industrial capitalism in the late nineteenth century. These included moral denunciations of a variety of perceived social ills said to be attributable to business: the marked social, economic, and political inequity of U.S. society; the routinization and trivialization of work; the worship of the big organization and the pervasive social conformity this was said to engender; the identification of personal and social well-being with the ever increasing accumulation of material possessions; and the prosecution of foreign military adventures, said to be fostered in part by business's greed and willingness to accept lucrative gain from any source. Of course, these kinds of systemic critiques were fueled regularly with journalistic and scholarly reports of sensational scandals suggesting malfeasance, misfeasance, and corruption on grand scales in the higher circles of business and government. Business's reputation was called into serious question by reports of price fixing, bid riggings, stock manipulation, insider trading, falsification of test data, the marketing of dangerous drugs, industrial accidents, severe occupational health problems allegedly caused by negligence, bribery both domestic and international, and, in a national administration known to be strongly linked to business, the whole grab bag of somewhat seamy practices that was called Watergate.[20]

Such reports recalled for some memories of earlier eras in American business history—of private armies and detectives and union busting; of abysmal and dangerous working conditions; of huge swindles of stock, land, and other equity; of the growth of massive trusts and cartels; of political bossism, graft, patronage, and payoffs on a grand scale; of routinely adulterated foods and completely untested drugs. Such practices became the fodder of muckraking magazines at the turn of the century, alternately titillating and outraging a rural nation poised on the edge of urbanization. The Progressive movement took such practices as some of its targets and demanded and got government regulation of business in key areas.[21] In much the same way, the latest big cycle of government regulation, which began around 1970 and has made its strongest marks in occupational safety and health, regulation of the environment, and protection of the consumer, drew its early energy from broadly based social movements coupled with the public outrage generated by the increase in, or perhaps increased reporting of, recent business scandals.

However, with the aid of a massive expansion of public relations programs, business has been able to overcome most of its reputational crises of this century by relying on the extraordinary vitality of the American economy. Except for the Great Depression, business and government alike have always tried to solve social problems and nullify competing social claims by expanding the economy.

Since 1970, however, many of the fundamental premises of our economic world have changed. Energy is no longer cheap; America can no longer claim to be the undisputed leader of technological know-how or of managerial expertise; the nation's rate of labor productivity increase has suffered a notable and as yet largely unexplained decline; Trotsky's and Veblen's law of uneven development seems to be coming to life as the nation's old industrial heartland has become known as the "Rustbelt," and economic dominance and concomitant social affluence have shifted to new geographical areas, many in the West and Southwest, where new high technology industries are based. And, with only brief respites, the economy has been plagued since 1970 with recurring bouts of inflation, sluggish growth, a combination of the two dubbed stagflation, relatively high rates of unemployment and underemployment, a sharp decline in the increase of real earnings even among middle-class white-collar employees, high interest rates, serious trade deficits and negative international balance of payments, and alarmingly high government deficits. In short, instead of providing the lofty ground suitable for prolonged defense, the American economy has more often in the last fifteen years resembled a quagmire that leaves businessmen vulnerable to attack.

Second, the inherently ambiguous legacies of science and particularly of its applications in technology have caught up with and, in some cases, overrun the glowing promises made for them and the hopes that those promises have nourished with serious consequences for the corporation's claims to legitimacy. This has happened on different levels. For the most part, of course, the American public reveres science. The public attitude toward technology is more tempered but only ideologists of a certain ilk deplore the enormous benefits that science, applied by business, can bring society. Modern life as we

know it—our medical technology, transportation systems, food production
and distribution, information processing and communications networks, to
name only a few obvious examples—depends increasingly on the systematic
commercial application of knowledge won by rational experimental inquiry.
But sometimes particular scientific developments, or more usually, particular
applications of science have, or are seen possibly to have, unintended consequences that make technology and even science seem suddenly perilous as
well as beneficial.[22]

The technological application of scientific knowledge seems double-edged
when the painstakingly produced chemical compounds that constitute effective cooling agents in refrigerators come to be feared as potential destroyers
of the earth's stratospheric ozone; when gene-splicing technology that can
dramatically improve, say, food production is feared to be capable as well of
unleashing microorganisms perilous to humans; when the computer technology that has already dramatically altered our command of information is
thought, if only in science fiction, to be capable of also accidentally triggering
a nuclear war; when a chemical plant in Bhopal, India, producing useful compounds and providing employment in a poor country, suddenly has an emis-
sion that kills 2,000 people; or when nuclear power, heralded since World
War II as the key to pollution-free energy abundance becomes seen, in the
aftermath of Three Mile Island or Chernobyl, as a menace. The issue here is
usually posed as one of control. Who will decide how particular scientific
knowledge is to be applied and what safeguards will govern its application?
The whole burgeoning field of risk analysis[23] is closely tied to such a technical
formulation of the dilemmas posed by science. Risks can, it is argued, be measured, compared, and quantified. Choices, sometimes difficult ones, can be
posed and recommendations proffered to minimize risk in, of course, the most
cost-efficient manner possible. But, as risk analysts will readily admit, no
amount of rational analysis of risks or even redundant systems of control to
prevent accidents can entirely eliminate the possibility of, say, human error.
Moreover, it is a byword in the chemical industry at least that it is precisely
in those technological areas where accidents have seldom occurred that the
largest potential catastrophes loom; the very lack of practice in responding
quickly to untoward incidents can precipitate uncontrollable events.

More generally, modern science and technology epitomize the exaltation
of the human intellect and the ability of rationally calculated action to sweep
away the dark and tangled mysteries of the world. The world becomes an
object of systematic investigation, of carefully reckoned probabilities, of
planned manipulation. In the process, science and technology systematically
divest the world of the inexplicable, of the magical, of the mysterious. One
does not, of course, know or even care how everything in one's daily life has
come to be or functions—say, how styrofoam coffee cups are made from
chemicals or how the durability of oxford broadcloth depends on the expert
blending of cotton and polyester. But, in a world where science is a god, one
knows that one can find out. The surety that the rational/technical habit of
mind produces disenchants the world, as Max Weber pointed out,[24] and

undermines nonrational, irrational, or suprarational explanations for the way things are. It devalues myth, poetry, and religion.

This process of disenchantment becomes problematic, however, when some turn of events upsets a taken for granted acceptance of the benefits of science or of a particular technology and tinges something generally thought to be wondrous or at least beneficial with malevolence. When wonder becomes horror in the public eye, particular scientific advances and the industries based on them get called into serious question. Unanticipated consequences of technological advances seem especially to precipitate such a reaction. When, for instance, a manufacturer of feminine hygiene products introduced an extremely absorbent fiber into tampons a few years ago, the resultant "toxic shock syndrome" deaths among young women almost decimated that product line among all manufacturers. Such incidents shake, if only briefly, the whole positivistic faith that underpins our civilization and that helps constitute business's high ground of defense.

The matter becomes still more complicated.[25] When some unanticipated event or the unforeseen consequences of some decision involving science and technology results in harm to human beings, those injured at least and sometimes their relatives as well seek explanation and demand accountings for what occurred. Scientific reasoning can, however, offer only rational causal explanations of how something happened, of the statistical probability of its reoccurrence, of the likelihood of lasting damage. Neither science nor the promise of technological improvements can provide solace, meaning, significance, sympathy, or comfort to human beings who feel injured or bereaved. In fact, as part of its general disenchantment of the world, scientific rationality undercuts traditional religious attempts to provide consoling theodicies, that is, comforting theories of the justice of God, that might explain suffering, death, or the unequal distribution of good and bad fortune brought about by scientific or technological advances.

Latent fears about the possible uses and consequences of scientific knowledge coupled with the collapse of traditional religious theodicies breed the ever present potential for public rage that managers see as irrational. I mean here the sentiment that seems common in our public life, a mixture of moral indignation and resentment not necessarily tied to specific events though often triggered by them. In the areas of science and technology, rage becomes directed against those institutional orders thought to control the applications of science. Both government and business become objects of such rage, with the latter often singled out for special opprobrium because of business's unabashed self-interest. This kind of rage cannot be explained by the outside agitator theories implicit in managers' caricatures of perceived adversaries.

The outside agitator thesis is also propagated in various ways, one should note, by some academic champions of business. Such writers suggest that leadership cliques of special-interest groups, working adroitly with a "sectarian" ideology that among other things stresses "purity of heart and mind," keep themselves in power in their voluntary organizations by exploiting their members' and the general public's fears, particularly of industrial pollution.[26]

Though one can hardly dispute that the public is manipulated to some extent by special-interest groups with the lucrative collaboration of the media, such a view does not explain either the latent public fears about some applications of science, or particularly the phenomenon of public rage that has produced a proliferation of legal claims against corporations. The last point is particularly important since the growing demand on corporations for monetary restitution for perceived injuries suggests a more complicated relationship between business and the public.

Part of the folklore of the modern corporation, in fact, consists of a catalog of stories about how big corporations are being victimized by the courts in what amounts to a radical transformation of tort law. Managers repeat variations of cases—for instance, of a man who purchased a thrice-owned punch machine, altered it, and after losing a finger, sued the original manufacturer for negligent construction; of a farmer who, despite clearly marked warning labels, coated his animal feed troughs with a toxic wood preservative, sold milk from contaminated cattle, and then when he himself was sued by irate parents whose children had drunk the milk, sued the chemical company who produced the preservative; or of a student research assistant inexplicably asked to carry dangerous acid in glass containers on a faulty elevator which lurched and caused the young woman to break a container, showering her with acid and permanently disfiguring her. Although she is said to have sued her university, her supervising professor, the elevator manufacturer, and the chemical company that provided the acid, managers had few doubts that the jury would "pin the tail on business" because of the "abiding conviction that corporations have vaults filled with gold bars called profits." At some level, even managers who repeat such stories and thus reinforce their own shared sense of beleaguerment, recognize the profound and profoundly felt dependence of most people in our society on those large organizations that claim to control the scientific genie.

The rational/technical habit of mind at the core of the modern corporation produces the vast material benefits that engender such dependence at the same time that it sweeps away the cobwebs of old faiths. The new faith of scientific rationality and rational control of technology always causes, however, considerable dangers, at least for those who claim to be its ministers. When things go wrong, one might well be accused of betraying promises made to one's flock.

Third, in a world of collapsed theodicies, one denuded, therefore, of ultimate significance, the quest for inner-worldly salvation of a sort becomes intense. Such quests for salvation assume many different forms, often totally incongruous with the functionally rational, pragmatic positivism at the core of the bureaucratic ethos that dominates public life in our society. One of the most important of these in contemporary American society is the quest for self-perfection through the ascetic conditioning and care of the body, a development which, as it happens, has been a boon to some industries and a scourge to others. The fashion, health-care, cosmetics, sporting goods and other physical fitness industries, certain food enterprises, as well as certain cultural forms, that is, dance in general, ballet in particular, owe much of their upsurge in recent years to the sacralization of the body among the American middle classes. There seems to be a growing obsession with preserving, improving, and beautifying the body, which in some circles has assumed the status of a sacramental object. The impulse for this kind of salvation through self-control, self-discipline, and self-abnegation directly parallels the self-rationalization and self-promotion endemic to the corporate world, where only the most naive expect reward as just deserts for effort. Some segments of the bureaucratic new middle classes in particular carry the sacralization of the body to quite far reaches. Nowhere is this tendency more evident than in the diverse and widespread attempts to protect the body's purity against external contamination. The whole drift in recent years toward what are thought to be natural foods, the minimization of additives and preservatives in food, the surge in popularity of lighter alcoholic beverages, the changes in public perceptions toward the effects of even secondary tobacco smoke inhalation, are only a few of the practical consequences of the ideology of sacramental bodily purity. One may, of course, abuse one's body in a myriad of ways—for example, through drug use—while maintaining such an ideology. The key here is the perceived source of contamination. Involuntary contamination thought to be imposed by external agents, particularly by powerful institutions like business or government, becomes, under such an ideology, intolerable. This ideology, even in muted form, seems almost designed to clash with the hopeful positivistic creed of American business, although it is important to note that a great many businessmen hold to the ideology in private where their own particular industries or special areas of expertise within an industry are not concerned. As it happens, chemical pollution—which one cannot see, hear, or often even smell, let alone control—completely undercuts the ideology of salvation through bodily control and consequent purity and casts people back into a threatening world from which even an inscrutable god has disappeared. The public outrage against the chemical industry in the last fifteen years—consider, for instance, the perceptual distance between the long-held and widespread acceptance of Dupont's promise of "Better Living Through Chemistry" to the public hysteria over Love Canal—reflects not only the public redefinition of formerly accepted practices, or even the discovery of actual industrial abuses, but also the frustration of a salvation ideology. The stories that fill newspapers about chemical pollution, always, managers say, complete with pictures showing half-decayed drums, become daily reminders to many that one's fate in a threatening world depends largely on the same bureaucracies that have not only destroyed old gods but undermined new secular theodicies.

The irrationality that emerges from such ideological frustration continually clashes with managers' own worldviews and sometimes fuels managers' acerbic sense of humor. I do not mean to suggest that managers' worldviews in this area are monolithic. Organizational proximity to actual production processes, for instance, shapes managers' attitudes in distinctive ways, providing, say, plant managers, even those in entirely different industries, with beliefs more in common with each other than with their own organizational colleagues in, say, sales and marketing. But, as a general rule, managers' familiarity with and pragmatic acceptance of inevitable industrial mishaps breeds in them a certain cavalier attitude toward them that outsiders, especially those who adopt the ideology of bodily purity, might see as grave peril. Consider a story told by a senior manager at Alchemy Inc., recounted with great gusto to an appreciative audience of juniors and peers:

> I was at this party the other night and I was sitting next to this older lady and she said: "My God, did you people see the paper tonight? There's leakage from some chemical plant and it's infecting the drinking water around here." So I asked if I could see the paper and the article said that there was some seepage out of a pond that a chemical plant used for disposal but that the EPA was monitoring the situation as well as all 25 wells in the area. In the meantime, the company was remedying the situation. I pointed this out and she looked at me, her eyes narrowed, and she asked, "Who do you work for?" I said I worked for a large chemical firm and she burst out laughing and asked if I expected her to believe me. She laughed right in my face! I asked her what she was worried about. You have to drink the water for 25 years before anything would happen—I mean, she was already a grandmother—but that didn't seem to help her much.

Such incongruities of perspective commonly mark managers' encounters with various segments of the public. Chemical company managers are only the paradigmatic case here. My interviews are filled with stories of managers who claim to have been verbally assaulted not only by strangers at cocktail parties, but by their children's teachers when they visit schools, and even by their children themselves at the breakfast table for being supposedly callous and insensitive to the social consequences of business activity. Perhaps more than anything else, managers are puzzled by such attacks, though they pounce quickly on any inconsistencies that they perceive in their opponents. For example, one manager whose firm produced a pesticide that became caught up in a widely publicized episode of mishandling and illegal disposal was attacked by his brother-in-law, a lifelong military man, for his very association with the company. The manager found it grimly ironic that "things have reached a point where a trained killer is berating me for producing something useful." More generally, managers view the irrational fear of contamination evinced by those who espouse an ideology of bodily purity with some derision. One can, after all, referring to the same pesticide, "eat handfuls of the stuff with no lasting adverse effects." Moreover, they point out as only one example of the alchemy that science and ingenuity can produce, how the filthiest crankcase oil can be filtered through sulfuric acid to produce a lotion gentle enough for a baby's skin. To insist primly on bodily purity not only betrays an unwarranted squeamishness in an industrial age, but a lack of faith in the magic of science, let alone in the resilience and recuperative powers of the human body.

All of these factors come together to produce managers' sense of beleaguerment. I can best illustrate the social psychological meaning of these larger historical trends for managers by repeating the account of one middle-level production manager in the chemical company. He describes how actual scientific discoveries and shifting social definitions have repeatedly over the last three decades turned the personal meaning of his work upside down:

Well, from 1957 through 1962, I was intimately involved with the manufacture of DDT. During that time, we doubled production and sold almost all of it to Africa and India. And I knew and went home *knowing* that I was saving more lives than any major hospital was capable of doing. I *knew* that I was saving thousands of lives by doing this.

Then Rachel Carson's *Silent Spring* came out and not only did I become a murderer of falcons and robins, but also one of the mass murderers of the world. I was now doing evil things to the world.

Then I went to a plant which was manufacturing [chlorofluorocarbons] and we increased production by 20–25 percent; a lot of it went into hair sprays. We also used vinyl chloride and found out that it was causing liver cancer. Then I found out that I was destroying the whole ozone layer of the earth and doing it for personal gain.

Then I went into soda ash. Without it, there wouldn't be a window pane in the whole United States. But at the time, because of the Clean Air Act and the Clean Water Act, suddenly I became a polluter. Children learned in school that chemicals killed. And, of course, there was no question in the academic community that I was perceived as an evil person doing evil things. And that became true even in the corporation. Plants became a *liability*, rather than the source of wealth. The perception was: Wouldn't it be nice if we could just sell chemicals without producing them? So the profession of producing things became a *low* profession and the good people were those who were producing services. Manufacturing people became evil. I think this is one reason that marketing people became ascendant in the competition for advancement.

Then I went into making sulfuric acid and that involved the whole issue of water pollution.

He goes on to describe his reaction to all of this:

I guess I'm more bemused than anything else. It's the same type of feeling that I would have if I were an MD who had been doing radical mastectomies and then someone says—hey, you didn't have to do that. It's a feeling of disappointment without a feeling of shame. *I know that I have done some useful things.* I know that the only source of money is taking something out of the ground and making something. That's where money comes from—making something out of nothing. Without that type of activity, civilization wouldn't exist. So, on something like DDT, I'll leave the judgment to Europe after World War II and all the people saved by the widespread use of it.

The very significance of one's work, like many other aspects of organizational life, becomes ambiguous. One reaches out, of course, for whatever solid meanings are at hand. But one recognizes that, in a moment, one's best efforts can be called into question and perhaps even nullified. One of the few consolations available is the hope that those who reinterpret one's work and denigrate its value might someday be seen to be captive to a kind of moral smugness.

Within this context of perceived harrassment and shifting scientific and ideological winds, while always attending to the pressing and sometimes contradictory exigencies of business life, managers must address a multiplicity of audiences, some of whom are considered rivals, and some outright adversaries. These audiences are the internal corporate hierarchy with its intricate and shifting power cliques and competing managerial circles, key regulators, local and federal legislators, special publics that vary according to the issues, and the public at large, whose goodwill and favorable opinions are considered essential for a company's free operation. Managerial adeptness at inconsistency becomes evident in the widely discrepant perspectives, reasons for action, and presentations of fact that explain, excuse, or justify managerial behavior to these diverse audiences.

The cotton dust issue in the textile industry illustrates what I mean. Prolonged exposure to cotton dust produces in many workers a chronic and disabling pulmonary disease called byssinosis or, colloquially, brown lung. In 1979, according to an estimate from the U.S. Department of Labor, about 560,000 workers were exposed to cotton dust each year and 84,000 of these had byssinosis in some degree.[27] Bernadino Ramazzini, considered the father of occupational medicine, had pointed out lung disorders among flax and hemp workers in Italy in his great treatise *De Morbis Artificum*, published in 1713.[28] After the Industrial Revolution, observations of similar disorders were made throughout the world in the textile industry.[29] British medical researchers in particular thoroughly documented a high incidence of byssinosis among British textile workers, and it was made a compensable occupational disease in England under the Byssinosis Act in 1941.[30] By contrast, a major epidemiological study in the United States published in 1933, though it noted some disabling respiratory illnesses, did not specifically attribute such ailments to cotton dust.[31] Even as late at 1947, the Federal Security Agency of the U.S. Public Health Service said:

In the United States, however, the problem of serious dust disease among cotton workers is hardly known to exist. It is possible that it does exist but goes unrecognized or is ignored, or is obviated by worker turnover, i.e., workers leave the industry before disabling symptoms develop.[32]

Two British researchers, puzzled by the disparity between the British and American findings, undertook a pilot study in 1960 in two mills in the United States; they discovered that some byssinosis was indeed present in the American mills.[33] Since that time, there has been a plethora of studies on the subject both by independent or university-affiliated researchers and by specialists working for the textile industry.[34] In the early 1970s, the Occupational Safety and Health Administration proposed a ruling to cut workers' exposure to cotton dust sharply by requiring textile companies to invest large amounts of money to clean up their plants. The industry fought the regulation fiercely but a final OSHA ruling was made in 1978 requiring full compliance by 1984.[35]

The industry took the case to court. Reagan appointees in OSHA tried to have the case removed from judicial consideration and remanded to the agency they controlled for further cost-benefit analysis. This move produced a curious mixture of jubilation and private wariness among key managers in Weft Corporation; I shall comment on this shortly. The Supreme Court, however, decided in 1981 that the 1978 OSHA ruling was fully within the Agency's mandate, namely to protect workers' health and safety as the primary benefit exceeding all cost considerations.

During these proceedings, Weft Corporation was engaged on a variety of fronts and was pursuing a number of actions. For instance, it intensively lobbied regulators and legislators and prepared court material for the industry's defense, arguing that the proposed standard would crush the industry and that the cotton dust problem, if it in fact exists, should be met by increasing workers' use of respirators.

The company also joined the rest of the industry in hammering out, in public and private, an ideology with several main recurring themes aimed at special-interest groups as well as at the general public. The ideology went as follows. There is probably no such thing as byssinosis; textile workers suffering from pulmonary problems are all heavy smokers and the real culprit is the government subsidized tobacco industry. Even very healthy young men and women just graduated from high school cannot pass the pre-employment breathing test administered at the cotton mills, a clear indication of how debilitating smoking can be to lung capacity.[36] Besides, 20 to 25 percent of the general adult population has some form of chronic breathing problems with symptoms similar to byssinosis.[37] Therefore, if there is a problem, it is one almost impossible to diagnose accurately and fairly, since the pool of workers from which the textile industry draws already have lung disorders. The textile industry should not bear the burden of medical problems unrelated to work. Moreover, if there actually is a problem in the workplace, only a few workers are afflicted and these must be particularly susceptible to impurities or even biological agents in cotton. Clearly, cotton growers are deeply implicated since the cotton bales they deliver to the docks of textile factories might contain the real, though as yet unknown, microbiological causes of the alleged disease byssinosis. Rather than engineering controls, the more reasonable solution then would be increased medical screening of the work force to detect susceptible people and prevent them from ever reaching the mill floor. Reasonable medical surveillance should also be increased to detect and remove workers if breathing irregularities are later noticed. Byssinosis is, after all, 100 percent reversible if detected in its early stages. But the preshift and post-shift testing proposed by OSHA cannot easily be routinized, at least if the mills are to be kept running.

Further, the proposed regulation is based on faulty research containing errors in data selection, methodology, and analysis that seriously call its validity into question. In fact, the very instrument specified to measure cotton dust—the vertical elutriator—picks up all sorts of moisture, sizing, and oil-sodden, airborne particulates, making accurate measurement of actual cotton dust highly suspect.[38] At the least, the findings on which OSHA is relying are not generalizable to the whole textile industry. Regulation must be based on scientific grounds. Not only is OSHA's science faulty but all the important issues surrounding cotton dust have become obscured by the rampant emotionalism generated by self-serving special-interest groups like *The Charlotte Observer*, which produced the inflammatory series "Brown Lung: A Case of Deadly Neglect."[39] The very term "brown lung" is, in fact, a misnomer invented by Ralph Nader to suggest false parallels in the public mind between byssinosis and silicosis, or black lung. Besides, how can cotton cause brown lung when cotton is white? Only one of the sorry consequences of such misinformation is the misplaced public sympathy extended to former textile workers—mostly poor, ignorant, old people—who, coached in the sequence of symptoms to report by radical groups like the Brown Lung Association[40] and, of course, by lawyers, repay the generosity of their former employers with compensation suits, a tactic sure to disrupt the traditionally amicable community relations of mill towns. Moreover, compensation claims by workers are stirring up trouble between textile companies themselves. Workers can claim compensation after seven years' exposure to cotton dust, but that entire time need not be spent in one corporation. Since typically the last employer foots the bill, one manufacturer ends up paying for the disabilities caused by another. Finally, Weft Corporation, and the industry as a whole, claimed that if the regulation were imposed, most of the textile industry would move overseas, where regulations are less harsh.

In the meantime, Weft, as well as all the large and medium-sized American textile companies, was actually addressing the cotton dust problem, but in a characteristically indirect way. As part of a larger modernization effort, the firm invested $20 million in a few plants where executives knew such an investment would make money. Among other things, this investment automated with chutes the early stages of handling cotton—opening the bales and picking through the cotton—traditionally a very slow procedure, and substantially increased productivity. The new technology was not only faster, but produced fewer downtime periods and fewer operator errors. One should note that this relatively high rate of productivity has been the broad pattern throughout the industry for the last several years; even during the 1981 recession, textiles led all manufacturing sectors in rate of productivity increase.[41]

The investment also had the side benefit of reducing cotton dust levels to the new standard in precisely those areas of the work process where the dust problem is greatest. In fact, some of the new technology itself demanded a cleaner work environment because the machinery's lower dust tolerance required the installation of automatic traveling vacuums. One manager who was in charge of the project to evaluate investment alternatives for one large complex comments on whether dust control was a principal factor in the decision to spend $15 million modernizing several carding rooms:

> No, definitely not. Would any sane, rational man spend $15 million for a 2 percent return? . . . Now it does improve the dust levels, but it was that if we don't invest the money now, we would be in a desperate [competitive] position fifteen years from now. Our demonstrated cash flow situation was such that eventually we would have had even tougher decisions to make. None of these were clear-cut decisions. There are always several sets of inputs—like with our chute-fed cards. That had some complexities . . . like the cost of building them and the flow of production problems that they might create or resolve. Like at [Jackson plant], you could eliminate the dust problem without going to chute-fed cards or you could go to cost-saving modernizing for the long term which would improve quality as well *and* in addition deal with the dust issue. It was on these bases that the decision was made.

Publicly, of course, Weft Corporation, as do many other firms, claims that the money was spent entirely to eliminate dust, evidence of its corporate good citizenship. Privately, executives admit that without the productive return, they would not have—indeed, given the constraints under which they operate—could not have spent the money. And they have not done so in several other plants and only with great reluctance, if at all, in sections of otherwise renovated plants where it is more difficult to increase productivity with machinery to achieve simultaneous cost and dust reduction.

Indeed, the productive return is the only rationale that carries real weight within the corporate hierarchy. This is not seen narrowly. Executives are acutely aware that a major problem facing the textile industry is its pejorative image among younger workers who increasingly shun work that might bring upon themselves the old stereotypes applied to cotton mill workers of being a "linthead" or "woolhead." The industry has to modernize even to maintain its footing in the lower 40 percent of the labor pool from which it now draws its workers. Executives also admit, somewhat ruefully and only when their office doors are closed, that OSHA's regulation on cotton dust has been the main factor in forcing the pace of technological innovation in a centuries-old, hidebound, and somewhat stagnant industry. It has also been a major factor in forcing executives to think in the long run rather than continually succumbing to short-term pressures. This is one of the reasons why the shrewdest among them only feigned elation at the attempts by Reagan's OSHA appointees to remove the cotton dust regulation from the purview of the

Supreme Court. If such a move were successful, it could only encourage the traditionally reactionary elements of the textile industry who refuse to recognize on principle that government regulation, within reason, can be the businessman's best friend. A high-ranking Weft executive explains:

> See, from the start, it had been put into perspective by the industry that we should take advantage of any loopholes. And this is the typical corporate response pattern—to hedge, dodge, and try to avoid the issue in every possible way. You know, [use] the old line: "Nobody has conclusively proved that. . . ." Or to adopt the old smoking and byssinosis line. And all this when anyone who has ever been in a cotton mill, especially back in 1958, or spent some time in the mill villages, knows goddam well there was a problem. We *know* that there is something in cotton dust that causes byssinosis. I often feel that if we had not hollered and shouted and had just spent the money on technology that we wouldn't have a problem today. To some extent, this is a southern knee-jerk reaction . . . to government. We still have a lot of old-timers who think that Calvin Coolidge is still in the White House.

Even other, more moderate managers make the serious mistake of believing the industry's press releases and thus getting tangled in the flypaper of their own ideologies. But shrewd, flexible managers know that appeals to inevitability, like the cotton dust rule, as long as they are invoked with a kind of controlled exasperation, are the safest way to break internal organizational deadlocks, bring substantive critical rationality into play in managerial work, and get things done.

Such adeptness at inconsistency, without moral uneasiness, is essential for executive success. Done over a period of time, in fact, it seems to become a taken for granted habit of mind. As one executive at Covenant Corporation says:

> Now some people don't understand this. . . . But as you move up the ladder, you don't have people who don't understand. And the people up high don't necessarily do it consciously. They are able to speak out of both sides of their mouth without missing a step.

It means being able to say, as a very high-ranking official of Weft Corporation said to me without batting an eye, that the industry has never caused the slightest problem in any worker's breathing capacity. It means, in Covenant Corporation, propagating an elaborate hazard/benefit calculus for approval of dangerous chemicals while internally conceptualizing "hazards" as business risks. It means publicly extolling the carefulness of testing procedures on toxic chemicals while privately ridiculing animal tests as inapplicable to humans.

It means publicly demanding increased self-regulation of industry while privately acknowledging that the competitive welter of corporate life and of the market consistently obscures attention to social needs. It means lobbying intensively in the present to shape government regulations to one's immediate advantage and, ten years later, in the event of a catastrophe, arguing that the company acted strictly in accordance with the standards of the time. It means claiming that the real problem of our society is its unwillingness to take risks. Why not, for instance, cover sidewalks because some pedestrians get hurt by runaway cars? Why the clamor about possible radiation from nuclear power plants when people in Denver are exposed every day to higher levels of natural radiation in their air? In the thickets of one's bureaucracy, of course, one avoids risks at every turn. It means publicly denouncing those who, like Tom and Daisy in F. Scott Fitzgerald's novel "smashed up things and creatures . . . and let other people clean up the mess they had made . . . ,"[42] such as the paper mill upstream from Weft's main finishing operation that spews bilious waste into the river or the "midnight dumpsters" who illegally bury toxic chemical waste, leaving Covenant and other big corporations holding the bag under Superfund. In the furtherance of one's own career, of course, one assiduously follows the "take the money and run" ethos. It means, as well, making every effort to socialize the costs of industrial activity, arguing that one is furthering the common weal, while, of course, striving to privatize the benefits. Only those men and women who can accept the world as it is with all of its irrationalities and who can say what has to be said in order to do what has to be done for one's organization and for oneself have a true calling to higher corporate office.

Finally, those truly adept at inconsistency can also interpret with some accuracy the inconsistent machinations of their colleagues and adversaries. This is not a mean skill. At the very beginning of my fieldwork, the top lawyer of a large corporation was discussing an issue that I had raised when he said:

> Now, I'm going to be completely honest with you about this.

He paused for a moment and then said:

> By the way, in the corporate world, whenever anybody says to you: "I'm going to be completely honest with you about this," you should immediately know that a curveball is on the way. But, of course, that doesn't apply to what I'm about to tell you.

In a world of cheerfully bland public faces, where words are always provisional, intentions always cloaked, and frankness simply one of many guises, wily discernment, being able, as managers say "to separate the honey from the horseshit," becomes an indispensable skill.

7

The Magic Lantern

I

The need for symbolic dexterity, particularly the ability to fashion, quickly and readily, appropriate legitimations for what must be done, intensifies as one ascends the corporate ladder. Since the success of large commercial bureaucracies depends to a great extent on the goodwill of the consuming public, ambitious managers recognize that great organizational premiums are placed on the ability to explain expedient action convincingly. Public opinion, of course, constitutes one of the only effective checks on the bureaucratic impulse to translate all moral issues into practical concerns. Managers not only face the highly specific and usually ideological standpoints of one or another "special-interest" group but, even more fearsome, the vague, ill-formed, diffuse, highly volatile, and often irrational public opinion that is both the target of special-interest groups and the lifeblood of the news media. Those imbued with the bureaucratic ethos thus make every effort to mold public opinion to allow the continued uninterrupted operation of business. Moreover, since public opinion inevitably affects to some extent managers' own conceptions of their work and of themselves, public goodwill, even that which managers themselves create, becomes an important part of managers' own valued self-images. In this sense, both moral issues and social identities become issues of public relations.

Public relations serves many different functions, some of them overlapping. Among the most important are: the systematic promotion of institutional goals, products, images, and ideologies that is colloquially called "hype," a word probably derived from hyperbole or, perhaps, from hypodermic; the direct or, more often, indirect lobbying of legislators, regulators, special publics, or the public at large to influence the course of legislation; the creation, through a whole variety of techniques, like matchmaking money with art or social science, of a favorable awareness of a corporation to provide a sense of public importance to otherwise anonymous millionaires; and the manufacture and promulgation of official versions of reality or of benign public images that smooth the way for the attainment of corporate goals or, in special circumstances, that help erase the taint of some social stigma affixed to a corporation. In short, the goal is to get one's story out to important publics. In such ways, managers can at least try to shape and control the main dimensions of public opinion in an unsettled social order where values, leadership, and even the direction of the society itself often seem up for grabs. This attempt to establish some sort of rationality and predictability over potentially tumultuous public opinion parallels exactly the corporate rationalization of the workplace itself through the techniques of scientific management and the rationalization of employee relationships through the human relations movement and its latter-day progeny.

Most corporations try to get their stories out on a regular sustained basis, intensifying their efforts, of course, during crisis periods. For the most part, corporations allot this work to special practitioners of public relations within the firm who consult regularly with the highest officials of the organization. These practitioners, and quite often the highest officials themselves, also employ public relations specialists in agencies. With some important differences that I shall discuss later, the views of public relations specialists both in corporations and in agencies correspond closely with those of corporate executives and managers, though typically the outlook of specialists is more detached. In particular, public relations work gives its specialists a fine appreciation of how the drama of social reality is constructed because they themselves are usually the playwrights and the stage directors. Public relations specialists may then be considered sophisticated proxies for those corporate managers sensitive to public opinion. Their work, which consists essentially of creating and disseminating various ideologies, the ethics that they fashion, and in particular the basic habit of mind that underpins all of their efforts, provide some insight into how moral issues get translated into issues of public relations.

II

From the modern beginnings of their occupation, men and women in public relations have been acutely aware that social reality and social reputations are not given but made. Modern public relations began with the ballyhoo of the circus and carnival barkers whose job it was to pull crowds into the big tent or the sideshow or point out to the assembled multitude the derring-do of performers. Some carnival barkers had to dazzle crowds long enough—by keeping, for instance, everyone's neck craned while the crowd looked up at the high diver poised before flight—in order to allow the pickpocket concession time enough to work their light-fingered magic.[1] Later, press agents built on the simple and effective messages of propaganda that P. T. Barnum enunciated in his autobiography.[2] They developed a wonderworld of publicity stunts that delighted, amazed, and amused millions of people and drew public attention to clients or to other wares. Harry Reichenbach, by his own admission the greatest publicist of them all, tells in his autobiography, among a great many other tales, the story of how he elevated, on a wager, "an unknown girl with hardly any ability and in ten days had her name in electric lights on Broadway at a star's salary,"[3] and how he arranged to have Rudolph Valentino's beard shaved off at a national barbers' convention and the remains deposited in a museum, thereby benefiting both the barbers and Valentino's sagging popularity.[4] His promotional work for the infant motion-picture industry consumed a great part of his career. In pushing one movie or another, he organized a delegation of Turkish notables (actually recruited from the Lower East Side) to visit New York on a secret mission to find the "Virgin of Stamboul," a fabled heiress who had been whisked from her native land on an American freighter in a romantic intrigue.[5] He arranged for a lion to be smuggled into a posh New York hotel in a piano case and appear later with its "owner," one T. R. Zann.[6] In two other stunts, both unfortunately aborted, he organized a cannibal tribe in Tarrytown, New York,[7] and had the ossified salt body of Lot's wife, complete with a certifying letter from an English archaeologist in Egypt, discovered by a night watchman in a vacant field.[8]

It is worth looking past what seem today to be sophomoric stunts to dwell briefly on Reichenbach's career. Behind his disarming optimistic ingenuousness, itself an occupational characteristic of public relations practitioners, lies a hard appraisal of the malleability of social reality and of people themselves that is also typical of the occupation. Reflecting, for instance, on how he had arranged for an oversized orangutan dressed in a tuxedo and high silk hat to drop in on New York's 400 at the Knickerbocker Club, Reichenbach says:

> The idea that it would be possible for a monkey dressed in natty clothes to crash into society was something unusual, unbelievable, and when it happened, it furnished front-page material. The fact that I had planted this episode and used it to promote the Tarzan picture, established more firmly in my mind that the whole difference between the things one dreamed about and reality was simply a matter of projection. Many publicity stunts that occurred later on in my work took on this magic-lantern effect. An idea that would seem at first flush, extravagant and impossible, became by the proper projection into life, a big item of commanding news value.[9]

He observes that some kinds of fabricated episodes, like that of the Turkish sheiks searching for the lost heiress, exert a powerful hold on the public mind:

> There was that quality of fascination about the incident that made it almost better than truth. It had become romance, illusion. It was one

of those episodes which gave public and press alike the feeling that if it didn't happen, it should have happened![10]

The news media collaborate with publicists to exploit these kinds of public fancies.

> Wish-news is a type of publicity that nearly always breaks on the front page. It is news so thrilling, melodramatic and heart-gripping that every city editor wishes it were true. There was a time when publicity men would concoct this kind of news in dark corners for fear of being exposed. Today some tabloids don't wait for publicity men to concoct it. They make it up themselves.[11]

Playing with the magic lantern demands, of course, a pliable audience, and Reichenbach discovered at an early age the seemingly inexhaustible gullibility of the crowd and, indeed, its complicity in its own deception. Professional solicitors of the crowd's approval were not much different. Even a boy from Frostburg, Maryland, like Reichenbach, could concoct stories from "simple backwoods recipe(s)" that "wise newspapermen" from the "mighty cosmopolitan press" would eagerly devour.[12] In time, even those whose fame had been entirely fabricated with skillful artifice came to believe their own press clippings.

> [T]he irony of all publicity [is that] ... No matter how fantastic the ruse by which an unknown actor was lifted to fame, he'd come to believe it was true and the poor press agent would be shocked to find that he had never told a lie.[13]

Reichenbach came to see himself at the center of a vast matrix of influence. Given what he saw as the gullibility of most people, this had broad ramifications.

> Publicity is the nervous system of the world. Through the network of press, radio, film and lights, a thought can be flashed around the world the instant it is conceived. And through this same highly sensitive, swift and efficient mechanism it is possible for fifty people in a metropolis like New York to dictate the customs, trends, thoughts, fads and opinions of an entire nation of a hundred and twenty million people.[14]

In this view, "the mass is always a magnified reflection of some individual."[15]

> Take apart the average individual, dissect his mind, his manner, his attitudes and you will find that every idea, every major habit and trend in his makeup is a reflection of the fifty outstanding personalities of the day.[16]

In the average person's mind, Rockefeller's new dimes exemplify thrift; Zieg-feld's Follies girls female beauty; and Irving Berlin's latest tune the standard of popular music.[17] The wise publicist need only find the right personalities of the moment and tie his client's needs to their luster.[18] Moreover, Reichen-bach saw publicity as a wholly neutral tool, a "blind disseminating force" that worked for anyone who knew how to use it, as effective for inspired reform-ers as for racketeers. He noted that the latter, in fact, had come to appreciate the value of a good front and the great utility for business of being well-dressed, living a genteel lifestyle, and of being known as a good family man.[19] In such a view, reality dissolves into appearances and becomes chimerical. Notions of substance get lost in a welter of shadowy images, of staged events, of carefully arranged fronts. The publicist sits in the wings of a theater he has fashioned, amidst all the rigging and props, and watches with detached bemusement and eventually with a growing private cynicism,[20] masked always by public ingenuousness, the plays he has written, the actors he has put on stage, and the warm appreciation of an audience he has assembled precisely by creating illusions.

In time, the circus barker and the ballyhoo expert became transformed into the more dignified public relations counsel. Other writers have detailed the main stages and themes of what was a tangled and uneven development.[21] I shall mention here only some highlights of the main drift of this history.

1. To counter the moralistic antibusiness broadsides of muckraking jour-nalists early in this century, businesses began to hire their own press agents to plant favorable stories in newspapers and magazines, both with and without attribution. Businesses also withdrew advertising revenues from leading muckraking journals, forcing some to cease publication.[22] At the same time, some enlightened business leaders and their counselors, led by the Guggen-heims and the Rockefellers, began to develop the more sophisticated tech-niques of the frank open statement toward one's enemies and the grand con-ciliatory gestures like benefices to the public, that preempt all discussion.[23] The leading public relations man of the pre-World War I era, Ivy Lee, coun-selor to the Rockefellers, advocated in fact the supremacy of public opinion in a democracy and the necessity for corporate leaders to court it in a rational open way, with the public relations counselor as an interlocutor.[24] In this view, public relations could play a useful role in persuading business to make actual substantive reforms rather than merely paper over real concerns with talk and gestures. Though Lee's public philosophy was not entirely consistent with his actual practice, this idealized image of the profession persists today among some public relations practitioners and it is occasionally fulfilled.

2. The crucible of World War I saw the melding of the three emerging professions of symbol manipulation and management—journalism, public relations, and advertising—through the institutional mechanism of the Com-mittee on Public Information, headed by George Creel. This vast sprawling propaganda organization brought former muckraking journalists, like Creel himself, together with promoters of corporate privilege, like Harry Reichen-bach and Ivy Lee, in the higher cause of mobilizing ideas to carry the "Gospel

of Americanism to every corner of the globe."[25] A whole generation of opinion-shapers, storytellers, publicity experts, and image-makers honed their already well-developed skills in symbol manipulation to a fine point in selling the war to end all wars to the American people, the idea of America to the world, and the idea of surrender to enemy soldiers.[26] As Richard Tedlow has pointed out,[27] many of the participants in Creel's committee went on to become leaders in public relations and related fields.

The apparent success of wartime propaganda heightened interest in the professional possibilities of molding public opinion in peacetime. One of Creel's committee, Edward Bernays, the man who displaced Ivy Lee and became the prototype of the 1920s public relations man, commented later on how key figures perceived the successes of World War I propaganda and its possible lessons:

> It was, of course, the astounding success of propaganda during the war that opened the eyes of the intelligent few in all departments of life to the possibilities of regimenting the public mind. . . . [T]he manipulators of patriotic opinion made use of the mental clichès and the emotional habits of the public to produce mass reactions against the alleged atrocities, the terror and the tyranny of the enemy. It was only natural, after the war ended, that intelligent persons should ask themselves whether it was not possible to apply a similar technique to the problems of peace.[28]

Where Ivy Lee had advocated, at least in public, the desirability of open rational discourse, Bernays, at least at this stage of his career, straightforwardly adopted simply a more genteel version of Reichenbach's notion of impressionable masses. Dim conceptions of the masses were in the air at the time. In 1925, Walter Lippmann critically analyzed a public's ability to appreciate the intricacies of any issue or indeed to keep its attention on anything but crises. He adds:

> [S]ince [a public] acts by aligning itself, it personalizes whatever it considers, and is interested only when events have been melodramatized as a conflict.

> The public will arrive in the middle of the third act and will leave before the last curtain, having stayed just long enough perhaps to decide who is the hero and who is the villain of the piece.[29]

Around the same time, advertising began to emphasize nonrational appeals to consumers. Many advertising men came to feel that their craft had to be based not so much on reasonable grounds but on suggestive appeals to the unconscious.[30] Bernays echoed all of these theories. His early work in particular is pervaded with the imagery of herds of people shepherded by those expert in the "mechanisms and motives of the group mind."[31] The public relations counselor was a creator of events, a man in a position to make things happen.[32] Bernays favored indirect ways of appealing to the public, and he developed many of the tactics and devices that are now stock in trade for public relations practitioners. These include third-party endorsements by authoritative figures; the identification and cultivation of "opinion leaders" or "trend setters"; the use of public events—for example, contests or displays—that highlight one thing, like beautiful women or great art, and simultaneously sell another, like floppy hats on the beautiful women or the corporate sponsor of the art exhibit; pretesting public opinion with psychological tests and surveys; and the thoughtful speech by the corporate or political leader that makes private interests appear to be public goods.

3. The Depression and all the ills that accompanied it—economic catastrophe, the growing success of the labor movement in presenting its own case to the public, the spectre of leftist political radicalism, the appeal of cooperative enterprise, and the gigantic apparatus of the New Deal spearheaded by a president who was himself a master publicist—led key business leaders to launch a massive public relations counterattack so that business could tell its story. The campaign was centered in a newly revitalized National Association of Manufacturers (NAM) and it evinced in nearly classical form what has been called the "American business creed."[33] The espousal of the classical business creed was not restricted to the NAM campaign. Individual corporations, particularly giants like General Motors, U.S. Steel, Dupont, and Ford, expanded their own internal public relations staffs and launched their own campaigns reiterating or echoing the same kind of message. The extent and range of all of these efforts were impressive. They included extensive institutional advertising campaigns extolling in various ways free opportunity, initiative, and competition; a massive advertising campaign entitled "Prosperity Reigns Where Harmony Dwells"; special editions of in-house magazines designed for public distribution; the placement of probusiness editorials in small dailies across the country; the syndication for several hundred papers of a cartoon series with a probusiness stance; the sponsorship of radio programs of every variety complete with probusiness homilies; and the massive production of short motion pictures telling the story of one or another industry for distribution as trailers to movie theaters or to educational or recreational organizations.[34] It was during this period too that businesses began to develop systematic internal communication efforts directed at their own employees; well-informed workers with correct perspectives were deemed a company's best ambassadors to the world.

NAM and its allied adherents to the classical business creed were not, of course, the only corporate petitioners for the public ear. During World War II and after, more liberal business voices, often identified with those segments of managerial capitalism that appreciated the great economic opportunities presented by the adoption of Keynesian economic policies, began to find expression principally through the public relations campaigns of the Committee for Economic Development (CED).[35] Not long after, the NAM campaign was ridiculed by William H. Whyte, then an editor for *Fortune* magazine.[36] These particular ideological splits between different wings of the business elite centered on the proper role of government in economic affairs. One may notice similar ideological clashes in more recent years, say, on the issue of the social responsibility of business. The CED campaign is important in another respect. Reflecting perhaps the improving fortunes of its own constituency, it dropped the somewhat defensive tone that had marked the NAM effort; its optimistic buoyancy and assertiveness restored to public relations its historical and, one might argue, proper role—that is, as "prophet of good fortune."[37]

4. During World War II and in the postwar years, public relations became and has remained a major institutional force in American society. There are no systematically compiled data to support such a claim;[38] one must rely rather on a number of disparate though related indices. For instance, corporate and trade association expenditures on what is called corporate or public relations advertising—that is, advertisements that do not sell a particular brand of product but rather try to establish a good image for a company or for a generic product, like milk or cotton—seem to be on the rise. Moreover, the number of public relations agencies has grown, the revenues of the largest public relations firms have kept abreast of economic growth, many colleges and universities across the country now offer degrees or courses in public relations, and virtually every large organization in all orders of our society—whether business, government, religious, educational, or military—now has a public relations division.[39] Finally, attempts at professionalization of the field, while less than successful because of the peculiarities of the occupation, especially the sharp competition for clients between agencies, have nonetheless been regularly renewed. In the last decade, probably in response to the opportunities presented by the growth and consolidation of the electronic media, many public relations firms have been acquired by large powerful advertising houses that wish to provide their clients with wholly coordinated double-barreled offensives. The new alliance between these twin but historically somewhat antagonistic sources of image management might signal a whole new phase in public relations history.

It is, in any event, no exaggeration to say that public relations practices and techniques pervade every nook and cranny of our social order. In the course of a single day, the average middle-class citizen might easily hear on radio snatches of several speeches given by government or corporate officials but ghostwritten by a public relations wordsmith; tune in to the plethora of staged media events that dot his television screen, for instance, press conferences, talk-show panel discussions, celebrations of achievement such as the Emmy presentations or the Academy Awards, the pregame, postgame, and even midgame interviews with players and coaches that have transformed sporting events, or interviews of "spokesmen" or "spokeswomen" for books, companies, self-improvement courses, social causes, or even scientific theories; see in passing on the screen a few of the thousands of "news clips," the electronic descendants of press handouts that report feature stories related to a company's business—like a feature on daylight saving time by a watch company, or a series on the medical uses of procedures utilizing small amounts of radioactive materials by a group of nuclear physicians; visit a museum to see an exhibit of, say, Egyptian art sponsored by a design corporation that, coincidentally, has just released its latest line of apparel featuring the new Egyptian look; receive newsletters from some of the thousands of organizations, public or private, politically conservative, liberal, or radical, eleemosynary, educational, or religious, that routinely manufacture official or counterofficial versions of reality suiting their needs; read in *The Wall Street Journal* or *The New York Times* accounts of specific events or larger trends attributed to "informed sources," the code name for public relations men and women; or see in the same journals the results of the latest public opinion poll on the most serious or the most banal topic conducted by an "independent research firm," actually a wholly-owned subsidiary or a subcontractor of a public relations agency. Such a welter of images and ideologies even comes to assume for many men and women in our society a comfortable air of solidity, a development that would not, of course, have surprised Harry Reichenbach. Paradoxically, the more artifice used in constructing social reality, the more does that reality come for many to seem commonplace, natural, and taken for granted.

III

Men and women in public relations are not generally taken in by their own artifice. Rather, the very nature of their work continually reminds them that the world is put together, often in the most arbitrary fashion. Whether in a corporation or an agency, a public relations practitioner, in addition to meeting the normal bureaucratic fealty requirements of his station, must above all satisfy his clients' desires to construct the world in certain ways.[40] Clients always want certain versions of reality propagated. These should: enable them to accomplish whatever practical tasks are at hand as expeditiously as possible; and convey a favorable public image, and implicitly a preferred self-image, to some crucial publics. The organizational success of public relations practitioners depends on remaining attentive to clients' desires. As one vice-president at Images Inc. says: "Even if your viewpoint is 180 degrees from his [the client's], you have to see which track his mind is on." In general, moreover, clients want to believe the best about themselves; in this sense, they, rather than targeted publics, become the public relations practitioner's best customer.

There are, of course, good clients and bad clients. A good client keeps his public relations specialists adequately informed, provides "feedback" and "constructive criticism," and recognizes that public relations depends on time-billing rather than on product billing and provides enough funds to do the job properly. A good client "takes stock of himself," that is, dispassionately objectifies his company's products, his company's organizational structure and personnel, and, say, in the case of a top corporate official, himself, to make them all more readily manipulable and therefore marketable commodities. Above all, a good client is flexible and therefore able rapidly to shift ground and actual policies as well to meet new needs or new pressures. A bad client, by contrast, either does not understand or chooses to ignore the peculiarly indirect approach of public relations and wants immediately observable results in terms of press clippings or TV time; uses a public relations program as a vehicle for self-aggrandizement within his own corporation, placing the public relations specialist in danger of "getting caught in a pissing contest between executives"; demands the release of press statements that are only marginally "newsworthy" and then blames the public relations specialist when nothing at all gets printed or aired; conceals crucial aspects of his story from his public relations advisers and refuses them adequate access to his staff and facilities to get the full story; comes to the public relations agency with trumped-up data and fake photographs—as happened, for instance, at Images Inc. when a client falsely claimed the efficacy of a product to remove tar from despoiled beaches—and ends up declaring bankruptcy, leaving the public relations agency liable for a multimillion-dollar lawsuit; wants the public relations agency, as in the case of some single-party foreign governments, to put a good public face on practices like the "persuasion" and "elimination" of opponents; expects the public relations agency to be the "bag man" to pay off government officials or newspaper editors; and, perhaps especially, insists on an indefensible or totally unbelievable version of reality or expects the public relations specialist to tell outright lies.

Agency personnel are the most vulnerable to clients' wishes. Typically, work in agencies is organized around accounts, with teams of practitioners with particular expertise, often drawn from different lines of authority, being assigned to service an account; or, if an account is large and diversified, various specialists deal with particular needs of a client. In an agency, interesting work, prestige, money, perquisites for oneself and one's friends, like tickets to the opera, ballet, theater, symphony, and major sporting events, as well as invitations to the chic receptions where businessmen mingle socially with figures from the literary and artistic worlds, all depend on holding and satisfactorily servicing lucrative accounts. To some extent, working for a prestigious client even if the account itself is not lucrative—being, for instance, the spokesman on a specific issue for a well-known international watch manufacturer—can be a source of internal organizational leverage for a practitioner, but only because one's colleagues assume that an account with such a well-known and respected company very likely involves big money.

When big accounts, or portions of them, "take a walk," agency staff quite often are asked to follow them out the door. As it happens, accounts in the public relations world circulate continually and only sometimes because of actual or alleged dissatisfaction with public relations service. The pattern of continual mergers, upheavals, and power struggles in corporations, that I have argued earlier is at the core of American corporate life, directly affects public relations agencies. When a new CEO or divisional president assumes power in a corporation, he will quite often change public relations and advertising agencies as part of a larger strategy of shedding the past or to assert his own "new vision" of the future. When this occurs, almost invariably, he will move his account to an agency whose leaders he knows and with whom he feels comfortable. This continual circulation of accounts means that agency personnel are constantly searching for new accounts and constantly devising ways to hold present clients, despite the knowledge of the inevitability of their eventual departure. Both exigencies create the fundamental condition of public relations work, that is, the necessity to be continually attentive to clients' desires. An anecdote from Images Inc. illustrates the point. One day, an executive vice-president in the agency was lavishly praising a bright young man who was currently "on a roll." When I asked if this person would be promoted because of his work, the executive vice-president looked at me with some surprise and said: "Well, just because he's great today doesn't mean he'll be great tomorrow. Anything can happen. He has to keep his clients happy if he wants us to stay happy with him." One's future, at least in public relations agencies, depends almost entirely on creating and sustaining particular versions of reality.

As a rule, corporate public relations specialists lead somewhat more secure lives. However, during the controversies endemic to the great industries today, their positions can also become suddenly precarious. It is they who have to hammer out and offer to the public the customarily bland and delicately phrased versions of reality thought necessary to dampen public ire or at least keep special-interest groups at bay while corporate leaders grapple with exigencies in back rooms. The very pace of events, however, and the choices events demand often leave corporate public relations specialists scrambling to invent appropriate ways to explain what has to be done.

Such enforced attentiveness to others' desires to portray the world a certain way breeds a distinctive habit of mind that characterizes the ethos of public relations and, through the influence of public relations, the ethos of American business. In the world of public relations, there is no such thing as a notion of truth; there are only stories, perspectives, or opinions. One works, of course, with "facts," that is, selected empirically verifiable statements about the world. But as long as a story is factual, it does not matter if it is "true." One can feel free to arrange these facts in a variety of ways and to put any interpretation on them that suits a client's objectives. Interpretations and judgments are always completely relative. The only canons binding this process of interpretation are those of credibility or, more exactly, of plausibility. If an interpretation of facts, a story, is taken as plausible by a targeted audience, it is just as good as "true" in any philosophical sense, indeed better since it furthers the accomplishment of an immediate goal. Insofar as it has any meaning at all, truth is what is perceived. Creating the impression of truth displaces the search for truth.

Since all events are stories, one must develop a sensitivity to the nuances of language and to the familiar twists of plot that allow these stories to be told as simple, living dramas. This does not require a meditative reflectiveness or, least of all, any historical inquisitiveness about the origins of events. Indeed the past is useful only insofar as a selective recasting of it might help one to grasp and present events as popular novelists do, that is, in broad brush-strokes. Avoiding undue complexities, one learns to craft the little stories that will engineer at least acquiescence if not consent and allow a client's operations to proceed without undue interruption. After all, most people's understanding of the world consists precisely of such little stories, pieced together or accepted outright from a myriad of other constructions of reality.

Men and women in public relations are, of course, acutely aware that their advocacy of certain positions makes them somewhat suspect to an increasingly media-savvy public, a suspicion that they feel is unwarranted. In their view, the public has been unduly influenced by, if it has not swallowed whole, the occupational ideology of the journalistic media, an ideology that they know well both because of their continual interaction with journalists and especially because many people in public relations have "crossed the street" from journalism, to, of course, a mixed chorus of envy and contempt from their former colleagues. From the standpoint of public relations, the journalistic ideology closely resembles the social outlook of most college seniors— a vague but pious middle-class liberalism, a mildly critical stance toward their fathers in particular and authorities in general; a maudlin championship of the poor and the underclass; and especially the doctrine of tolerance, open-mindedness, and balance. In fact, public relations people feel, the news media are also constructing reality. They are always looking for a "fresh" and exciting angle; they have an unerring instinct for the sentimental that expresses itself in a preference for "human interest" rather than substance; and they arrange facts in a way that purports to convey "truth," but is in fact simply another story. In reality, news is entertainment. And, despite the public's acceptance of journalistic ideologies, most of the public watch or read news not to be informed or to learn the "truth," but precisely to be entertained. There is no intrinsic reason, therefore, why the constructions of reality by public relations specialists should be thought of as any different from those of any group in the business of telling stories to the public. Everyone is telling stories and everyone has a story to tell. Public relations men and women are simply storytellers with a purpose in the free market of ideas, advocates of a certain point of view in the court of public opinion. Since any notion of truth is irrelevant or refers at best to what is perceived, persuasion of various sorts becomes everything.

Before discussing some of the particular persuasive techniques of public relations, two general remarks are in order. First, the essential task of public relations in all of its operations is to invent better ways and especially to devise better explanations and accounts for what has to be done; in short, its role is to transform expediency into altruism or even statesmanship. Second, the genius of public relations, a gift that it shares with advertising, consists to a great extent in its dexterity at inverting symbols and images. Whether it is hyping products, influencing legislation, transforming reputations, or erasing stigma, public relations tries to transform actually or potentially perceived weaknesses into strengths and subvert or at least call into question the strengths or particularly the credibility of opponents. Thus, the lowly bottom-feeding catfish, a food for generations of poor southern whites and especially blacks, when commercially farmed, is promoted as the "cultivated catfish," complete with a long-tailed tuxedo and starched shirt. Or, in an era dominated by television, radio executives launch a campaign to alter the idea of radio as a nonvisual medium by emphasizing the power of the imagination; they distribute posters showing a fish smoking a pipe or a banana dancing, both with the tagline, "I just saw it on radio." The textile industry, under great market pressure from well-made and cheaper Asian imports, pushes for restrictive tariffs, extolling the virtues of traditional American craftsmanship. A diversified conglomerate seeking a "unified corporate identity" commissions a major path-breaking study on what is actually an inversion of a somewhat embarrassing private obsession of the chief executive officer. The CEO's house, it is said, in the aftermath of a mugging of a friend, is an arsenal stocked with weapons and booby-trapped against the night when some unfortunate burglar wanders into his yard. A public relations firm fashions a study on how the quality of American life is affected by the fear of crime and names the report and the corporation itself after the CEO. An asbestos manufacturer declares bankruptcy and changes its name to end a flood of worker compensation suits arguing that, far from being an avoidance of responsibility, such a strategy is actually the first step in establishing an industry and government fund that will ensure equity in payments to all, not just those disabled workers who are first in line. And a corporation that produces plastic containers, regularly under assault from various groups for littering the environment, considers a public relations communications program to explore and extol the role of packaging goods throughout human history. The subversion of an opponent's credibility takes various forms but, generally speaking, it tries to undercut the legitimacy of opposing claims. The most common example is to question the particular scientific data that underpin a position that counters one's own interests.

Both the general aim and the genius of public relations may be observed in its persuasive techniques. As it happens, following the legacy of Edward Bernays, indirect means of persuasion are thought to be particularly effective ways of reaching deeply into the many publics that can influence a business. In this, public relations contrasts sharply with the direct hard sell of advertising. By all odds, the classical indirect method of public relations is the creation of a corporate persona, a kind of fictive reality, known colloquially in the field as a "front." This technique helps mobilize or defuse public support for a position while concealing or at least obscuring the principal interests initiating action.

An example from Alchemy Inc. illustrates how the front works. The chemical company is one of the leading producers of chlorofluorocarbons (CFCs), extremely useful inert chemicals that have wide applicability both for industrial and consumer use. In 1974, a major scientific controversy developed about the possible erosion by these chemicals of stratospheric ozone, a broad zone of the earth's atmosphere that extends from about 8 to 30 miles above the earth and that filters out cancer-producing and otherwise harmful ultraviolet solar rays. Aerosols using CFCs were banned by regulation in 1978, causing substantial losses to the big producers of the substances, among them Alchemy, and wiping out in the process the whole industry that produced aerosols. In 1980, a new Advanced Notice to Propose Rulemaking (ANPR) was issued by the Environmental Protection Agency (EPA) proposing a further regulation of CFCs, this time capping production at certain levels, utilizing a market share allocation mechanism to determine the maximum amount of CFCs a firm would be allowed to produce in a year. The aim of the proposed legislation was to create artificial shortages, drive up prices for the chemicals, and finally to control what was termed the "banking" of CFCs. Because CFCs are inert and have extremely long life, they would in time, it was argued, when released from millions of refrigerators, foam cushions, car or home air conditioners, or as waste after use as industrial solvents, find their way into the stratosphere and attack the ozone. Great arguments raged in the scientific community about the ozone depletion theory. For instance, in the course of eight years, the National Academy of Sciences issued several reports alternately supporting the theory, having second thoughts, and then retreating from the field in ambiguity. Advocates of the ozone depletion theory were quite forceful in pushing the proposed regulation. Some went so far as to assert that the continued unregulated production of CFCs was laying the groundwork for a new and even more catastrophic Love Canal. Advocates for the business position argued that, in the absence of scientific surety, production should continue unabated while further research proceeded. In fact, some scientists in the business community worked on developing early warning systems that would signal a worsening of ozone erosion and provide ample lead time for response. At the chemical company, line managers directly charged with or familiar with CFCs privately scoffed at the ozone depletion theory and argued that the scientists who cooked it up had their own eyes on the main chance. Up the ladder, key business leaders felt that the real issue in the whole dispute was the proposed market share allocation device that might serve as a model for still other and possibly more damaging regulation in different areas.

With the help of a public relations firm and together with another principal producer of CFCs, Alchemy Inc. created a group called the Alliance for Responsible CFC Policy. On the surface, the Alliance seemed to be a coalition of the industrial consumers of CFCs, that is, small manufacturers who used the substances to produce commodities like polyurethane foam, plastics, and air conditioners. In reality, the chemical company and the other big producers of CFCs bankrolled and controlled the whole operation, made and broke different executive directors of the Alliance, organized speaking tours of young, personable, and attractive managers armed with "speaking packages" with multicolored tabs for quick reference during question periods, and coordinated a national campaign of sober scientific dissent and of outraged letters to congressmen and regulators protesting the proposed regulation. Near the end of the initial period of comment to the ANPR, managers at

Alchemy gleefully congratulated each other on their efforts—an entire room at the EPA was said to be overflowing with the mountain of paper generated by their write-in campaign. It would be a long time, they said, before anybody heard or even saw the relevant program officer at the agency. In the end, shortly after President Reagan's appointee took over the EPA, the regulation was quietly buried, although the Alliance failed in its attempt to drive a stake through the ozone depletion theory itself and thus forestall possible future regulation.[41]

Of course, none of the major players in such a drama—that is, regulators, environmental activists, politicians, or businessmen themselves—are really fooled by such a classic maneuver. One should note, however, that the heat of battle, the continual necessity to act in public forums outside the corporation as if a particular front were indeed an independent entity, and the sometimes requisite stance of indignation toward one's opponents, sometimes cause many businessmen to half-believe realities they know to be fictive. In any event, one's direct opponents are not the target of fronts. Rather, fronts are devised for the broader public whose support is deemed crucial in the struggle against opponents. In this arena, the most credible or plausible organizational public face is thought to have the best chance of winning the day. Practically speaking, this means finding and marketing the most salable organizational image while simultaneously undermining or at least calling into question the image of one's chief adversaries. In the CFC case, managers and their public relations advisers calculated correctly that, among those images available, the one with the widest public appeal and with the best chance of striking terror into the hearts of regulators and congressmen alike was that of small businessmen, rather than corporate giants, valiantly joining forces to struggle against bureaucratic tyranny, regulators who precipitously jump to conclusions before all the scientific data are assessed, and self-promoting professors of chemistry whose ambition clouds their scientific objectivity.

Fronts are particularly suited to furthering private interests under the guise of another organizational image, that of the "constructive alternative." For instance, Images Inc. worked for a coalition of manufacturers and small grocery store owners who were fighting a bottle bill referendum requiring a deposit on beverage containers. The firm organized a committee of eminent, well-known, and well-placed people that: invoked a variety of appeals, including hidden costs and inconvenience to the consumer and the likelihood of an explosion of pests in the small stores and bodegas that under the proposed bill would have to receive returned containers; and worked for a Total Litter Control program, advertised with the acronym TLC, instead of "focusing narrowly" on bottles and cans. As it happens, the committee existed only on expensive and well-illustrated stationery. The multitudinous press releases warning of the horrors that would follow public approval of the referendum, the red-and-white, heart-adorned TLC stickers that began to litter building walls and subway cars, and the spokesmen and women with high-sounding, but in one case wholly fictional, academic degrees who trooped the talk show circuit, were all products of the public relations imagination. Apart from the creation of fictitious credentials, one should note that this use of the front differs not at all from the way the device is employed by thousands of political, social, cultural, and religious organizations of every ideological and social stripe. Public relations men and women, whether on the right, center, or left, whether in the service of God, the state, art, human rights, or commercial gain, know that in a society of media markets the magic of a glittering name, respected accomplishment, and the cultural authority that accompanies established professional or institutional position are far more persuasive than reasoned arguments.

Finally, a very frequently encountered organizational image among front groups in these days of heated scientific controversy is that of the disinterested scientific institute. For instance, the Formaldehyde Institute, basically a trade association of formaldehyde producers and industrial users of the chemical, was formed in 1979 to counter growing public and scientific concern about the chemical. Formaldehyde is a highly reactive, colorless, and low-cost substance that has widespread applicability in a great number of industries— for instance, in cosmetics, explosives, paints, leathers and furs, and medicines to name only a few. Serious problems had emerged with urea formaldehyde foam insulation in homes, and some studies strongly suggested the possibility of nasal cancer in humans exposed to the substance for prolonged periods. At the time, regulation governing the foam insulation was pending before the Consumer Product Safety Commission, and the big fear was that other industrial users of the chemical might be regulated by still other agencies. The textile industry, in particular, which relies wholly on a formaldehyde-based resin to produce permanent press polyester/cotton fabrics, feared that OSHA would impose a standard reducing workers' allowable time-weighted average (TWA) exposure to the chemical from the current two to three parts per million (ppm) to one ppm, a reduction that would cause severe operating problems in finishing plants.[42]

The stated purpose of the Formaldehyde Institute "is for the sound science of formaldehyde and formaldehyde-based products and to ensure that the data are used and interpreted properly."[43] To this stated end, the Institute has, among other activities, amassed a variety of independent studies on formaldehyde, collaborated with various regulatory agencies and groups like the National Cancer Institute on other related research, compiled an extensive bibliography of studies on the chemical, held workshops and seminars on formaldehyde, sent out mailings with summary results of data to directors of health departments in all fifty states, and published a wide variety of pamphlets and brochures for the general public on the benefits to society of this "building block" chemical. The themes in all this literature constitute a paradigm of sorts of the basic message of other disinterested scientific institutes focusing on similarly complex scientific issues:

1. There is no scientific evidence that formaldehyde causes cancer in humans.

2. Animal tests on rats that have shown incidences of nasal cancer are inapplicable to humans. First, rats have a predisposition to nasal irritations.

Second, the extremely high levels of exposure to which test rats are subjected span almost the whole lifetime of a rat, an unrealistic test that cannot be extrapolated to humans.

3. The only reliable data are long-term epidemiological studies of workers regularly exposed to formaldehyde. The only major study of this kind provides no evidence that formaldehyde causes cancer in humans at the levels of exposure to the chemical experienced in the workplace, let alone the much lower levels of the chemical released in such consumer products like textiles or pressed wood.

4. Regulation must be based on firm, generally accepted science. In the absence of such science, any interference with the production and use of formaldehyde constitutes unwarranted restriction and betrays, in fact, an unscientific cast of mind.

5. Our society cannot live without formaldehyde. Without it, not only would more than a million American workers directly involved in making formaldehyde and formaldehyde-based products, in industries earning more than $18 billion a year, be thrown out of work, but many other crucial industries, like textiles, the automotive and machine industries, and the construction industry, would be severely curtailed with direct economic penalties to individuals and society as a whole.

6. Besides, a multitude of natural as well as man-made sources produce massive amounts of formaldehyde, including the human body, vegetation, and automobile emissions. The chemical is, in fact, essentially part of the natural environment of any society, particularly an industrial social order.[44]

Scientific fronts thus gather together under the rubric of science a host of arguments that try to discredit opponents' positions while establishing the reasonableness and plausibility of scientific interpretations favorable to a certain practical application of knowledge. Of course, the Institute does not discourage somewhat more colorful and pointed arguments to the public made by various users of the chemical. Opponents of regulation on formaldehyde often point out, for instance, that morticians who use a lot of formaldehyde suffer not from an excess of nasal cancer but rather from cirrhosis of the liver, an ailment caused by other pickling substances. Executives at Weft Corporation argue that permanent-press shirts are the mother of women's liberation and that banning formaldehyde would result in sending newly career-minded women back to their ironing boards. They also argue that they feel caught in a double bind. The industry has moved as far as consumer preferences will allow it to polyester blends, at least partly because of the cotton dust issue. But polyester blends require treatment with formaldehyde to meet consumer preferences. Do government threats to regulate formaldehyde mean that it wants the industry to move back to the use of more cotton?

Scientific fronts often conceal complicated political strategies. For instance, the Edison Electric Institute, an umbrella organization for energy producers and consumers ranging from the very conservative National Independent Coal Operators' Association to the moderate National Association of Manufacturers, recently formed the Alliance for Balanced Environmental

Solutions. The Alliance's principal task is to counter the growing domestic and international public concern about acid rain, that is, the deposit of harmful chemical pollutants through precipitation that alters the pH balance in soil and bodies of water. A principal, though by no means the only, source of acid rain in the eastern part of North America seems to be the air-borne transmission of sulfur dioxide from coal-burning electrical plants. As it happens, these plants are located in the midwestern United States. However, because of extremely high smokestacks installed in the 1950s, precisely to carry pollution away from local communities, and because of the vagaries of wind patterns, air-borne sulfates from these plants are, apparently, helping to "acidify" and thus to despoil the lakes, streams, and forests of the northeastern United States and southern Canada. The situation raises complicated jurisdictional disputes and particularly questions of interregional equity and liability. Put simply, the real issue is: Who pays for other people's troubles when responsibility is blurred? Through a series of reports, conferences, and newsletters, the Alliance is making *mutatis mutandis* essentially the same arguments as the Formaldehyde Institute. In particular, it stresses the need for continued scientific research into the origins of acid rain, the actual extent of supposed damage, and the harmfulness of any regulatory or legislative solutions before scientific certitude is established.[45] In reality, it is likely that the Edison Electric Institute is playing for time through the Alliance. First, the future direction of national energy policy is deeply uncertain in the wake of the operational mishaps and financial disasters suffered by the nuclear energy industry in recent years. Second, the massive coal-burning electrical plants in the Midwest have many years to go before exhausting the huge investments made in them after World War II. The rhetoric of the quest for scientific surety helps to postpone political choices until money already spent is well used and until investment alternatives become clear.

One can scarcely dispute the importance of reliable science as a basis for regulation. As noted earlier, the whole framework of our society depends on rational scientific inquiry and its technological application. Faulty or fraudulent science can only impede the quest for what one might call a civic rationality. Most men and women cannot make informed assessments of scientific data. Moreover, when they try to make such judgments, they rarely have a forum within which to articulate their appraisals. Still further, if articulated, their judgments are likely to be dismissed as being insufficiently expert. Men and women in public relations know therefore that, as a rule, science is as science seems. By their nature, scientific data are always tentative and subject to revision. And, in fact, practical men and women who understand the pivotal role of public opinion welcome scientific ambiguity unless they themselves can claim certainty to their own benefit. Uncertainty provides the requisite space to maneuver, provided that one invokes the hallowed canons of science in a measured and respectable way and provided, of course, that one surrounds oneself with a group of experts, preferably with impeccable credentials, who will testify to the probity of one's position. Since credentials influence credibility, they must include not only proper certification and established position but also freedom from ostensible conflict of interest that might allow others to interpret scientific judgment as biased.

An example from Images Inc. brings these themes together. Images Inc. represented for a time a pharmaceutical firm that was under criticism for a weight-control pill that in certain cases, it was charged by a well-known public health group, had the unfortunate side effect of death. Executives at the pharmaceutical firm cited their own experts to argue that such charges were not only absurd but malicious. Executives at Images Inc. had no interest whatsoever in trying to master the chemical complexities of the dispute. Here, as in many other cases, they threw up their hands and argued that their own lack of expertise meant that they certainly could not adjudicate any scientific ambiguities. However, one PR executive who was troubled by the public health group's evidence, investigated the issue on her own and reached a negative judgment about the drug. She voiced her concern at a meeting that I attended and urged the agency to consider resigning the account. A top agency official pointed out that, although she was entitled to her private and individual viewpoint, experts disagreed about the drug. The real problem facing Images Inc., he went on to say, was the public image of the head scientist at the pharmaceutical firm. The man's slight public awkwardness underlined his lack of established professional achievement; regrettably, he was also the brother-in-law of the drug firm's president. The chief order of business for Images Inc. was not therefore to discuss complicated scientific quandaries but to persuade the president to dump his brother-in-law and to figure out which articulate experts could be lined up to convince the public that the weight-control pill posed no unnecessary or unreasonable dangers to health.

Closely related to fronts are other methods of persuasion that promote products, causes, people, or organizations in a similarly indirect way. Thus, one creates marathon and cross-country events to promote running shoes and children's bubble-gum blowing contests with school scholarships as prizes to push bubble gum. In the aftermath of a series of politically motivated murders of tourists, one plants articles in key upscale magazines on exotic birds, summer camping, tropical fruits and vegetables, and native cuisine to stimulate tourist interest in a Caribbean island, as well as arranging well-publicized celebrity visits to the "resort paradise." Or one produces short news features giving a behind-the-scenes look at how the commercials for a client's products are made and arranges for such films to be shown to captive audiences on airplanes at no charge.

"Landmark studies" of various sorts constitute another crucial indirect public relations device today. At the suggestion of a public relations firm, a corporation will commission a study to be carried out by the PR firm's research wing. Most commonly, these focus on issues directly related to a company's marketing areas. Thus, a PR firm does an analysis of American reading habits for a book industry group, a study of fashion consciousness for a leading clothes store, studies of changing perceptions of women's roles both for a feminine hygiene products firm and for a cigarette company out to capture the young female market, and an appraisal of sports in American life for a beer firm that advertises heavily during sports events. Often, too, "path breaking" studies that are designed to put corporate leaders "out in front" of important public issues are commissioned. For instance, an insurance company funds a study of changing values in American life that argues, with an assurance that only comes with a certain innocence of historical knowledge, that the level of an individual's religious commitment more strongly determines personal values than economic status, age, sex, race, or political belief and that the "increasing impact of religion on social and political institutions may be . . . a trend that could change the face of America"; and a leading producer of office furniture funds a study of how the tastes and styles of the baby-boom generation are shaping "corporate cultures" and the environment and decor of the contemporary office. Such reports are always conducted "under the aegis of a distinguished advisory panel" of both men and women of affairs and particularly of the higher reaches of the academic world who help legitimate the entire enterprise, win accolades for the public spiritedness, social vision, and social sensitivity of corporate leaders, and, of course, gain more extensive name recognition for the sponsoring organization.

Typically, such studies use the standard polling techniques developed and perfected since the mid-1930s by the Gallup, Roper, and Harris organizations. As it happens, the methodology of polling techniques ideally matches the underlying habit of mind of public relations. Public relations studies dip into the rapidly moving stream of public opinion. Since the premium, especially as established by clients, is always on current opinion, the studies are either ahistorical or use historical facts in a highly selective way. They make only low-level empirical generalizations uninformed by any clear theoretical position. Public opinion itself becomes both the primary datum and the interpretive yardstick of material. The notion of historical structures or continuities has no significance nor, for that matter, do shifts in public opinion except for the assumption that today's poll results erase and invalidate yesterday's opinions. Without a historical consciousness and some firm criteria to locate materials and to help make discerning judgments, the wheat and chaff of "the million bits of information," the "hard data" produced by "sophisticated statistical techniques," are not separated and are presented with equal seriousness or equally cheerful, upbeat blandness.

It is somewhat inaccurate to say that there are no firm criteria in public relations with which to assess public opinion data. One framework that always matters is the client's assessment of what data mean or, more precisely, should mean. As a general rule, few clients wish to be associated with "gloomy" reports unless, in so doing, they can stake out positions of corporate leadership and point to clear programmatic solutions for the problems noted. Such solutions should not, it goes without saying, upset too many people. Further, few executives will sponsor a report that counters their own organization's interests or for that matter their own personal ideologies. Clients' desires thus place some strictures or "parameters" on the interpretations of data available to public relations practitioners.

An example from Images Inc. illustrates the way such interpretive parameters work. In the early 1980s, the agency talked one of its big clients, a major container producer, into sponsoring a "breakthrough" study on perceptions of the "trade-offs" between environmental protection and economic growth. Data were to be gathered from the public at large, avowed environmentalists, top corporate executives, small businessmen, and several communities facing specific tensions between the environment and economy. In the heady days of neoconservative triumph following President Reagan's first election, executives at the container corporation fully expected to receive a report that highlighted the public's abandonment of the environmentalist sentiments of the 1970s and an espousal of a "new realism" about the regrettable exigencies that inevitably accompany economic growth. After analyzing the data, however, the research group and account team at the public relations agency felt compelled to write a draft arguing that although the public wanted a return to economic growth, it did not want, in any event, growth at the expense of environmental decline. In fact, the draft said that the country seemed gripped by a pervasive "earth concern" that put economic growth in a distinctly secondary role. As it happened, the draft provoked such consternation at the highest levels of the container corporation that the entire project and future projects as well were jeopardized. Top officials at the public relations firm became more actively involved at this point. After several rewritings, a much blander document emerged that stressed the public's desire for a finely poised balance between growth and preservation of the environment. Rumors circulated freely in the public relations firm about the near reversal of emphasis, and both junior and senior people said privately that whole sections of data contrary to the thesis of balance had either been omitted or reported in an undecipherable way in the final version. The chief researcher for the project and a top official both adamantly deny this and argue that all the data were reported. The researcher, however, allows that "a lot of soul-searching was necessary in order to achieve the broadest perspective possible on this issue." The top official, in a written document prepared for a meeting to discuss the issue, argued that:

> [T]he final report was better than it would have been if it had not gone through [the] process of reexamination. It was stronger, it was more important, it was more constructive. . . . At the same time, there is no doubt that pressures were brought on us to come to the kind of conclusions we finally reached.

At the meeting, he added, somewhat more pithily: "We tried to be honest but, believe me, it wasn't easy."

In this context, the notion of honesty becomes ambiguous and elusive since it is unclear by what standards honesty is being measured. Here the notion of truth treated earlier becomes crucial. The same top executive defines truth:

I sometimes sit back and think that if we could make up a list of all the viewpoints of all our clients and somehow fit them together, then that would be truth. That would be what we are as a firm.

Another executive in the same agency says:

Everyone out there is constructing reality. We and our clients have perceptions too. Who is telling the truth? Is there anyone out there who has the time and the inclination to sit down and truly evaluate the many situations?

Yet another executive from the same firm puts a fine point on the issue when one of his colleagues raised a question about the truth of a position advocated by one of the firm's clients:

Truth? What is truth? I don't know anyone in this business who talks about "truth."

To some extent, these views simply reflect the particular habit of mind, the kind of marked relativism, already described, that undergirds public relations work and the ethos that public relations helps shape for corporate managers. This relativism has, as it happens, a close though largely unappreciated affinity with views currently propagated in literary and philosophical circles. Here truth is also either an irrelevant concept or one that is wholly kaleidoscopic. It is pointless to seek for underlying structural unities or even determinate partial truths, because there are only differences. The objective world dissolves into subjective consciousness and is projected outwards. Just as Harry Reichenbach came to see things, reality consists precisely of projected perspectives. Law, for instance, becomes literature; morality becomes public convention; social life becomes a text subject to infinite hermeneutical exegesis.[46] As one public relations executive puts it, in commenting on another rearrangement of data to move closer to a client's viewpoint: "It's called 'interpretation.'" As long as a kind of plausibility is maintained, one perspective is as good as any other. In discounting in advance any intrinsic significance of ideas or, one might add, of moral values that flow from them, this habit of mind meshes nicely with the bureaucratic virtues of adeptness at inconsistency and alertness to expediency. Within such a framework, public relations specialists usually conclude very pragmatically that one might as well "sing whatever song the client wants to hear."

IV

Public relations work both demands and fosters in its practitioners a characteristic occupational virtue, that is, a highly self-conscious, reflexive ability to "doublethink," to borrow Orwell's term, to hold in one's mind and be able to voice if necessary completely contradictory versions of reality. Successful doublethinking demands, first, a talent for the intricate casuistry needed to broker whatever differences may exist between one's sense of self and the exigencies of immediate situations and, second, the ability to externalize one's casuistic ability to help others invent better reasons for doing what has to be done. One should note that this occupational virtue is a highly refined version of the adeptness at inconsistency that marks the symbolic dexterity of successful corporate managers and to the extent that corporate managers rely on public relations practitioners, it is one seedbed of that adeptness.

Public relations practitioners sometimes define their ability to doublethink as a personal hazard of sorts even as they recognize its professional value. They see, for instance, the systematic distancing of oneself both from the symbols that one manipulates and from the people that one serves—a distancing that they know makes doublethink possible and effective—as a kind of cynicism. The aphorism in the field is: "You come into this business an idealist; you leave a cynic." Practitioners' view of the malleability of truth is the touchstone for their recognition of the hazardous virtue that their work requires. One public relations executive explains:

> Most PR people are very cynical indeed. For them, truth is relative, completely relative. They can see relativity in any situation. They can look at truth from many different angles and switch viewpoints often and rapidly.

One must, of course, bring form out of such plasticity in order to accomplish the practical goal of helping clients forge a particular public stance. But even as one doublethinks to help others rationalize themselves, one becomes drawn deeper into an ambiguity where nothing is certain and where nothing commands, or can command, a lasting commitment. The same executive says:

> You have to be able to understand how people think. To really do this, you have to objectify people; you have to be able to press people and go deeper into their motives than you normally would. You have to be able to recognize the diversity of perspectives on things and you have to be able to say the opposite point of view from what you might have yourself.

Like the notion of truth, ideas as such are irrelevant or only become useful and important when they have an immediate practical use. For this reason, even more than in other areas of business, deeply held convictions, whether political, religious, or moral, can only be a hindrance to big success in public relations. However, Images Inc., and some other public relations firms as well, do not require their executives to work on accounts with which they feel "uncomfortable." Such a policy honors individuals' private reservations whatever their source. It also prudently recognizes that psychological discomfort could undermine the emotional conviction, or its convincing semblance, thought necessary to sell a client's viewpoint to a public. Such a separation of individual conscience from corporate action institutes a particular kind of casuistry, one that allows individuals to enjoy the benefits of corporate responses to exigencies while permitting personal feelings of moral purity. As it happens, the peculiar angle of vision that public relations work affords its practitioners demands continual casuistry. Greater proficiency in doublethink not only increases the ability to shape usable practical ideas but it also increases the sense of distance that practitioners experience between themselves and their occupational roles. Practitioners come to see how their own carefully crafted rationales cloak self-interest even as they, like Harry Reichenbach before them, see their clients coming to believe the promotional stories that they fashion. They see too the propensity and willingness of large sectors of a presumably literate public to "believe in the tooth-fairy" and they often ask themselves: If the public will accept, say, this, what won't they accept? In this sense, the more successful one becomes at public relations, the greater the likelihood of seeing oneself as cynical, though, as suggested earlier, any such self-conception is always, except perhaps to some close colleagues, masked with public faces of optimistic ingenuousness and buoyant vitality. Moreover, as also mentioned earlier, public relations practitioners, attuned as they are to public opinion, are acutely aware of the often pejorative public views of their profession. Both because they see their own virtues as hazardous and know that others see their profession as suspect, they apply their abilities of inventing better ways of legitimating what has to be done to their own work. It is worth noting some of the main directions such legitimations take.

Public relations practitioners sometimes claim an identification with the interests of their clients, say, advocacy of textile tariffs or construction of a political action committee. Here, the situation of corporate in-house public relations practitioners differs somewhat from those in agencies. Continual efforts for a unitary set of interests can provide corporate practitioners with a readier basis for organizational faith than the necessarily variegated advocacies of men and women in agencies. The depth of such faith depends largely on the extent to which corporate practitioners help make the decisions they have to defend publicly, that is, on the extent to which they take on the managerial role and become liable to its cognitive consequences. Agency practitioners not only defend multiple interests but face repeatedly the experience of even well-served clients switching agencies. Especially unsettling are the departures of clients who decide that, since they are as they have been portrayed, they have no future need to construct reality. The continual circulation of client accounts in agencies diminishes the possibilities of comforting, long-held allegiances to organizations, products, or causes.

Alternatively, and by contrast, practitioners in both settings sometimes justify their efforts by appealing to a professional ethos that celebrates the exercise of technical skill separated from any emotional commitment to one's clients. A dignified version of this legitimation is the often repeated analogy between public relations practitioners and lawyers; both occupations, it is argued, fulfill important advocacy roles in a free society. Only the practice of the professional virtue of public relations, however hazardous to individual practitioners, can assure the continued diversity of opinion that marks our democracy. Practitioners evince a somewhat more direct version of this stance when they refer to themselves as "hired guns," a characterization often accompanied with sardonic irony. For instance, when his firm had just taken the account of a corporation engaged in a widely publicized ploy to thwart workers' attempts to gain compensation for debilitating occupational illnesses by declaring bankruptcy, one executive says: "Well, after all, these bastards have got a story too!" Another executive muses: "I often ask myself: 'What is the going price for my soul today?'" Here, verbal irony symbolizes and expresses the professional virtue of cynicism but more in celebration than in defense. For the most part, hired guns accept the world as it is, without qualms, and tell stories for those who can pay the storytellers. As one executive explains:

> That's the *reality* of our society. There's no question that their story is being told because they have the money and power. I've got to recognize that I'm part of this society and just come to live with that. Our society *is* the way it is. It's run on money and power, it's that simple. Truth has nothing to do with it. So we just accept the world as it is and live with it.

Seeing oneself as a hired gun extols technical virtuosity while affording the emotional distance that allows the thorough, rational application of that virtuosity to clients' interests. At the same time, it guards one against the wounded idealism that seems to make requisite cynicism emotionally corrosive.

Public relations practitioners also justify their work by pointing to the social goods that are the by-products of the corporate stories that they fashion. Images Inc., for instance, regularly arranges corporate sponsorship of a variety of art, sculpture, and photography exhibitions and collaborates as well in publishing books on them. The agency literally creates these realities by matchmaking artistic talent and accomplishment with money. In the process, up-and-coming junior corporate executives get the kind of exposure to refined, sophisticated artistic and intellectual circles that will help prepare and polish them for higher posts. Artists, in turn, as long as their work is not too avant-garde, receive the benefits of a latter-day Medici-like patronage. Public relations people claim a double accomplishment—they help civilize businessmen, not least by inspiring in them a "passion for greatness" rather than self-interest as the important motive for patronage of the arts; and they provide the public with access to high culture. The same firm has also arranged corporate sponsorship of dance and musical performances, helped develop important educational programs such as one on infant nutrition, conducted some useful surveys such as one on the problems facing ethnic minorities, and done a lot of *pro bono* work for philanthropic, community, and public service organizations in the bargain. One tries, then, to move some clients in directions that seem socially desirable while at the same time playing with the magic lantern to serve their interests. Sometimes, too, the ability to accomplish any good at all in this world seems to depend on the willingness to serve even clients with no apparent redeeming features in order to seize capricious opportunities to channel other clients' resources into work deemed socially worthwhile.

Sometimes, finally, men and women in public relations legitimate what they have to do with virtuoso displays of their special legerdemain in symbolic reversal. By definition, public relations is concerned with actions and particularly language in the public sphere of social life, with professional and institutional performance in somewhat ritualized social drama. However, public relations practitioners often argue that their real concern is simply "basic human interaction, helping people to communicate with one another," that is, sharpening the most rudimentary and ordinary human skills. In this view, what is important in the wholly secular sphere of public social life are abilities originally shaped in intimate, private, and somewhat sacred social settings. Historically, of course, public relations has been at the forefront of the many social forces breaking down the separation between public and private in our society. Public relations has, for instance, furthered the already strong democratic impulse to level social distinctions by encouraging both political and corporate leaders to appear before the public as "regular guys." Moreover, its many promotional techniques have been responsible to an important extent for the celebrity phenomenon in this century, which depends largely on creating and fostering a ravenous public appetite for glimpses of intimate details of the private lives of the rich, famous, and powerful. The legitimation at issue appeals precisely to such a merger of public and private. In this view, public relations simply embodies in a professional way the intricate subterfuges, the explanations, excuses, and justifications that mark all social intercourse. What seems to be public and peculiarly professional is at bottom private and universal, that is, part of human nature. In discussing why public relations is often viewed by the public with suspicion, one executive says, for example:

You know, PR is dealing with all the things that we deal with every day in our private lives, but on a much larger level. I mean, there is a certain beauty to it. It's reflective of what we all do each day. We do something wrong and we try to explain it. We get drunk and we act badly; we have a fight and we use abusive language. Well, [Company X] got drunk, drunk with money and power and abused its employees and then covered it up. That's a terrible thing, but it's not all that different from what we all do. I think that what people don't like about PR is that we remind them of themselves, on a grand scale, on a large screen where they can see all the ploys they use to manipulate others

in the little dramas of their own lives. They see all the duplicity and
all the storytelling of their own lives writ large. It makes them very
uncomfortable because we remind them of themselves.

Men and women in public relations simply utilize their own intuitive and
experiential understandings of the quandaries, negotiations, and brokered and
bungled solutions of private lives as the stuff to shape the scripts of public
drama. They succeed precisely when the stories they fashion have emotional
resonance in the private lives of broad sectors of the public, even though such
resonance might precipitate a recoiling jolt of self-recognition and consequent antagonism toward the storyteller. In this sense, public relations performs a quasireligious symbolic role, most closely approximated by the traditional role of priest or minister or in our more secular world by the
psychotherapist. This quasireligious function reconciles business to the public by providing businessmen with acceptable vocabularies to confess their
sins and do repentance if necessary and with the opportunity to receive from
the public, regulators, and legislators alike, a kind of absolution.

However, I should reiterate that, because of the occupational role structure that binds them together, the most important audience and customer for
public relations are managers themselves. The premium on alertness to expediency demands, of course, an ability and readiness to doublethink one's way
through the contradictory irrationalities of everyday problems. But standing
at the middle of events grappling with exigencies, especially in a hierarchical
milieu that requires authorities to display sincere conviction in their actions,
seems to foster at least a kind of half-belief, and sometimes more, in one's
efforts to do what has to be done. In helping managers invent better reasons
for expedient action, public relations counselors, and less directly the techniques and the casuistic habit of mind they institutionalize in management
circles, reduce the distance managers experience between requisite moral
flexibility and the occupationally induced urge to believe sincerely in the value
of one's own actions. The central institutional mechanism in managerial circles for this process, from the middle levels to the very top of the corporation,
is what might be called a rehearsal.

Rehearsals mark all of social life. I shall focus here only on a special kind
of rehearsal, that is, the rehearsal of legitimations for what has to be done.
Within their own organizational circles, managers regularly rehearse their
explanations and accounts for actions decided upon. On one hand, such
rehearsals may prepare one principally for the ongoing internal organizational
drama. In this case, rehearsals often focus on developing "defensible" rationales for action which can, of course, assume widely varying forms depending
on which criteria and ideologies hold sway in an organization at a particular
time. Alternatively, rehearsals may be geared to honing rationales for the
broader extra-organizational audiences that managers at certain levels and in
particular positions must sometimes address. But whether rehearsals of legitimation are designed to prepare managers for internal or external audiences,
they typically go through a three-stage sequence. First, managers cast around

a variety of perspectives in order to "cover all the bases" and see the situation at hand from many angles of vision. In this stage, there is little formality and often a fair amount of levity, usually in the form of parody by offering, for instance, burlesque rationales for action with mock seriousness. Certain viewpoints fall of their own weight, others get discarded as wholly implausible, and still others are entertained for long periods but in a provisional manner.

The second stage of such a rehearsal begins when it becomes clear, often but not always by the edict of the presiding authority, that certain explanations rather than others should be the point of focus. Given managers' sensitivity to interactional and verbal cues, particularly from bosses, the shift to a more focused discussion is not usually precipitous or forced. Rather, one or more possible rationales become subject to a kind of devil's advocacy in which potential weaknesses of arguments are explored. The manner of discussion shifts during this stage toward a more formal etiquette of debate. One manager will say, for instance, "Well, we could say that ...," elaborating a set of reasons for action. Another manager will counter, "But, if you say that, it could be argued that ... Why not put it this way ... ?" And still another will say, "But if we say that, how do we explain ... ?" Except during a precipitous crisis, this second stage of a rehearsal can last for long periods and extend over many meetings until viewpoints begin to crystallize.

The final stage of a rehearsal of legitimations begins, almost imperceptibly, when a certain viewpoint seems convincing to a circle and begins to assume coherent and elaborate form. Sometimes an individual manager will articulate a rationale in a manner that suddenly "puts all the pieces together"; sometimes a public relations counselor assumes this interactive symbolic role. However, the decisive moment in the third stage of a rehearsal and, in fact, the point of the whole process comes when a managerial circle, or key members of it, decide that a certain rationale "is the way to go," one with which they "feel comfortable." Here morality becomes one's personal comfort vis-à-vis the anticipated views of others. The measure of that comfort becomes a confidence in the casuistry necessary to persuade others that one's stories are plausible and one's choices reasonable. Such anticipatory confrontations with the viewpoints of certain publics make rehearsals, on one hand, a forum for a kind of accountability. On the other, in helping managers master the public relations technique of playing with the magic lantern, rehearsals also encourage the most subtle form of hype, namely convincing oneself of one's own rectitude.

Despite their thoroughgoing skepticism, even public relations men and women can become dazzled by their own technique. The magic lantern produces both light and shadows. What matters on the screen are convincing impressions of reality, plausible representations, and a conformity to conventional manners, faces, and tastes. The images cast upon the screen do not so much displace substance, notions of truth, and principles as leave them in the dim periphery of the theater. Public relations becomes public-relations-mindedness, a circuitous institutional logic that makes placating various publics the principal and, at times, the only goal. Some years ago, Images Inc. came under vigorous journalistic and public assault for some questionable practices of its own. The firm's instinctive institutional response suggests the habit of mind that public-relations-mindedness creates. Executives at the firm held, of course, their own rehearsal to frame appropriate responses to the charges being made. As public pressure mounted, the public relations firm created a position and then appointed a director of public relations.

8

Invitations to Jeopardy

I

The ethic that emerges in bureaucratic contexts contrasts sharply in many respects with the original Protestant ethic. The Protestant ethic was a social construction of reality of a self-confident and independent propertied social class. It was an ideology that extolled the virtues of accumulating and reinvesting wealth in a society organized around property and that accepted the stewardship responsibilities entailed by property. It was an ideology where a person's word was his bond and where the integrity of the handshake was crucial to the maintenance of good business relationships. Perhaps most important, it was connected to a predictable economy of salvation—that is, hard work will lead to success, which is a sign of election by God, a taken for granted notion also containing its own theodicy to explain the misery of those who do not make it in this world. This economy of salvation was, in my view, the decisive conscious meaning of the ideology, a meaning that linked even antagonistic segments of the old middle class. At the core of the middle class's righteous, some would say smug, faith in itself, of its inexhaustible drive, of its unremitting pragmatism, was the conviction that hard work necessarily had its just rewards here and now as a token of divine favor in the hereafter. This conviction was also the bedrock of a profound guilt mechanism that impelled one to fulfill personal and social obligations; failure to do so, like a failure to work hard, was thought to be a sin against both God and self.

Bureaucracy and the ethic it generates undercuts the crucial premises of this classic ideology and strips it of the powerful religious and symbolic meaning it once had. Bureaucracy breaks apart the ownership of property from its control, social independence from occupation, substance from appearances, action from responsibility, obligation from guilt, language from meaning, and notions of truth from reality. Most important, and at the bottom of all of these fractures, it breaks apart the older connection between the meaning of work and salvation. In the bureaucratic world, one's success, one's sign of election, no longer depends on an inscrutable God, but on the capriciousness of one's superiors and the market; and one achieves economic salvation to the extent that one pleases and submits to new gods, that is, one's bosses and the exigencies of an impersonal market.

In this way, because moral choices are inextricably tied to personal fates, bureaucracy erodes internal and even external standards of morality not only in matters of individual success and failure but in all the issues that managers face in their daily work. Bureaucracy makes its own internal rules and social context the principal moral gauges for action.

Formerly, the businessmen of the old independent middle class turned to the Protestant sects in their communities for moral certification. A sect's acceptance of a person testified to his ethical probity, vouched to others that he was honest and, more to the point, credit-worthy. One can still see the cultural vestiges of this crucial mechanism of social and moral approbation through religious affiliation on Sunday mornings in the small southern community where Weft Corporation has its headquarters. The front pews of the local Presbyterian church are always crowded with local businessmen, corporate managers, and their families. Some Weft managers still insist, in fact, that one's prospects in the corporate hierarchy depend on one's membership and, more exactly, on one's standing in that congregation.

But the probationary crucibles that managers face in their bureaucratic milieux are much more ambiguous and demanding. Instead of relatively stable councils of elders who guard doctrine and dictate behavioral norms, the basic framework of managerial work is formed by structures of personalized authority in formally impersonal contexts, fealty with bosses and patrons, and alliances shaped through networks, coteries, cliques, and work groups that struggle through hard times together. It is always subject to upheaval and the consequent formation of new ties and alliances. Each circle of affiliation in this world, while it lasts, develops its own criteria of admission, its own standards of trustworthiness, its own gauges of emotional comfort, and even its own etiquette, all within the general structure and ethos of a particular corporation. The dominant clique in a hierarchy at any given time establishes the general tone for other groups.

Of course, the segmented work patterns of bureaucracy underlie these larger structures. Managers' cognitive maps to the thickets of their world contain sharp, sometimes absurd, caricatures of the style and ethos of different occupational groups. These suggest some of the ways in which managers appraise the myriad of character types whom they see peopling their world. Production types, for instance, are said to be hard-drinking, raucous, good-time charlies; engineers, always distinguishable by the plastic pen containers

in their shirt pockets, are hostages to an outdated belief in a pristine mathematical rationality; accountants are bean counters who know how to play the
shell game; lawyers are legal eagles or legal beagles in wool pinstripes who, if
they had their way, would tie managers' hands completely; corporate staff are
the king's spies, always ready to do his bidding and his dirty work; marketing
guys are cheerful, smooth-talking, upbeat fashion plates who must nonetheless keep salesmen under their thumbs; salesmen are aggressive loudmouths
who feel that they can sell freezers to penguins in Antarctica and who would
sell their grandmothers just to make a deal. Salesmen hate the restraints that
marketers put on their work and on their ego gratification. Financial wizards,
on the ascendancy everywhere, are tight-mouthed, close to the vest poker
players who think that a social order can be built on paper deals. And outside
consultants are men and women who borrow one's watch and then charge for
telling the time. Different occupational groups meld with each other through
regular work assignments, or special task forces, or through the vagaries of
power shifts that subordinate one group to another. Within each group,
whether based strictly on occupational expertise or emerging as the result of
other melding, more general patterns of personalized authority, fealty, alliances, conflict, and power seeking prevail. Managers thus experience the corporation as an intricate matrix of rival and often intersecting managerial circles. The principal goal of each group is its own survival, of each person his
own advancement. As one rises in the organization, one necessarily spends
more and more time maintaining networks and alliances precisely in order to
survive and flourish, a skill that, when well-developed, is usually called leadership. The unintended social consequence of this maelstrom of competition
and ambition is the public social order that the corporation presents to the
world.

Within such crucibles, managers are continually tested even as they continually test others. They turn to each other for moral cues for behavior and
come to fashion specific situational moralities for specific significant others
in their world. But the guidance that they receive from each other is as profoundly ambiguous as the social structure of the corporation. What matters
in the bureaucratic world is not what a person is but how closely his many
personae mesh with the organizational ideal; not his willingness to stand by
his actions but his agility in avoiding blame; not his acuity in perceiving fal-
sity or errors but his adeptness at protecting others; not his talent, his abilities,
or his hard work, but how these are harnessed with the proper protocol to
address the particular exigencies that face his organization; not what he
believes or says but how well he has mastered the ideologies and rhetorics
that serve his corporation; not what he stands for but whom he stands with
in the labyrinths of his organization.

In short, bureaucracy creates for managers a Calvinist world without a
Calvinist God, a world marked with the same profound anxiety that characterized the old Protestant ethic but one stripped of that ideology's comforting
illusions. Bureaucracy poses for managers an intricate set of moral mazes that

are paradigmatic of the quandaries of public life in our social order. Within this framework, the puzzle for many individual managers becomes: How does one act in such a world and maintain a sense of personal integrity?

II

Bureaucratic work itself, of course, provides powerful frameworks that can and often do obscure tensions between requisite actions and idealized self-images, sometimes even for considerable periods. In particular, the continuous, standardized regularity of bureaucratic work tends to routinize personal experiences and helps shape taken for granted frameworks even on issues that outsiders might find unsettling. Managers at Alchemy Inc., for instance, simply shrug at many of the widely trumpeted hazards of toxic waste; here, one person's hysteria and cause for moral outrage is another's familiar and somewhat dull routine. Moreover, bureaucratic compartmentalization, with its concomitant secrecy and fragmentation of consciousness, often prevents the passing from one level of an organization to the next, indeed from one managerial circle to another, of the actual knowledge of troublesome issues—say, the burial of important data, or the double-crossing of an associate, or payoffs to officials or to employees who threaten to "sing about where the bodies are buried," or the outright theft of ideas or strategies. At the least, compartmentalization provides wholly acceptable rationales for not knowing about problems or for not trying to find out. It also seems to be a structural inducement to private irrationalities, generating, for instance, suspicions, wild rumors, and even attributions of calculated malevolence that often, given the public roles that managers must play, get projected into the public arena in disguised forms. In this sense, the very rationality of bureaucracy may stimulate remarkable patterns of irrationality. Finally, despite the organizational premium on symbolic dexterity, some managers often come to believe, as noted earlier, their own public relations about their organizations and about themselves. The attainment of such a degree of sincerity inhibits critical reflection, especially about moral dilemmas.

Sooner or later, however, almost all managers experience clashes between the requirements of their world and aspects of their valued self-images. Such tensions arise most predictably when organizational upheavals cause an unraveling of the social and moral ties that secure one's status and social identity or when public attacks on one's organization call one's organizational morality into question. But even the everyday ambiguities and compromises of managerial work often pose invitations to jeopardy. Some of the recurring dilemmas that managers face test their own preferred self-definitions. All of these revolve in one way or another around the meaning of work. Those managers who respond fully to the organizational premiums on success are especially important here because their ambition not only drives themselves but continually regenerates the structure of their world.

First, some of the fundamental requirements of managerial work clash with the normal ethics governing interpersonal behavior, let alone friendship in our society. Our egalitarian ideology couples here with remnants of Judeo-Christian beliefs counseling honesty, loyalty, and compassion toward other people. But at bottom, a great deal of managerial work consists of ongoing struggles for dominance and status. Real administrative effectiveness flows, in fact, from the prestige that one establishes with other managers. Prestige in managerial hierarchies depends not only on position as determined by the crucial indices of rank, grade, title, and salary, and the external accoutrements that symbolize power. Even more fundamentally, it consists of the socially recognized ability to work one's will, to get one's way, to have the say-so when one chooses in both the petty and large choices of organizational life. At one level, the superordination and subordination of bureaucratic hierarchies guarantee clashes between the egos of men and women who "like to control things," whose choice of occupation, in fact, has been at least partly shaped by their orientation and habituation to control. For instance, an administrative coordinator describes the daily battles between Beach, the president of one of Weft's divisions, and Schultz, his talented vice-president:

> I feel every knife turn between [Beach] and [Schultz]. [Beach] enjoys lording it over [Schultz]. For instance, in a dispute, [Beach] will say: "I'll make the final choices." And this drives [Schultz] crazy. And then the whole department is drawn up on either side of the battle. . . . [I]n the morning, I'll come in and try to cope with the latest issue. I'll be thinking: "What did [one] mean about this? How will the other guy react when he finds out?" The way things are now is that [Schultz] can work heavily toward influencing things, but if [Beach] felt that he could make some decision which would turn out well and would at the same time be against [Schultz], he would make it in a minute.

At another level, the struggle for dominance is an inevitable by-product of the pyramidal construction of bureaucracies that fuels managers' driving competitiveness. A divisional vice-president at Weft comments:

> There just aren't that many places to go when you get up as high as I am. . . . [T]he competition that does occur is within the division. You're not competing for jobs with another division.

> Now within the division, there's a limited number of positions, of spots, and after you're here for awhile and know the score, you don't have three guys after one spot. . . . [T]he competition is not necessarily for the jobs that open up, since they are so few. Rather the ongoing competition is *for your way of doing things*. We all want things to go our way and the competition, dilemmas, and problems are when it doesn't go my way but somebody else's. I've competed and lost on that

issue. . . . That's where there is real pressure. It's in the competitiveness in trying to have it your way. You have to be able to swallow the
defeat.

Defeat at the middle and upper-middle levels produces in the losers feelings
of frustration and of being "boxed in." Such disappointments must be concealed and the ideology of team play often affords a convenient cover for
defeat, one that might even be translated later into organizational credit. But
one cannot, of course, lose too often without risking permanent anonymity.
At the top of an organization, the loss of prestige occasioned by a major policy
defeat leaves the loser with the hard choice between resignation or the daily
humiliation of cheerfully doing something someone else's way. Defeat in such
circumstances seems especially difficult when the victor insists on being mag-
nanimous. In such a case, the victor enjoys plaudits for big-hearted sensitivity
while his defeated opponent often finds such generosity more oppressive than
vindictiveness. On the other hand, winning carries with it the knowledge of
others' envy and the fear that one's defeated opponents are lying in wait for
an opportunity to turn the tables. One adopts then a stance of public humility,
of self-effacing modesty that helps disguise whatever sense of triumph one
might feel. Moreover, winning, say, on a policy dispute, carries the burden
of implementation, sometimes involving those whom one has defeated. One
must then simultaneously protect one's flanks and employ whatever wiles are
necessary to secure requisite cooperation. Here the disarming social grace
that is a principal aspect of desirable managerial style can be particularly useful
in making disingenuousness seem like "straight arrow" behavior. Finally,
winning sometimes requires the willingness to move decisively against others,
even though this might mean undermining their organizational careers. These
may be neighbors on the same block, members of the same religious com-
munion, longtime work colleagues, or, more rarely, members of the same
club. They may be good, even excellent, employees. In short, managerial
effectiveness and others' perceptions of one's leadership depend on the willingness to battle for the prestige that comes from dominance and to make
whatever moral accommodations such struggles demand. In the work world,
those who adhere either to secular democratic precepts as guides rather than
guises or, even more, to an ethic of brotherly love, run the risk of faltering
in those struggles. But those who abandon the ethics of *caritas* and hone themselves to do what has to be done must accept the peculiar emotional aridity
that is one price of organizational striving and, especially, of victory.

Second, managers at the middle levels in particular also have to come to
grips with the peculiar inequities of the corporate world that call the meaning,
purpose, and value of their work into question. They take for granted, of
course, the material and symbolic inequities embedded in their bureaucratic
hierarchies, hoping as they do that they themselves will one day benefit from
the opportunities to appropriate credit from subordinates, command others'
deference, and enjoy the generous salaries, company cars, year-end bonuses,
big offices, attractive secretaries, and golden parachutes and golden handcuffs

(financial ties that bind) that are seen to be the prerogatives of high rank, prestige, and power. However, the institutionalized inequities that result from what managers see as a pervasive mediocrity in big organizations do pose dilemmas. One measure of the troublesome character of such mediocrity is the widespread emotional resonance tapped by the recent widely heralded managerial consultant slogan of "excellence in management."[1]

As managers see it, mediocrity emerges out of the lack of fixed criteria within an organization to measure quality, whether of products or performance. In a world where criteria depend entirely on the interpretive judgments of shifting groups in an ever-changing social structure, where everyone's eyes are fixed on each other and on market exigencies, the construction of notions of quality becomes highly political since individual fates depend on the outcome. Clearly, skillful leadership and mobilization of organizational resources can impose a consensus about appropriate standards. However, to do so, one has to: resist pressures for short-term expedient solutions to problems that compromise one's notion of desirable standards; be willing to confront others, both in private and in public, who espouse or embody in some way variant, undesirable standards; and enforce one's judgment with organizationally approved sanctions. But given the bureaucratic ethos, such insistence on standards of excellence can quickly earn one enemies and the feared label of being "inflexible." As it happens, when it is socially difficult to extol or uphold high standards, a kind of leveling process occurs that produces a comfortable mediocrity, a willingness to settle for, say, whatever the market will bear, or to tolerate shoddiness of products or performance, provided there is no undue social disruption. In such situations, among those managers who wish for clearer, higher standards, quasifictional images of the supposed superiority of different organizations or of the purported technical and managerial prowess of the Japanese often abound, usually invoked with wistful longing and sometimes with rueful envy.

Perceptions of pervasive mediocrity breed an endless quest for social distinctions even of a minor sort that might give one an "edge," enable one to "step out of the crowd," or at least serve as a basis for individual claims to privilege. More specifically, an atmosphere of mediocrity erodes the hope of meaningful collective achievement and encourages, at least among more aggressive managers, a predatory stance toward their organizations, that is, a search for private deals, a working of the system for one's own personal advantage. This may mean, variously, winning the assignment of a valued account, product, or client; wrangling one of the coveted discretionary places on a bonus scheme; or getting the inside track on promotions through the exposure gained by chairing a crucial committee or task force. A system of deal making places a premium on maximizing one's organizational leverage in order to make claims on those with power to dispense perquisites. In such a system, "big numbers" may help reduce organizational vulnerability but do not necessarily help maximize leverage. Rather, the social factors that bind managers to one another, whether in conflict or in harmony, are the chief sources of deals. Such a system is thus principally characterized by the exchange of personal favors and the dispensation of patronage to seal the alliances that give one "clout"; by the systematic collection of information damaging to others and particularly about deals struck and favors won in order to argue more effectively the propriety and legitimacy of one's own claims; and, on the part of those in power, by pervasive secrecy, called confidentiality, that attempts to cordon off the knowledge of deals already made lest the demands on the system escalate unduly. It is worth noting that most middle managers' general detestation of affirmative action programs, apart from their resentment at yet another wild card in the corporate deck and at being asked to bear cheerfully the burdens of others' neglect and mistakes, is rooted in the perception that such arrangements symbolically legitimate the perceived inequities of their world, cloaking simply a new kind of expedient favoritism with self-righteous ideologies. Seen from this perspective, the corporation resembles for many a jerry-built structure, like a boardwalk erected on pilings of different heights, that, when viewed from a distance over sandy stretches in baking summer heat, shimmers rickety and swaying to the eye.

In such a world, notions of fairness or equity that managers might privately hold, as measures of gauging the worth of their own work, become merely quaint. One fluctuates between a frustrated resentment at what seems to be a kind of institutionalized corruption and systematic attempts to make oneself a beneficiary of the system. Being a "good soldier" may carry for some the private satisfactions of work well done, of bargains kept, or of organizational goals attained through one's best efforts. But such dedication may also make one unfit for the maneuvers that can bring organizational privilege and reward.

Third, managers at every level face puzzles about the overall meaning of their work in a business civilization in which the old notion of stewardship has been lost and in which work in business is alternately regarded with at times adulation, at times tolerant condescension, and at times outright suspicion. Sooner or later, most managers realize, as Thorstein Veblen did many years ago, that there are no intrinsic connections between the good of a particular corporation, the good of an individual manager, and the common weal. Stories are legion among managers about corporations that "devour" individuals, "plunder" the public, and succeed extravagantly; about individual managers whose predatory stances toward their fellows, their organizations, and society itself only further propel their skyrocketing careers; about individual managers desiring to harness the great resources of private enterprise and address social ills only to end up disillusioned by their colleagues' attention to exigencies; and about corporations that have espoused noble public goals only to founder in competitive markets and endanger the occupational security of their employees by failing to concentrate on the bottom line.

Meaningful connections between organizational well-being, individual fates, and the common weal can, of course, be forged both by individual managers and by organizations at the level of policy. But, where they exist, such connections proceed from some ideological standpoint backed by institutional mechanisms. Law and regulation usually shape only the broad parameters of action and allowable public discourse in such matters. As I have suggested earlier, law and regulation can be quite important in providing requisite appeals to inevitability on controversial issues that break political deadlocks within organizations. But typically such external compulsions cannot offer the meaningful rationales that sustain the hard organizational work of coordinating diverse, sometimes opposing, managerial interests. Properly enforced, assertions of values by top management can do this, at least for periods of time until organizational reshuffling alters organizational premiums. Some corporations, for instance, espouse policies of product responsibility, tying organizational rewards to sustained vigilance over the uses and possible uses to which a product might be put. Such programs thus try to link individual success, reduction of corporate liability, and consumer safety. These programs can, of course, never be wholly successful. As the several poisonings of over-the-counter drugs in early 1986 suggest, even relatively farsighted product safety policies cannot anticipate the potential depth of individual irrationalities, whether these proceed from psychopathology or, perhaps more disturbing, from the didactic self-righteousness of those privileged to receive some ideological enlightenment. Moreover, to sustain the links between the corporation, the individual, and the common good over the long haul, important conditions must obtain within an organization. Specifically, the ideology incorporating certain values must be continuously and forcefully articulated by key authorities who are ostensibly committed to its premises, and, at the same time, the ideological links between the good of the corporation and the common weal in particular must be plausible both to managers and to important external publics. As it happens, both conditions are difficult to meet. Day-to-day exigencies, the personnel transitions of large organizations, the endless circulation of new rhetorics of innovation among top managers, the entrenched cynicism of middle managers on whose backs the burdens for any such policies will fall, and of course, the "take the money and run" ethos, make it difficult to sustain organizational commitment to goals defined as socially important.

Even more difficult is fashioning some working consensus about the meaning of "corporate social responsibility," a consensus that includes top management, external publics that top management is trying to appease, and middle management that must implement a policy. Here the precariousness of ideological bridges over the chasm between the interests of a corporation, individual managers, and the public are most apparent. Some years ago, for example, Alchemy Inc. was producing a food-grade chemical used principally as a meat preservative. The company was, in fact, one of the chief suppliers of the chemical to the processed food industry. Although the business was small in comparison to other company operations, its oligopolistic position in this particular market made the preservative a very lucrative commodity. Suddenly, a newly released government study fingered the food preservative as carcinogenic. The report received great and widespread publicity, coinciding as it did with a public debate about carcinogens in food and with a nationwide health food fad that stressed, among other things, natural diets uncontaminated with artificial ingredients. Moreover, Covenant Corporation was recovering at the time from the bad publicity of an environmental catastrophe. In light of both developments, the CEO of Covenant, who was nearing retirement, ordered the immediate sale of the preservative business, arguing that the recent scientific evidence made such a divestiture an act of corporate social responsibility. This position earned him plaudits from several environmental and health groups.

Alchemy managers, by contrast, argued privately that the CEO's real motivation was simply the avoidance of any further public relations hassles at that stage of his career. After the managers in charge of the preservative business had divested, they had more material grounds for their skepticism as they watched the company that bought the operation "make money hand over fist." They wondered whether the CEO had not simply "caved in." Is, they asked, "supine acquiescence" to special-interest groups or to suspect or perhaps even bogus government research the meaning of corporate responsibility? Of course, they discounted the animal tests that suggested the preservative's carcinogenicity. But so what, they argued, if the preservative did in fact pose some risk of cancer? Better, they said, the risk of a slight long-run increase in the rate of stomach and intestinal cancer than the certainty of a precipitous spurt in the incidence of botulism, particularly in the lower-income black and Hispanic groups that typically consume large amounts of processed meat and, both because of poverty and cultural practices, often leave food uncovered and unrefrigerated for considerable periods. Is corporate social responsibility, they asked, maintaining a private sense and public image of moral purity while someone else does necessary but tainted work? Or is real social responsibility the willingness to get one's hands dirty, to make whatever compromises have to be made to produce a product with some utility, to achieve therefore some social good, even though one knows that one's accomplishments and motives will inevitably be misinterpreted by others for their own ends, usually by those with the least reason to complain? Besides, they pointed out, consumers continue to purchase artificially preserved meats in large quantities. Is not the proper role of business "to give the public what it wants," adopting the market as its polar star, as the only reliable guide in a pluralistic society to "the greatest good for the greatest number," as the final arbiter not of values, which are always arguable, but, more importantly, of tastes, about which there can be no reasonable dispute?

In short, managers' occupational roles are such that they simply cannot please everybody, even fellow managers. What seems socially responsible from one perspective may seem irresponsible or just plain venal from another angle. In fact, exercises in substantive rationality—the critical, reflective use of reason—are not only subject to infinite interpretations and counterinterpretations but also invite fantastic constructions of reality, including attributions of conspiracy. Thus a major corporation provides a gift of $10 million to establish new foundations that will materially aid South African blacks and is promptly accused by a black American leader of bolstering apartheid.[2] Weft managers create an elaborate recreational complex for Weft employees in the corporation's southern community and are charged with perpetuating traditional textile company paternalism. Some executives at Images Inc. donate their time to bring together several institutional sectors of a local town in which they live for community betterment and are charged with trying to grab headlines and line up future business. Managers often feel that, however genuine it may be, altruism is a motive that is always denied them by others. To complicate matters still further, the necessary self-promotional work of presenting private goals as public goods, or the self-defensive work within the corporation of presenting public goods as hardheaded business decisions, or managers' knowledge that bureaucracy insulates them from the real consequences of their actual choices, often make their protestations of socially responsible actions suspect even to themselves.

This context helps one understand why many managers feel, particularly as they grow older, that much of the actual work of management is senseless. Of course, big victories, pleasing deals, the seizure of capricious opportunities to accomplish something one thinks is worthwhile, the intrinsic pleasure, when it occurs, of harmonious orchestration, and, with personal success, the opportunity for leading roles in philanthropic, artistic, or social organizations of various sorts, trusteeships at elite colleges and universities, directorships in other corporations and the concomitant opportunity to mingle with other powerful peers, and the respectability that money and status afford, all punctuate and mitigate such senselessness. But the anonymity that is the lot of most corporate managers exacerbates it. Moreover, the successful propagation of professional ideologies of service or truth-seeking by occupations like medicine or the professoriate often make businessmen view their own attention to the material world as base or crass.

Yet attention to the material world can anchor one's sense of self. In fact, the problem of the senselessness of managerial work increases as the work itself becomes more abstract, typically as one advances. With increasing seniority, one retreats from concrete tasks, say, overseeing the manufacture of sheets or shirting material or running the production of hydrofluoric acid. One thus loses immediate connections to tangible human or industrial needs. For those who came up through the plants, one also loses regular contact with the renewing drama of industrial work. A plant manager at one of Alchemy's largest and most troublesome operations, a man who regularly goes in at all hours "to fight the dragons," tells how often he does not even wait for trouble:

Sometimes I'll wake up in the middle of the night thinking about the plant. And if I can't get back to sleep, I'll slip out of bed and walk over to the plant and just walk around the machinery and talk to the guys. I love the smell of the oil and the grease and the sound of the machines. For me, that's what life is all about.

But to advance, one must leave behind such a comforting concreteness, indeed the visible enactment of one's rational schemes, where materials, labor, and machinery are brought together to produce value.[3] One leaves behind as well the technical knowledge or scientific expertise of one's younger years, lore now more suited for the narrower roles of technicians or junior managers. One must, in fact, put distance between oneself and technical details of every sort or risk the inevitable entrapment of the particular. Salesmen too must leave their bags and regular customers and long boisterous evenings that seal measurable deals behind them and turn to marketing strategies. Work becomes more ambiguous, directed as it is toward maneuvering money, symbols, organizational structures, and especially people. The CEO at Weft Corporation, it is said, "doesn't know a loom from a car." And the higher one goes, the more managers find that "the essence of managerial work is cronyism, covering your ass, [and] pyramiding to protect your buddies."

The more abstract work becomes, that is, the less one actually does or oversees concrete tasks, the greater the likelihood that one's rational efforts to improve an organization will meet with and even beget various kinds of irrationality. One's rational systems, say, in Weft Corporation for measuring loom efficiency, or in Covenant for designing a grid appraising the relative strategic potentials of a cluster of businesses, fall to others for implementation and become hostage to their own private and organizational agendas, or become the cross hairs of others' gunsights. One's best laid plans are always subject to ambush by random events, fickle markets, recalcitrant or, worse, well-intentioned but incompetent subordinates, rival managers, or simply the weariness that work produces. One's best intentioned schemes sometimes produce exactly the opposite of what one wanted to achieve. One's best efforts at being fair, equitable, and generous with subordinates clash both with a logic that demands choices between people, inevitably producing hatred, envy and animosity, and with the plain fact that, despite protestations to the contrary, many people do not want to be treated fairly. In short, the increasingly abstract quality of managerial work as one advances both symbolizes and exacerbates the structural fragmentation of corporate, individual, and common goods. Such conundrums often produce nostalgic yearnings for simpler times, for the concrete work of one's younger years, even for fabled crisis periods when "everyone pulled together and got the job done," and perhaps especially for a society that unambiguously, it is thought, extolled work in business as socially honorable and personally salvific.

III

For most managers, especially for those who are ambitious, the real meaning of work—the basis of social identity and valued self-image—becomes keeping one's eye on the main chance, maintaining and furthering one's own position and career. This task requires, of course, unrelenting attentiveness to the social intricacies of one's organization. One gains dominance or fails depending on one's access to key managerial circles where prestige is gauged precisely by the relationships that one establishes with powerful managers and by the demonstrated favor such relationships bring. Even beyond their practical and crucial importance in furthering careers, the social psychological lure of entrance into such select groups is, of course, powerful and layers the drive to get ahead with complicated overtones. Such acceptance means, variously, no longer being relegated to marginality; having one's voice heard and opinion count in matters small and weighty; experiencing the peculiar bonds with one's fellows produced by shared secrecy, hard decisions and hard times, a sense of shared emotional aridity, and competition with rival cliques; penetrating the many layers of consciousness in the corporation that baffle outsiders and marginal managers alike; and being able to dispense at times, usually in the heat of battle and only within one's tried and trusted circle, with the gentlemanly politesse and requisite public advocacy of high-minded beliefs and, always with relief and sometimes with comic vulgarity, to get down to brass tacks. What one manager calls "our surrender of ourselves to groups" has its emotional touchstone in the sense of professional intimacy that acceptance into a managerial circle affords. Group intimacy, especially with powerful others, rewards and seals the self-directed transformation of self that makes one come to accept the ethos of an organization as one's own. But the process is rarely simple, precisely because such acceptance depends on developing and maintaining personal relationships with powerful others. Mastering the subtle but necessary arts of deference without seeming to be deferential, of "brown nosing" without fawning, of simultaneous self-promotion and self-effacement, and occasionally of the outright self-abasement that such relationships require is a taxing endeavor that demands continual compromises with conventional and popular notions of integrity. Only those with an inexhaustible capacity for self-rationalization, fueled by boundless ambition, can escape the discomfort such compromises produce.

But self-rationalization, even for those willing to open themselves up fully to institutional demands, produces its own discomforts and discontents. As in all professional careers, particularly those dependent on large organizations, managerial work requires a psychic asceticism of a high degree, a willingness to discipline the self, to thwart one's impulses, to stifle spontaneity in favor of control, to conceal emotion and intent, and to objectify the self with the same kind of calculating functional rationality that one brings to the packaging of any commodity. Moreover, such dispassionate objectification of the self frames and paces the rational objectification of circumstances and people that alertness to expediency demands. In its asceticism, self-rationalization curiously parallels the methodical subjection to God's will that the old Protestant ethic counseled. But instead of the satisfaction of believing that one is acquiring old-time moral virtues, one becomes a master at manipulating personae; instead of making oneself into an instrument of God's will to accomplish His work in this world, one becomes, variously, a boss's "hammer," a tough guy who never blinks at hard decisions, or perhaps, if all goes very well, an "industrial statesman," a leader with vision.

On one hand, such psychic asceticism is connected to the narcissism that one sees in executives of high rank. The simultaneous need for self-abnegation, self-promotion, and self-display, as managers work their way through the probationary crucibles of big organizational life, foster an absorption with self and specifically with self-improvement. Managers become continually and self-consciously aware of their public performances; they measure themselves constantly against others; and they plot out whatever self-transformations will help them achieve desired goals.

On the other hand, over a period of time, psychic asceticism creates a curious sense of guilt, heightened as it happens by narcissistic self-preoccupation. Such guilt, a regret at sustained self-abnegation and deprivation, finds expression principally in one's private emotional life. One drinks too much; one is subject to pencil-snapping fits of alternating anxiety, depression, rage, and self-disgust for willingly submitting oneself to the knowing and not knowing, to the constant containment of anger, to the keeping quiet, to the knuckling under that are all inevitable in bureaucratic life. One experiences great tensions at home because one's spouse is unable to grasp or unable to tolerate the endless review of the social world of the workplace, the rehearsals of upcoming conversations, or the agonizing over real or imagined social slights or perceptions of shifts in power alignments. One wishes that one had spent more time with one's children when they were small so that one could grasp the meanings of their adolescent traumas. Or one withdraws emotionally from one's family and, with alternating fascination and regret, plunges ever deeper into the dense and intimate relationships of organizational circles where emotional aridity signals a kind of fraternity of expediency. Many try at times to escape the guilt with Walter Mitty-like fantasies of insouciant rebellion and vengeful retaliation; but one knows that only if and when one rises to high position in a bureaucratic hierarchy does one have the opportunity to turn the pain of self-repression against one's fellows.

However, for those with the requisite discipline, sheer dogged perseverance, the agile flexibility, the tolerance for extreme ambiguity, the casuistic discernment that allows one to dispense with shopworn pieties, the habit of mind that perceives opportunities in others' and even one's own misfortunes, the brazen nerve that allows one to pretend that nothing is wrong even when the world is crumbling, and, above all, the ability to read the inner logic of events, to see and do what has to be done, the rewards of corporate success can be very great. And, of course, those who do succeed, those who find their way out of the crowded, twisting corridors and into the back rooms where the real action is, where the big games take place, and where everyone present is a player, shape, in a decisive way, the moral rules-in-use that filter down through their organizations. The ethos that they fashion turns principles into guidelines, ethics into etiquette, values into tastes, personal responsibility into an adroitness at public relations, and notions of truth into credibility. Corporate managers who become imbued with this ethos pragmatically take their world as they find it and try to make that world work according to its own institutional logic. They pursue their own careers and good fortune as best they can within the rules of their world. As it happens, given their pivotal institutional role in our epoch, they help create and re-create, as one unintended consequence of their personal striving, a society where morality becomes indistinguishable from the quest for one's own survival and advantage.

AUTHOR'S NOTE

Chapter 1 discusses some of the main dimensions and ambiguities of my field-work in the corporate world. This note simply details the data that frame the book.

1. I have treated some data as preliminary. These include elaborate con-versations, negotiations, and discussions with a range of managers in half of the thirty-six corporations that refused permission for the study. In several cases, these interactions led me to the top of the companies I approached. I have also treated as preliminary seven in-depth interviews with top officials in a medium-sized chemical company and in a large defense contractor. More extensive access in these two companies could not be arranged.

2. The core data are 143 intensive, semi-structured interviews with man-agers at every level in the companies I have called Weft Corporation (50), Alchemy Inc. and its parent Covenant Corporation (53), and Images Inc. (40). Each interview usually lasted between two and three hours but sometimes went much longer. In particular, I re-interviewed more than a quarter (40) of my interviewees, and many of these a third and fourth time. Among those re-interviewed, I also selected a stratified group of twelve managers. I regularly asked these managers to interpret materials that I was collecting. I met with these managers more than a half dozen times each.

I conducted all interviews personally. Most were arranged by appointment and done in the workplace during regular office hours. A few took place in restaurants, cafeterias, or bars; one was held in a private home. I recorded all interview data by hand and typed them myself into interview records, usually the same day. The fieldwork in both Weft and Alchemy Inc./Covenant began in fall 1980 and lasted until mid-1982 and mid-1983, respectively. The entire month of May 1981 was spent in southern states studying Weft's corporate headquarters and its manufacturing facilities, to which I had extensive access. While in the South, I also interviewed some textile workers from Weft mills. I also visited one of Alchemy Inc.'s plants, and I interviewed executives in another operating company of Covenant Corporation, located elsewhere, to check out findings made at corporate headquarters. I also visited Washington, D.C. both to interview Covenant's government lobbyists and to talk with government officials in different regulatory agencies to improve my understanding of the complex technological issues that managers in both Alchemy Inc. and Weft Corporation face. The fieldwork in Images Inc. began in a regular way early in 1982 and lasted through 1985. It continues in sporadic form today.

3. The interview data are complemented by extensive nonparticipant and participant observation. These observational data include attendance at some management meetings, informal conversations and discussions over meals, coffee, and drinks, and participation in a range of social events. The latter include a church picnic and various celebratory receptions. Through the good offices of the executive who granted me access to Alchemy Inc., I was able to attend two seminars for up-and-coming managers in that company, each lasting several days. These occasions not only enabled me to meet managers from all over the country but also to meet Alchemy and Covenant executives to whom I had no previous access. It was often in such informal settings that I gained the best insights during my fieldwork, ideas that I then pursued more formally through interviews. In all the firms that I studied, I also reviewed the company literature directed at managers, as well as internal documents detailing organizational actions or stances on specific issues.

4. Finally, one other set of data has informed my work. As my study proceeded, I began to see that an investigation of organizational morality should also explore managerial dissenters, so-called whistleblowers, many of whom take stands against their organizations on grounds that they define as moral. Since whistleblowers are scarce in the corporate world, I focused on dissenters in bureaucratic contexts, both corporate and governmental. Beginning in 1982 and continuing to the present, I have done thirteen case studies of organizational dissenters, interviewing eighteen whistleblowers in the process. Each case study has involved the review of considerable amounts of documentary evidence. I have used these data here principally to help me understand more fully corporate managers' occupational morality. I did this by presenting several whistleblower cases to the stratified group of twelve managers mentioned earlier, asking them to assess the dissenters' actions and motives by their own standards.

Notes

Introduction. Business as a Social and Moral Terrain

1. For a comprehensive listing of these works, see Donald G. Jones, *A Bibliography of Business Ethics, 1971–1975* (Charlottesville, Va.: University Press of Virginia, 1977); and Donald G. Jones and Helen Troy, eds., *A Bibliography of Business Ethics, 1976–1980* (Charlottesville, Va.: University Press of Virginia, 1982).

2. These include the Center for the Study of Applied Ethics at the Darden Graduate Business School, University of Virginia; the Center for the Study of Values at the University of Delaware; the Center for Business Ethics at Bentley College; the Center for the Study of Ethics in the Professions at the Illinois Institute of Technology; the Center for Applied Philosophy at the University of Florida; and the Center for Public Philosophy at the University of Maryland. A comprehensive list of such centers is available from the Ethics Resource Center, 1025 Connecticut Avenue, N.W., Suite 1003, Washington, D.C. 20036.

3. See, for instance, the *Report of the Committee for Education in Business Ethics* sponsored by the National Endowment for the Humanities (Skokie, Ill.: Fel-Pro Incorporated, 1980); Charles W. Powers and David Vogel, *Ethics in the Education of Business Managers* (Hastings-on-Hudson, N.Y.: The Hastings Center, 1980); and Opinion Research Corporation, *Codes of Ethics in Corporations and Trade Associations and the Teaching of Ethics in Graduate Business Schools*, a survey conducted for the Ethics Resource Center (Princeton, N.J.: Opinion Research Corporation, June 1979). Sixteen percent of graduate schools of business responding to this survey (57 out of 134 schools, or 43 percent) offered a separate course in ethics; almost all claimed that ethics was included in other courses. In early 1987, the Harvard Business School received a gift of $30 million to support a program on ethics in its curriculum. Most of the gift

came from John S. R. Shad, the outgoing chairman of the Securities and Exchange Commission. See Alison Leigh Cowan, "Harvard to Get $30 Million Ethics Gift," *The New York Times,* Tuesday, March 31, 1987, D1, cols. 3–5 and D8, cols. 5, 6. According to the article, one purpose of the gift was to help the Harvard Business School " . . . forge a weapon to curb abuses on Wall Street."

4. For a useful listing of some of the main works in this tradition going back to 1900, see Portia Christian with Richard Hicks, *Ethics in Business Conduct: Selected References from the Record—Problems, Attempted Solutions, Ethics in Business Education* (Detroit, Mich.: Gale Research Company, 1970).

5. Wherever there are human moral quandaries, there is, of course, casuistry; it is as ancient as human thought itself. For two fine summaries of the main historical developments in moral casuistry, see R. M. Wenley, "Casuistry," *Encyclopedia of Religion and Ethics,* Vol. 3 (Edinburgh: T. T. Clark, 1910), pp. 239–247; and Benjamin Nelson, "Casuistry," *Encyclopedia Britannica,* Vol. 5 (1973 edition), pp. 51–52.

Chapter 1. Moral Probations, Old and New

1. Max Weber, *The Protestant Ethic and the Spirit of Capitalism,* translated by Talcott Parsons (New York: Charles Scribner's Sons, 1958), p. 172.

2. See, for instance, Bernard Bailyn, *The New England Merchants in the Seventeenth Century* (Cambridge, Mass.: Harvard University Press, 1955), pp. 16–44.

3. The case of Robert Keayne, a New England Puritan merchant, suggests the personal vicissitudes that differences in doctrinal interpretation mixed with social splits, could create for an individual. Keayne's troubles all began with a bag of nails that, as far as he was concerned, he had sold for a very fair price. However, as he tells us in his last will and testament, *The Apologia of Robert Keayne: The Self-Portrait of a Puritan Merchant,* edited by Bernard Bailyn (Gloucester, Mass.: Peter Smith, 1970), there was a seeming, though not actual, mix-up in his own ledger entries on the transaction owing to a mistake in the size of the nails originally delivered (pp. 53–54). The buyer of the nails, himself a magistrate, accused Keayne of gouging unjust profits from honest citizens, though Keayne points out that the buyer did not see fit to render payment for the nails for more than two years (p. 52). Keayne found himself the lightning rod in a community squall. He was hauled before the high civil court and excoriated not only about the nails but about a number of other items—some gold buttons and a bridle—for which, it was said, he had overcharged and, in pursuing his own interests, had harmed the whole community. It was suggested as well that he had falsified his business records in the matter of the nails. The court levied a stiff fine of 200 pounds, and there were those, Keayne felt, who would have exacted much more, who pressed their accusations " . . . with such violence and pretended zeal as if they had had some of the greatest sins in the world to censure." (p. 46) Keayne escaped excommunication at the hands of the church authorities but he was obliged to do penance to regain the godly fellowship.

The whole experience left Keayne filled with resentment and remorse. On one hand, Keayne wondered why he had been singled out to be pilloried. Was the selling of the nails at rates that " . . . were cheap pennyworths in comparison of what hath been taken since [p. 48] . . . such a crying and oppressing sin?" (p. 52) On the other hand, he brooded about the private torment and sense of shame such public accusations, however unjust in his view, brought him. He says:

... I was much grieved and astonished to be complained of in Court and brought publicly to answer as a grievous malefactor. . . .

I confess still as I did then and as I have said before, that the newness and strangeness of the thing, to be brought forth into an open court as a public malefactor, was both a shame and an amazement to me. It was the grief of my soul . . . that any act of mine (though not justly but by misconstruction) should be an occasion of scandal to the Gospel and profession of the Lord Jesus, or that myself should be looked at as one that had brought any just dishonor to God. . . . And if it had been in my own power I should rather have chosen to have perished in my cradle than to have lived to such a time. . . . Yet I do say still as I have often done before, that those things for which I was questioned . . . did deserve no such proceedings as was carved out to me, though some blew up those sparks into a great flame. (pp. 58–59)

Doctrine, like contemporary law and regulation, depended entirely on how it was interpreted and enforced.

See also Bernard Bailyn's treatment of Keayne's story in *The New England Merchants in the Seventeenth Century*, pp. 41–44.

4. Max Weber, "The Protestant Sects and the Spirit of Capitalism," in *From Max Weber*, translated and edited by Hans Gerth and C. Wright Mills (New York: Oxford University Press, 1958), p. 321.

5. See Illsoo Kim, *New Urban Immigrants: The Korean Community in New York* (Princeton, N.J.: Princeton University Press, 1981), pp. 205–207.

6. Max Weber, "The Protestant Sects and the Spirit of Capitalism," in *From Max Weber*, pp. 302–322. See especially pp. 302–308.

7. Two notable works on the importance of the idea of success in American society are John G. Cawelti, *Apostles of the Self-Made Man* (Chicago, Ill.: University of Chicago Press, 1965); and Richard M. Huber, *The American Idea of Success* (New York: McGraw-Hill, 1971). Many popular biographies, particularly of men and women who have become celebrities, are in fact celebrations of the idea of success, seasoned with moral admonitions about its perils. Autobiographies of public figures usually mine the same rich cultural lode, although with a naturally greater emphasis on self-dramatization. A recent very popular work in this genre is Lee Iacocca with William Novak, *Iacocca: An Autobiography* (New York: Bantam, 1984).

The literature providing practical advice to reach the heights of the corporate world is voluminous and ever-growing. A visit to a small bookstore in June 1986 yielded the following catch of titles related to the subject: Dr. Srully Blotnick, *The Corporate Steeplechase: Predictable Crises in a Business Career* (New York: Facts on File, 1984); Dr. Srully Blotnick, *Otherwise Engaged: The Private Lives of Successful Career Women* (New York: Penguin, 1985); Eugene Bronstein and Robert Hirsch, *The MBA Career: Moving on the Fast Track to Success* (Woodbury, N.Y.: Barron's Educational Service, 1983); Charles Paul Conn, *The Winner's Circle* (New York: Berkley Books, 1983); Martha Friedman, *Overcoming the Fear of Success* (New York: Warner Books, 1980); George Mazzei, *Moving Up: Digging in, Taking Charge, Playing the Power Game and Learning to Like It* (New York: Pocket Books, 1986); Ross and Kathryn Petras, *Inside Track: How to Get Into and Succeed in America's Prestige Companies* (New York: Vintage, 1986); Henry C. Rogers, *Rogers' Rules for Success* (New York: St. Martin's/ Marek, 1984); Mark H. McCormack, *What They Don't Teach You at the Harvard Busi-*

ness School: Notes From a Street Smart Executive (Toronto and New York: Bantam, 1986); Roberta Roesch, *You Can Make It Without a College Degree* (Englewood Cliffs, N.J.: Prentice-Hall, 1986); W. Clement Stone, *The Success System That Never Fails* (New York: Pocket Books, 1980); Thomas Chorba and Alex York, *Winning Moves: Career Strategies for the Eighties* (Garden City, N.Y.: Anchor Press/Doubleday, 1986); Clinton McElmore, *Good Guys Finish First: Success Strategies for Business Men and Women* (New York: Jove, 1983); and Thomas Friedman, *Up the Ladder: Coping with the Corporate Climb* (New York: Warner Books, 1986).

8. I have drawn heavily here on the magisterial work of Alfred D. Chandler, Jr., *The Visible Hand: The Managerial Revolution in American Business* (Cambridge, Mass.: The Belknap Press of Harvard University Press, 1977). See especially pp. 207–283.

9. For a lively and informative analysis of how government bureaucracies grow, see Herbert Kaufman, *Red Tape, Its Origins, Uses, and Abuses* (Washington, D.C.: The Brookings Institution, 1977).

10. In 1900, white-collar employees constituted 17.6 percent of all American workers; in 1920, 24.9 percent; in 1940, 31 percent; in 1960, 40 percent; and in 1980, 51 percent. The percentages for 1900, 1920, 1940, and 1960 are calculated from figures given in the U.S. Bureau of the Census, *Historical Statistics of the United States, Colonial Times to 1970,* Bicentennial Edition, Part 1 (Washington, D.C., 1975), Series 182 and 183, p. 139. The percentage for 1980 is calculated from figures given in U.S. Bureau of the Census, *Statistical Abstract of the United States: 1985,* 105th Edition (Washington, D.C., 1984), Table 673, p. 400.

11. See Max Weber, "Bureaucracy," in *From Max Weber,* translated and edited by Hans Gerth and C. Wright Mills (New York: Oxford University Press, 1958), pp. 196–244.

12. The literature on managers is, of course, vast. I mention here only those works that have been most important in framing my own understanding of managers' role in the ascendancy of the new middle class. See Emil Lederer, *The Problem of the Modern Salaried Employee: Its Theoretical and Statistical Basis,* translated by E. E. Warburg, WPA Project No. 165-6999-6027 (New York: Columbia University, 1937); Carl Dreyfuss, *Occupation and Ideology of the Salaried Employee,* 2 vols., translated by Eva Abramovitch, WPA Project No. 465-97-3-81 (New York: Dept. of Social Science, Columbia University, 1938); Thorstein Veblen, *Absentee Ownership* (New York: B. W. Huebsch, Inc. 1923); Thorstein Veblen, *The Theory of Business Enterprise* (New York: Charles Scribner's Sons, 1904); Adolph A. Berle and Gardiner C. Means, *The Modern Corporation and Private Property* (New York: The Macmillan Company, 1932); James Burnham, *The Managerial Revolution* (New York: The John Day Company, 1941); Hans Gerth and C. Wright Mills, "A Marx for the Managers," in *Ethics: An International Journal of Social, Political, and Legal Philosophy,* Vol. 52, No. 2 (January 1942), pp. 200–215; Joseph Schumpeter, *Capitalism, Socialism and Democracy* (New York: Harper & Brothers, 1942); William H. Whyte, *The Organization Man* (New York: Simon and Schuster, 1956); David Riesman in collaboration with Reuel Denney and Nathan Glazer, *The Lonely Crowd: A Study of the Changing American Character* (New Haven, Conn.: Yale University Press, 1950); C. Wright Mills, *White Collar* (New York: Oxford University Press, 1951); Melville Dalton, *Men Who Manage* (New York: John Wiley & Sons, Inc., 1959); and Joseph Bensman and Arthur J. Vidich, *The New American Society* (Chicago, Ill.: Quadrangle Books, 1971).

Chapter 2. The Social Structure of Managerial Work

1. A highly elaborated theory of decentralized administration of the corporation dates back at least to the immediate post-World War II era. See William B. Given, Jr., "Freedom Within Management," *Harvard Business Review*, Vol. 24, No. 4 (Summer 1946), pp. 427–437. Attempts at the actual practice of decentralization seem to have a longer history and often follow periods of rapid expansion and centralization. Gabriel Kolko, for instance, notes that many corporations, in the aftermath of the period of great industrial concentration at the turn of the century, " . . . found their overcentralization unprofitable, and tried to reduce plant sizes and distribute plants more widely throughout the nation." At United States Steel " . . . the organizational structure was centralized only at the very highest policy level, and autonomous operating units and specialized staffs have been a general trend in the large corporate structure since the turn of the century." See Gabriel Kolko, *The Triumph of Conservatism* (New York: Free Press of Glencoe, 1963), p. 29. As I suggest in the text, I am somewhat skeptical about the extent of the larger historical significance of decentralization within corporate hierarchies. The current rhetoric of decentralization may simply mask the tremendous concentration of capital presently taking place through mergers, acquisitions, takeovers, and so on, and the organizational consolidation of such expansion through administrative mechanisms.

2. Organizational upheavals seem to have become commonplace by the early 1960s in this country. See D. Ronald Daniel, "Reorganizing for Results,"*Harvard Business Review*, Vol. 44, No. 6 (November–December 1966), pp. 96–104. Daniel reports that "[d]uring a three year period from 1962 through 1964, no fewer than 66 of the nation's top 100 industrial companies reported major organizational realignments to their stockholders—an average rate of one change per company every 54 months." (p. 96) He goes on to estimate on the basis of his consulting experience that, since unreported changes must also be numerous, the real rate of reshuffling is probably one major realignment per major company every two years (p. 96). He also provides a rule of thumb that even a casual perusal of the business press suggests is as salient today as it was when he wrote: the larger the company, the greater the likelihood of major change within a specified period.

3. The term "network" seems to have entered social science usage during the 1950s in British social anthropology. See, for instance, Elizabeth Bott, *Family and Social Network* (London: Tavistock, Social Science Paperback, 1971), 2nd edition (first published in 1957). Bott's later edition contains an interesting overview of the development of the term in social science literature. Bott used the term "network" as opposed to "organized group" to describe the set of relations she was studying. She says: "In an organized group, the component individuals make up a larger social whole with common aims, inter-dependent roles, and a distinctive sub-culture. In network formation, on the other hand, only some, not all, of the component individuals have social relationships with one another. . . . In a network, the component external units do not make up a larger social whole; they are not surrounded by a common boundary." (p. 58) Formulated in such a way, the concept is not especially useful for understanding informal managerial groupings within a highly formal organizational structure. An earlier formulation by J. A. Barnes in his essay "Class and Committees in a Norwegian Island Parish," *Human Relations*, Vol. 7, No. 1 (February 1954), pp. 39–58, provides a somewhat more open-ended, though highly structural definition. Barnes

writes: "Each person is, as it were, in touch with a number of people, some of whom are directly in touch with each other and some of whom are not. . . . I find it convenient to talk of a social field of this kind as a *network*. The image I have is a set of points some of which are joined by lines. The points of the image are people, or sometimes groups, and the lines indicate which people interact with each other." (p. 43) Finally, J. Clyde Mitchell in his essay "The Concept and Use of Social Networks," in *Social Networks in Urban Situations,* edited by J. Clyde Mitchell (Manchester, U.K.: Manchester University Press, 1969), pp. 1–50, stresses his concern with the morphological characteristics and interactional criteria of networks in a highly formal way.

With the exception of the mathematical sociologists, the usage in American sociology is more informal. It is often used in discussions of social movements, as in Jo Freeman, "The Origins of the Women's Liberation Movement," *American Journal of Sociology,* LXXVIII, 4 (January 1973), pp. 792–811; or in David Snow et al., "Social Networks and Social Movements: A Microstructural Approach to Differential Recruitment," *American Sociological Review,* Vol. 45, No. 5 (October 1980), pp. 787–801. Some sociologists use it, like Bott, to describe relationships within community settings. For instance, Elliot Liebow in *Tally's Corner* (Boston, Mass.: Little, Brown and Co., 1967) uses the concept to describe social relationships centered on a street corner, although he later substitutes the notion "personal community" for network. For any individual, he says, "his personal community . . . is not a bounded area but rather a web-like arrangement of man-man and man-woman relationships in which he is selectively attached in a particular way to a definite number of discrete persons. In like fashion, each of these persons has his own personal network." (p. 162) Liebow emphasizes the fluid nature of these networks. He says: "The overall picture is one of a broad web of interlocking, overlapping networks in which the incumbents are constantly—however irregularly—shifting and changing positions relative to one another." (p. 203) One may infer that some social scientists, like Barnes, would object to Liebow's use of the term as too personal or ego-centered in nature.

The term has passed over into everyday parlance and, in the managerial world at least, often seems to have a metaphorical resonance with new electronic technology. Thus one "gets connected" with others, "plugged into" groups, or "makes contact" with others.

4. The notion of social circles probably originated with Georg Simmel, *The Web of Group Affiliations,* translated by Reinhard Bendix (Glencoe, Ill.: Free Press, 1955) although, as Charles Kadushin notes, Bendix systematically translates the word "circle" as "group." Simmel argued that social circles develop around focal points like age and sex statuses, intellectual and cultural interests, self-interest, family, religion, and a variety of other statuses. Perhaps the most thorough discussion of the notion of social circles is Charles Kadushin, "The Friends and Supporters of Psychotherapy: On Social Circles in Urban Life," *American Sociological Review,* Vol. 31, No. 6 (December 1966), pp. 786–802. Kadushin sees circles as characterized by high density and indirect chains of interaction, interest as the basis for interaction, moderate institutionalization, and informal leadership. In a later article, "Power, Influence and Social Circles: A New Methodology for Studying Opinion Makers," *American Sociological Review,* Vol. 33, No. 5 (October 1968), pp. 685–699, he suggests that the notion may be a suitable framework for studying elites and power. He writes:

A social circle has three defining characteristics, two of which are positive and one, negative: (1) A circle may have a chain or network of indirect interaction such that most members of a circle are linked to other members, at least through a third party. It is thus not a pure face-to-face group. (2) The network exists because members of the circle share common interests—political or cultural. (3) The circle is not formal—i.e. there are: (a) no clear leaders, although there may be central figures; (b) no clearly defined goals for the circle, though it almost always has some implicit functions; (c) no definite rules which determine modes of interaction, though there are often customary relationships; and (d) no distinct criteria of membership. (p. 692)

Here Kadushin equates "network" and "circle" but not, one should note, as the British social anthropologists use the former term. Kadushin also suggests that the structure of a social circle differs according to type; circles concerned with power and influence can be "pyramidal."

Other writers have used the term in studying elites. See, for instance, Gwen Moore, "The Structure of a National Elite Network," *American Sociological Review*, Vol. 44, No. 5 (October 1979), pp. 673–692. Moore implicitly distinguishes between the notions of clique, circle, and network and focuses on elite circles, adopting for the most part Kadushin's usage of the term, as a way of gauging the social cohesiveness of a national elite network. Finally, Michael Useem uses the concept of circles in his book *The Inner Circles: Large Corporations and the Rise of Business Political Activity in the U.S. and the U.K.* (New York: Oxford University Press, 1984).

5. In the sociological literature, the notion of "gang" is usually associated with juveniles, delinquency, or juvenile delinquency. The earliest major treatment of the notion of gangs is Frederic M. Thrasher, *The Gang: A Study of 1313 Gangs in Chicago* (Chicago, Ill.: University of Chicago Press, 1927), and most subsequent usages do not differ substantially from Thrasher's definition. Thrasher distinguishes a gang from other forms of collective behavior—play groups, crowds, clubs, rings, and secret societies—through a number of factors. Gangs are spontaneous and unplanned and entail frequent face-to-face relations. They are marked by "expressive" behavior. They "move through space" and eventually meet some hostile element that precipitates conflict. They are characterized by informal organization shaped through interaction in social situations. Finally, they have a home territory. Thrasher does not see gangs as inherently criminal, although they may become so in addition to becoming socialized into any number of possible forms. William Foote Whyte, *Street Corner Society* (Chicago, Ill.: University of Chicago Press, 1943) adopts the same neutral usage and sees the gang as an informal arrangement that serves a variety of social functions. Whyte pays particular attention to the social organization of the gang. For Whyte, the gang grows out of boyhood friendships in a neighborhood setting, has a leader and hierarchical structure, and a commonly understood though never discussed set of social relationships.

The decade of the 1950s saw a marked increase in interest in deviant youth culture, but not much development in the concept of the gang. Albert K. Cohen, *Delinquent Boys: The Culture of the Gang* (Glencoe, Ill.: Free Press, 1955); and Richard Cloward and Lloyd E. Ohlin, *Delinquency and Opportunity* (Glencoe, Ill.: Free Press, 1960) do not add much to Thrasher's work except perhaps to confuse it by mixing the notion of gang with that of subculture. Harrison E. Salisbury in *The Shook-up Generation* (New York: Harper and Brothers, 1958) identifies the gang specifically with juvenile, delinquent, violent, and male groups. In other works, this identification of the phenomenon with lower-class, adolescent, male delinquents is fairly common. The notion of gang is not usually applied to elite groups, except pejoratively. See, for instance, Richard Ney, *The Wall Street Gang* (New York: Praeger Publishers, 1974);

David Bonavia, *Verdict in Peking: The Trial of the Gang of Four* (New York: G. P. Putnam's Sons, 1984); Philip Roth, *Our Gang* (New York: Random House, 1971); and, implicitly, Bertolt Brecht, *The Threepenny Opera*, translated by Desmond Vesey and Eric Bentley (New York: Grove Press Inc., 1964).

Chapter 3. The Main Chance

1. See Robert Jackall, *Workers in a Labyrinth: Jobs and Survival in a Bank Bureaucracy* (Montclair, N.J.: Allanheld, Osmun and Co., 1978). See especially pp. 44–63.

2. John T. Molloy, *Dress for Success* (New York: Warner Books, 1976).

3. Colonial Books, Clinton, Massachusetts. The firm was bought by a conglomerate in the late 1970s and subsequently dismantled. I did fieldwork in Clinton in the summer of 1978.

4. Some sociologists, following Pierre Bourdieu's work, would call such *savoir faire* an aspect of social or, especially, "cultural capital." See, especially, Pierre Bourdieu, *Distinction: A Social Critique of the Judgement of Taste,* translated by Richard Nice (Cambridge, Mass.: Harvard University Press, 1984). In my own view, the notion of cultural capital is a concept that may obscure more than it reveals about managers' actual social world while adding little to one's real understanding of what makes that world work. See, for instance, Michael Useem and Jerome Karabel, "Pathways to Top Corporate Management," *American Sociological Review,* Vol. 51, No. 2 (April 1986), pp. 184–200. Although managers are not unfamiliar with the notion of capital, they use it in a social sense only in talking about accumulated "political capital," debts that others owe to oneself, credibility established, and so on, that must be expended wisely. Style, on the other hand, is something that one "has," something that is thought to be part of one's personality. Bourdieu would consider it part of one's habitus, the capital one gains through one's socialization into a particular social position, something that is not therefore easily gained or shed. Managers, at least American managers, tend to think about the matter differently. They recognize, of course, the crucial importance of social breeding, particularly exposure to the proper social manners that the right schools afford. But one can try to acquire the "right style" by altering one's personality through self-rationalization. In any event, one does not accumulate style.

5. This viewpoint is put forth most completely in William H. Whyte, *The Organization Man* (New York: Simon and Schuster, 1956); and in David Riesman, in collaboration with Reuel Denney and Nathan Glazer, *The Lonely Crowd: A Study of the Changing American Character* (New Haven, Conn.: Yale University Press, 1950).

6. Karl Mannheim, *Man and Society in An Age of Reconstruction* (London: Paul [Kegan], Trench, Trubner & Co. Ltd., 1940), p. 55.

7. See especially Joseph Bensman, "The Advertising Man and His Work, Its Organization, Ethics, and Meaning," in *Dollars and Sense* (New York: Macmillan, 1967), pp. 9–68.

8. The same manager goes on to explain why the curve is used:

Why do they insist on the curve? Simple. It saves money. Your raises are tied to where you come out on the curve and the corporation can save a lot of money by giving a guy—or a lot of guys—a raise of, say, $5,000 in 15 months, rather than in nine months or a year. You get your raises at the *end* of the period which has been set for you. This is a game that is played everywhere. If you give someone a raise, most people look at the amount given. But in terms of disposable income, the spacing of your raise is the most crucial thing. So, if you get a raise but at 18 months, well, over your lifetime, you're making a lot less money than you think you are. And this is a classic way to reduce the corporate payroll.

9. Max Weber, "Religious Rejections of the World and Their Directions," in *From Max Weber*, edited and translated by Hans Gerth and C. Wright Mills (New York: Oxford University Press, 1958), p. 330.

Chapter 4. Looking Up and Looking Around

1. See Max Weber, *Economy and Society*, edited by Guenther Roth and Claus Wittich (Berkeley, Los Angeles, and London: University of California Press, 1978), pp. 85–86. Karl Mannheim, *Man and Society in an Age of Reconstruction* (London: Paul [Kegan], Trench, Trubner & Co. Ltd., 1940), pp. 52–55.

2. For a contrasting view, at least as far as women are concerned, see the psychologist Carol Gilligan's *In a Different Voice* (Cambridge, Mass.: Harvard University Press, 1982). This widely cited work is based on structured interviews with men and women and on literary analogies. The book argues that women, specifically because of gender, adopt moral stances fundamentally different than men's. In this view, women's morality is marked by a particularity and responsibility emerging out of the nurturing social roles traditionally assigned to women. To a great extent, the book is a debate with the developmental psychology of Lawrence Kohlberg, who postulates a sequence of moral development that Gilligan finds problematic. See, for example, Lawrence Kohlberg, *The Philosophy of Moral Development: Moral Stages of the Idea of Justice* (San Francisco, Calif.: Harper & Row, 1981).

The example of women weavers cited in the text suggests that the matter may be more complicated than Gilligan or other writers following her lead in postulating a specifically feminine morality allow. The exigencies of modern occupational roles may cause moralities associated with gender, that do perhaps prevail in certain social contexts, to be bracketed at work in the same way that traditional religious beliefs and precepts become irrelevant in bureaucratic milieux. What Gilligan and others argue is a different morality may simply be a greater adeptness at moral casuistry, a skill honed perhaps by the requirements of traditional female roles. In connection with this, it is worth noting that a very large and growing percentage of public relations practitioners, at least in public relations agencies, are women, a development that is causing some fear of female overrepresentation in executive circles in the field. In my own view, the question of whether women have a different morality than men can only be resolved with a systematic comparative analysis of women's actual occupational ethics in a variety of work settings—say, the academy, business, science, and clerical and blue-collar work—as contrasted with their ethics in social roles clearly ascribed by gender.

Chapter 5. Drawing Lines

1. See Robert Alex Baron, *The Tyranny of Noise* (New York: Harper Colophon, 1971), pp. 40–41. The "C" scale measures sound pressures on a flat scale. The "A" scale was adopted when it was discovered that humans are not as sensitive to the lower frequencies as to the higher. The "A" scale is the measure used in the textile industry.

2. Department of Labor, Occupational Safety and Health Administration, *Occupational Noise Exposure, Hearing Conservation Amendment; Final Rule. Federal Register*, Vol. 48, No. 46 (Tuesday, March 8, 1983), Part II, 9738–9785.

3. Karl Mannheim, *Ideology and Utopia* (New York: Harcourt, Brace & World, Inc., 1936), p. 118.

4. In addition to a lengthy interview in October 1983 with the man that I have named Joseph Wilson, I have used a number of documents in preparing this case. Among these is: U.S. House of Representatives, Committee on Interior and Insular Affairs, Subcommittee on Energy and the Environment, *Oversight Hearing: Current Status of the Three Mile Island Nuclear Generating Station, Units 1 and 2*, 98th Congress, 1st Session, April 26 (Washington, D.C.: U.S. Government Printing Office, 1983). Other documents are cited as appropriate.

5. Wilson's suspicion in this regard was confirmed in a later investigation conducted by the NRC's Office of Investigations, which found that: "The NRC has contributed to TMI-2 organizational problems by not acting in a conventional regulatory mode for the facility." See Nuclear Regulatory Commission, Office of Investigations, *Three Mile Nuclear Generating Station, Unit 2 Allegations Regarding Safety Related Modifications, Quality Assurance Procedures and Use of Polar Crane. Docket No. 050 320. Summary*, p. 2. September 1, 1983.

6. On January 20, 1983, Wilson wrote a memo to one of his two superiors, the GPUN deputy director, trying to ensure that documentation for Bechtel's refurbishment of the crane would be provided to Site Operations. The memo concludes: "If the crane is turned back over to Site Operations, it is expected that adequate documentation will be provided to ensure its requalification." See Nuclear Regulatory Commission, *Op. Cit. Docket No. 050 320. GPU Nuclear Inter-Office Memorandum*.

7. Richard D. Lyons, "Crews at Reactor Criticize Cleanup," *The New York Times*, March 28, 1983, A1, col. 1 and A10, col. 1.

8. Ben B. Hayes, Director, Office of Investigations, Nuclear Regulatory Commission, *Memorandum for Chairman Palladino, Subject: Three Mile Island NGS, Unit 2 Allegations Regarding Safety Related Modifications and QA Procedures (H-83-002)*, September 1, 1983, p. 1.

9. Ibid., p. 2.

10. Nunzio J. Palladino, letter to Mr. William Kuhns, Chairman of the Board, General Public Utilities Service Corporation, October 7, 1983, p. 2.

11. See *Safety Evaluation By the Office of Nuclear Reactor Regulation, Three Mile Island Program Office, Facility Operating License No. DPR-73, GPU Nuclear Corporation, et. al. Three Mile Island Nuclear Station Unit-2 (TMI-2). Docket No. 50-320. Refurbishment of the Reactor Building Polar Crane, Load Test and Recertification for Use.* November 18, 1983.

12. Since I presented this case to corporate managers for their evaluation, there have been a number of developments. In July 1984, GPUN successfully used the polar crane to lift the head from the TMI-2 reactor. In August 1984, GPUN inspectors spotted a problem with a manual brake release on one of the crane's two redundant brake units; the brake release had been installed in November 1982 during the refurbishment of the polar crane. According to a GPUN press release, this was done " . . . under the supervision of Bechtel personnel. The mechanisms were fabricated and installed without normal engineering oversight because of administrative deficiencies that existed while an integration of GPU Nuclear and Bechtel management was being completed at TMI-2. Those deficiencies have been corrected." (GPU Nuclear, News Release, January 10, 1985, #5-85N) The crane was taken out of operation and the hand release mechanisms removed. The crane was later put back into service and

GPUN claims to have instituted an expanded program of preventive maintenance and pre-operational testing for the crane.

In February 1985, *The Philadelphia Inquirer* ran a three-part series on TMI that reports in a journalistic way many of the events described in this chapter. See *The Philadelphia Inquirer*, "Three Mile Island: Accident Without an End: The Lethal Legacy Inside TMI" by Jim Detjen and Susan Fitzgerald (February 10, 1985), pp. 1A, 18A, 19A, 20A, 21A; "At the Crippled Plant, Workers Face Invisible Dangers" (February 11, 1985), pp. 1A, 6A, 7A; and "TMI Critics Who Paid a Price" (February 12, 1985), pp. 1A, 8A. GPUN responded to the series both with press releases and with a two-page advertisement that appeared in several central Pennsylvania newspapers disputing *The Inquirer*'s facts and interpretations. These materials are available from GPU Nuclear Corporation, Public Affairs Department, Three Mile Island Nuclear Station, P.O. Box 480, Middletown, Pa. 17057.

In its series, *The Inquirer* reports that the manager that I call Wilson received an undisclosed monetary settlement from GPUN and was last reported working as an inspector at a nuclear facility in the southern United States. GPUN continues to maintain that this manager was fired only because of a conflict of interest.

13. See Opinion Research Corporation, *Codes of Ethics in Corporations and Trade Associations and the Teaching of Ethics in Graduate Business Schools*, a survey conducted for the Ethics Resource Center (Princeton, N.J.: Opinion Research Corporation, June 1979) for a sense of the extent of this corporate trend. Seventy-three percent of the 248 companies responding to the survey said that they had a written code of ethics. The return rate was a fairly low 38 percent.

Chapter 6. Dexterity with Symbols

1. These terms were culled from a much longer list that was posted on a prominent bulletin board in Alchemy Inc. with no source given. I showed the list to a dozen of my interviewees at Alchemy to gauge how accurately the terms present the incongruities between words and contextual meaning in the corporate world. There was strong general agreement that the list was uncannily accurate, although tinged with bitter humor. I published part of the list in 1983 (see Robert Jackall, "Moral Mazes: Bureaucracy and Managerial Work," *Harvard Business Review*, Vol. 61, No. 5 (September–October 1983, pp. 118–130). The following summer, while doing secondary research in preparation for this book, I came across a similar, though shorter, list of euphemisms that seems to have been the basis for the list posted at Alchemy. See Jack Mabley, "'Personnel Code' Not a Laughing Matter," *Chicago Tribune*, October 29, 1981, Section 1, p. 21, col. 2. Since Mabley's article was based on an interview with the president of a personnel consulting firm, it is likely that similar lists have appeared in a myriad of other publications read by businesspeople. Stories and jokes that accurately reflect behavioral and emotional truths make the rounds repeatedly in the business world, altered to suit particular contexts. In the list presented here, I have starred those phrases that appeared only on the Alchemy list.

For an excellent sociological analysis of the subtle uses of language, see Hans Speier, "The Communication of Hidden Meaning," *Social Research*, Vol. 44, No. 3 (Autumn 1977), pp. 471–501.

2. Stephen Hilgartner, Richard C. Bell, and Rory O'Connor, *Nukespeak: The Selling of Nuclear Technology in America*, (San Francisco, Calif.: Sierra Club Books, 1982), p. xiii.

3. National Council of Teachers of English, Committee on Public Doublespeak,

Quarterly Review of Doublespeak (Urbana, Ill.: National Council of Teachers of English, 1111 Kenyon Road, Urbana, Ill.), Vol. VII, No. 4 (July 1981), p. 1.

4. *Quarterly Review of Doublespeak*, Vol. X, No. 2 (January 1984), p. 1.

5. *Quarterly Review of Doublespeak*, Vol. IX, No. 2 (January 1983), p. 1.

6. *Quarterly Review of Doublespeak*, Vol. XI, No. 2 (January 1985), p. 1. Issue misnumbered as Vol. IX.

7. See Frederick Winslow Taylor, *The Principles of Scientific Management* (New York and London: Harper & Brothers Publishers, 1929 [Copyright 1911]). See also the interesting recent treatment of Taylor and Taylorism by Judith A. Merkle, *Management and Ideology: The Legacy of the International Scientific Management Movement* (Berkeley, Los Angeles, and London: University of California Press, 1980).

8. The classic statement of the human relations school is Elton Mayo, *The Human Problems of an Industrial Civilization* (Boston, Mass.: Division of Research, Graduate School of Business Administration, Harvard University, 1946).

9. As it happens, morale and productivity are probably unassociated. See Victor H. Vroom, "Industrial Social Psychology," in *The Handbook of Social Psychology*, edited by Gardner Lindzey and Eliot Aronson (Reading, Mass.: Addison-Wesley Publishing Company, 1969), Vol. V, p. 199.

10. See Loren Baritz's analysis of the origins and practice of psychological testing in industry in *The Servants of Power* (Westport, Conn.: Greenwood Press, Publishers, 1974).

11. Consultants News, *A Cross-Section of the Management Consulting Business* (Fitzwilliam, N.H.: Consultants News, 1979).

12. Joel Dean, "The Place of Management Counsel in Business," *Harvard Business Review*, Vol. 16 (1937–1938), pp. 451–465, especially pp. 451–453. See also his more extended monograph *The Management Counsel Profession* (Bloomington, Ind.: Indiana University Publications Social Science Series, No. 2, 1940).

13. James H. Kennedy, "An Overview of Management Consulting in the United States Today" (Fitzwilliam, N.H.: Consultants News, 1981), p. 5.

14. John A. Byrne, "Are All These Consultants Really Necessary?" *Forbes*, October 10, 1983, pp. 136–144.

15. I am indebted to Gerald L. Moore, "The Politics of Management Consulting," Ph.D. Diss., Department of Sociology, Graduate Center, City University of New York, 1982, and especially to several conversations with Joseph Bensman for alerting me to many of the issues in the analysis that follows. I am indebted too to Elizabeth S. Tice and Frank J. Navran for providing me with the occasion to draw together my field data on management consultants and managers' experiences with consultants in a paper entitled "The Vicissitudes of Organizational Tinkering," Sixth Organizational Effectiveness Professional Development Clinic, BellSouth Corporation, Atlanta, Georgia, December 7, 1983.

16. See Terrence E. Deal and Allen A. Kennedy, *Corporate Cultures: The Rites and Rituals of Corporate Life* (Reading, Mass.: Addison-Wesley Publishing Company, 1982), *passim*, but see especially pp. 85–103.

17. See, for example, Rosabeth Moss Kanter, *The Change Masters* (New York: Simon and Schuster, 1983), *passim*.

18. A note with methodological implications may be apposite here. Precisely because managers have such a sharply defined responsiveness to authoritatively established criteria evident to them in a given situation, they are often unconcerned with facts as facts are normally conceptualized. In one company, in which nonconfidential surveys of all sorts relating to business matters are regularly circulated, managers say

that they often "pull numbers out of the air" to satisfy the perceived demands of higher-ups. This makes data from, say, surveys administered through hierarchies somewhat problematic. Unless complete confidentiality is promised, one may not be measuring an individual's perception of reality but rather his perception of what reality is expected to be or what he wishes others to think his perception is.

19. An example from the medical profession illustrates the point. Peter Gott, a Connecticut physician, writes a regular medical advice column for a small-town local paper which occasionally pokes fun at the inconsistencies of those in the medical profession. In a couple of columns, however, Gott seems to have crossed a line between poking fun and drawing blood. He writes:

> Any patient can attest to the fact that a physician's waiting room is aptly named. It's a place where you pay the doctor for the privilege of waiting . . . and waiting . . . and waiting.
>
> I am constantly amazed to discover how much guff intelligent people will put up with. Housewives, who organize with exact precision a family vacation for five members at Cape Cod, sit for hours looking at their nail polish in these waiting rooms. High-powered, busy executives whose businesses depend on split-second accuracy for appointments and meetings, cool their heels in dingy waiting rooms; they haplessly check their digital watches as precious minutes tick by.
>
> Where is the doctor? What on earth is he *doing* that is so important? Patients apprehensively lounge for hours while babysitters collect time and a half and harassed bank secretaries field telephone calls which the boss promised he would be back for at 3 o'clock. In what other business can you keep valued clients and paying customers waiting interminable periods? What *is* the doctor doing?
>
> He has an emergency. Someone in greater need than you, esteemed attorney or corporation president, requires the unscheduled attention of the doctor. He has an emergency! Can you believe it?
>
> Well, I don't believe it. It's pure bunk. I am going to let you in on a little trade secret. The doctor keeps people waiting because he is so disorganized that he has over-scheduled himself. He is hungry to keep his office filled and it really doesn't matter who is caught in the game . . . providing the doctor himself doesn't have to wait. Furthermore, he hasn't had the courtesy to allow proper time for each patient.
>
> You see, he was already 35 minutes late to the office because he received, at the hospital, a very disturbing 20-minute call about his stock portfolio. That was shortly followed by a 15-minute discussion, with another doctor in the hospital parking lot, about the relative merits of a Porsche 944 over a Datsun 280Z.
>
> Of course, once he arrived at the office and noted—with supreme satisfaction—that patients were starting to pile up like 747s over Kennedy Airport, he had to have a couple of telephone conversations with other doctors about sick patients. And, doctors being what they are, the talk eventually got around to golf scores and did you have a super time in St. Croix last March and how

are the kids; you know, *vital* stuff like that. Emergencies. [See Peter Gott, "Doctor in the House: The Waiting Room," *The Lakeville Journal*, Lakeville, Conn., August 4, 1983.]

In a column describing some of the benefits that a medical degree confers on doctors, in addition, of course, to allowing one to heal the sick, he says in part:

> . . . [T]he MD degree permits the bearer to become a member of The Club . . . the club of doctors. Of course, once a doctor is a member of the club, he has certain obligations: he must refer constantly to how little money he has, yet live in a large and well-manicured house; become pompous and arrogant but not speak badly about his colleagues; make sure that "his" hospital is run for the benefit of doctors, not patients; not allow patient convenience to compromise his own; and never write newspaper columns which criticize The Club. In return, the doctor may not be charged for routine medical care, can obtain enough free drugs (from pharmaceutical companies) to supply his own modest requirements for codeine, drink too much, raise a little hell (when off duty), and generally indulge himself to whatever extent he pleases.

> . . . [T]he MD degree is [also] an open invitation to borrow money without collateral. The poor slob down at the factory has to hock his car to pay for Triscuits. The doctor, on the other hand, has an unlimited line of credit; in fact, some lending agencies actually woo doctors for mortgages and that little extra cash needed for a new BMW. Friends, the MD degree is a license to steal. [See Peter Gott, "Doctor in the House: Perquisites," *The Lakeville Journal*, Lakeville, Conn., October 27, 1983.]

The column was popular with the public but when it was picked up by a larger daily in neighboring Dutchess County, New York, it so provoked some medical professionals there that they threatened to censure Gott with a reprimand from a county medical association. The controversy was first reported by Susan Chira, "Physician's Column Roils Colleagues," *The New York Times*, February 10, 1984, B2, col. 4. After a brief show of publicity, the complaints against Gott were quietly dropped. See "Physician-Columnist Is Not Reprimanded," *The New York Times*, February 23, 1984, B8, col. 6. I am indebted to Ms. Chira of *The New York Times* and to Dr. Gott for providing some additional information on the incident in phone conversations.

20. The literature on the corporate and governmental scandals of the last few decades is quite enormous though very uneven in its quality. I note here only a few examples on a few issues. On the electrical price-fixing conspiracy, see John G. Fuller, *The Gentlemen Conspirators* (New York: Grove Press Inc., 1962); Gilbert Geis, "The Heavy Electrical Equipment Antitrust Cases of 1961," in *White-Collar Crime*, edited by Gilbert Geis and Robert F. Meier (New York: Free Press, 1977), revised edition, pp. 117–132; United States Committee on the Judiciary, Subcommittee on Anti-Trust and Monopoly, 87th Congress, 2nd Session (1961), "Administered Prices," in U.S. *Senate Committee Hearings*, Part 27, Vol. 1479, pp. 16507–17966; Richard Austin Smith, "The Incredible Electrical Conspiracy," *Fortune*, Vol. 63 (April 1961), pp. 132–137 and (May 1961), pp. 161–164. On financial manipulations, see William Blundell, *Swindled* (New York: Dow Jones Books, 1976). On the falsification of test data in a famous case involving airplane brakes, see Kermit Vandivier, "Why Should My Conscience Bother Me?" in Robert L. Heilbroner et al., *In the Name of Profit* (Garden

City, N.Y.: Doubleday, 1972), pp. 3–31; and U.S. Congress, Joint Economic Committee, Subcommittee on Economy in Government, 91st Congress, 1st Session (1969), "Air Force A–7D Brake Problem," August 13. For an example of test data falsification in the development of a drug, see Sanford J. Ungar, "Get Away With What You Can," in Robert L. Heilbroner et al., *In the Name of Profit* (New York: Doubleday, 1972), pp. 106–127. On the marketing of dangerous drugs, see the accounts of the famous thalidomide scandal by Henning Sjostrum and Robert Nilsson, *Thalidomide and the Power of the Drug Companies* (Middlesex, U.K.: Penguin, 1972); and especially Insight Team of *The Sunday Times of London, Suffer the Children: The Story of Thalidomide* (New York: The Viking Press, 1979). On industrial accidents and occupational health issues, see Ray Davidson, *Peril on the Job* (Washington, D.C.: Public Affairs Press, 1970); Paul Brodeur, *Expendable Americans* (New York: The Viking Press, 1974); Rachel Scott, *Muscle and Blood* (New York: E. P. Dutton & Co., 1974); Nicholas Ashford, *Crisis in the Workplace: Occupational Disease and Injury* (Cambridge, Mass.: MIT Press, 1976); Willard S. Randall and Stephen D. Solomon, *Building 6: The Tragedy at Bridesburg* (Boston, Mass.: Little, Brown and Co., 1977); and Daniel M. Berman, *Death on the Job* (New York: Monthly Review Press, 1978). On bribery, see William E. Blundell and Stephen Sansweet, "On the Give: For U.S. Firms Abroad Bribery Can Often Be Routine Cost," *The Wall Street Journal,* Vol. 185, No. 91 (May 9, 1975), p. 1, col. 1 and p. 10, cols. 3–5; and Robert Shaplen, "Annals of Crime: The Lockheed Incident I & II," *The New Yorker,* January 23, 1978, pp. 48–74 and January 30, 1978, pp. 74–91. On industrial pollution, Michael Brown, *Laying Waste: The Poisoning of America by Toxic Chemicals* (New York: Pantheon, 1980); and David Zwick and Marcy Benstock, *Water Wasteland* (New York: Grossman Publishers, 1971). Finally, on Watergate, the autobiographies of some of the main figures make interesting reading. See, in particular, John W. Dean III, *Blind Ambition* (New York: Simon and Schuster, 1976); H. R. Haldeman with Joseph DiMona, *The Ends of Power* (New York: Times Books, 1978); and Jeb Stuart Magruder, *An American Life: One Man's Road to Watergate* (New York: Atheneum, 1974).

There is little question that such literature, at least that which is journalistic, plays an important role in stirring up public moral outrage. There seems to be an inexhaustible market for scandal, and writers who serve that market may be thought of as "moral entrepreneurs," to borrow a phrase used by Joseph Bensman and Robert Lilienfeld among other sociologists. As a general rule, such literature helps one understand the complexities of moral issues in corporations in inverse proportion to the moral fervor of the writer.

21. A number of books have dealt with these and other vicissitudes of turn-of-the-century American capitalism. See, in particular, Henry D. Lloyd, *Wealth Against Commonwealth* (New York: Harper & Brothers Publishers, 1894); Lewis Corey, *The House of Morgan* (New York: G. Howard Watt, 1930); John Flynn, *God's Gold: The Story of Rockefeller and His Times* (New York: Harcourt, Brace and Company, 1932); Burton Hendrick, *The Life of Andrew Carnegie,* 2 vols., (Garden City, N.Y.: Doubleday, Doran & Co. Inc., 1932); and John Moody, *The Masters of Capital* (New Haven, Conn.: Yale University Press, 1919) and *The Railroad Builders* (New Haven, Conn.: Yale University Press, 1919). Many of these works have a marked animus against big business. Matthew Josephson drew heavily on these studies among others in writing his great trilogy: *The Robber Barons: The Great American Capitalists 1861–1901* (New York: Harcourt, Brace and Company, 1934); *The Politicos, 1865–1896* (New York: Harcourt, Brace and Company, 1938), and *The President Makers: The Culture of Politics and Leadership in an Age of Enlightenment, 1896–1919* (New York: Harcourt, Brace

and Company, 1940). Despite their occasional heavy-handedness and doctrinaire slant, his books present a remarkable period of our history in such a lively, colorful, and sweeping way that they have had a lasting impact both on historians and on the public consciousness. For thorough scholarly analyses of the main social forces of the period, see Richard Hofstadter, *The Age of Reform* (New York: Vintage, 1955); Robert Wiebe, *The Search for Order 1877–1920* (New York: Hill and Wang, 1967) and *Businessmen and Reform: A Study of the Progressive Movement* (Cambridge, Mass.: Harvard University Press, 1962); and Gabriel Kolko, *The Triumph of Conservatism* (New York: Free Press of Glencoe, 1963).

22. One can gain some measure of the changes in public perceptions of science and technology by contrasting Don K. Price, *The Scientific Estate* (Cambridge, Mass.: Harvard University Press, 1967), which depicts the joint scientific and technological communities as the "established dissenters," with the report ten years later by Todd LaPorte and Daniel Metlay, *They Watch and Wonder: Public Attitudes Toward Advanced Technology* (Berkeley, Calif.: Institute of Governmental Studies, University of California, December 1975), Final Report to the Ames Research Center, National Aeronautics and Space Administration, Grant NGR 05-003-0471. LaPorte's and Metlay's data suggest the growth of a skeptical ambivalence toward technology.

23. See, for instance, Edmund A. C. Crouch and Richard Wilson, *Risk/Benefit Analysis* (Cambridge, Mass.: Ballinger Publishing Co., 1982); Baruch Fischhoff et al., *Acceptable Risk* (Cambridge, U.K.: Cambridge University Press, 1981); Charles Perrow, *Normal Accidents: Living With High-Risk Technologies* (New York: Basic Books, Inc., 1984); and Nicholas Rescher, *Risk: A Philosophical Introduction to the Theory of Risk Evaluation and Management* (Washington, D.C.: University Press of America, 1983). William Lowrance, *Of Acceptable Risk* (Los Altos, Calif.: William Kaufmann, Inc., 1976) is particularly engaging and thought-provoking. As early as 1940, Hans Speier wrote a thoughtful and provoking essay that lays out many of the issues currently being discussed in the field of risk analysis. The essay was published later in a collection of his work. See Hans Speier, "Risk, Security and Modern Hero Worship," in *Social Order and the Risks of War* (New York: George W. Stewart, Inc., 1952), pp. 112–128.

Risk, of course, is a wholly socially constructed concept. Managers working in this area distinguish between "demonstrable" and "theoretical" risk. The notion of "demonstrable risk" refers to areas or substances that one concedes are hazardous; the idea of "theoretical risk" applies when one feels comfortable arguing about whether a hazard exists at all or, if admitted, how far one should go in controlling it. The choice of definition is almost always influenced not only by practical exigencies but by one's perception of how plausible and defensible one's "risk assessment" is. Some industries, like the tobacco business, to a mixture of amusement and chagrin from managers in other businesses, ignore the issue of plausibility altogether and simply "stonewall" it.

24. Max Weber, "Science as a Vocation," in *From Max Weber*, translated and edited by Hans Gerth and C. Wright Mills (New York: Oxford University Press, 1958), p. 155.

25. I am indebted to Arthur J. Vidich for sparking some of the ideas that follow. See, in particular, his brief piece "Hiroshima's Legacy: The Theodicy of Man-Made Hazards," *Anthropology Newsletter* (September 1980), p. 3.

26. Mary Douglas and Aaron Wildavsky, *Risk and Culture* (Berkeley, Los Angeles, and London: University of California Press, 1982).

27. U.S. House of Representatives, Committee on Science and Technology, *A*

Review of the Scientific and Technological Issues in the Regulation of Cotton Dust in Primary Cotton Textile Industry, 98th Congress, 1st Session, House Report No. 98-215 (Washington, D.C.: U.S. Government Printing Office, 1983). See *Letter of Transmittal* by Albert Gore, Jr., pp. v–vi.

28. See *De Morbis Artificum*, Bernardini Ramazzini Diatriba. *Diseases of Workers.* The Latin text of 1713, revised, with translation and notes by William Cave Wright (Chicago, Ill.: University of Chicago Press, 1940). Ramazzini notes:

> . . . [L]ikewise those who card flax and hemp so that it can be spun and given to the weavers to make the fabric find it very irksome. For a foul and poisonous dust flies out from these materials, enters the mouth, then the throat and lungs, makes the workmen cough incessantly, and by degrees brings on asthmatic troubles.
>
> About the beginning of winter hemp-carders arrive in swarms from the parts of France nearest to the Italian border and scatter over the whole country on both sides of the Po; for our workers are not so skilled in this craft of combing hemp. One may see these men always covered with dust from the hemp, pasty-faced, coughing, asthmatic, and blear-eyed. Moreover, they work mostly in confined rooms because of the severe cold of winter which is their regular season for this work, hence while they comb the hemp which has been well smeared with grease they cannot help taking in foul particles by the mouth; these pollute the spirits and stuff up the organs of respiration; hence arise serious ailments. . . . They say that they suffer more from combing flax than hemp, perhaps because its dust is finer and enters the respiratory organs more easily and provokes them more to try to cough up the poisonous stuff. (pp. 257, 259)

29. For a comprehensive and instructive review of this literature, see Federal Security Agency, U.S. Public Health Service, *A Review of the Literature Relating to Affections of the Respiratory Tract in Individuals Exposed to Cotton Dust,* Public Health Bulletin, No. 297 (U.S. Public Health Service, Washington, D.C., 1947), pp. 1–86.

30. See, in particular, R.S.F. Schilling, "Byssinosis in Cotton and Other Textile Workers," *The Lancet,* August 11, 1956, pp. 261–265 and August 18, 1956, pp. 319–325 for an interesting historical overview with particular emphasis on the British experience.

31. R. H. Britten, J. J. Bloomfield, and J. C. Goddard, *The Health of Workers in a Textile Plant,* U.S. Public Health Bulletin, No. 207, Washington, D.C., 1933.

32. Federal Security Agency, U.S. Public Health Service, *A Review of the Literature Relating to Affections of the Respiratory Tract in Individuals Exposed to Cotton Dust,* Public Health Bulletin No. 297, pp. 71–72.

33. C. B. McKerrow and R.S.F. Schilling, "A Pilot Enquiry into Byssinosis in Two Cotton Mills in the United States," *Journal of the American Medical Association,* Vol. 177, No. 12 (September 23, 1961), pp. 850–853.

34. A few of the best known studies by independent or university-affiliated researchers are A. Bouhuys, "Byssinosis in a Cotton Weaving Mill," *Archives of Environmental Health,* 6 (1963), pp. 465–468; A. Bouhuys, L. J. Heaphy, Jr., R.S.F. Schilling, and J.W. Wellborn, "Byssinosis in the United States," *New England Journal of Medicine,* Vol. 277, No. 4 (1967), pp. 170–175; and Gerald J. Beck and E. Neil Schachter, "The Evidence for Chronic Lung Disease in Cotton Textile Workers,"

The American Statistician, Vol. 37, No. 4 (November 1983), pp. 404–412. The best known industry study is H. R. Imbus and M. W. Suh, "Byssinosis: A Study of 10,133 Textile Workers," *Archives of Environmental Health,* 26 (1973), pp. 183–191.

35. Department of Labor, Occupational Safety and Health Administration, "Occupational Exposure to Cotton Dust," Final Mandatory Occupational Safety and Health Standard, *Federal Register,* Vol. 43, No. 122 (Friday, June 23, 1978), Part III, pp. 27350–27463.

36. The two most systematic and comprehensive studies of the relationships between smoking, exposure to cotton dust, and lung impairment are A. Bouhuys, J. B. Schoenberg, G. J. Beck, and R.S.F. Schilling, "Epidemiology of Chronic Lung Disease in a Cotton Mill Community", *Lung,* Vol. 154 (1977), pp. 167–186; and G. J. Beck, L. R. Maunder, E. N. Schachter, and R.S.F. Schilling, "Follow-up of Active and Retired Cotton Textile Workers," Part I–III Report ASPER/CON-78/0168/A (April 1981) for U.S. Department of Labor, Office of the Assistant Secretary for Policy, Evaluation, and Research, National Technical Information Service, Springfield, Va. These studies indicate that both exposure to cotton dust and smoking pose important risks to the lungs. The effects of each risk are "additive and often equally important." Even when statistically controlling for smoking, cotton textile workers had many more pulmonary dysfunctions than expected.

37. The claim that 20–25 percent of the general adult population has some form of chronic lung disease seems to have originated with a letter to *The Charlotte Observer* from the Mecklenberg County (North Carolina) Medical Society. The claim is regularly repeated by Weft Corporation executives and is cited widely in industry literature. See, for example, the pamphlet by Burlington Industries, Inc., "A Cotton Dust Progress Report," (Greensboro, N.C.: Burlington Industries, January 1981) or the brochure from the American Textile Manufacturers Institute, "Some Facts About Cotton Textile Industry and the Cotton Dust Problem From the People Most Directly Involved" (Washington, D.C.: ATMI, no date). The American Lung Association disputes this claim, citing the unpublished data summary of a national survey of the civilian, noninstitutionalized population by the National Center for Health Statistics in 1981. That survey indicates "that about 1 in 12 Americans have one or more chronic lung diseases (CLDs) inclusive of asthma, chronic bronchitis, emphysema, and interstitial lung conditions." Berton D. Freedman, Director, Epidemiology and Statistics Unit, Medical Affairs Division, American Lung Association, New York, N.Y. Personal correspondence, January 19, 1984, p. 1.

38. The key studies linking byssinosis to exposure to cotton dust are A. Bouhuys, J. B. Schoenberg, G. J. Beck, and R.S.F. Schilling, "Epidemiology of Chronic Lung Disease in a Cotton Mill Community," *Lung,* Vol. 154 (1977), pp. 167–186, already cited; and Dr. James Merchant et al., "Byssinosis and Chronic Bronchitis among Cotton Textile Workers, *Annals of Internal Medicine* 76 (1972), pp. 423–433. Merchant is the author of some fifteen papers on aspects of byssinosis, and his work, which was crucial to the OSHA regulation, was singled out for attack by the textile industry in court proceedings. See *Brief for Petitioners,* American Textile Manufacturers Institute, Inc. et al., vs. Ray Marshall, Secretary of Labor, U.S. Department of Labor et al., in the Supreme Court of the United States, October Term, 1980 (Page Proof, No. 79–1429), pp. 8–11.

39. This series appeared in *The Charlotte Observer,* Sunday, February 3, 1980, to Sunday, February 10, 1980. The *Observer* was awarded a Pulitzer Prize for the series in 1981.

40. This was a community organization based in Greenville, S.C. It was com-

prised of former and present textile workers assisted by paid and unpaid organizers, VISTA volunteers, and others. During the height of the controversy over cotton dust, it had chapters throughout the Carolinas and published a regular newsletter called *Brown Lung Blues.*

41. See U.S. House of Representatives, Committee on Science and Technology, *A Review of the Scientific and Technological Issues in the Regulation of Cotton Dust in Primary Cotton Textile Industry,* 98th Congress, 1st Session, Report No. 98–215 (Washington, D.C.: U.S. Government Printing Office, May 24, 1983), p. 21. Dr. Ruth Ruttenberg's testimony is cited:

> The textile industry, largely due to its new capital investments, is leading U.S. manufacturers in productivity growth. It was astounding to me to realize that during the period 1948–1979, textile manufacturing had the highest productivity growth rate of the 19 major manufacturing categories in SEC category 20–38, which represent the manufacturing sector. At an average increase of 4.87 percent a year, it led chemicals, petroleum refining, electronic equipment, and all those manufacturing sectors which we tend to think of as leaders in productivity growth. Its 4 percent annual increase during the recession of 1981 is high above the national average of just over 2 percent. (p. 21)

See also *Compliance with the OSHA Cotton Dust Rule: The Role of Productivity Improving Technology,* Final Report for the Office of Technology Assessment (Contract No. 233-7050-0) (Washington, D.C.: Ruttenberg, Friedman, Kilgallan and Associates Inc., March 1983) for an industrywide analysis of the link between capital investment, increased productivity, and compliance with the cotton dust regulation.

42. F. Scott Fitzgerald, *The Great Gatsby* (New York: Charles Scribner's Sons, 1925), pp. 180–181.

Chapter 7. The Magic Lantern

1. See Harry Reichenbach, *Phantom Fame,* as told to David Freedman (New York: Simon and Schuster, Inc., 1931), pp. 46–47.

2. Phineas T. Barnum, *Barnum's Own Story: The Autobiography of P. T. Barnum, Combined & condensed from the various editions published during his lifetime by Waldo R. Browne* (New York: The Viking Press, Inc., 1927). For a thoughtful and provoking essay on the social significance of Barnum's art and ideology, see Neil Harris, *Humbug* (Boston, Mass.: Little, Brown and Company, 1973).

3. Reichenbach, *Phantom Fame* (New York: Simon and Schuster, Inc., 1931), p. 8.

4. Reichenbach, pp. 203–204.

5. Reichenbach, pp. 106–113.

6. Reichenbach, pp. 55–58.

7. Reichenbach, pp. 178–183.

8. Reichenbach, p. 184.

9. Reichenbach, p. 29. The first magic lantern was a simple projective device consisting essentially of a box with a concave mirror at the rear, a candle for a light source, an aperture to insert silhouette slides, and a lens to magnify the image. Later, slides mounted in a circle or in an enclosed mobile cylinder enabled motion to be simulated on the screen. The motion picture is the direct descendant of the magic lantern. A

Jesuit priest, Athanasius Kircher, invented the magic lantern around 1644; he was considered by many to be engaged in necromancy because he could make images and shadows appear where none had been before. For a fascinating treatment of the whole history of magic lanterns, see Martin Quigley, Jr., *Magic Shadows: The Story of the Origin of Motion Pictures* (Washington, D.C.: Georgetown University Press, 1948).

One should note that extravagant stunts, like those concocted by Reichenbach, are still used by public relations firms. Television coverage, of course, provides an even greater magic lantern effect than Reichenbach could have imagined. The following item appeared in the in-house newsletter of Images Inc.:

> [S]taffer [Jim Jenkins] recently assisted in the coordination of a "hanging" by
> . . . a dance troupe out of Japan, on behalf of [a major Japanese corporation].
> Prior to a performance at the Warner Theater in the Nation's Capital, the
> troupe performed a "hanging" from the National Theater . . . [as] four members, with their ankles bound, were lowered by ropes, from the top of the
> building. Dressed in white, and with their heads shaven, the dancers stopped
> traffic during the noontime event as they performed a brief dance, suspended
> in the air. The event received extensive network and local affiliate attention.

10. Reichenbach, p. 112.
11. Reichenbach, p. 123.
12. Reichenbach, pp. 99 and 113.
13. Reichenbach, p. 92.
14. Reichenbach, p. 165.
15. Ibid.
16. Reichenbach, p. 166.
17. Reichenbach, p. 167.
18. Reichenbach, p. 169.
19. Reichenbach, pp. 168–169.
20. Reichenbach, p. 173.

21. One should examine in particular Leila A. Sussmann, *The Public Relations Movement in America,* unpublished M.A. Thesis (University of Chicago, Department of Sociology, March 1947); Richard S. Tedlow, *Keeping the Corporate Image: Public Relations and Business, 1900–1950* (Greenwich, Conn.: JAI Press Inc., 1979); and Alan R. Raucher, *Public Relations and Business, 1900–1929* (Baltimore, Md.: The Johns Hopkins Press, 1968).

22. See C. C. Regier, *The Era of the Muckrakers* (Chapel Hill, N.C.: The University of North Carolina Press, 1932), pp. 173 ff. Regier's work is a good social history of the whole era.

23. In 1912, for instance, Daniel Guggenheim testified before a hostile industrial relations commission in the aftermath of fierce strikes by workers in Guggenheim mines who claimed a number of abuses, including twelve-hour work days, low wages, poor living conditions, and an extremely high rate of disabling injuries. Under the guidance of Bernard Baruch and Sam Untermeyer, Guggenheim told an astonished commission and audience of labor organizers and socialists that workers are justified in organizing, entitled to more material goods, entitled to a greater voice in determining work conditions, and entitled to share in industry's profits. Guggenheim went so far as to assert that the government should facilitate these goals by taxing the estates of the rich. The last sentiment outflanked Miss Ida Tarbell, the woman considered, to her own chagrin, the scourge of the Rockefellers. She criticized Guggenheim's pro-

posal for inheritance taxes as somewhat too radical, though she lauded him as a fine captain of industry. See Harvey O'Connor, *The Guggenheims: The Making of an American Dynasty* (New York: Covici-Friede Publishers, 1937), pp. 314–323. Ida M. Tarbell was, of course, the author of *The History of the Standard Oil Company*, 2 vols. (New York: McClure, Phillips & Company, 1904), one of the earliest and most important muckraking tracts. As Richard Hofstadter points out, Tarbell, the daughter of an oil-rich Pennsylvania family whose fortunes suffered from Rockefeller's push for monopoly, was an accidental muckraker of sorts, as was true of many of her colleagues. She ended her career publishing a hagiography of the industrialist Judge Gary. See Richard Hofstadter, *The Age of Reform: From Bryan to F.D.R.* (New York: Vintage, 1955), pp. 193–194.

In 1914, the Rockefellers, under great public criticism because of the massacre of striking workers and their families at Ludlow, Colorado, hired Ivy Lee, then a counsel with the troubled Pennsylvania Railroad. Shortly thereafter, John D. Rockefeller, Jr., toured the strike areas of Colorado, spoke with the workers, an event that received wide press coverage, and later shook hands with the fabled Mother Jones before the same labor commission that Guggenheim had outmaneuvered. Both the Guggenheims and the Rockefellers, of course, also developed wide-ranging philanthropic programs. See Alan R. Raucher, *Public Relations and Business, 1900–1920*, pp. 25–27, and Leila A. Sussman, *The Public Relations Movement in America*, p. 16. See also the account in the biography of Lee by Ray Eldon Hiebert, *Courtier to the Crowd* (Ames, Iowa: Iowa State University Press, 1966), pp. 97–108.

24. See, for instance, Ray Hiebert, *Courtier to the Crowd*, p. 12. Throughout his career, Lee adopted the public stance that leaders should be frank and direct with the masses. See, for instance, Ivy Lee, Occasional Paper-No. 3, *The Problem of International Propaganda*, An Address by Ivy Lee Before a Private Group of Persons Concerned With International Affairs, in London, July 3, 1934 (New York?: 1934).

25. George Creel's autobiography *Rebel At Large* (New York: G. P. Putnam's Sons, 1947) describes his early career, which included campaigns against child labor, bribery of public officials, and Rockefeller's difficulties at Ludlow, Colorado. Louis Filler, *Crusaders for American Liberalism* (Yellow Springs, Ohio: Antioch Press, 1961), among others, notes the irony of the wholesale incorporation of the muckrakers into the Committee on Public Information. Creel's own unofficial recounting of the CPI is *How We Advertised America: The First Telling of the Amazing Story of the Committee on Public Information That Carried the Gospel of Americanism to Every Corner of the Globe* (New York: Harper & Brothers, 1920).

In a short eighteen months, among other activities, the CPI published large numbers of pamphlets for worldwide distribution; commanded the services of 75,000 speakers in 5,200 communities giving 755,190 speeches, each of four-minutes duration; mobilized artists and advertising men both to produce pictorial publicity and to disseminate it in every conceivable way; issued a daily newspaper to 100,000 people; produced a wide range of feature and shorter length films, as well as photographic and slide displays; gathered together the "leading novelists, essayists, and publicists of the land" who produced articles on the war and American life for press syndication; established a Bureau of Cartoons that mobilized and directed the cartoonists of the country for constructive war efforts; and supervised the censorship of newspapers, periodicals, cables, and films to ward off any misleading impressions of American life. For some general treatments of the work of the Committee on Public Information, see U.S. Committee on Public Information, *The Creel Report* (New York: DaCapo Press, 1972); Detlef R. Peters, *Das "US-Committee on Public Information"* (Inaugural-Dissertation

Freie Universität, Berlin, 1964); and James R. Mock and Cedric Larson, *Words That Won the War* (Princeton, N.J.: Princeton University Press, 1939). For an inside under-standing of the organizational workings of the CPI, one should consult the correspon-dence of Carl Byoir, Creel's associate chairman. The vast part of the daily business of the CPI went through Byoir, and it is in his letters and directives that one can begin to sense the sprawling nature of the organization, the inevitable petty bickerings, the currying of political favor, and the development of the often ingenious methods used to develop public support for the war. See National Archives, Record Group 63, *Records of the Committee on Public Information*. CPI 1 A-4, CPI 1 A-5, CPI 1 A-6, and CPI 1 A-7. Byoir, of course, went on to found a prosperous public relations agency that bore his name until late in 1986, when it was absorbed by Hill and Knowlton, another large public relations firm.

26. Harry Reichenbach, a member of Creel's Committee, describes some of the techniques used to demoralize the enemy and encourage surrender. These included sending a million letters to Italian soldiers at the front telling them that their wives were adulterously involved with those exempted from armed service, dropping "diplo-mas" over German lines that qualified any German private to go over to the Allies and be immediately promoted to officer status, and smuggling small pocket Bibles into Ger-many that contained propaganda tracts inside. See Reichenbach, *Phantom Fame*, pp. 236 and 246–248.

27. Richard Tedlow, *Keeping the Corporate Image*, p. 40.

28. Edward L. Bernays, *Propaganda* (New York: Liveright, 1928), pp. 27–28. Harry Reichenbach also comments on his own realization of the importance of prop-aganda during the war:

> The vast extent of propaganda only dawned on me now. It was almost as much a war of printing presses as of machine guns. Instead of one spieler on a plat-form in front of the Koutch tent, there were a hundred and fifty thousand spielers,—spielers as far as the eye could reach, spielers that could show you black is white and night is day without stumbling a single word or interrupting the smooth and glossy flow of their language: "Come here folks! The greatest war on earth! We've got the deadliest gases, the biggest cannons, the most tangled barbed wire, the fastest aeroplanes, the surest torpedoes, the finest soldiers to send over the top—and what is more, the enemy is all wrong!" (Reichenbach, *Phantom Fame*, p. 240.)

29. Walter Lippmann, *The Phantom Public* (New York: Harcourt, Brace and Company, 1925), p. 65.

30. See Merle Curti, "The Changing Concept of 'Human Nature' in the Litera-ture of American Advertising," *Business History Review*, Vol. 41, No. 4 (Winter 1967), pp. 335–357, especially p. 356. See also Daniel Pope, *The Making of Modern Adver-tising* (New York: Basic Books, 1982), pp. 237–251.

31. Edward Bernays, *Propaganda*, p. 47.

32. Edward Bernays, *Propaganda*, p. 152.

33. See Francis X. Sutton, Seymour E. Harris, Carl Kaysen, and James Tobin, *The American Business Creed* (New York: Schocken Books, 1962). Stated briefly, some of the main themes of the NAM campaign were:

> (a) Business has been systematically misrepresented to the American people by self-interested groups—labor, radicals, and those bent on socialism. This

misinformation has created a serious misunderstanding of the vital role that business plays in the American system.

(b) No matter how bad things are at the moment, Americans still enjoy the best standard of living on earth, and this is a direct result of the genius of American business. Moreover, the great political freedom we enjoy here is inextricably tied to our economic freedom; only the free market system can provide political freedom. We cannot deceive ourselves with the idea that government encroachments on the economy can be allowed without endangering our basic political rights.

(c) Moreover, Americans are all in this together. Business, labor, and government are not, at bottom, antagonists. They all share the common interest of rebuilding America. Businessmen want and need to be successful for everyone's benefit. What hurts business hurts everyone.

(d) The real leaders of our country are therefore businessmen and business managers. It is they who are seeking harmony and progress and working for everyone's interests. People should not impede them in this task but rather assist them. Businesses need to make a fair profit to continue their work on behalf of the society.

See Sutton et al., pp. 19–52. See also S. H. Walker and Paul Sklar, *Business Finds Its Voice* (New York: Harper and Bros., 1938), pp. 1–16.

34. See Walker and Sklar, *Business Finds Its Voice,* pp. 19–40.

35. Richard Tedlow, *Keeping the Corporate Image,* pp. 122–125, gives a good description of the split between the NAM and the CED.

36. William H. Whyte, *Is Anybody Listening?* (New York: Simon and Schuster, Inc., 1952).

37. The term is Max Weber's to describe one of many types of ancient prophets, specifically those whose predictions "evoked timely expectations" in royal court circles. See *Ancient Judaism,* translated by Hans Gerth and Don Martindale (Glencoe, Ill.: Free Press, 1952), p. 325 and *passim.* In our era, public relations is, of course, only one of the many professions that act as prophets of good fortune. In this category, one must also include any group that puts its empirical and interpretive legerdemain at the disposal of established authority. See Joseph Bensman, "Hans Gerth's Contribution to American Sociology," in *Politics, Character and Culture: Perspectives from Hans Gerth,* edited by Joseph Bensman, Arthur Vidich, and Nobuko Gerth (Westport, Conn.: Greenwood Press, 1982), pp. 221–274. See especially p. 247.

38. Exact data on public relations are hard to obtain because the indirect character of the public appeals that mark the field obscures the real extent of public relations activities. Corporate budgets for the salaries of internal public relations staff are, for instance, a poor index of the real amount of money spent on public relations work. That same staff may be coordinating portions of various budgets, such as those allocated for government lobbying, corporate donations to the arts, and advertising.

39. From 1974 to 1984, corporate expenditures for what is called corporate or public relations advertising in the six main media outlets (consumer magazines, newspaper supplements, network television, spot television, radio, and outdoor) rose by 249 percent to total $782,985,000 in 1984. Trade association advertising of the same sort showed an even larger increase, rising 397.4 percent over the same period; associations spent $435,168,500 in the same six media in 1984. See Josephine Curran,

"The 14th Annual Review of Corporate Advertising Expenditures," *Public Relations Journal,* Vol. 41, No. 12 (December 1985), p. 28 ff. One should note that some people in public relations would dispute using any advertising figures to measure public relations. But public relations personnel are often involved in planning out this particular kind of advertising.

Gross revenue figures for the largest public relations firms are perhaps a better index of the growth of the field. *Jack O'Dwyer's Newsletter,* the most widely read publication in the field, publishes annually a list of the top public relations firms and their gross fee income. For the top 15 firms in 1969, the total combined fee income was $46,215,000; in 1983, it was $265,223,000 (my calculations, rounded and unadjusted figures). The growing educational respectability of public relations is another measure of the field's growth. Albert Walker, *Status and Trends in Public Relations Education in United States Senior Colleges and Universities* (New York: Foundation for Public Relations Research and Education, 1981) lists more than 300 colleges and universities that offer courses in public relations; 65 of these offer degrees in public relations or in closely related fields with a pubic relations emphasis.

40. The word "client," as used in both the public relations and advertising worlds, has a multitude of meanings depending on the context. It is used to refer variously to a corporation whose account one services, one's opposite number at the corporation, or an entire group of individuals at the corporation charged with overseeing and evaluating agency work. It can also describe a generalized other with whom one has a sometimes friendly, sometimes antagonistic, but always dependent relationship. The best treatment of the multifaceted and inferential use of the word, as well as of the far-reaching consequences for agency personnel having multiple interpretive arbiters of one's work, has been done by Janice M. Hirota in her analysis of the "approval process" in advertising agencies. See her "Cultural Mediums: The Work World of 'Creatives' in American Advertising Agencies," unpublished Ph.D. Diss., Department of Anthropology, Columbia University, 1987.

41. The scientific literature on the ozone depletion controversy is vast and highly technical. However, one can grasp the main dimensions of the issue by examining the principal reports that have come out of the National Academy of Sciences on the issue. These are National Research Council, Committee on Impacts of Stratospheric Change, *Halocarbons: Effects on Stratospheric Ozone* (Washington, D.C.: National Academy of Sciences, 1976); National Research Council, Committee on Impacts of Stratospheric Change, *Halocarbons: Environmental Effects of Chlorofluoromethane Release* (Washington, D.C.: National Academy of Sciences, 1976); National Research Council, Committee on Impacts of Stratospheric Change and Committee on Alternatives for the Reduction of Chlorofluorocarbon Emissions, *Protection Against Depletion of Stratospheric Ozone by Chlorofluorocarbons* (Washington, D.C.: National Academy of Sciences, 1979); National Research Council, Committee on Chemistry and Physics of Ozone Depletion and the Committee on Biological Effects of Increased Solar Ultraviolet Radiation, *Causes and Effects of Stratospheric Ozone Reduction: An Update* (Washington, D.C.: National Academy of Sciences, 1982); and National Research Council, Committee on Causes and Effects of Changes in Stratospheric Ozone, *Causes and Effects of Changes in Stratospheric Ozone: Update 1983* (Washington, D.C.: National Academy Press, 1984).

As it happens, a hole in the ozone the size of the continental United States was only recently discovered above Antarctica. A multination meeting sponsored by the United Nations Environmental Program agreed in principle (in April 1987) to freeze and eventually to reduce the production and consumption of chlorofluorocarbons and other industrial chemicals that purportedly attack the ozone. See Thomas W. Netter, "U.N. Parley Agrees to Protect Ozone," *The New York Times*, Friday, May 1, 1987, A1, col. 1 and A10, cols. 3–4. In an interview in late 1986, an Alchemy executive commented on the finding in Antarctica: "We weren't aware that penguins used that much hairspray."

42. At Weft Corporation's huge finishing plant, the obstacles to reducing workers' exposure to formaldehyde do indeed seem to be formidable. At that plant, Weft applies a formaldehyde-based resin to raw cloth, along with a variety of other mixtures such as blueing agents and softeners, depending on customer specifications, on nineteen finishing ranges located in the middle of the plant. The ranges are between 150 and 200 feet in length and handle fabric up to 200 inches wide. Each range is fed by two feeder vats located in an enclosed room above the ranges; these vats themselves are fed from a warehouse through a piping system.

The problem of workers' exposure to free formaldehyde—that is, formaldehyde that has escaped the resin and returned to a gaseous state—occurs in the upstairs room as well as downstairs at each range. The vats upstairs could be totally encased without too much trouble, but only the few workers who mix the resin work around them. The real problem is in the downstairs ranges, which because of their size cannot be easily or inexpensively encased. Moreover, in order to get exposure down to one ppm, the level that Weft executives at the time of my field research feared OSHA would impose, the present four exhaust systems that carry off fumes and emissions from production would have to be dramatically improved. Essentially this would require the erection of a massive smokestack to eject the hot moist air from production high enough above the plant to prevent any recirculation of ejected air while at the same time pumping enough fresh air into the plant to prevent a quasivacuum from being created. But another entire manufacturing operation is located in the same building, on the floor directly above the finishing ranges. This would have to be closed down or moved to another location. In effect, were the exposure to formaldehyde to be lowered to one ppm, the real choices facing Weft would be to build a new plant with both completely encased machinery and a wholly new ventilation system, or to find a substitute for formaldehyde. Similar dilemmas face other manufacturers. The textile industry has been scrambling to find a substitute for formaldehyde, but no really cost-effective one has yet been discovered.

43. James W. Giggey, "Chairman's Report," *1983 Annual Report, Formaldehyde Institute* (Scarsdale, N.Y.: Formaldehyde Institute, 1983), p. 3.

44. See Formaldehyde Institute, *Formaldehyde Information Kit* (Scarsdale, N.Y.: Formaldehyde Institute, no date), *passim*. In the last several years, there have been several studies done by different groups on the health dangers posed by formaldehyde. Evidence for the carcinogenicity of formaldehyde was first presented in 1979. See Chemical Industry Institute of Toxicology, *Statement Concerning Research Findings*, Docket No. 11109 (Research Triangle Park, N.C.: CIIT), October 8, 1979. These data and other evidence are reviewed in Joint NIOSH/OSHA Current Intelligence Bulletin 34, *Formaldehyde: Evidence of Carcinogenicity* (Cincinnati, Oh.: National Institute for Occupational Safety and Health, April 15, 1981). More recently, OSHA issued a notice prior to rulemaking that further reviews previous studies and proposes lowering permissible exposure levels to the chemical. See "Occupational Exposure to Formaldehyde," *Federal Register*, Wednesday, April 17, 1985, Vol. 50, No. 74, pp. 15179–15184. On December 10, 1985, OSHA proposed a final rule with two regulatory alternatives, depending on whether it decided finally whether formaldehyde is an irritant or a carcinogen. The Formaldehyde Institute, of course, took the position

that its members should support the notion that the chemical is an irritant; this would involve lowering the permissible exposure limit to between one and two ppm. The Institute told its members to urge OSHA "not to conclude that low levels of exposure (3 ppm 8-hour TWA) of formaldehyde should be regulated as a potential occupational carcinogen unless there is evidence of occupational cancer in man as opposed to laboratory animals under high dose conditions." See Formaldehyde Institute, *Formaldehyde Newsletter*, Vol. VI, No. 1 (March 3, 1986), p. 1. (The newsletter and other materials are available from the Institute at its new address, 1330 Connecticut Avenue, N.W., Washington, D.C. 20036.) The Institute received a big boost for its position with the release in June 1986 of a long-term epidemiological study conducted by the National Cancer Institute together with a consortium of producers and users of formaldehyde. The study concluded that the data from its historical cohort study of 26,561 workers in ten formaldehyde-producing or using facilities "provide little evidence that mortality from cancer is associated with formaldehyde exposure at levels experienced by workers in this study." (p. 1071) See Aaron Blair et al., "Mortality Among Industrial Workers Exposed to Formaldehyde," *Journal of the National Cancer Institute*, Vol 76, No. 6 (June 1986), pp. 1071–1084.

But subsequent studies, including another by Dr. Blair (see Aaron Blair et al., "Cancers of the Nasal Pharynx and Oral Pharynx," *Journal of the National Cancer Institute*, Vol. 78, No. 1 [January 1987], pp. 191–192), have left the matter still very controverted. In the late spring of 1987, the Environmental Protection Agency issued a risk assessment of formaldehyde saying that there is limited evidence that exposure to formaldehyde causes cancer in humans. There was, of course, a chorus of scoffs and boos from segments of the business community. See, for instance, the editorial "Scaring the Public" in *The Wall Street Journal*, July 7, 1987. The Formaldehyde Institute's position remains unchanged. A final OSHA rule on workplace exposure to formaldehyde is expected late in 1987, with implementation due sometime in 1988.

45. For an overview of the acid rain dispute, see Congress of the United States, Office of Technology Assessment, *Acid Rain and Transported Air Pollutants: Implications for Public Policy* (Washington, D.C.: Government Printing Office, 1984); National Research Council, Committee on Atmospheric Transport and Chemical Transformation in Acid Precipitation, *Atmospheric Processes in Eastern North America: A Review of Current Scientific Understanding* (Washington, D.C.; National Academy Press, 1983). See also Robert H. Boyle and R. Alexander Boyle, *Acid Rain* (New York: Schocken Books, 1983).

The Alliance's viewpoint is put forward in a series of newsletters available from the organization at 1225 19th Street N.W., Suite 270, Washington, D.C. 20036. The moderate, genteel tone of these newsletters shows sophisticated public relations work. Exactly the same arguments, expressed, however, much more crudely, may be found in *The National Independent Coal Leader*, the monthly publication of the conservative National Independent Coal Operators' Association. See, for instance, "Acid Rain: VPI Professor Says Coal Is Not to Blame," Vol. 15, No. 8 (March 1981), p. 27; "Many Reputable Scientists Disagree on the Acid Precipitation: Coal is Not the Culprit," Vol. 16, No. 3 (October 1981), p. 1 ff.; "Cause and Effect of Acid Rain Needs Research," Vol. 16, No. 11 (June 1982), p. 14; "Experts Question Acid Rain Theories," Vol. 17, No. 4 (October 1982), p. 14 (issue misnumbered; should be No. 3); "Acid Lakes Traced to Soil, not Rain," Vol. 17, No. 8 (March 1983), p. 16; "Acid Rain Bill Would Harm Industry, Economy," Vol. 17, No. 10 (May 1983), p. 16; "Acid Precipitation and Acid Lakes; Is Coal the Whipping Boy for Oil's Pollution Contribution?" Vol. 18, No. 4 (November 1983), p. 1 ff.; "Expert Says Acid Rain Issue Distroted [sic] by

Press," Vol. 18, No. 6 (February 1984), p. 1 (issue misnumbered; should be No. 7); "Environmentalists Accused of Trying to Kill Mining," Vol. 18, No. 5 (December 1983), p. 6; "Based Entirely on Theory: Acid Rain—Fact or Fiction?", Vol. 18, No. 6 (January 1984), p. 1 ff.; "Ky. Official Sees Little Benefit From Acid Rain Controls," Vol. 19, No. 6 (March 1985), p. 20; and "Studies Find No Acid Precipitation," Vol. 20, No. 2 (September 1985), p. 8.

46. The literature of poststructuralist, postrealist criticism is enormous and covers a variety of fields. For a few salient examples, see Stanley Fish, *Is There a Text in This Class? The Authority of Interpretive Communities* (Cambridge, Mass.: Harvard University Press, 1980); Mark C. Taylor, "Deconstruction: What's the Difference?", *Soundings*, Vol. LXVI, No. 4 (Winter 1983), pp. 387–403; and Sanford Levinson, "Law As Literature," *Texas Law Review*, Vol. 60, No. 3 (March 1982), pp. 373–403. For some counterviews, see Gerald Graff, *Literature Against Itself* (Chicago, Ill.: The University of Chicago Press, 1979); Steven Knapp and Walter Benn Michaels, "Against Theory," *Critical Inquiry*, Vol. 8 (Summer 1982), pp. 723–742; and Gene Bell-Villada, "Northrop Frye, Modern Fantasy, Centrist Liberalism, Anti-Marxism, Latin Leftism, Passing Time, and Other Limits of American Academic Criticism," *Berkshire Review*, Vol. 19 (1984), pp. 40–55.

Chapter 8. Invitations to Jeopardy

1. The stress on excellence in management boomed with the publication of Thomas J. Peters and Robert H. Waterman, Jr., *In Search of Excellence: Lessons from America's Best-Run Companies* (New York: Warner Books, 1982), a book that is another classic paradigm of managerial consultant writing, complete with a handy list of eight attributes of excellence. Two years later, a follow-up study by *Business Week*, November 5, 1984, pp. 76–83, argues that at least fourteen of the forty-three corporations cited by Peters and Waterman as excellent had "lost their luster." The article notes that Peters at least is undeterred by such troubling news and is planning other works showing managers how to implement the attributes of excellence.

2. See Kathleen Telsch, "Coca Cola Giving $10 Million To Help South Africa Blacks," *The New York Times*, March 24, 1986, A13, col. 2.

3. Take, for instance, the scene that one encounters on the main floor of Weft's large finishing plant, called "The Bleachery." The cloth from the greige mills comes to loading docks at the rear of the building in huge rolls, tinted different colors to distinguish different weights—for instance, white for shirting material and pink for heavy trouser cloth. All of the cloth contains polyvinyl alcohol (pva), one agent that facilitates the weaving process. The first operation is to remove the pva by washing the cloth in "rope" form—that is, twisted into long strands. The cloth is then untwisted and run at incredibly high speeds in flat form through gas flames on both sides. This helps remove other impurities still left in the cotton part of the cloth. Then the cloth is put back into rope form and whipped by ropes and pulleys through holes in the wall into an adjacent room where it is put into huge vats with a biologically active enzyme that removes the "sizing," the starch that gives the yarn requisite tensile strength for weaving. After the cloth sits in the vats for four hours, it is once again pulled up in rope form into a series of baths, for instance, of hot water and of caustic soda, and at each stage is dried over drying cans. After this, the cloth is often mercerized, that is, put again in a caustic soda bath to heighten its receptivity to dyes. After drying, it then goes to the dyeing ranges, and perhaps later, to the printing ranges.

All of this is an astonishing sight. At any given moment, thousands and thousands of yards of cloth in rope form swirl overhead on pulleys moving from one operation to another; here cloth is racing through flames, here over drying cans, there entering the finishing ranges a dull gray and emerging any of a series of muted or brilliant colors. At one level of their consciousness, those who work in the plant come to take for granted what seems extraordinary to an outsider. At another level, they make connections between product and process—say, the shirt that one wears and how it was made—generally unavailable to those outside a particular occupational community. Even after years of work in such a setting, some managers still find their daily exposure to the drama of coordinating human toil with technology an exhilarating experience.

Suggestions for
Further Reading

There is scarcely an occupational group about which more has been written than that of corporate managers, and this brief essay makes no attempt to cover the whole range of these materials. The notes to individual chapters provide titles on some of the specific professional, organizational, and personal issues that managers face. I mention here only some works that I think are particularly useful for developing a sociological understanding of their world.

The growth of managers as an occupational group is inextricably linked to the emergence of the large organization and the consequent transformation of Western capitalism, developments first noted by German social theorists. The starting point for understanding these great changes is Max Weber's *The Protestant Ethic and the Spirit of Capitalism,* translated by Talcott Parsons (New York: Charles Scribner's Sons, 1958), a work that Weber first published in 1904–1905. The book describes the worldview of the independent, propertied old middle class that propelled the West into industrial capitalism. Weber extends his analysis in an essay called "The Protestant Sects and the Spirit of Capitalism," in *From Max Weber,* translated and edited by Hans Gerth and C. Wright Mills (New York: Oxford University Press, 1958, pp. 302–322). The essay recounts some observations from his trip to the United States in 1904. In describing the process of moral probation and approbation in the southern Protestant sects, he provides deep insights into both the social psychology of organizations and the sociology of ethics. Around the same period, other German thinkers pointed out how the growth of large centralized bureaucracies in both the private and public sectors was generating the emergence of a propertyless salariat of white-collar workers, a "new middle class," wholly dependent on big organizations for their livelihoods. See, in particular, Emil Lederer, *The Problem of the Modern Salaried Employee: Its Theoretical and Statistical Basis,* translated by E. E. Warburg (New York: Columbia University, 1937). Carl Dreyfuss gives one of the richest and most detailed portraits of this burgeoning white-collar sector in *Occupation and Ideology of the Salaried Employee,* 2 vols., translated by Eva Abramovitch (New York: Department of Social Science, Columbia University, 1938). In a book originally scheduled for publication in 1933 but then suppressed by a Nazi editor, Hans Speier discusses the social psychology of the new middle classes and the political consequence of their ascendance in Germany. See his *German White-Collar Workers and the Rise of Hitler* (New Haven, Conn.: Yale University Press, 1986). Speier disseminated some of the main themes of his work in essays both before and after he fled Germany. Of particular importance were his "The Salaried Employee in Modern Society," *Social Research,* Vol. 1, No. 1 (February 1934), pp. 111–133, and *The Salaried Employee in German Society* (New York: Columbia University, 1939).

   C. Wright Mills took this German social theory, to which he had been introduced by his mentor Hans Gerth, who was also an émigré from Nazi Germany, and applied it to the American scene in *White Collar: The American Middle Classes* (New York: Oxford University Press, 1951). Mills utilized as well the powerful frameworks for understanding American capitalism developed early in the century by Thorstein Veblen in *The Theory of Business Enterprise* (New York: Charles Scribner's Sons, 1904) and in *Absentee Ownership* (New York: B. W. Huebsch, Inc., 1923). The big shift from entrepreneurial to bureaucratic capitalism, and the social and cultural consequences of that shift, became main themes of American writers. Some, like James Burnham in *The Managerial Revolution* (New York: The John Day Company, 1941), saw the shift heralding a technocratic future dominated by administrative experts in which property relations and therefore class divisions would be transformed. Others like Hans Gerth and C. Wright Mills in "A Marx for the Managers," *Ethics: An International Journal of Social, Political, and Legal Philosophy,* Vol. 52, No. 2 (January 1942), pp. 200–215, scoffed at such notions and argued that, in fact, bureaucracies mediate, mask, and even intensify class conflict. Joseph Schumpeter in *Capitalism, Socialism and Democracy* (New York: Harper & Brothers, 1942) saw in the growing "obsolescence of the entrepreneurial function" that marks our bureaucratic era the end of the simultaneously creative and destructive dynamism that historically had propelled capitalism. William H. Whyte later popularized Schumpeter's theme in his book *The Organization Man* (New York: Simon and Schuster, 1956), arguing that traditional rugged individualism had given way to a "social ethic." David Riesman in collaboration with Reuel Denney and Nathan Glazer captured for a whole generation at mid-century the main social psychological dimensions of this situation in *The Lonely Crowd: A Study of the Changing American Character* (New Haven, Conn.: Yale University Press, 1950), a book that argues that Americans have become less "inner-directed" and more "other-directed." Riesman, however, attributed the change largely to demographic and child-rearing trends rather than to changes in the organizational basis of society. Arthur J. Vidich and Joseph Bensman, building on their own analysis of a small community in *Small Town in Mass Society* (Princeton, N.J.: Princeton University Press, 1957), synthesize a great many studies of the bureaucratization of our social order in *The New American Society* (Chicago: Quadrangle, 1971). For a huge and meticulous business history of the emergence of American managers as an occupational group, one should also see Alfred D. Chandler, Jr., *The Visible Hand: The Managerial Revolution in American Business* (Cambridge, Mass.: The Belknap Press of Harvard University Press, 1977). A comparative look at how the process has worked itself out in some other countries may be gained by examining Ezra F. Vogel, *Japan's New Middle Class: The Salary Man and His Family in a Tokyo Suburb* (Berkeley, Los Angeles, and London: University of California Press, 1971), as well as Michael Crozier, *The Bureaucratic*

Phenomenon (Chicago: University of Chicago Press, 1964) on France. Of course, long before any of these writers, Karl Marx had written with great insight about the social and political impact of bureaucratization, focusing particularly on the subjection of French society to military-bureaucratic domination after the collapse of the absolute monarchy. See *The Eighteenth Brumaire of Louis Bonaparte* (New York: International Publishers, 1967).

To understand managers, one must also appreciate the inner workings of bureaucracies. The sociology of formal or complex organizations has become, in America at least, essentially another branch of administrative science; as a rule, it provides insights into bureaucracy in inverse relation to its advocacy of organizational tinkering of various sorts. The classic treatment of bureaucracy is Max Weber's "Bureaucracy," in *From Max Weber* (pp. 196–244), as well as his regular return to the subject in *Economy and Society*, 2 vols., edited by Guenther Roth and Claus Wittich (Berkeley, Los Angeles, and London: University of California Press, 1978). Weber's dispassionate treatment of the institution, and his Germanic admiration of the thoroughness made possible by rationalization, are often taken as an apology for bureaucracy. In fact, perhaps better than anyone, Weber recognized the profound dilemma of modern life. Industrial society as we know it is impossible without large-scale, highly rationalized organizations, but these organizations often shape our lives in the most troubling ways. Many other writers have followed the leads that Weber provides and have explored the underside of bureaucracies. In particular, one might look at Robert K. Merton, "Bureaucratic Structure and Personality," *Social Forces*, Vol. XVII (1940), pp. 560–568; Harry Cohen, *The Demonics of Bureaucracy* (Ames, Iowa: Iowa State University Press, 1965); and Joseph Bensman and Bernard Rosenberg, "The Meaning of Work in Bureaucratic Society," in *Identity and Anxiety: Survival of the Person in Mass Society*, edited by Maurice R. Stein, Arthur J. Vidich, and David Manning White (New York: The Free Press, 1960, pp. 181–197). For an instructive explanation of one of bureaucracy's most disliked features, see Herbert Kaufman, *Red Tape, Its Origins, Uses, and Abuses* (Washington, D.C.: The Brookings Institution, 1977). And Alfred Weber, Max's younger brother, wrote a sobering appraisal of bureaucracy's long-term political impact in "Bureaucracy and Freedom," *Modern Review*, 3–4 (March–April 1948), pp. 176–186. The darker side of bureaucracy is also a major theme in some of the literature of the twentieth century. One should see in particular Franz Kafka, "In the Penal Colony," in *The Penal Colony: Stories and Short Pieces*, translated by Willa and Edwin Muir (New York: Schocken Books, 1970, pp. 191–227) and *The Trial*, translated by Willa and Edwin Muir (New York: Vintage Books, 1969). These works were originally published in 1919 and 1925, respectively. More recently, some novels by Joseph Heller create wild parodies of bureaucracy. See *Catch 22* (New York: Dell, 1961) and *Something Happened* (New York: Alfred Knopf, 1974).

The impact of the big organization on the person is a crucial and enduring issue. Authoritarian bureaucracies, such as those described by Erving Goffman in "Characteristics of Total Institutions," in *Asylums: Essays on the Social Situation of Mental Patients and Other Inmates* (Garden City, N.Y.: Doubleday Anchor, 1961, pp. 3–124), either overwhelm the individual or provoke his overt or covert resistance. The subtler and far more important case for understanding managers is the voluntary integration of a person into an organization through his response to organizational premiums. Erving Goffman's classic essay "The Moral Career of the Mental Patient," also in *Asylums* (pp. 127–169), brilliantly describes such self-rationalization. The dilemmas that patients face in adjusting their selves to alter hospital staff's views of them are paradigms of the puzzles encountered by a great many men and women in our modern organizational society. Goffman also treats the theme of the chameleonic self in *The Presentation of Self in Everyday Life* (Garden City, N.Y.: Doubleday Anchor, 1959). Karl Mannheim's seminal treatment of self-rationalization, set in the context of a whole discussion of rationality and irrationality in modern life, is still very worthwhile. See *Man and Society in an Age of Reconstruction* (London: Paul [Kegan], Trench, Trubner Ltd., 1940, pp. 39–75). Few sociologists have written about the meaning of modern work and its impact on the person with greater thoughtfulness than Everett C. Hughes in *The Sociological Eye: Book II Selected Papers on Work, Self, and the Study of Society* (Chicago: Aldine-Atherton, 1971) or Joseph Bensman and Robert Lilienfeld, *Craft and Consciousness: Occupational Technique and the Development of World Images* (New York: Wiley, 1973). Two studies of the world of business and its impact on executives are particularly important. These are Melville Dalton, *Men Who Manage* (New York: John Wiley & Sons, 1959) and especially Joseph Bensman, "The Advertising Man and His Work," in *Dollars and Sense* (New York: Macmillan, 1967, pp. 9–68). Bensman's book is also one of the few works that, following Weber, studies occupational ethics from a strictly sociological standpoint as an analysis of actual moral rules-in-use. The anthropologist F. G. Bailey does the same for the academy in *Morality and Expediency: The Folklore of Academic Politics* (Chicago: Aldine Publishing Company, 1977).

Finally, as I argue in the text, managers' lot is to do work and make choices that will inevitably make some people, even other managers, unhappy. In a world that has broken apart overarching and unifying belief systems and theodicies, choices based on one set of values inevitably clash with desired choices based on other values. And, all the while, salvation ideologies proliferate as men and women try to fashion a meaningful cosmos for themselves. The theoretical framework for understanding these fundamental conflicts and quandaries comes from Max Weber's dense but powerful essays in *From Max Weber*, "Religious Rejections of the World and Their Directions" (pp. 323–359) and "The Social Psychology of the World Religions" (pp. 267–301). The crucial and growing importance of public relations in our epoch stems, in part, from this clash of values, as everyone tries to mobilize support for his or her own viewpoints or ideologies. But public relations is also, and especially, the elaboration of official versions of reality. A good general treatment of public relations in American business is Richard S. Tedlow, *Keeping the Corporate Image: Public Relations and Business, 1900–1950* (Greenwich, Conn.: JAI Press Inc., 1979). Good introductions to the sociology of wordsmithing, public relations' distinctive stock in trade, are Hans Speier, "The Communication of Hidden Meaning," *Social Research*, Vol. 44, No. 3 (Autumn 1977), pp. 471–501, and Dwight Bolinger, *Language—The Loaded Weapon* (New York, Longman, 1980). The social and political use of language is, of course, a pervasive theme in the work of the incomparable George Orwell. See especially his "Politics and the English Language," in *The Collected Essays, Journalism and Letters of George Orwell, Volume 4: In Front of Your Nose 1945–1950*, edited by Sonia Orwell and Ian Angus (New York: Harcourt Brace Jovanovich, Inc., 1968, pp. 127–140). One can also still profit from Walter Lippmann's ruminations on the conundrums of public opinion in modern democratic societies marked by increasingly centralized executive power. See *The Phantom Public* (New York: Harcourt, Brace and Company, 1925).

Index

Acid rain, 178–79, 232 *n.* 45. *See also*
    Fronts, public relations, scientific
Advertising, 10, 139, 148, 171, 173, 174
    and Committee on Public Information,
        166–67. *See also* Public relations
Alchemy Inc. (chemical company), 20, 24,
        34, 35, 36, 42, 43, 44, 45, 50, 51,
        52, 53, 54, 56, 57, 58, 59, 61, 62,
        63, 64, 65, 66, 72, 73, 76, 79, 84,
        86, 88, 119, 123, 127, 132, 154,
        155–56, 194, 201
    and chlorofluorocarbons, 174–76
    and coking plant, 81–82, 84–85
    fieldwork in, 15–16, 205–6
    Kelly, case study of, 121–22
    and meat preservative, 199–200
    milking of plants in, 91–94
    and natural gas, 87–88
    as operating company of Covenant, 17–18
    Patterson, case study of, 67–70
    and pesticide plant, 94–95
    and shake-ups at Covenant, 24–32. *See
        also* Covenant Corporation
Alliance for Responsible CFC Policy,
        175–76. *See also*
        Chlorofluorocarbons; Fronts, public
        relations

Alliances, 24, 28, 30, 52, 80, 133, 135, 198
    and cliques, 39
    and coteries, 38
    as defense, 27
    defined, 38
    and networks, 38
    and patronage structure, 62
    and social structure of organizations,
        192, 193. *See also* Circles,
        managerial
Anxiety, 13, 21, 142
    as basic aspect of managerial life, 40,
        73–74, 204
    as characteristic of old Protestant ethic
        and bureaucratic ethic, 191
    description of, in Young, 99
    and drawing lines, 120, 123
    as fueled by management consultants,
        141
    and organizational upheavals, 4, 26, 31
    and perceived lack of connection
        between work and results, 70–71
    and probation, 40
Aridity, emotional, 4, 196, 203, 204
Asceticism, secular, 7, 8
    psychic, 203, 204. *See also* Self-
        rationalization

I am indebted to Janice M. Hirota for her invaluable help in preparing this index. RJ

Authority, 4, 34, 39, 41, 45, 46
    ambiguity of, at Three Mile Island, 113–
        14
    authoritative definitions and management
        consultants, 140–41
    and blame, 85–88
    of chief executive officer, actual and
        symbolic, 21–23, 36
    and commitment system and fealty, 18–
        19
    cultural, and persuasion, 177
    and decision making, 75–82, 84–85
    and details and credit, 20–21, 81, 196
    exercise of, 27, 69
    levels of, and abstractness of viewpoints,
        124–26
    necessity to please, and probation, 40
    and official definitions of reality, 52–55
    patrimonial, characteristics of, 19–20, 23
    personalized, in American bureaucracies,
        11–12
    personalized, in corporate hierarchies,
        17, 18–19, 192, 193
    prerogatives of, 27, 49, 204
    and rehearsals, 189
    relationships, etiquette of, 111
    and responsibility, 88–89
    simultaneous centralization and
        decentralization of, in corporations,
        17–19, 36
    subordination to, 5
    and technical disputes, 118
    use of staff by, 35

Barnum, P. T., 164
Bechtel Corporation, 113–18
Beleaguerment, managers' sense of, 147–
    56
Bell, Daniel, 139
Bensman, Joseph, 61
Bernays, Edward, 167–68, 174
Black (pseudonym for lawyer at
    Covenant), 122–23
Blame, 21, 25, 27, 28, 99, 110, 118
    avoidance of, 90–95, 193
    blamability, 114
    "blame-time," 85, 88, 134
    circle of, 98
    issue in gut decisions, 85
    varieties of, 85–90
Brady (pseudonym for whistleblower),
    105–11. See also Comfort, notion of
Brown (pseudonym for executive at
    Alchemy), 27, 28, 30–32, 39

Brown lung. See Byssinosis
Brown Lung Association, 158
Bureaucracy, 7, 16, 101, 112, 116
    and abstract view of problems, 124
    American, 4, 11–12
    authority in, 17–23
    classical model, 11
    communications apparatus typical in,
        36–37, 146
    conflicts and tensions in, 34–36, 195
    at Covenant, 90
    diffusion of responsibility in, 86–90, 201
    ethic of, 191–92
    fragmentation of work and knowledge
        in, 80
    freedom in, 88
    genius of, 6, 52–53
    institutional logic in, 112
    and managerial groups, 12–13
    mediocrity and institutionalized
        inequities in, 197–98
    and moral consciousness, 3, 192
    moral ethos of, 110, 119, 162
    and moral mazes, 193–94
    patrimonial, 11–12, 19, 23, 24
    probationary crucibles in, 192–93
    and psychological distance from
        problems through impersonality,
        127
    and rationalization of public faces, 46–
        48
    segmented work patterns of, 192–93
    and separation of people from
        consequences of their actions, 127–
        28
    and significance of political struggles in,
        24
    and situational moralities, 193
    sociology of, 4, 10–11, 138
    as system of organized irresponsibility,
        95
    and transformation of moral issues into
        practical concerns, 111–12. See also
        Premium(s)
Bureaucratic work, 11
    abstractness of, with advancement, 201–
        2
    and bracketing moralities, 6
    compartmentalization and secrecy in,
        194
    and looking up and looking around, 80
    moral dilemmas posed by, 12, 13
    and multiple ideologies and mythologies,
        146–47

patterns and social structure of
corporation, 192–93
and people's consciousness, 5–6. *See also*
Managerial work
Bureaucratization
decline of old and ascendance of new
middle class, 9–10
of economy, 9
Business ethics, field of, 4–5
Business schools, 4, 41–42, 141
Byssinosis, 103, 136, 156–60. *See also*
Cotton dust

Capriciousness, of organizational life, 63,
73–74, 77, 79, 88, 144, 192
Casuistry, 131, 184, 185, 188–89, 204
defined, 5
CED. *See* Committee for Economic
Development
CEO. *See* Chief Executive Officer
CFC(s). *See* Chlorofluorocarbons
Charlotte Observer, The, 158
Chief executive officer (CEO), 17, 35, 40,
43, 51, 63, 76, 79, 82, 87, 89, 104,
122, 143, 144, 171, 174, 200, 202
and Brady, 105–11
and commitment system, 18–19, 21–23
and shake-ups in Covenant/Alchemy,
25–32, 37, 67
and shake-up in Weft, 32–33
Chlorofluorocarbons, 15, 155
and ozone depletion theory, 127, 150,
230–31 *n.* 41
and public relations fronts, 174–76
Circles, managerial
access to, 103, 104, 108, 131, 202
at Covenant/Alchemy, 27, 70
criteria for admission to, 39–40
criteria universally important in, 46–
65
defined, 38–39, 212–13 *n.* 4
moral ethos of, 101, 127–28
and organizational structure, 193
ouster from, 105–11, 112–19
professional intimacy in, 203, 204
and protection against contingencies,
69
rule(s) of, 29, 96–97, 118, 128–33
and self-rationalization, 6, 14, 16, 23–
25, 43, 58, 59–61, 117, 120, 135,
145, 147, 156, 188, 193
at Weft, 41, 104
wider, 38, 141, 148

Clients, 18, 116, 146, 147, 197
management consultants' relationship to,
137–44
public relations practitioners'
relationship to, 164, 166, 169, 170–
73, 180–87
relationships with patrons within an
organization, 19–20, 25, 50, 53,
61–62, 104. *See also* Fealty
Cliques
and alliances, 39, 192
criteria for admission, 62
power, 32, 39, 128, 156
and rivalry, 53, 202
and social structure of organizations, 56.
See also Circles, managerial
Code
dress, 46–47
formal, of ethics, 132
linguistic, 135, 170
moral, of managers, 4, 31, 38, 97
moral, of profession, 109, 110. *See also*
Ethics, occupational; Rules (-in-use)
Cognitive maps, 30, 64, 65, 67, 68, 80, 88,
128, 135
and caricatures of different occupational
groups, 192–93
defined, 23–24
Coking plant, gut decision, case study of,
81–82, 84–85
Comfort, notion of, 14, 15, 136
as criterion for admission to circles, 39,
128, 192
defined, 13, 56
importance of, in shake-ups, 26, 33, 70,
172
and rehearsals, 189
and style, 58
uncomfortable, notion of, 14, 26, 52, 54,
76, 78, 104, 105, 110, 111, 184, 188
Committee for Economic Development
(CED), 168–69
Committee on Public Information (CPI),
166–67, 227–28 *n.* 25
Conflict, in organizations, 33, 53, 55, 133,
197
and everyday competition, 35–36, 195–
96
between line and staff, 34–35, 132
masked by social ambiance, 36–37, 38
between occupational groups, 34, 193
between powerful managers, 35
Consumer Product Safety Commission,
177

Contingency, sense of, 33, 40, 63, 67, 70,
    73, 79, 135
Coteries
    and alliances, 38–39, 192
    criteria for admission to, 62
    defined, 38
    and social structure of organizations, 56.
        See also Circles, managerial
Cotton dust, 16, 103, 136, 178
    case study in textile industry, 156–60.
        See also Inconsistency, adeptness at
Covenant Corporation, 22, 39, 41–42, 43,
    51, 53, 55, 60, 63–64, 71, 76–77,
    78, 82–83, 85, 88, 89, 90, 91, 127,
    139, 144, 146, 160, 161, 202
    Black, case study of, 122–23
    fieldwork in, 15–16, 22, 205–6
    Kelly, case study of, 121–22
    and meat preservative, 199–200
    and natural gas, 87–88
    organizational structure of, 17–18
    Patterson, case study of, 67–70
    Reed, case study of, 123
    shake-ups in, 24–35
    social ambiance in, 36–37
    Young, case study of, 96–100. *See also*
        Alchemy Inc.
"Cover your ass" (CYA), 88–90
Credibility, 174
    displacement of notion of truth by, 204
    importance of, in organizations, 26, 35–
        36, 62, 85
    loss of, 70–71, 99
    and plausibility, in public relations, 172,
        179–80. *See also* Persuasion
Creel, George, 166. *See also* Committee on
    Public Information (CPI)
CYA. *See* "Cover your ass"

Decision making, 6, 14, 64, 75–100
    (Chapter 4), 141
    gut decisions, 77–85
    ideologies about, 75
    routine decisions, 75–77
    and vocabularies of rationality, 76–77.
        See also Responsibility
        (accountability)
Depression, Great, 149
    growth of public relations during, 168–
        69
Disenchantment
    and collapse of traditional theodicies,
        151–52

as product of science and technology,
    149–51
    and salvation ideologies, 152–53
Dissent, 133, 175
    and team play, 54–55
    in technical disputes, 118
    and voicing bad news, 118. *See also case
        studies of* Brady; White; Wilson,
        Joe
Doublethink
    defined, 183–84
    and irrationalities of everyday problems,
        188
    as personal hazard and professional
        virtue, 184–85. *See also*
        Inconsistency, adeptness at
Drawing lines, 101–33 (Chapter 5)
    in relations with customers, 120–22
    as trade-off between principle and
        expediency, 119
    when information is scarce, 122–23
Durkheim, Emile, 139

Edison Electric Institute, 178–79. *See also*
    Fronts, public relations, scientific
Environmental Protection Agency (EPA),
    31, 82, 84, 136, 148, 154, 175, 176
EPA. *See* Environmental Protection
    Agency
Ethic
    bureaucratic, 4, 12, 13, 191–94
    of environmental vigilance at Alchemy,
        119
    professional, tenuousness of in
        bureaucracy, 111
    Protestant, 7–11, 59, 191, 193, 203
    of self-control, among managers, 48
    success, 9
    Tucker's, 132
    work, 9. *See also* Ethos
Ethics
    business, 4–5
    of *caritas*, and irreconcilable opposition
        with exigencies of public life, 68–
        69, 196
    code(s) of, 119, 132
    Judeo-Christian, 105, 195
    Sunday school, 118
Ethics, occupational, 15
    of colleagues, 122–23
    of corporate managers, 4, 6, 12, 13, 14,
        15, 16
    defined, 4

of public relations practitioners, 163
toward and of customers, 120–22
transformation into etiquette, 204. *See also* Rules (-in-use)
Ethos, 204
of bureaucracy, 12, 110, 119, 152, 162, 197
of corporations, 44, 45, 46, 109, 132, 172, 183, 192, 203
as institutional logic, 95
of management consulting, 137, 138, 140
managerial, 101, 129
professional, 106, 110, 185
of public relations, 172, 183
of rapid mobility, 91
short-term, 82–85, 96, 143–44
"take the money and run," 96, 99, 161, 199
of team play, 50
Etiquette (protocol)
and alertness to expediency, 128, 193
of authority relationships, 111
of circles, 192
of debate, in rehearsals, 189
of fealty relationships, 103
of management consultants, 144
organizational (general), 6, 38, 80, 130
transformation of ethics into, 204
Euphemisms. *See* Language
Expediency, 117
alertness to, defined, 112
alertness to and self-objectification, 119, 203
bureaucratic premium on alertness to, 123–24
characteristics of manager alert to, 133
fraternity of, 204
and public relations, 173, 183, 188
self-rationalization and alertness to, 124–28
social acceptance and alertness to, case studies, 128–33
vs. principle, 118–19. *See also* "What has to be done"

Failure, 8, 41, 55, 61, 62, 77, 85
and bureaucratic ethic, 192
and mobility panic, 67
as nonpromotability, 65–67
and old Protestant ethic, 191
significance and social consequences of, 67–70

Fealty, 32, 39
and alliance structure, 45, 49, 103, 193
and alliances, 38
and commitment system, 18–19
rearrangement of during shake-ups, 25, 26, 30, 114
between subordinates and bosses, 19–21, 70, 104, 170, 192
Fieldwork, 3, 7–16 (Chapter 1), 161, 205–6 (Author's Note)
gaining access for, 13–16
Fitzgerald, F. Scott, 161
Football, as metaphor. *See* Language
Forbes, 51, 139
Formaldehyde, 71, 177–78, 231–32 *n*. 44
Formaldehyde Institute, 177–78. *See also* Fronts, public relations, scientific
Fortune, 169, 204
reversals of, 33, 135
theodicies, and good and bad, 151. *See also* Luck
Fortune, 168
Fragmentation, 75
of consciousness, 84, 194
of corporate, individual, and common goods, 198–202
of issues, 20
Freud, Sigmund, 139
Fronts, public relations, 166, 174–80
defined, 174
scientific, 177–80

Gang, notion of, 39, 213–14 *n*. 5. *See also* Circles, managerial
General Public Utilities (GPU), 113, 116, 117
General Public Utilities, Nuclear (GPUN), 112–17
GPU. *See* General Public Utilities
GPUN. *See* General Public Utilities, Nuclear
Green (pseudonym for manager at Alchemy), 86
Guggenheim, family, 166
"Gut" decisions, 77–85

Harvard Business Review, 51
Harvard University, 138
Human relations movement, 138, 163
and management consulting, 138. *See also* Scientific management

Ideology, 36, 37, 105, 142, 146, 151, 188, 193, 195, 198, 201
  and assertion of values in an organization, 198–200
  journalistic, as seen by public relations, 173
  meritocratic, 62
  of old Protestant ethic, 8, 145, 191
  of planning and control, 70–71
  and public relations, 162, 163, 170, 181
  of sacramental bodily purity, 152–54
  salvation, 153
  of team play, 52–54, 196
  of textile industry on cotton dust, 157–58, 160
Images Inc., 22–23, 58, 184, 189–90, 201
  and corporate sponsorship of artistic endeavors, 186–87
  fieldwork in, 15–16, 205–6
  and fronts, 176–77
  organizational structure of, 18
  and pragmatic character of social science surveys, 138–39
  and public opinion study of environmental protection vs. economic growth, 181–83
  and relationships with clients, 170–72
  and weight-control pill, 180
Inconsistency
  adeptness at, 146–56, 156–61, 183, 184
  and consistency in public life, 146, 219–20 *n.* 19
  everyday inconsistency among managers, 146–47
Institutional logic, 35, 38, 69, 95, 96, 100, 117, 124, 189, 204
  defined, 112. *See also* Etiquette (protocol)
Intimacy, professional, 51, 203, 204. *See also* Circles, managerial
Iran-contra affair, 5
Irrationality, 74, 146, 199
  and adeptness at inconsistency, 161
  as affected by science and technology, 150–51
  and bureaucratic compartmentalization, 194
  as consequence of ideological frustration, 153–54
  and doublethink, 188
  generated by rationality, 12, 194, 200
  of markets, 71, 118
  perceived, of ideology of bodily purity, 154

  perceived, of some behavior, 48–49
  perceived, of some decisions, 22, 76–77, 81–85
  of public opinion, 162
  rational attempts to control, 12, 14, 35, 76. *See also* Rationality, functional; Rationality, substantive

Kelly (pseudonym of manager at Alchemy), 121–22

Language
  bureaucratic ethic and separation from meaning, 192
  euphemistic, 14, 25, 134–37, 172
  football as metaphor for managerial team work, 49–50
  of management consultants, 141–42
  metaphorical resonance of, of top boss, 22
  provisional, 134, 136, 147, 161, 188–89
  rational/technical, 104
  symbolic reversal as special legerdemain of public relations, 173–74, 187–88. *See also* Inconsistency
Lee, Ivy, 166, 167
Lippmann, Walter, 167
Looking up and looking around, 75–100 (Chapter 4), 77, 79–80
Love Canal, 153, 175
Luck
  right place at the right time, 72–73
  and success, 3, 70, 73
  supremacy of chance over merit, 16
  wrong place at the wrong time, 72–73

Magic lantern, 162–190 (Chapter 7)
  as mechanical device, 225–26 *n.* 9
  as metaphor, 164, 165, 187, 189–90
Main chance, the, 3, 41–74 (Chapter 3), 175, 202
Management consulting
  ethos of, 137–44
  historical roots and growth of, 137–39
  managerial caricatures of, 143, 193
  as paradigm of ambiguous expertise, 137, 140
  and shake-ups at Covenant/Alchemy, 25, 27, 32
Managerial work, 7, 14, 16, 24, 30, 40, 42, 51, 56, 110, 123, 132, 134, 138, 160
  basic structures and experiences of, 20, 33–40, 83–84, 192

meanings of, 194–204, 233–34 *n.* 3
uncertainties in, 23, 33, 37–38, 40, 63, 70–73, 80. *See also* Probation
Mannheim, Karl, 24, 59, 75, 111
Marx, Karl, 139
Mayo, Elton, 138
Merton, Robert K., 139
Milking of plants, 91–95, 96–100
Mills, C. Wright, 95, 139
Mistakes
    and blame, 85–88
    consequence of major public, 65
    covering up, 86, 128
    diverting blame for past, 25
    fear of admitting, 122
    fear of making, 26, 78, 80
    necessity to avoid, 42
    outrunning, 90–96, 100
    privilege of authority to declare, 20
    protecting boss (or patron) from, 19, 62
    resentment at bearing burden of others', 132, 198
    and team play, 52
    watching for those of others, 128
Mobility panic, 14, 67, 91–95
Morality, 7, 204
    bracketing of traditional, in workplace, 6, 105
    bureaucracy and erosion of standards of, 111–12, 192
    occupational (organizational), 3, 4, 6, 11, 13, 15, 61, 109, 110, 194, 206
    as shaped in rehearsals, 189
    situational character of, in bureaucracies, 59, 101, 183, 193
    traditional, 4, 6, 10, 105. *See also* Rules (-in-use)

Nader, Ralph, 147, 158
NAM. *See* National Association of Manufacturers
Narcissism, of managers, 61, 203–4
National Academy of Sciences, 175. *See also* Chlorofluorocarbons
National Association of Manufacturers (NAM), 168, 169, 178, 228–29 *n.* 33
National Transportation Safety Board, 137
Networks, 15
    and alliances, 38, 192
    criteria for admission to, 62
    defined, 38, 211–12 *n.* 3
    political, 64, 82, 144
    and rivalry, 53

and social structure of organizations, 56, 193
    wider, 141. *See also* Circles, managerial
New York Times, The, 32, 51, 116, 170
Noise and hearing loss in textile industry, 101–5, 126
Noll (pseudonym for manager at Covenant), 96–100
Nonaccountability, 111
    abstractness of viewpoint with advancement and, 124–27
    social dimensions of, 128–33
    trust and cooperative, 118. *See also* Responsibility, lack of tracking of
NRC. *See* Nuclear Regulatory Commission
Nuclear Regulatory Commission (NRC), 113–17

Occupational Safety and Health Administration (OSHA), 86, 94, 97, 147, 177
    and cotton dust regulation in textile industry, 157–60
    and noise and hearing loss in textile industry, 101–5
Orwell, George, 184
OSHA. *See* Occupational Safety and Health Administration

Patrons, 19–20, 40, 65, 67, 73, 103–4, 192
    and patronage, 11–12, 24, 32, 38–39, 63, 103–5, 197–98. *See also* Clients, relationships with patrons within an organization
Patterson (pseudonym for executive at Alchemy), 67–70
Persuasion, 75, 171, 173
    indirect means of, in public relations, 173–83
    of self, in rehearsals, 189. *See also* Story, notion of in public relations
Polar crane (at Three Mile Island-2), 114–17. *See also* Expediency; Wilson, Joe
Pragmatism, 52, 138, 191
    bureaucracy and social origins of, in managers, 111–12
    as occupational virtue for managers, 105
Premium(s), 21, 73
    on ability to explain expedient action, 162
    on adeptness at inconsistency, 146–47
    on alertness to expediency, 112, 123–24, 188

Premium(s) (*continued*)
    ambition and internalization of, 16, 194
    on buoyant optimism, 56
    of bureaucratic work, 5–6
    on current opinion in public relations
        studies, 181
    on flexibility, 101
    on immediate personal gains,
        consequences of, 96
    on maximizing personal leverage, 197–
        98
    on return on assets, 91
    on seeming innovative, in higher circles,
        141
    and self-rationalization, 37, 46, 80
    on "sensitivity to others," 135
    shifting of, with organizational change,
        61, 199
    on success, 194
    on symbolic dexterity, 194
    on wily discernment, 161. *See also* Self-
        rationalization; Virtues
        (bureaucratic/managerial)
Principle(s), 101, 123, 131, 135, 204
    subordination to social intricacies of
        organizations, 118–19. *See also*
        contrasting cases of Brady; Tucker;
        Wilson, Joe
Probation, 7–16 (Chapter 1)
    and anxiety in managers, 40
    inclusion in managerial circles, 13, 16,
        131
    and managerial work, 42, 46, 47, 70,
        71–72, 130
    and old Protestant ethic, 8. *See also*
        Probationary crucibles
Probationary crucibles, 40, 72, 84
    of bureaucratic milieux, 192–93, 203.
        See also Anxiety
Propaganda, 164
    and Committee on Public Information,
        166–67. *See also* Public relations
Protestant ethic, 7, 59, 191, 193, 203
    assault on, 8–10
    enduring significance of, 8
    Korean-Americans and, 8
Public faces, 38, 55, 59, 61, 80, 119, 122,
        161, 185
    social mastery and, 46–48. *See also* Self-
        rationalization; Style
Public opinion, 179, 185
    attempts to mold, 162–63, 166–70
    polls, 180–81
    shifts in, 35
    and uncertainties for managers, 71

Public relations, 6, 10, 108, 148, 162–90
        (Chapter 7), 194, 200, 204
    clients in, 170–72, 181–82, 188
    development of, 149, 166–70
    distinctive habit of mind, 172–73, 183
    and doublethink, 183–85
    essential task of, 173
    fieldwork in, 15–16, 205–6
    fronts, 174–80
    functions of, 162–63
    genius of, 173–74
    legitimations for work in, 185–88
    and rehearsals, 188–90

Rage, public, 151–52
Ramazzini, Bernadino, 156
Rationality, functional, 146, 193
    as applied to self in self-rationalization,
        59–61, 203
    and bureaucracy, 11, 12, 72
    of conceptual tools for managers, 82,
        127
    contrasted with substantive rationality,
        75–76
    defined, 75–76
    and irrational markets, 118
    language of, 104
    planning as ceremony of, 70
    and public opinion, 163
    and quests for salvation, 152–54
    scientific, and disenchantment, 150–52
    and scientific management, 137–38
Rationality, substantive
    and adeptness at inconsistency, 160
    civic, 179
    and decision making, 82, 160
    defined, 76
    and irrationalities, 200–1
    as subverted by "take the money and
        run" ethos, 96–100
Reagan, President Ronald
    appointee in Environmental Protection
        Agency, 176
    appointees in Occupational Safety and
        Health Administration, 157, 159
    era, 31
    managerial triumph after first election
        of, 26, 29, 148, 182
Reed (pseudonym for lawyer at Covenant),
        123
Regulation (governmental), 81, 82, 83,
        149, 198, 199
    on acid rain, 178–79
    as businessman's best friend, 160
    on chlorofluorocarbons, 15, 174–76

on formaldehyde, 71, 177–78
in nuclear industry, 117
Occupational Safety and Health
  Administration, on cotton dust,
  156–60
Occupational Safety and Health
  Administration, on noise and
  hearing loss, 101–5
science as basis for, 179–80
and uncertainties for managers, 71
Rehearsal(s), 204
stages of, 188–90
Reichenbach, Harry, 164–67, 170, 183,
  185
Responsibility (accountability), 28, 42, 49,
  56, 61, 62, 101, 107, 110, 113, 118,
  174
avoidance of, 80
and decentralization of authority, 17, 36
diffusion of, 64, 78–85, 179
diffusion of and blame, 86, 114
lack of tracking of, 87–88, 89, 90
and mobility panic, 67
outrunning mistakes, 90–91, 95
rehearsals and, 189
separation of actions from consequences,
  127–28, 192, 201
social, of business, 169, 199–200. *See
  also* Milking of plants
Risk
analysis, field of, 76, 150, 160–61, 222
  n. 23
internal organizational, for managers, 26,
  43, 51, 52, 55, 82, 84, 85, 86, 92,
  105, 132, 140, 160–61, 196, 202
of others' money, 108, 110
technological, 150, 160–61, 200
zero-risk mentality, 117
Rockefeller, John D., 8
family, 166
Rules (-in-use), 4, 5, 7, 62, 112, 133
and assessment of others, 13, 14
and bureaucracy, 6, 52
bureaucratic, as guides for behavior, 6,
  12, 46–49, 192
of bureaucratic life, 109–10, 118
bureaucratic vs. professional, 105–11,
  112–19
of combat, 35
of corporate politics, 28
for gut decisions, 78–79
learned from others, 37–38
and management consultants, 137, 142
as occupational ethics or morality, 3, 4,
  145, 204

of "take the money and run" ethos, 99–
  100. *See also* Ethics, occupational

Scandals, corporate and governmental, 5,
  148–49, 220–21 *n.* 20
Scientific management, 137–38, 163
Secrecy, 80, 122, 198
compartmentalization and, 194
at core of managerial circles, 133
and drawing lines, 123
as managerial virtue, 118
and professional intimacy, 203
Self-abnegation, 8, 48, 119, 153, 203,
  204
Self-control, 8, 47, 48, 49, 80, 153
Self-control and sexual behavior in
  corporations, 48–49
Self-effacement, 19, 203
Self-objectification, 119, 203
Self-promotion, 3, 34, 74, 153, 203
Self-rationalization, 4, 47, 59–61, 74, 119,
  124, 153, 203
Shake-ups (upheavals and reorganizations),
  4, 16, 24, 36, 43, 73, 171, 194
in Covenant/Alchemy, 25–32, 61, 87
in Images Inc., 139
and rearrangement of fealty, 25, 26, 30
at Three Mile Island, 113
and uncertainty, 33, 63
in Weft, 32–33
Short-term ethos, 24, 197
becoming captive to, 96–100
and management consultants, 143–44
and milking, 91–96
reasons for, in managerial work, 82–85
regulation as safeguard against, 159–60.
  See also Mobility panic
Smith (pseudonym for president of
  Alchemy), 25–30, 43, 67, 68, 70,
  79, 93, 95
Social responsibility, corporate, 169, 199–
  200
Story, notion of in public relations, 163,
  165, 166, 168, 169, 171, 172–73,
  185, 186, 188, 189
Style, 12, 19, 28, 62, 67, 135, 141, 192,
  196, 214 *n.* 4
of leadership, 22, 23, 25, 36
as a selective criterion, 45, 46, 56–59
Success (advancement), 3, 4, 6, 7, 9, 24,
  44, 75, 111, 135, 137, 155, 193,
  194, 209–10 *n.* 7
and adeptness at inconsistency, 145–46,
  160–61
and alliances, 38–39

Success (advancement) (*continued*)
  and attentiveness to clients in public
    relations, 170
  and the bureaucratic ethic, 192
  criteria for, in managerial circles, 46–65
  hard work as key to, ideology of, 3, 44–
    45, 72, 191
  lack of necessary connections between
    work and, 62–63, 70, 79, 198
  and luck, 70–73
  in old Protestant ethic, 8, 191
  outrunning mistakes as key to, 90–96
  as related to authority and decision
    making, 75–82
  rewards of, 201, 204
  and short-term ethos, 143–44
  striving for, as moral imperative, 43–46.
    See also Failure

"Take the money and run" ethos, 94, 161,
  199
  becoming captive to, 96–100
  defined, 96
  and piecework system in textile mills,
    95–96
Taylor, Frederick, 137–38
Team play, 21, 59, 62, 116, 196
  main dimensions of, 50–56
  metaphorical basis of, in football, 49–50.
    See also Dissent
Tedlow, Richard, 167
Theodicy
  disenchantment and collapse of
    traditional, 151–53
  and old Protestant ethic, 191
Three Mile Island (TMI, TMI-1, TMI-2),
  112–17, 136, 150
TMI. *See* Three Mile Island
TMI-1. *See* Three Mile Island
TMI-2. *See* Three Mile Island
Tönnies, Ferdinand, 139
Trotsky, Leon, 149
Truth, notion of, 108, 111, 164, 172–73,
  182–83, 184–85, 186, 189, 192,
  204. *See also* Story, notion of in
  public relations
Tucker (pseudonym for manager), 128–33.
  See also Circles, managerial; Virtues
  (bureaucratic/managerial)

Veblen, Thorstein, 149, 198
Virtues (bureaucratic/managerial), 38
  ability to make others comfortable, 56
  adeptness at inconsistency and alertness
    to expediency, 183

  backtracking, filling in, evasion,
    subterfuge, and secrecy, 118
  covering up, 86, 128
  doublethink as hazardous, in public
    relations, 183–85, 186
  flexibility, 51, 59, 101, 145, 188, 204
  old moral, 72, 191, 203
  pragmatism, 105
  silence, 47–48, 66–67, 128, 130–33
Vocabularies, 74
  and cognitive maps, 24
  of excuses, 86, 121
  of explanation, 147
  managerial, as frameworks, 12
  of motive and accounts, 134
  in philosophical circles, 5
  pragmatic, 120
  of rationality, 78
  of reconciliation (public relations), 188

Wall Street, 25, 60, 87, 141
Wall Street Journal, The, 28, 32, 51, 170
Watergate, 5, 148
Weber, Max, 139
  on classical notion of bureaucracy, 11
  on formal or functional rationality, 75–
    77
  on the Protestant ethic, 7–9
  on rational/technical habit of mind and
    disenchantment, 150–51
  on tensions between demands of *caritas*
    and public life, 68–69
Weft Corporation, 21, 23, 35, 37, 38, 41,
  44, 45, 50, 52, 64, 65–66, 70, 71,
  73, 77, 78, 80, 84, 91, 119, 136,
  142, 161, 192, 195, 200, 202
  cotton dust issue at, 156–60
  ethics toward and of customers in, 120–
    21
  fieldwork in, 15–16, 205–6
  formaldehyde resin issue in, 71, 178,
    231 *n.* 42
  noise and hearing loss at, 101–5
  organizational structure of, 18
  piecework system, consequences of, 95–
    96
  presentational style at, 57, 58
  probation of promising young manager
    in, 42
  and scientific management in mills, 137–
    38
  shake-up in, 32–33
  views of workers by managers at
    different levels, 124–26
White, case study of, 101–5

"What has to be done," 53, 112, 117–18, 133, 134, 146, 162
  and adeptness at inconsistency, 160–61
  and organizational success, 204
  and public relations, 172, 173, 184, 185, 188
  and self-rationalization, 196. *See also* Institutional logic
Whistleblowers (dissenters), 146
  fieldwork with, 206. *See also case studies of* Brady; White; Wilson, Joe

White (pseudonym for manager at Weft), 101–5
Whyte, William H., 168
Wilson, Joe (pseudonym for whistleblower), 112–19, 216–17 *n.* 12. *See also* Expediency
World War II, 33, 150, 168, 169, 179
  militarization and bureaucratization of society during, 9

Young (pseudonym for manager at Covenant), 96–100